The Economics of Structural Racism

This extensive and comprehensive book tracks persistent racial disparities in the United States across multiple regimes of structural racism. It begins with an examination of the economics of racial identity, mechanisms of stratification, and regimes of structural racism. It analyzes trends in racial inequality in education and changes in family structure since the demise of Jim Crow. The book also examines generational trends in income, wealth, and employment for families and individuals, by race, gender, and national region. It explores economic differences among African Americans, by region, ethnicity, nativity, gender, and racial identity. Finally, the book provides a theoretical analysis of structural racism, productivity, and wages, with a special focus on the role of managers and instrumental discrimination inside the firm. The book concludes with an investigation of instrumental discrimination, hate crimes, the criminal legal system, and the impact of mass incarceration on family structure and economic inequality.

PATRICK L. MASON is Professor of Economics and Economist at the Political Economy Research Institute, University of Massachusetts, Amherst. His research interests include racial inequality, educational achievement, income distribution, unemployment, social identity, family well-being and structure, racial profiling, and computerization, innovation, and employment.

Cambridge Studies in Stratification Economics: Economics and Social Identity

Series Editor

William A. Darity Jr., *Duke University*

The Cambridge Studies in Stratification Economics: Economics and Social Identity series encourages book proposals that emphasize structural sources of group-based inequality, rather than cultural or genetic factors. Studies in this series will utilize the underlying economic principles of self-interested behavior and substantive rationality in conjunction with sociology's emphasis on group behavior and identity formation. The series is interdisciplinary, drawing authors from various fields including economics, sociology, social psychology, history, and anthropology, with all projects focused on topics dealing with group-based inequality, identity, and economic well-being.

The Economics of Structural Racism

Stratification Economics and US Labor Markets

PATRICK L. MASON
University of Massachusetts, Amherst

Shaftesbury Road, Cambridge CB2 8EA, United Kingdom

One Liberty Plaza, 20th Floor, New York, NY 10006, USA

477 Williamstown Road, Port Melbourne, VIC 3207, Australia

314–321, 3rd Floor, Plot 3, Splendor Forum, Jasola District Centre, New Delhi – 110025, India

103 Penang Road, #05–06/07, Visioncrest Commercial, Singapore 238467

Cambridge University Press is part of Cambridge University Press & Assessment, a department of the University of Cambridge.

We share the University's mission to contribute to society through the pursuit of education, learning and research at the highest international levels of excellence.

www.cambridge.org
Information on this title: www.cambridge.org/9781009290807

DOI: 10.1017/9781009290784

First published 2023

A catalogue record for this publication is available from the British Library.

Library of Congress Cataloging-in-Publication Data
NAMES: Mason, Patrick L., author.
TITLE: The economics of structural racism : stratification economics and US labor markets / Patrick L. Mason, University of Massachusetts, Amherst.
DESCRIPTION: Cambridge, United Kingdom ; New York, NY : Cambridge University Press, 2022. | Series: Cambridge studies in stratification economics | Includes bibliographical references and index.
IDENTIFIERS: LCCN 2022053492 (print) | LCCN 2022053493 (ebook) | ISBN 9781009290807 (hardback) | ISBN 9781009290777 (paperback) | ISBN 9781009290784 (epub)
SUBJECTS: LCSH: African Americans–Economic conditions. | Racism–Economic aspects–United States. | Discrimination in employment–United States.
CLASSIFICATION: LCC E185.8 .M345 2022 (print) | LCC E185.8 (ebook) |
DDC 331.6/396073–dc23/eng/20221116
LC record available at https://lccn.loc.gov/2022053492
LC ebook record available at https://lccn.loc.gov/2022053493

ISBN 978-1-009-29080-7 Hardback
ISBN 978-1-009-29077-7 Paperback

To Winifred, Kim, Corey, and Kikora – who made this journey possible;

– to the ancestoral families who warred against enslavement and Jim Crow to make me possible: Nathan & Minda Brown Mason, Henry & Ann Sinclair McNeil, John & Julia Proctor Rollins, William "Pink" & Helen Hayward Bradwell;

– to James & Estella Green – whose family became my family, too;
– to Marcellus, Mary, Marcellus, Cassandra, Maynard – co-authors; and,

– to the next generations (*A luta continua; vitória é certa*): Nyrkeria, Marcus, Corey, Shizaia Mary, Inyla, Keveun, Trinity, Justice, Ja'Nayh, Haden, Cassandra, Kyra Diana, Sincere, Demiere, Lyla.

Contents

Figures

Tables

PART I

FOUNDATIONS

1

Introduction

1.1 STRUCTURAL RACISM AND STRATIFICATION ECONOMICS

African American family income is 63 percent of White family income. African American family wealth is 4–14 percent of White family wealth. African American women and men earn 84 percent and 68 percent, respectively, of the weekly wages earned by White women and men; both ratios are lower than during the mid-1970s. It is a multi-decade truism that the African American unemployment rate is twice the White unemployment rate.

Structural racism is undervalued within the dominant US economic narrative and its derivative public policies related to persistent racial disparity. The dominant narrative instead offers an individualist perspective on racial disparity. Individualist reasoning is committed to explaining racial disparities in economic well-being as primarily the outcomes of individual decisions by workers regarding skill acquisition, labor force participation, employment, hours, occupational selection, and risk-taking. Therefore, racial differences in earnings and other labor market outcomes are explicated as the result of differences in the individuals' marketable skills, behaviors, and culture.

Individualist scholars de-emphasize racial discrimination as a substantial force in the labor market (Heckman, 2011). Within this framework, "race" is confined to non-market activities and racial identity is not often distinguished from values, behaviors, or culture. When it comes to persistent racial disparity, the individualist framework is supported by a largely Libertarian frame: competition creates a level playing field, persons with identical skills and market-functional values and behaviors will receive identical treatment in the market. By extension, this view holds that individuals or racial groups who achieve superior economic well-being are endowed with higher-quality market-functional values, behaviors, and culture. Groups that have lower levels of economic well-being have inferior market-functional attributes. Despite the popularity of the individualist framework, the empirical evidence has not provided strong support for this perspective (Mason, 1997, 2007; Darity and Mason, 1998; Bertrand and Mullainathan, 2004; Neumark, 2012).

Stratification economics offers an alternative to individualist economics. Stratification economics takes the idea that people with identical skills and market-functional behaviors will *not* necessarily receive identical treatment in the labor market seriously. Within this framework, race is a strategically determined economic norm that facilitates differential access to resources and opportunities (Darity, Mason, and Stewart, 2006). Persistent racial discrimination is consistent with market competition and the accumulation of capital. Rather than a level playing field, the competitive pursuit of profit creates differentiation and inequality. Historically, slavery and Jim Crow formalized both racial identities and enormous racial inequalities in wealth. The privileges of wealth sustain and reinforce both wealth inequalities and racial identities, so that racialized competition within markets and persistent wealth inequalities continue to combine to reproduce structural racism.

Structural racism has been a permanent feature of the US political economy, culture, and society. Structural racism is the result of an interconnected collection of social norms, policies, institutions, identity strategies, and ideologies designed to preserve White supremacy. It is possible to have a future without racism: we have to choose to abolish racism, which requires fundamental structural transformation. Historically, we have chosen to preserve racism – or, at least, the multigenerational struggle seeking to make the fundamental structural changes necessary to permanently rid America of racism has not yet succeeded.

Permanent structural racism is instrumental, but it is not immutable. Racism under chattel capitalism (1619–1865) was different from racism under servitude capitalism (1865–1965), which was different from racism under racialized managerial capitalism (1933–present). Racism "is a critically important stabilizing force that enables Whites to bind across a wide socio-economic chasm. Without the deflecting power of racism, masses of Whites would likely wake up and revolt against the severe disadvantage they suffer in income and opportunity when compared with those Whites at the top of our socio-economic heap" (Bell, 1992: 571).

Bell is hardly the first scholar to understand the instrumental nature of racism. Benjamin Franklin, a major architect of American democracy and economy, stated that English colonization of the American continent provided a great economic opportunity for common Whites to achieve a high measure of economic well-being. To protect this opportunity, Franklin (1751) wanted American immigration to be limited to "purely white people," which for Franklin meant only English and German Saxons. Groups to be excluded from America included: Africans, because they are either Black or tawny; Asians, because they are tawny; Indigenous Americans, because they are tawny; and, swarthy complexion Europeans such as *Spaniards*, *Italians*, *French*, *Russians*, *Swedes*, and all Germans except Saxons.

The instrumental racial division that Franklin helped to build was a sufficiently prominent feature of the American political economic architecture that led W. E. B. Du Bois to conclude, "The problem of the twentieth century is the problem of the color-line, – the relation of the darker to the lighter races of men in Asia and Africa, in America and the islands of the sea. It was a phase of this problem that caused the Civil War" (Du Bois, 1903: 15). The color-line does not separate individuals; it separates groups. It is a social norm that regulates the relationship between Whites and Non-Whites. For Du Bois, the color-line was supported by a permanent White racial contract – White workers willingly tradeoff racial disparity in labor market outcomes and higher profit for capital in order to obtain a racially advantageous social wage for White workers (Du Bois, 1935: 700). Racially discriminatory practices to preserve privilege are likely to persist rather than fade since racial discrimination within the labor market is consistent with the competitive process. Du Bois addressed the question of why lower class Whites stayed in the White racial coalition rather than joining with Blacks to challenge the White elite. His answer begins with the suggestion that, in the immediate aftermath of Reconstruction, lower class Whites received a "public and psychic benefit" from their racial status: "... the white laborers, while they received a low wage, were compensated in part by a sort of public and psychological wage ..." His discussion of the specifics of the "public and psychological wage" delineates tangible relative benefits that can be assigned monetary values:

> They were given public deference and titles of courtesy because they were white. They were admitted freely with all classes of white people to public functions, parks, and the best schools. The police were drawn from their ranks, and the courts, dependent upon their votes, treated them with such leniency as to encourage lawlessness. Their vote selected public officials, and while this had small effect upon the economic situation, it had great effect on their personal treatment and the deference shown them. White schoolhouses were the best in the community, and conspicuously placed and they cost anywhere from twice to ten times as much per capita as the colored schools. The newspapers specialized on news that flattered the poor whites and almost entirely ignored the Negro except for crime and ridicule.
>
> On the other hand, in the same way, the Negro was subject to public insult; was afraid of mobs; was liable to the jibes of children and the unreasoning fears of white women; and was compelled almost continuously to submit to various badges of inferiority. (Du Bois, 1935: 700)

Persistent joblessness and unequal labor market treatment create anxiety for working class persons and their families. Workers seek protection from these severe risks to their families' current and future well-being. Per Du Bois, racial identity norms are outcomes of instrumentally strategic behavior. Even if White workers do not get the highest possible wages, they get other valuable outcomes: better schools and therefore higher quality and quantity of skills for their children, lower probability of joblessness, better public parks for collective entertainment and higher home values, greater access to public functions and greater quality and quantity of social capital, better treatment by the police and the courts, and greater access to public officials responsible for providing valuable public services, as well as a host of psychological benefits. On the other hand, Black workers receive lower pay than White workers within the labor market and less favorable outcomes than White workers outside the labor market.

Nobel laureate Dr. Martin Luther King, Jr. famously argued that "Racism, economic exploitation, and militarism" are the "triple evils" of American capitalism (Washington, 1986: 250). In America, "profit motives and property rights are considered more important than people" (Washington, 1986: 629). Social justice for the oppressed is a non-issue. Reverend King explained,

> A nation that will keep people in slavery for 244 years will "thingify" them, make them things. Therefore they will exploit them, and poor people generally, economically. And a nation that will exploit economically will have to have foreign investments … will have to use its military might to protect them. (Washington, 1986: 251)

Continuing, King stated, "For years I labored with the idea of reforming the existing institutions of the society, a little change here, a little change there. Now I feel quite differently. I think you've got to have a reconstruction of the entire society." Further, "Something is wrong with capitalism as it now stands in the United States. *We are not interested in being integrated into this value structure … a radical redistribution of power must take place*" (Fairclough, 1983: 122–123, emphasis added).

Using more colorful language, Malik Shabazz (Malcolm X) described capitalism as a "bloodsucking" system. Shabazz argued that, "It's impossible for a white person to believe in capitalism and not believe in racism. You can't have capitalism without racism (Breitman, 1965: 69)." He further stated that

> This is the *worst* racist society on this earth. There is no country on earth in which you can live and racism be brought out in you – whether you're white or black – more so than this country that poses as a democracy. This is a country where the social, economic, political atmosphere creates a sort of psychological atmosphere that makes it almost impossible, if you're in your right mind, to walk down the street with a *white* person and not be self-conscious. It almost can't be done, and it makes you *feel* this racist tendency that pops up. But it's the society itself. (Breitman, 1965: 214)

Thus, both the supposed "integrationist" King and the alleged "Black separatist" Shabazz agreed that Black identity is separate from White identity. Both were hostile to capitalism. However, neither King nor Shabazz saw Black identity as behaviorally or otherwise inferior to White identity and neither suggested that acculturation into Whiteness is something Blacks should aspire to. Rather, both saw capitalism as inherently racist. Simultaneously, both encouraged African Americans to have a positive attitude toward hard work and achievement, strong family values, a moral and ethical lifestyle, and to continue the struggle to reconstruct America's political economy.

Much has changed about America and the world since the mid-to-late 1960s heyday of King and Shabazz, when the Civil Rights and Black Power movements succeeded in destroying servitude capitalism (Jim Crow). Nevertheless, popular African American political economic thought and culture continue to be characterized by an unyielding ambivalence toward American political and economic institutions and great skepticism regarding Whites' willingness to aggressively pursue actions that will make America a racially just society.[1]

Donald Harris made the important point that joblessness is one of the causal factors of racial discrimination (Harris, 1972). Most workers have no or few financial assets. Their sole source of income is wages and salaries. Unemployment and involuntary part time employment are major risks to the security of families. The intensity of racial discrimination is correlated with the interracial competition for employment. Further, racial discrimination is correlated with the wages and compensation of jobs: African Americans are pushed into jobs with lower pay.

This text examines African American social and economic outcomes, with an emphasis on the American labor market. The statistical analysis focuses on the years after the high point of the Civil Rights movement. Post-1965, for the first time in the twentieth century but for the second time in American history, African Americans had formal equality before the law. After the Civil War ended chattel capitalism, African Americans had a brief but highly contested period of formal equality before the law, that is, the Reconstruction years 1865–1877. Similarly, after the Civil Rights movement ended servitude capitalism associated with Jim Crow, African Americans once again experienced a period of formal equality before the law. But, just as freedmen found themselves trying to integrate into a totally racialized political economy during Reconstruction, African Americans emerging from under Jim Crow found themselves trying to integrate into a totally racialized political economy during 1965–1974. Chattel capitalism and servitude capitalism were political economies designed to transfer wealth from Blacks to Whites. The systems worked as planned. After the elimination of both chattel capitalism and servitude capitalism, there were vast disparities in wealth, family income, and individual earnings between (and among) Americans of African descent and Americans of European descent.

Total racialization implies that, in addition to persons selecting economic strategies as specific individuals and members of particular families, they also select economic strategies as members embedded in mutually exclusive racial

[1] In a nationally representative survey of African American political economic ideologies, Dawson (2001: table 2.8, p. 83) shows that 37 percent of African Americans subscribe to the basic tenets of Black nationalism; 34 percent are comfortable with the core ideas of Black Marxism; 40 percent of African Americans are disillusioned liberals; 19 percent of African Americans accept feminist ideology; and, only 1 percent of African Americans accept the ideological beliefs of Black conservatism.

groups. Groups are more than summations of individuals; the group acts within the individual. Deviations from social norms, whether by persons acting alone or within small clusters, are punished by the group. Racial identities are social norms and actions that reinforce racial identity norms and relative well-being are supported by own-group members, while actions that challenge racial identity norms and relative well-being are punished by own-group members. Understanding persistent structural racism requires understanding the actions of groups and persons.

African Americans represent 14.2 percent (47.6 million) of America's total population of 335 million persons. Similarly, the census of 1860 shows that Blacks were 14.1 percent of the national population, numbering 4,441,790 persons out of a total population of 31,443,790. From the end of chattel capitalism in 1865 to the eve of World War I in 1910, 90 percent of African Americans resided in the Southern states of the United States of America. Blacks constituted about 37 percent of the Southern population in 1860.[2] In 1870, the percentages for the individual Southern states were: Alabama (48 percent), Arkansas (25 percent), Delaware (18 percent), District of Columbia (33 percent), Florida (49 percent), Georgia (46 percent), Kentucky (17 percent), Louisiana (50 percent), Maryland (23 percent), Mississippi (54 percent), North Carolina (37 percent), Oklahoma (8 percent in 1890), South Carolina (59 percent), Tennessee (26 percent), Texas (31 percent), and Virginia (42 percent).[3] From 1910 to the mid-1960s the percentage of African Americans residing in the South declined; nevertheless, the majority of African Americans have continued to reside in the South. About 58 percent of African Americans currently reside in the South.

1.2 REGIMES OF STRUCTURAL RACISM

The evolution of Black economic status is the product of complex political economic interactions among permanent racism, aggressive self-help among people of African descent, public policy, capitalist competition and the pursuit of profit, egalitarian social movements, and the social construction of racial identities. Intertemporal and intergenerational changes in racial disparities in income and wealth vary according to regimes of structural racism (see Table 1.1).

1.2.1 Chattel Capitalism

Chattel capitalism in America was characterized by the transatlantic slave trade and by White enslavement of Africans. Enslavement in America existed from

[2] www2.census.gov/library/publications/decennial/1870/population/1870a-04.pdf. Last accessed December 12, 2022.

[3] www2.census.gov/library/publications/decennial/1870/population/1870a-04.pdf. Last accessed December 12, 2022.

TABLE 1.1. *Regimes of structural racism*

	Years	Period: Governmental policy and racial regime	Race gap: Income & wealth	Governmental policy
I.	1619–1865	Chattel capitalism	Increasing	Support slavery
II.	1865–1965	Servitude capitalism	Increasing	
	1865–1877	Black codes and Reconstruction	Decreasing	Support equality
	1877–1914	The Nadir	Increasing	
	1877–1965	Jim Crow	Increasing	Support capital, take away Black civil rights
III.	1941–present	Racialized managerial capitalism	Decreasing	New Deal, Fair Deal, New Frontier & the Great Society
	1914–1965	Great Migration & Urbanization	Increasing	
	1945–1973	Second Reconstruction	Decreasing	
	1973–2008	The 2nd Reversal: Stagnation and decline	Stagnation	
	1981–present	Racialized managerial capitalism	Stagnation	Conservatism and libertarianism

1619 to 1865. During this period, Africans were commodities: they were beings who were hunted, harvested, and exchanged for profit by European and American traders. African family structure and family functioning were outcomes dominated by enslavers' concern for profit. International shipping, banking, insurance, shipbuilding, and the rise of great universities were enabled by the slave trade (Darity and Mullen, 2020). Although slavery existed in all of the states, it was in the plantation economies of the South where slavery was most extensively developed, where the racial identities required for a slave society received their most complete development, where White supremacy and animosity toward Blacks was most intense, and where 90 percent of African Americans resided.

The plantation economy was a system of production for profit, as is always the case under any capitalist system. Capital was allowed to move into and move out of plantation production. Plantation output (cotton, sugar, tobacco, rice, coffee, and sometimes the services of the enslaved) was traded nationally and internationally.

Enslavers had complete control over the labor process and complete control over the lives of their commodities. Enslaved workers on a plantation expanded (decreased) when plantation production expanded (decreased). White workers were mobile, but Non-White workers were commoditized and not free (Africans) or free and de-humanized and threatened with extinction (Native Americans). Immigration and citizenship were totally racialized: only Whites were eligible for citizenship. Non-White immigrants were unwanted. White workers had the ability to sell their labor but very limited economic assets.

The public policy framework supporting chattel capitalism was simple: White monopoly of political power. This required a combination of political conservatism and economic libertarianism. The federal, state, and local government provided instruments of force to support private ownership of persons. Government provided laws to determine eligibility for enslavement and citizenship. However, plantations and all businesses were free to operate with minimal or no governmental regulation or oversight. On the plantation, the enslaver was the criminal legal system. Government did not provide social programs under chattel capitalism. The role of government was to help Whites extract land from Native Americans and extract uncompensated labor from Africans.

The era of chattel capitalism provided the socioeconomic and institutional context for the historical transformation of Africans in America into African Americans. This process was initiated with 20 Africans who entered indentured servitude in Jamestown, Virginia in 1619. They came to America with an African history, an African value system and psychology, an African culture and conception of the family, an African cosmology, an African understanding of economics, and – ultimately – an African way of being. They were incorporated violently into a society constructed for the enrichment of Europeans. At the very beginning of the nation, their African identity, their Non-European otherness, was subverted into the source of putative Black inferiority.

Initially, Africans in America married and co-mingled with similarly situated Europeans (Higginbotham, 1978). However, by the middle of the 1600s the foundation was set for a racialized society: a race-based slave economy through 1865 and a society constructed on de jure racial segregation for the next 100 years thereafter. As the American political economy moved forward from 1619 to 1865, African otherness was transformed into "Black." To be Black was the antithesis of White. Whiteness was the key to crucial elements of personhood: citizenship, owning property, and voting rights, along with the protection of and service by the state and its police/military power. "Black" and "slave" became synonyms, as did "White" and "free." Whiteness entitled a person to preferential treatment, in particular, singular access to public resources and a virtual monopoly over private resources. Affluent Whites were entitled to the special privileges of wealth and Whiteness while the least affluent Whites were entitled only to the privileges of Whiteness. Racial identity became a form of property and Whiteness was the highest yielding identity property. Among European Americans, "Blacks" were persons to be excluded; but, among persons of African descent, Blackness created a culture of self-help, protection from and resistance to racism, and affirmation of African American personhood.

Consider the racial public policies of Thomas Jefferson and Andrew Jackson. Both are lionized social icons and both have their images printed on the national currency. The former was a slave-owner, philosophical architect of Indian genocide, planter, author of the Declaration of Independence, major contributor to the Constitution, and second President of the United States of America, while the latter was an amoral and unethical land speculator, genocidal murderer, extender of democracy and the privileges of Whiteness to lower income Whites, and seventh president of the United States of America (Takaki, 1990). The careers of these two men illustrate the relationship between public policy, economic development, the operation of competitive markets, and the function of racial identity as property.

Jefferson wanted to create a White agrarian market economy. There were at least two resource shortages that imperiled the Jeffersonian vision: a shortage of labor and a shortage of commodified land. Land was in short supply because it was under the control of Native Americans, who did not view land as a commodity to be bought and sold by individuals. Labor was in short supply because there were too few laborers available at sufficiently low wages for the profitable operation of the burgeoning plantation economic system. To solve the land shortage problem Jefferson encouraged White–Indian intermarriage, hoping to destroy the socio-cultural identities of indigenous populations by assimilating them into European institutions and values of privatized individual land ownership. To the extent that assimilation failed, Jefferson favored relocation of native peoples to land unwanted by Whites or extermination of native peoples who did not wish to acculturate or relocate.

Jefferson discouraged intermarriage between Whites and Africans. Assimilating Africans into Americans would undermine the supply of persons available for slave labor on plantations and work against the social, economic, and political stability of chattel capitalism. Jackson cared little for assimilation of Indians, especially via intermarriage with Southern Whites; instead, he perfected what is now called "ethnic cleansing." Then and now, ethnic cleansing is a process for achieving through extreme violence that which cannot be achieved cheaply (if at all) through market buying and selling; it is a violent process for transferring ownership and control of the land and natural resources from one ethnic group to another ethnic group.

1.2.2 Servitude Capitalism (Black Codes and Jim Crow)

The competitive forces of the market did not bring chattel capitalism to an end; the competitive pursuit of profit failed to create a level playing field for all persons. Chattel capitalism was suddenly and violently ended by government policy: the US civil war of 1861–1865. The abolition of chattel capitalism gave way to servitude capitalism: a period characterized by White expropriation of Black citizenship. White monopolization of Black citizenship allowed agricultural production for profit to take place with forced labor of nominally free persons. Also, both farm and factory employers had complete control over the labor process.

Public policy remained officially racist: there was a White monopoly of political power; the government had control over the process of racial domination; the government provided instruments of force to support racial domination; there was racialized citizenship; the government permitted White employers to use violence to maintain control over the labor process and permitted White citizens to use violence to maintain racial dominance; there was de jure racial segregation; anti-Black racial discrimination in market transactions was legal (discrimination in housing, employment, credit, etc.); and there was anti-Black discrimination in access to public resources and opportunities (education, military, burials, parks and public facilities, etc.).

Servitude capitalism existed from 1865 to 1965. The Reconstruction era of 1865–1877 was also the beginning of servitude capitalism. Nominally, for a brief period, radical Reconstructionists within the federal government sought to create a plural race society where all citizens were equal before the law. It did not happen. Simultaneously, state governments across the South created Black codes designed to effectively re-enslave African Americans.

The Nadir (1877–1917) and cryto-slavery (1872–1942) mark the rise and consolidation of Jim Crow. The Nadir is the post-slavery low point for African American civil liberties. Cryto-slavery refers to the various institutions White Southerners used to maintain involuntary servitude and political domination of African Americans within the context of servitude capitalism. This racial institution was supported by libertarian capitalism.

1.2.3 Racialized Managerial Capitalism

The rise of the most recent regime of structural racism overlaps with the final stages of servitude capitalism. In particular, racialized managerial capitalism emerged between the New Deal and Great Society federal programs of Presidents Franklin D. Roosevelt (1933–1945) and Lyndon B. Johnson (1963–1968). Racialized managerial capitalism is characterized by the tremendous racial disparity in wealth created by the racism of 1619–1965, along with substantive White control of managerial financial, informational, and decision-making resources. The worker–manager racial identity match in firms, organizations, and institutions is the point of reproduction of racial disparity, as managers use their discretion to distribute resources across racial groups differentially.

Notably, government policy rather than the competitive forces of the market is responsible for abolishing Jim Crow. The New Deal started at the end of servitude capitalism and the Great Society ended Jim Crow. The New Deal–Great Society governmental era encouraged the rise of social and economic managers within the public sector. Political managers were an important force for ending servitude capitalism. African American self-help also played a major role in destroying Jim Crow. In particular, during the era of African American migration and urbanization, that is 1914–1965, millions of African Americans moved from the South to the rest of the country and from rural areas to urban areas, both within and outside of the South. This remains the largest internal migration in America's history and is an exceptional example of both individual and social group self-help. Also, the end of migration and urbanization, 1945–1965, represents the high point of the Civil Rights movement and the emergence of the Black Power movement of 1965–1973, along with White reaction to Black progress and advocacy for racial equality.

Historian C. Vann Woodward (1973) has labeled the 1955–1968 civil rights years the "Second Reconstruction." The "Second Reversal," that is, 1973–2008, occurred after this period of progress. The second reversal includes nearly all of the major recessions since the end of Jim Crow, that is, from 1965 to the present. African American social and economic progress is neither linear nor automatic. Rather, it is tidal, ebbing and flowing, while rising and falling according to the nature and extent of changes in the business cycle, changes in the extent and intensity of social movements, the nature and extent of individual and group self-help among African Americans, and changes in the racial animus of federal, state, and local public policies. The Second Reversal has been a period of prolonged economic stagnation and decline for African Americans.

1.3 SUMMARY AND DISCUSSION

Proponents of *individualism* assert that racial disparities are not a reflection of pervasive racism nor unjust class privilege. Instead, individualists assert: (1) members of the economic elite are deserving of their economic and social advantages; and (2) African American–White racial inequalities in wealth are caused by differences in income, savings, and family functioning; racial differences in income are caused by differences in ability, acquired skill, that is, the quantity and quality of education, and family functioning; racial differences in family functioning are caused by differences in racial identity, in particular, African American racial identity is characterized by dysfunctional individual behaviors, weak family values, and anti-intellectual racial culture. The individualist perspective is summarized by the claim that African Americans have a "counter-culture" that requires non-conformance with the White emphasis on market functional values and family behavior. According to the individualist perspective, the pursuit of profit by privately owned firms operating in perfectly competitive ("textbook") markets has the ancillary benefits of breaking down racial barriers and creating a meritocratic labor market. But, a racially level playing field leads to persistent racial inequality because of African American behavior.

Among proponents of individualism the economics of race is defined by a singular objective – locating the source of Black inferiority that is responsible for persistent racial disparity. Explanations of African American inferiority include genetic inheritance (Murray and Hernstein, 1994), educational quality (Maxwell, 1994; Neal and Johnson, 1996), dysfunctional or pathological families, communities, and culture (Moynihan, 1965; Sowell, 1975; Loury, 1984), and government policy (Williams, 1982). Regardless of the ultimate source of racial differences in skill acquisition, income, employment, and wealth – biology, family and community behavior, or culture – individualists argue that it is the average behavior of individual African Americans that is the primary cause of lower average income, wealth, and socioeconomic status that perpetually plagues Black Americans. Among individualists, the assertion of African American inferiority is persistently reproduced as the canonical framework for evaluating racial differences in socioeconomic status and the formation of racial identity.

Stratification economics offers an alternative perspective. From the stratification point of view persistent racial discrimination and markets characterized by strategic competitive rivalry are interconnected processes. The stratification perspective offers a distinct political economy of racism: (1) persistent racial socioeconomic disparity occurs because of persistent differences in wealth and power, not because of racial disparity in any alleged element of Black inferiority; (2) it presents an economic theory of the formation of racial identities based on differential access to resources rather than differential behavior; (3) it presents a theory of racial discrimination whereby discriminatory behavior may be profit-increasing and therefore an element of competitive managerial strategies by firms; (4) it is consistent with the historical development of racial disparity and racial conflict; and (5) it establishes a connection between persistent racial discrimination and class privilege.

Both racial identity and wealth bestow strategic advantages in capitalist markets as well as within the political process. The inequities of mid-twentieth century America were handed down from the racist political economies of chattel capitalism and servitude capitalism, that is, the policies, institutions, and outcomes of 1619–1965. These inequities provided a solid political economic foundation for racial disparity to be reproduced in perpetuity – unless specific action is taken to redistribute wealth. Simultaneously, the long history of racism and racial conflict has combined with the internal dynamics of cultural heritage and identity formation to continuously reproduce an African American social identity and consciousness that has strong and obvious African roots – though it is not African and is most certainly American – but is also greatly differentiated from the social identity and consciousness of Americans of European descent. Our reading of the data show positive changes have occurred since the end of Jim Crow, even as racial disparity in socioeconomic well-being has remained large with no indication that it will be ending soon.

For stratificationists, Black social identity is an important political economic strategy for overcoming racial and class impediments to African American social and economic progress. This text favors a stratification perspective on persistent racial disparity in American society. Thereby, it suggests that racism remains a very real force that vitiates contemporary economic processes and American social relations and institutions. The presentation herein is economic but with historical context. In addition, we also incorporate gender, ethnic and social diversity, macroeconomic conditions, public policy, wealth inequality, a heterodox analysis of market competition, and social identity.

2

Racial Identity As an Economic Norm

Structural racism requires racialized economic agents. The actions of racialized persons are combined with other stratification mechanisms (involuntary joblessness, wealth inequality, exploitation and differentiation of workers, discretionary power) to reproduce structural racism. We discuss in this chapter only racial identity production, postponing our discussion of additional mechanisms of stratification to Chapter 3.

Racial identities are a strategically determined social norm, designed for governing differential access to resources, especially wealth, power, and information, as well as protection from other-group antagonism. When applied to the labor market, the differential power and information of racial groups means that racial identity is a sorting mechanism, such that persons of otherwise equal productive capacity will have racially differential access to employment, compensation, promotion, training, and the probability of layoff according to the manager–worker identity match.

The formation of a racial identity norm is derived from the strategic interactions of all persons in a society, both between and within ancestral groups. Once formed, personal and small group deviations from the social norm, that is, personal and small group mutations or social innovations, are punished in two ways: (1) reduced access to resources within a person's own-ancestral group; and (2) less protection from antagonistic actions from other-ancestral groups. In this way, the racial norm is not fixed but it is strongly resistant to change and, importantly, it is difficult to alter social norms through personal or small group coalitions. Further, no behavioral prescriptions are mandated for racial identities.

2.1 ECONOMICS OF RACIAL IDENTITY AS A SOCIAL CONSTRUCTION

Theories of racial identity are linked to theories of the distributions of income, wealth, and political power. Biological theories of race were used to justify the enslavement, colonialization, and massacres of peoples of African, Asian, and Indigenous American descent. Americans commonly assume that racial identity is easily determined by skin shade and other physical features. This biological perspective implies that characteristics for determining racial identity are fixed over time within the United States and the same characteristics determine racial categories in countries other than the United States. From this perspective, racial categories are facts of nature; they have a major influence on socioeconomic outcomes, but socioeconomic outcomes do not influence racial identities.[1] Race as biology allows for the possibility that racial disparities in socioeconomic outcomes are biologically determined.

Less odiously, racial categories may be biologically determined but differences in skin shade and other physical features are not responsible for differences in socioeconomic outcomes; instead, it is argued that there are racial differences in culture, values, and behavior that are responsible for racial differences in socioeconomic outcomes. Cultural theories of race are favored by proponents of individualism, that is, advocates of human capital theory (economics) and status attainment theory (sociology). Culture, in this instance, does not refer to the production of art, music, books, fashion, theology, etc., but refers to market-oriented actions and behaviors, for example, future orientation, achievement orientation, family functioning and stability, deferred gratification, goal orientation, willingness to sacrifice for individual and family success, and so forth. Cultural theories of race assume that racial groups differ in the intensity of attributes that positively and negatively contribute to income attainment and wealth accumulation; dominant groups have a superior (more market functional) culture, while subaltern groups have an inferior (less market functional) culture.

From this perspective, interracial variation in racial culture is correlated with skin shade, but differences in skin shade (or other biological features) do not cause differences in culture. Moreover, White identity does not have a social or economic advantage – rather, Blackness reduces a person's life-chances. The individualist cultural argument is that if Blacks only behaved like Whites racial inequality in income and wealth would disappear. An earlier generation of scholars also argued that persistent racial inequality occurs because of "pathological" Black families (Moynihan, 1965) and the "dysfunctional" behavior of low-income Blacks (Loury, 1984). A refinement of this argument indicates the cultural attributes of African Americans of low socioeconomic status are particularly dysfunctional; they have relatively lower social capital (market functional values) than other African Americans and Whites (Loury, 1989). Lower status Blacks have lower social capital than Whites because racial discrimination in relations of contact means that Blacks do not have access to superior White social capital, that is White values and behavior, through

[1] For a detailed discussion of biology and race, see Graves (2004).

marriage, social group membership, etc. This perspective suggests that Black cultural deficiency encourages a lower quantity and quality of education among African Americans in comparison to Whites.

In explicit models of identity, individualist cultural perspectives equate Black racial identity with the prescriptive behavioral requirements of "oppositional culture," while White racial identity is the same as the prescriptive requirements of the "dominant culture" (Akerlof and Kranton, 2000; Akerlof, 2002). This yields an unpleasant tradeoff. Blacks may choose an identity that adapts to the dominant culture, knowing that full acceptance by members of the dominant culture is unlikely and that the choice is psychologically costly, since it involves being "different" from family and friends, who are outside of and have negative attitudes toward the dominant culture. Or, Blacks may select a historically determined alternative identity, an oppositional culture. The prescriptions for oppositional identity are defined in terms of "what the dominant culture is not." Since the prescriptions of the dominant culture endorse "self-fulfillment," those of the oppositional culture are self-destructive (Akerlof, 2002). The dominant identity emphasizes educational excellence but the oppositional identity is anti-intellectual (Austen-Smith and Fryer, 2005). Hence, from the individualist cultural perspective, the lower quantity and lower quality of African American education relative to White Americans and the intergenerational reproduction of racial disparities are caused by Black identity, an "oppositional identity" that is opposed to educational achievement because educational achievement is prescriptive behavior associated with White identity. From this perspective, racial disparities in educational, wealth, and socioeconomic outcomes can be eliminated if African Americans are willing to abandon "Black culture." As such, the deficiency perspective yields a testable hypothesis: "successful" African Americans should be substantially less likely to self-identify with Black culture than African Americans of more moderate socioeconomic status. The data presented in this book rejects this hypothesis.

Within the stratification perspective, racial categories are economic norms established by strategies for gaining or limiting access to public and private resources. Racial identity norms are outcomes of strategic social interactions among all persons and they have strong effects on the material life-chances of persons (Darity, Mason, and Stewart, 2006). In particular, these norms are associated with privileged access to public and private resources for dominant groups. Racial identity norms are stable, since they are formed from strategic social interactions within and between members of alternative ancestral groups. In short, race is a group strategy for acquiring wealth, power, and information; racial boundaries separate dominant and subaltern groups. Personal innovations away from racial categories are punished and personal adherence to racial boundaries is rewarded.

Certainly, there are differences in physical appearances according to ancestral origin; for example, Ghanaians and Englishmen differ in hair color, eye color, skin shade, and facial features. These differences, however, are neither necessary nor sufficient to establish differing racial categories. Racial categories arise and persist in society because racism has an instrumental purpose: persons are sorted by their physical differences in order to differentially distribute access to wealth, power, and information. The collective social interactions of millions of persons produce stable and resilient racial identity norms. These norms are strongly resistant to personal and small group innovations because persons who violate racial identity norms will be worse off than those who adhere to racial identity norms – even if abolishing racism would improve the well-being of society as a whole.

Social interactions are productive: they create goods, provide services and information, create new knowledge, impart training, and establish relationships with a variety of individuals. Both workers and managers enter firms, organizations, and institutions with racial identities that are stable social norms. The manager–worker identity match within firms, organizations, and institutions influences the distribution of information and evaluation of performance. Personal innovations away from racial identity norms result in lower payoffs from social interactions within a person's own- and other-group.

Despite the strong resistance against personal or small group deviations from racial norms, there are times when racial identity norms change. Sometimes, large scale social movements, major political events, or public policies will reinforce racial identity norms, while at other times these political events or public policies will alter racial identity norms.

Racially discriminatory practices to preserve privilege are likely to persist rather than fade, since racial discrimination within firms, organizations, and institutions is consistent with the competitive process (Du Bois, 1935: 700). The racial contract – White worker tolerance of labor market racial disparity, higher profit for capital, and a racially advantageous social wage for White workers – still exists among Whites in the United States. Per Du Bois, the total material and psychic payoff to White workers of remaining within their racial coalition trumps their class interests of joining with Blacks to fight for higher wages and an end to discrimination. Whites of all social classes have a much lower likelihood of exposure to unemployment. Not only is the overall Black adult (25 years of age and older) unemployment rate consistently two times as high as the White rate, but at each level of educational attainment the Black rate also tends to be double the White rate. The unemployment rate for Blacks with some college education exceeds the rate for Whites who have not completed high school (Fletcher, 2012). Devah Pager's (2003) field experiments reveal that the odds of a White male with a criminal record receiving a call back for a job are greater than that for a Black male with no criminal record, given comparable age and educational attainment.

An individual's race is both a form of personal identity and a means of competing in the market (Stewart, 1994). Further, since racial identity is a means of competing for resources, there is a positive externality associated with the social stock of own-group racial identity in the market and a negative externality associated with the stock of other-group race–cultural identity in the economy. Persons have agency in the construction of their own-group social identity, but social identity formation is not a solo act (Darity, Mason, and Stewart, 2006). Identity provides persons both with a means of entering into groups (and therefore represents a source of personal satisfaction) and a means of attaining status within groups (and therefore is connected to wealth accumulation).

Many social groups are open to each person: family, neighborhood, social clubs, educational affiliation, religious institutional membership, professional organization, etc. Membership in each of these groups requires accepting the identity of the group, just as persons are frequently excluded in order to preserve the particular identity of the group. Within the United States, race is an encompassing identity that conditions entry into most other social groups and identities. Within other societies, caste, religious affiliation, national origin, etc., may be the dominant conditioning category.

Because wealth is the most consistent substantive measure of status attainment in social groups, the construction of racial identity has an impact on income, independently of any effect that it may have on skill accumulation. Some racial identities will raise a group's rate of return to skill above the social mean (social nepotism and protection against discrimination); others will push the group's rate of return below the social average (limited nepotism and limited protection against discrimination), while some other identities may have a direct effect on personal satisfaction without having an earnings effect (social neutrality). So, identity can affect skill accumulation without having a mediating relationship to family values or personal behaviors.

The social construction of racial identity norms is an evolutionary process reflecting the collective interactions of all persons in society. Persons cooperate and compete over a range of socioeconomic activities, for example, employment, education, housing, credit, mating opportunities, religious, political and other institutional leadership positions, and so forth. Each person utilizes his or her personal productive abilities in these social interactions and each person competes or cooperates by employing an identity strategy that allows him/her greater or lesser access to some portion of group resources that he or she may draw upon to enhance productive potential. In particular, people engage in social interactions with resources that are provided to them or withheld from them by their families, other nurturing groups, and those who support a particular identity strategy. People construct racial identities by adhering to specific identity strategies. Each person selects an identity strategy that increases his or her well-being, given the set of identity strategies selected by all other persons. Strategies that are wealth-increasing are imitated by others whose previous strategies may have been wealth-decreasing. Thereby, a racial norm is established.

The contention that racial identity is biologically meaningless does not imply that there are no constraints on a person's racial self-identification. On the contrary, there are norms associated with racial construction. For example, persons of African descent may decide whether they wish to establish a "Black" identity or whether they wish to interact with others solely as "individuals." But, prevailing social norms do not permit persons of African descent to become "White," at least not in the United States. Conversely, in Brazil persons of African phenotype may have the option of selecting "pardo" (brown) or "preto" (Black). So, there is an opportunity for African phenotype persons to select away from Blackness even if they cannot select into Whiteness.

Wealth inequality is the socioeconomic mechanism that transfers to living generations the circumstances, conditions, and traditions of "dead" generations. At a given point in time social norms establish the identity strategies that are available to individuals; yet, the competitive survival of the fittest strategies, that is, the identity strategy that has the most positive influence on wealth accumulation, will influence the construction and replication of social norms. In the historically-specific context of the United States, Americans of European descent have used their political economic dominance to construct barriers to entry into and barriers of exit from "Whiteness." Conversely, in this social context, "Blackness" is the ultimate Non-White social construct; it is an antithetical residual category for those persons with the least access to the presumptive privileges of the property rights inherent in Whiteness. Non-Whiteness then is a social construction for limiting competitive challenges for Whites.

If person-specific or small group violations of the economic canons of racial identity norms, that is, mutations, are sufficiently costly, these innovations will not be imitated by others and the norm will persist. Think, for example, of small restaurant owners in the Jim Crow South who would not serve Black customers – even though such sales *ceteris paribus* would increase the restaurant's profits. But all else would not be held equal; White customers would decrease their patronage, other businesses (banks, suppliers) may decide to restrict their market interactions with the restaurant owner, and church members and neighbors may become hostile. In short, Whites who are otherwise unaffected or even better off by the restaurateur's decisions to serve Black customers provide in-group resources and sanctions linked to strengthening group position.

Historically, "passing" was an individualistic strategy to arbitrage differences in the payoff to racial identities. The formation of so-called mixed-race identity strategies may also be understood as racial identity arbitrage. For individuals who lack the phenotypic characteristics to pass or claim mixed-race identity, the individualist arbitrage strategy may include acculturation.

2.2 SKIN TONE AND RACE

Americans use differences in skin tone to sort each other into mutually exclusive racial groups. Whites have the lightest skin shade, while African Americans

TABLE 2.1. *Skin tone by race*

	Race of Respondent							
	Frequency				Cumulative Distribution			
Skin tone	White	Black	Other	Total	White	Black	Other	Total
1 Lightest	880	3	21	904	0.593	0.009	0.095	0.440
2	481	12	63	556	0.918	0.043	0.380	0.711
3	96	41	82	219	0.982	0.160	0.751	0.818
4	15	57	34	106	0.993	0.324	0.905	0.869
5	3	65	18	86	0.995	0.510	0.986	0.911
6	3	55	2	60	0.997	0.668	0.995	0.941
7	1	55	0	56	0.997	0.825	0.995	0.968
8	1	44	1	46	0.998	0.951	1.000	0.990
9	0	17	0	17	0.998	1.000	1.000	0.999
10 Darkest	3	0	0	3	1.000	1.000	1.000	1.000
Total	1,483	349	221	2,053				
Mean (μ)	1.53	5.51	2.89	2.35				

Source: Author's calculations. General Social Survey, 2018

have the darkest skin shade and Other racial groups have skin tones somewhere between African Americans and Whites. The implicit assumption is that racial categories are determined by biological differences and skin tone is an efficacious marker of these differences. Yet, inspection of the correlation between skin tone and racial identity shows that racial identity groups have overlapping distributions of skin tone. For many persons, skin tone is not a reliable marker of racial identity.

The distributions of skin tone for three racial groups are presented in Table 2.1. The survey interviewer evaluated each respondent's skin tone, assigning a score of 0 to albinos, 1 to persons with the lightest skin shade,. . ., and 10 to persons with the darkest skin shade. The mean American has a skin tone of 2.35 and 71 percent have a skin tone of 1 or 2. Fifty-six percent of Americans have a skin tone of 2 or higher.

There is overlap in the distributions of skin tone across racial groups (Figure 2.1). "Other" is a residual racial category that includes Native Americans, Pacific Islanders, Latinx, Arabs, Asians, Hindu, and a host of persons of mixed-ancestral heritage. Some people who self-identify as Other or Black might easily pass as White. For example, 38 percent (84 of 221 persons) of Others and 4.3 percent of Blacks (15 of 349 people) have skin tones of 2 or lower, the same as 92 percent of Whites.

Some Whites and many Others have sufficiently dark skin tone to self-classify as Black. For example, 1 percent of Whites (11 of 1,483) and 9.5 percent of Others (21 of 221 persons) have a skin tone of 5 or higher, that is, a skin tone equal to the average or higher skin tone of Black Americans.

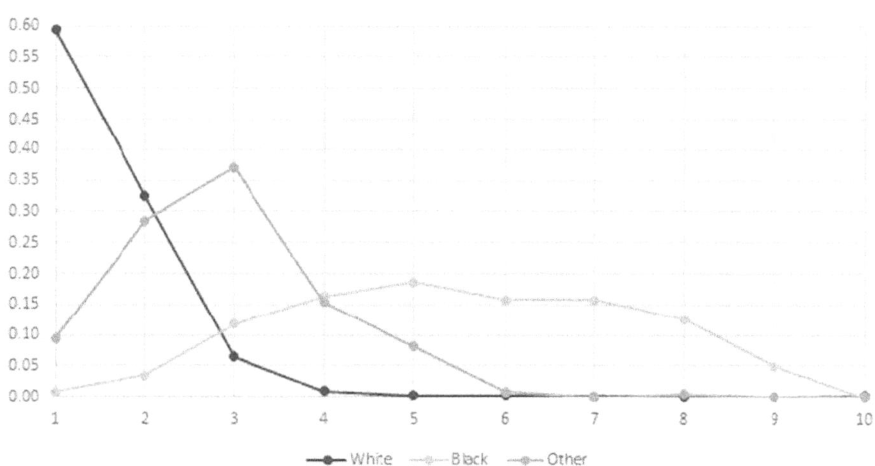

FIGURE 2.1. Distribution of skin tone by self-identified race
Source: Author's calculations. General Social Survey, 2018

On average, Others have a skin tone of 2.89. Sixteen percent of people who classify as Black have a skin tone of 3 or less and are able to pass as Other, while 8 percent of persons who self-identity as White have a skin tone of 3 or higher and thus are sufficiently dark to pass as Other.

The White skin tone distribution is L-shaped, with 91.8 percent having a skin tone of 1 or 2. Sixty percent of persons who self-identity as White have a skin tone of 1, only albinos are lighter. Sixteen of every 100 Black Americans has a skin tone of 3 or lower, the same as nearly 75 of every 100 Other Americans. Similarly, 18 of every 100 Other Americans have a skin tone of 4 or higher, compared to 96 of every 100 Black Americans. Many Black Americans have the skin tone to pass as Other and many Other Americans have the skin tone to pass as Black Americans.

The L-shaped White skin tone distribution is the result of a rigid social norm, whereby White status is a "pure" racial category; persons of mixed White and Non-White ancestry – and, thus darker skin tone – are excluded from Whiteness. The Black skin tone distribution is symmetric, because Blackness is an open racial category; no person of any known (or claimed) Black ancestry is excluded from Blackness; hence, the skin tone distribution has roughly similar probabilities for persons who are equally distant from the mean: roughly 15 percent of Blacks have a skin tone of 4 (a shade below the mean) and 15 percent have a skin tone of 6 (a shade above the mean). As a residual distribution, Others are often people who are excluded from Whiteness (because they are "impure") but who are uninterested in or too light be included in Blackness. By itself, skin tone is not an efficient mechanism for sorting persons into racial categories.

2.3 CENSUS DEFINITIONS OF RACE

The US decennial census has counted every American resident since 1790. For each of the 24 censuses between 1790 and 2020, every American resident has been assigned to or self-selected into at least one racial category. For most censuses, the enumerators were all White. Census classification rules and enumerator racial assignment are expressions of prevailing racial norms. Racial norms are resistant to change. In particular, two rules have remained constant across the censuses: (1) White purity, that is, mixed-race persons are excluded from White identity, regardless of whether race is assigned or self-selected; and (2) downward designation of mixed race persons, that is, mixed-race persons are designated the racial identity of the social group with the lowest socioeconomic status. Mixed-race designation may create social distance away from unmixed persons of the lowest social group, but it does not permit entry into the highest status group.

Starting in 1790, there were no specific census instructions on racial identification (Table 2.2). Census enumerators were to distinguish free White persons, all other free persons, and slaves. Racial identity determined access to important assets, viz., freedom, citizenship, ownership and protection of private property, and courts of law. Enslaved persons of African descent did not have access to either freedom, citizenship, ownership and protection of private property, or courts of law. Native Americans and other persons who were not White and not enslaved had nominal freedom, but they did not have access to citizenship, protection of property, or courts of law.

Prior to the end of chattel capitalism, White racial identity was a necessary condition for citizenship. But White political representation was determined by "the whole Number of free Persons, including those bound to Service for a

TABLE 2.2. *Racial identity and the US decennial census: 1790–1860*

Year	Instructions
1790	No specific instructions. Distinction between free white persons, all other free persons, and slaves.
1820	"Free colored persons" was added to census racial categories.
1850	Slave status was ascertained. Persons were recorded as "black" or "white" without instructions. Mulatto status is included for the first time.
1860	Color. "Color," in all cases where the person is White, leave the space blank; in all cases where the person is black without admixture insert the letter "B;" if a mulatto, or of mixed blood, write "M;" if an Indian, write "Ind." It is very desirable to have these directions carefully observed. "Chinese" is added to the California questionnaire.

Source: US Department of Commerce, Census Bureau, History, Through the Decades, Census Instructions, all years. www.census.gov/history/www/through_the_decades/census_instructions/. Last accessed December 20, 2022

Term of Years, and excluding Indians not taxed, three fifths of all other Persons" (United States Constitution, Article I Legislative Branch, Section 2 House of Representatives, Clause 3 Seats). Hence, enslavement of Africans increased the political power of all Whites in the states with the largest population of enslaved persons.

During 1790–1850, enumerators used their judgment to determine who was or was not White or Black. "Free colored persons" was added as a racial category in 1820 and mulatto was added in 1850. Only a free person of African descent with European features sufficient for passing for White – and actually passing – would be able to vote. The slave count increased Southern electoral college representation, that was further enhanced by the count of free colored persons in 1820 and mulattoes in 1850. Eugenicist Josiah C. Nott had lobbied for the mulatto category to be added to the census because he wanted data to verify his racist views that mulattoes were less fertile and had lower life expectancy than racially unmixed persons (Womack, 2017).

As the Civil War was approaching, in 1860 enumerators were given explicit instructions for racial classification. "Black" included persons who were Black-only, while "mulatto" included persons of "mixed blood." The racial designation "White" was reserved for persons who were White-only. Still, the enumerator used his judgment to determine who was White, Black, or mulatto. Neither Blacks nor mulattoes were eligible for citizenship.

Black persons represented nearly one in five Americans (19.3 percent) in 1790, though this had declined to about one in eight Americans (12.7 percent) by 1870 (see Table 2.3). Black representation was much higher in Southern states and increased during 1790–1850. For the median Southern states, Georgia and Maryland, Blacks comprised 35 percent of the population. The racial bar to freedom and citizenship benefitted the White elite because it gave them greater political power along with access to workers with reduced bargaining power (White workers were free but not wealthy), workers who were free but without bargaining power (free Africans), those who were free with land but no legal protection (Native Americans), or workers with no legal protection and no bargaining power (enslaved Africans). The racial bar to freedom and citizenship benefitted White workers because it gave them enhanced political power along with the right to vote, serve on juries, hold office, and obtain property; in the interracial competition for employment and public services it put them at the front of the line relative to enslaved Africans and non-citizens.

The 14th Amendment (June 13, 1866) established African American citizenship rights. The Censuses of 1870 and 1880 continued to define White as White-only. Mulatto was broadly defined to include quadroons (one grandparent is Black), octoroons (one great grandparent is Black), and all persons having any perceptible trace of African blood. Enumerators were told, "Important scientific results depend upon the correct determination of" persons who were mulattoes.

TABLE 2.3. *African American share of population: United States and selected States, 1790–1870*

	1790	1800	1810	1830	1850	1870
United States	19.3	18.9	19.0	18.1	15.7	12.7
South Carolina	43.7					58.9
Virginia	43.4					41.9
Georgia	35.9					46.0
Maryland	34.7					22.5
North Carolina	26.8					36.6
Delaware	21.6					18.2
Kentucky	17.0					16.8
Tennessee	10.6					25.6
West Virginia	9.5					4.1
Mississippi		41.5				53.7
Alabama		41.4				47.7
District of Columbia		30.4				33.0
Louisiana			55.2			50.1
Arkansas			13.0			25.2
Florida				47.1		48.8
Texas					27.5	31.0

Source: Gibson and Jung (2002).

Although the 1890 census is no longer extant, it marked yet another turning point in the government's racial classification of the US population: Black racial identity was dependent on the racial composition of a person's eight great grandparents. A person was Black if the person had "three-fourths or more black blood," that is, at least six of eight great-grandparents. Mulattoes were persons with three-eighths to five-eighths Black blood (or three to five great-grandparents), while quadroons had one-fourth Black blood (two great-grandparents), and octoroons were persons who had one-eighth or any trace of Black blood (at least one great-grandparent or any evidence of a Black ancestor).

The rationale for including expanded Black racial categories in 1890 is similar to the changes made in 1850, eugenicists wanted to collect data to support biogenetic theories that mixed-race Black persons had different life expectancies than pure Black persons. The census should therefore have published birth and death rates by pure and mixed race categories. It was popularly accepted "that mixed-race individuals were physically, mentally, and morally degenerate" (Hochschild and Powell, 2008: 69).

In the aftermath of the *Plessy* v. *Ferguson* "separate but equal" ruling of 1896, mixed race designations were dropped from the 1900 census; there were no instructions for identifying mulattoes, quadroons, or octoroons. Negroes or persons of Negro descent were identified as Black. Chinese, Japanese, and Indians (Native Americans) were also identified.

TABLE 2.4. *Racial identity and the US decennial census: 1870–1940*

Year	Instructions
1870	Color. It must not be assumed that, where nothing is written in this column. "White" is to be understood. The column is always to be filled. Be particularly careful in reporting the class Mulatto. The word is here generic, and includes quadroons, octoroons, and all persons having any perceptible trace of African blood. Important scientific results depend upon the correct determination of this class in Schedules 1 and 2.
1880	Color. It must not be assumed that, where nothing is written in this column, "white" is to be understood. The column is always to be filled. Be particularly careful in reporting the class mulatto. The word is here generic, and includes quadroons, octoroons, and all persons having any perceptible trace of African blood. Important scientific results depend upon the correct determination of this class in schedules 1 and 5.
1890	Whether white, black, mulatto, quadroon, octoroon, Chinese, Japanese, or Indian. Write white, black, mulatto, quadroon, octoroon, Chinese, Japanese, or Indian, according to the color or race of the person enumerated. Be particularly careful to distinguish between blacks, mulattoes, quadroons, and octoroons. The word "black" should be used to describe those persons who have three-fourths or more black blood; "mulatto," those persons who have from three-eighths to five-eighths black blood; "quadroon," those persons who have one-fourth black blood; and "octoroon," those persons who have one-eighth or any trace of black blood.
1900	Color or race. Write "W" for white; "B" for black (negro or of negro descent); "Ch" for Chinese; "Jp" for Japanese, and "In" for Indian, as the case may be.
1910	Color or race. Write "w" for white; "B" for black; "Mu" for mulatto; "Ch" for Chinese; "JP" for Japanese; "IN" for Indian. For all other person not falling into one of these classes, write "Ot" (for other), and write on the left-hand margin of the schedule the race of the person so indicated. For census purposes, the term "black" (B) includes all persons who are evidently full-blooded negroes, while the term "mulatto" (Mu) includes all other persons having some proportion or perceptible trace of negro blood.
1920	Color or race. Write "W" for white; "B" for black; "Mu" for mulatto; "In" for Indian; "Ch" for Chinese; "Jp" for Japanese; "Fil" for Filipino; "Hin" for Hindu; "Kor" for Korean. For all persons not falling within one of these classes, write" Ot" (for other), and write on the left-hand margin of the schedule the race of the person so indicated. For census purposes the term "black" (B) includes all Negroes of full blood, while the term "mulatto" (Mu) includes all Negroes having some proportion of white blood.
1930	Color or race. Write "W" for white; "Neg" for Negro; "Mex" for Mexican; "In" for Indian; "Ch" for Chinese; "Jp" for Japanese; "Fil" for Filipino; "Hin" for Hindu; and "Kor" for Korean. For a person of any other race, write the race in full.
	Negroes. A person of mixed white and Negro blood should be returned as a Negro, no matter how small the percentage of Negro blood. Both black and

(*continued*)

TABLE 2.4. (*continued*)

Year	Instructions
	mulatto persons are to be returned as Negroes, without distinction. A person of mixed Indian and Negro blood should be returned as Negro, unless the Indian blood predominates and the status as an Indian is generally accepted in the community.
	Indians. A person of mixed white and Indian blood should be returned as Indian, except where the percentage of Indian blood is very small, or where he is regarded as a white person by those in the community where he lives. For a person reported as Indian in column 12, report is to be made in column 19 as to whether "full blood" or "mixed blood," and in column 20 the name of the tribe is to be reported. For Indians, columns 19 and 20 are thus to be used to indicate the degree of Indian blood and the tribe, instead of the birthplace of father and mother.
	Mexicans. Practically all Mexican laborers are of a racial mixture difficult to classify, though usually well recognized in the localities where they are found. In order to obtain separate figures for this racial group, it has been decided that all persons born in Mexico, or having parents born in Mexico, who are not definitely white, Negro, Indian, Chinese, or Japanese should be returned as Mexican ("Mex").
	Other mixed races. Any mixture of white and nonwhite should be reported according to the nonwhite parent. Mixtures of colored races should be reported according to the race of the father, except Negro-Indian.
1940	Color or race. Any mixtures of white and nonwhite blood should be recorded according to the race of the nonwhite parent. A person of mixed Negro and Indian blood should be reported as Negro unless the Indian blood greatly predominates and he is universally accepted in the community as an Indian. Other mixtures of nonwhite parentage should be reported according to the race of the father. Mexicans are to be returned as white, unless definitely of Indian or other nonwhite race.

Source: US Department of Commerce, Census Bureau, History, Through the Decades, Census Instructions, all years. www.census.gov/history/www/through_the_decades/census_instructions/. Last accessed December 12, 2022

For 1910 and 1920, Black included all persons "who are evidently full-blooded negroes." Mulatto included all "persons having some proportion or perceptible trace of negro blood" in 1910 and "Negroes having some proportion of white blood" in 1920.

The census enumerators of 1930 were given the most extensive racial classification instructions up to that point in time. Mixed race categories were eliminated; persons of plural ancestral heritage were assigned to the racial category with the lowest status among the person's plural ancestral groups. For example, Negroes included: all persons of mixed White and Negro blood (regardless of how small the percentage of Negro blood); Blacks and mulattoes;

TABLE 2.5. *Racial identity and the US decennial census: Post–World War II*

1950	Determining and entering race. Write "W" for white; "Neg" for Negro; "In" for Indian; "Ch" for Chinese; "Jp" for Japanese; "Fil" for Filipino; "Hin" for Hindu; "Kor" for Korean. For a person of any other race, write the race in full. Assume that the race of a related person living in the same household is the same as the race of your respondent, unless you learn otherwise. Mexicans. Report white "W" for Mexicans unless definitely of Indian or other nonwhite race. Negroes. Report "Negro" (Neg) for Negroes and persons of mixed white and Negro parentage. A person of mixed Negro and Indian blood should be returned as a Negro, unless the Indian blood very definitely predominates and he is accepted in the community as an Indian. American Indians. Report "American Indian" (Ind) for persons of mixed white and Indian blood if enrolled on an Indian agency or Reservation role; if not so enrolled, they should still be reported as Indian if the proportion of Indian blood is one-fourth or more, or if they are regarded as Indians in the community where they live. In those counties where there are many Indians living outside of reservations, special care should be taken to obtain accurate answers to item 9.[1] Special communities. Report persons of mixed white, Negro, and Indian ancestry living in certain communities in the Eastern United States in terms of the name by which they are locally known. The communities in question are of long standing and are locally recognized by special names, such as "Croatan," "Jackson white," "We-sort," etc. Persons of mixed Indian and Negro ancestry and mulattoes not living in such communities should be returned as "Negro." Mixed parentage. Report race of nonwhite parent for persons of mixed white and nonwhite races. Mixtures of nonwhite races should be reported according to the race of the father. India. Persons originating in India should be reported as "Asiatic Indians."
1960	Self-described race. Country of birth of respondent and parents.
2000 & 2010	Self-described race; respondent may select multiple categories.

[1] Item 9 is the census question on the respondent's racial identity.
Source: US Department of Commerce, Census Bureau, History, Through the Decades, Census Instructions, all years. www.census.gov/history/www/through_the_decades/census_instructions/. Last accessed December 12, 2022

and, persons of Indian (Native American) and Negro blood (unless the Indian blood predominates and the status as an Indian is generally accepted in the community). Indians included all full-blooded Indians as well as persons of mixed White and Indian blood, "except where the percentage of Indian blood is very small, or where he is regarded as a white person by those in the community where he lives."

For Mexicans, national origin and racial identity were conflated into a single Non-White category. Census enumerators understood that the majority of Mexicans were Mestizo (various mixtures of persons with European, African, and Indigenous ancestral heritage) and a sizable minority of Mexicans are Indigenous or Native Americans. The instructions stated that "all persons born in Mexico, or having parents born in Mexico, who are not definitely White, Negro, Indian, Chinese, or Japanese should be returned as Mexican." Finally, any person of mixed White and Non-White heritage is reported according to the Non-White parent. "Mixtures of colored races should be reported according to the race of the father, except Negro-Indian." By 1940 Mexicans were considered White, "unless definitely of Indian or other nonwhite race."

The Civil Rights Movement reached its apex during the 1950s and 1960s. Once again, the decennial census changed its instructions for determining the racial affiliation of persons residing in America. Related persons living in the same household as the census respondent were assigned the same race as the respondent unless the enumerator "learns otherwise." Mexicans were White, unless the enumerator ascertained that a person of Mexican ancestry was "definitely of Indian or other nonwhite race." Negro was used instead of "Black." Negro included (pure) Negroes and all persons of mixed White and Negro parentage. Persons of mixed Negro and Indian blood were considered Negroes. Persons of mixed White and Indian blood were American Indians if they had at least one full-blooded Indian grandparent; otherwise, they were White. Persons living in special local commonly recognized communities and who had mixed White, Indian, and Negro ancestry were given whatever racial classification by which they were locally known. But, persons of White, Indian, and Negro ancestry who did not reside in these special communities were designated as Negro. East Indians (people from the country of India) were Caucasian. However, Caucasian status did not get them into Whiteness in the 1950 US census; instead, they were labeled Asiatic Indians.

From 1960 onward census respondents were allowed to select their own racial category. Respondents were allowed to select multiple categories in 2000. Despite multiple changes in the census' racial classification matrix, there are some consistent elements. First, White is a pure category, a category of exclusion, any known Non-White ancestry renders a person unqualified for White identity. Second, ancestral mixing pulls racial identity downward; persons of multiple ancestral heritages will be assigned the racial identity consistent with the race of the ancestral group with the least social status. Third, Black is an impure residual category, used to include anyone with any known African ancestry.

2.4 ACCULTURATION: RACIAL STRATEGIES FOR UPWARD MOBILITY

Chattel capitalism, servitude capitalism, and racialized managerial capitalism are regimes of structural racism. There are dissimilarities in the nature and extent of the racism. For example, White commodification of Black life (enslavement) is not the same as White monopolization of Black citizenship (Black Codes and Jim Crow), that is different from a regime with a pre-existing racial disparity in wealth created combined with substantive White control of managerial resources (racialized managerial capitalism). However, there are also important similarities. For each regime, there is a rule or system of rules for sorting individuals into mutually exclusive racial groups with differing amounts of political economic power, and individuals are punished for transgressing racial boundaries.

In a racialized economy, transracial acculturation by a single person or a small sub-group of persons is a social innovation. It is difficult for this innovation to spread and dislodge existing racial identity norms because individualist transracial acculturation reduces participation in own-group benefits and increases the costs borne by a single person or small sub-group of persons due to other-group antagonism. Yet, if there are differential rates of return to social group identities some persons may attempt identity arbitrage, that is, to find a mechanism that allows transracial acculturation into the group with the higher rate of return to social identity. If a person attempts transracial acculturation and the person is accepted into the alternative (greater resources) group, then the person's identity strategy will yield a higher payoff. In this case, a higher payoff means higher wages and better access to employment. If a person attempts transracial acculturation and is not accepted into the alternative group, then the person's identity strategy will yield a lower payoff. A failed attempt at transaction acculturation reduces access to both own- and other-group resources.

Historically, acculturation strategies within American society have included racial passing, "acting White," and mixed race identification (Burma, 1946).[2] Passing occurs when Euro-phenotype persons of African descent select a White racial identity or when Afro-phenotype persons of European descent select a Black social identity (Kennedy, 2001).[3] Persons might wish to pass in order to arbitrage differences in economic well-being associated with racial identities. If there is a large economic payoff to Whiteness, there will be strong incentives for European-featured Africans to identity as White and relatively little incentive for African-featured Europeans to identify as Black. Passing was particularly popular between the 1850s and 1940s, but appears to be much less prevalent today (Hobbs, 2014).

"Acting White" is ideological passing for those who lack the appropriate physical features to pass. If economic motives are the primary reasons for ideological passing, we should expect to see a relatively greater presence of

[2] African Americans sometimes refer to "Acting white" as Tomming. Passing may be situational, temporary, periodic, or permanent.

[3] African Americans who passed as White went to extreme lengths to make sure that they were never exposed. See Graham (1999).

ideological passing among the least wealthy social groups. Hence, African Americans acting White are not permitted to pass as White, but they are permitted to pass as individuals among Whites if they are sufficiently ideologically integrated into Whiteness.

2.5 COLORISM

Mixed-race identification is connected to the prevalence of colorism, a discriminatory process whereby the extent of racial disparity varies by skin shade (Goldsmith, Darity, and Hamilton, 2007). Colorism implies that lighter skin-shade Blacks may experience differential market payoffs relative to darker skin African Americans, but there is not a monotonic change in disparity as skin-shade changes from very dark to very light. Also, there is not a one-to-one mapping from skin shade to alternative racial self-classification categories. Most light complexion African Americans self-identify as Black-only, regardless of how they are seen by others. Similarly, some self-classified mixed-race African Americans may appear to be Black-only to others. Accordingly, empirical analysis on skin shade indicates how social perceptions of racial identity influences economic outcomes.

Historical economics, social psychology, sociology, and contemporary labor economics provide empirical evidence suggesting that colorism is an important feature of contemporary racial discrimination. These studies focus on both the United States and on the primary countries of origin for immigrants of African descent: the Caribbean, South America, and Africa. Some studies include self- or interview-reported measures of skin shade, while others utilize self- or interview-reported multi-racial classifications that are correlated with skin shade (Bodenhorn and Ruebeck, 2007).

Identity differences among African Americans were widespread during the nineteenth century. In their analysis of 1860 census data of the urban South, Howard Bodenhorn and Christopher Ruebeck found that mixed-race people, referred to as “mulattoes,” often had economic incentives to distinguish themselves from Blacks (Bodenhorn and Ruebeck, 2003). By rejecting Blackness and “acting White,” sometimes it was possible for mulattoes to obtain better education, higher occupational status, and greater wealth accumulation (Bodenhorn and Ruebeck, 2007). However, simply separating themselves from Black-only or darker African Americans was not sufficient for mulattoes to achieve greater socioeconomic well-being. The separation also had to occur in a context whereby it was beneficial to Whites. Further, the advantages of mixed-race identity varied by region and by the demographic composition of the population. For example, mixed-race individuals of the Lower South (and the Caribbean) most frequently were the children of affluent White males and free or enslaved Black women. Hence, they secured advantages not available to individuals who were Black-only, such as manumission, some degree of education, and inheritance from fathers (Bodenhorn, 2003). In contrast, mixed-race individuals of the Upper South were most frequently the children of poor White males and enslaved Black women. Hence, the mulatto–Black economic differential in the Upper South may have been less than the mulatto–Black economic differential in the Lower South.

Bodenhorn and Ruebeck (2007) further confirmed that there was a pattern of colorism in the 1860 urban South. They found that Black and mixed-race male heads of household accumulated 87 and 65 percent less wealth, respectively, than Whites. Similarly, Black and mulatto female heads of household accumulated 88 and 67 percent less wealth, respectively, than Whites.

The physical stature of a social group also has a positive correlation with the group's socioeconomic status. Differences in height provide another means to assess the relative status of mulattoes in comparison to Black-only persons. In an analysis of 23 counties in rural Virginia, Bodenhorn (2002) reported that light males attained an average terminal stature of 68.5 inches compared to a terminal stature of just 67.1 inches for dark males, while light women were, on average, more than 2 inches taller than women of dark complexion.

Both the sociology and social psychology literatures have documented strong empirical effects associated with skin tone colorism (Keith and Herring, 1991; Blair et al., 2002; Blair, Judd, and Chapleau, 2004; Herring, Keith, and Horton, 2004; Maddox, 2004). For example, using the 1979–1980 National Survey of Black Americans, sociologists Verna Keith and Cedric Herring constructed a continuous skin tone variable ranging from a value of 1 (very dark) to 5 (very light). They found that a one standardized unit increase in lightness was associated with greater years of education, higher occupational status, greater personal income, and greater family income.

A study by Arthur Goldsmith, Darrick Hamilton, and William Darity attempted to ascertain whether a preference for Whiteness influences inter- and intra-racial wage inequality.[4] Their work utilized samples from the 1979–1980 National Survey of Black Americans (NSBA) and the Multicity Study of Urban Inequality (MCSUI).[5] Goldsmith, Hamilton, and Darity found evidence in both the MCSUI and NSBA datasets that was consistent with weak

[4] Op. cit., Goldsmith, Darity, and Hamilton (2007).

[5] Similar studies include: Hersch (2006), that uses the 2003 New Immigrant Survey (NIS), the NSBA, MCSUI, and the 1995 Detroit Area Study: Social Influence on Health: Stress, Racism, and Health Protective (DAS); and Loury (2009), that uses the NSBA. Importantly, all of the interviewers for the NSBA are African Americans, which is not the case for the DAS (Hersch, 2006). For the DAS, both interviewer and interviewee provided skin tone assessments. The DAS shows that, for the sample of Black respondents, there was an agreement of interviewer- and self-reported skin tone only 65 percent of the time. In comparison to Black interviewers, Non-Black interviewers systematically reported darker skin tones for Black respondents. Conceivably, skin shade studies utilizing the MCSUI have errors-in-variables and thereby suffer from attenuation bias, that is, their coefficients on skin shade are biased toward the origin and thereby are less likely to detect colorism.

colorism.[6] In particular, African Americans as a whole suffered a market penalty relative to Whites, but the penalty for lighter African Americans was lower than the penalty for medium and darker shade African Americans.[7] Using the NSBA, Joni Hersch found no skin shade wage effects for women (Hersch, 2006). However, Hersch's analysis of the MCSUI data was consistent with colorism effects in the hourly wages of African American men and women.

The 2003 New Immigrant Survey (NIS) skin color variable contained greater and more precise measures of variations in skin shade than other skin shade variables available in large sample datasets, such as the NSBA and MCSUI populations. Interviewers were provided with a color scale that consisted of a series of hands with color increasing in darkness. Skin color was then reported on a scale of 0–10. Regardless of nation of origin, all immigrants received a skin shade assessment. Using the NIS, Hersch (2008) in this instance found that immigrants with the lightest skin tone earned 8–15 percent higher wages than darker immigrants with the same human capital, height, occupation, job characteristics, labor force attachment, spousal citizenship and visa status, race, gender, and national origin.[8] Including a standard set of human capital covariates (including English skills) and occupational controls to account for unobserved productivity variables, Hersch found that each one-point increase in skin tone scale lowered wages by 1.5 percent. The lightest skin immigrants earned 17 percent more than otherwise comparable immigrants with darker skin color.

Similarly, mixed-race persons are the largest Non-Black social group in Jamaica (Mason, 2007). Mostly, they are mixed race Black–White persons. Compared to otherwise identical Black Jamaicans, mixed race Jamaicans receive nearly 14 percent higher earnings. Historically, colorism has been the dominant expression of racial discrimination within Caribbean and South American countries. These considerations suggest that, relative to native-born African Americans, there may be a greater propensity toward mixed race self-identification among Caribbean and South American immigrants.

[6] An important limitation of both the NSBA and the MCSUI datasets is the very small number of observations of light complexion African Americans. For example, the Goldsmith et al. study has 331 observations on African Americans, but only 39 individuals are classified as light, with 154 and 133 classified as medium and dark, respectively. Their MCSUI sample includes 513 Whites, and 51, 177, and 207 light, medium, and dark complexion African Americans, respectively. Despite the very small numbers of very light and light complexion African Americans, the results obtained from the NSBA and MSCUI datasets are comparable to the results obtained from other datasets.

[7] There was no statistically significant difference between the penalties for the latter two groups. The absolute value of the skin shade coefficients depends on the method of estimation (ordinary least squares versus median regression), type of regression (standard versus ex ante), the number and type of wage covariates, and whether one is using the MCSUI or NSBA dataset.

[8] Hersch uses the New Immigrant Survey 2003.

2.6 INTO AND OUT OF WHITENESS

Phenotype remains an important predictor of racial identity (Golash-Boza and Darity, 2008). However, controlling for phenotype, racial identities are subject to change over time, regions, or countries (Ignatiev, 1995; Brodkin, 1998). Many groups Franklin (1751) wished to exclude from becoming American citizens because of their swarthy complexion are today considered "pure White."

The intensity of racial identity may vary within racial groups. Growth in the density of own-group identity is proportional to changes in the other-group antagonism (Mason, 2017). This suggests that the intensive and extensive margins of self-identification of a racial group (for example, African American self-identification as Black-alone versus mixed-race) will increase with an increase in other-group (White) antagonism, viz., an increase in racial or ethnic minority social and economic discrimination will increase the intensity of identification with the minority racial or ethnic group. This is a counter-intuitive result. With an increase in White antagonism there is a relatively large increase in the own-group protection benefit to self-identifying as Black-alone; hence, an increase in White antagonism will raise the incentive to self-identify as Black-alone.

Exogenous events, for example, an existential threat to the nation, may provide strong incentives to reduce racialization. Because the military is charged to protect the nation from this type of threat, it has sought to develop a military identity that dominates the pre-enlistment racial identities of persons joining the armed forces. But, currently existing institutional rules and procedures designed to reduce the intensity of pre-enlistment racial identity and to increase the intensity of post-enlistment military identity have limited efficacy (Stewart, 2009).

Arab ethnicity and Islamic religious affiliation were stigmatized by the public and private reaction to the Al Qaeda attacks of September 11, 2001 and a series of following events, viz., the US led invasion of Iraq during March 19, 2003–May 1, 2003, the long war following the Iraq invasion and the discussion of the war in the elections of 2004, the racially charged US presidential election of 2008, and the Congressional elections of 2010. Mason and Matella (2014) use interstate changes in the percentage of hate crimes targeted at Muslims to identify exogenous changes in the post-9/11 racial environment (Gould and Klor, 2016). They find that a one percentage point increase in anti-Muslim hate crimes is associated with a 9% increase in the odds an Arab or Islamic American will self-identify as Non-White, that is, either Black or Other-race. The point estimates for native-born persons and immigrants are 28% and 7%, respectively.

Mason (2017) uses changes in a state's fraction of White votes for Obama in 2008 relative to Kerry in 2004 to provide an empirical proxy for a change in White antagonism toward African Americans. This study finds that there is a positive and statistically significant Obama-effect on African American self-identification as mixed-race rather than as Black-alone. Point estimates of the Obama effect on African American racial identity range from a low of no statistically significant effect for elderly African Americans to a high of 1.09 percent marginal effect for young African Americans self-identifying as mixed-race. The Obama effect is strongest among the non-elderly (especially young adults), Latinx, and immigrants.

The racial identity effect of an increase in White antagonism depends on whether a group is under- or overrepresented in particular social and economic outcomes (Antman and Duncan, 2015). Specifically, the imposition of a state government ban on affirmative action policies in higher education, contracting, and employment, decreases the incentives for persons affiliated with under-represented ancestral groups to self-identity as a member of the racial group, while persons affiliated with overrepresented ancestral groups are more likely to self-identity as a member of the racial group. Hence, Antman and Duncan find that, when affirmative action bans are implemented, persons of African ancestral origin are less likely to self-identity as Black, while persons of Asian ancestral origin are more likely to self-identify as Asian.

Mason (2004) finds that, after controlling for skin shade and phenotype, English language fluency, and Spanish accent, that self-identification as Chicano and Spanish fluency has a negative effect on the earnings of Mexican Americans in comparison to persons who do not self-identify as Chicano and who are not fluent in Spanish. This is a clear Latinx identity penalty.

2.7 RACIAL IDENTITY, CULTURE, AND BEHAVIOR

There is no necessary link between racial identity and behavior. Within stratification economics, acting White is an acculturation strategy, completely divorced from assumptions regarding racial differences in market-functional personal behavior, values, and culture. But, within the individualist framework acting White is not an attempt at transracial acculturation. Rather, for individualists the acting White perspective is constructed on the notion that African American youth are anti-intellectual while White youth are academically oriented (Fordham and Ogbu, 1986). Hence, individualists assert that Blacks who are studious are violating African American cultural prescriptions and therefore are negatively perceived as "acting White." Studious African American students will then be punished by the anti-intellectual Black majority. There is no punishment for Whites who are studious. Per Fordham and Ogbu, African Americans' anti-intellectual culture is an important cause of the Black–White gap in academic achievement and, therefore, also the Black–White gap in labor market outcomes (Mason, 2004).

With reference to racial identity and associated cultural norms, a study by Ruebeck, Averett, and Bodenhorn (2009) is especially illuminating. In that work, they compared the risky behaviors and academic success of Non-

Latinx White, Black, and Black–White biracial youth. If we accept individualist reasoning, if African American youth who self-identify as biracial wish to establish that they are authentically Black, then they, too, will adopt an anti-intellectual (or "oppositional") culture. Ruebeck and colleagues hypothesized that self-identified bi-racial youth and Black youth are more likely to "act out," and high achieving (i.e., high GPA) bi-racial and Black youth will be even more likely to "act out" as a compensating mechanism for being high achievers within a group that is alleged to have an anti-intellectual culture. In fact, however, Ruebeck, Averett, and Bodenhorn found no evidence to support the individualist version of the "acting-White" hypothesis, finding instead evidence that is directly contradictory to the individualist perspective. Ruebeck and colleagues went on to conclude that the evidence suggests that self-identified bi-racial youth are constructing an identity that is neither Black nor White.

Economist Ronald Ferguson also pointed to data inconsistent with individualist economics (Ferguson, 2008). Instead, in agreement with the Darity/Mason/Stewart model, Ferguson's results showed that, when young African Americans label another African American youth as acting-White, the student is often quite literally acting White, frequently listening to "White" music, or speaking in a manner similar to Whites. An article co-authored by sociologist Tyson, Darity, and Castellino (2005) likewise concluded that the individualist acting-White hypothesis is not valid. Instead, Tyson and colleagues argued that all high achieving students are to some extent labeled "nerds" or "geeks," regardless of race.

2.8 SUMMARY AND DISCUSSION

Racial identity norms evolve from social interactions between and among persons of alternative ancestral, religious, or other social groups. Within these interactions, persons select strategies that strengthen or weaken racial identity norms. These social interactions increase the productivity of persons if they are mutually altruistic, that is, both persons are willing to share their personal and affiliational resources in order to accomplish a joint goal. Mutually antagonistic social interactions reduce each person's productivity. Racialization – the creation, abolition, and altering of racial categories – is an ongoing process of social and economic evolution.

The socioeconomic evolution of racial norms carries with it a process of racial labeling, that is, deciding on the matrix of rules describing the boundaries between mutually exclusive racial groups and allocating persons to those groups. To the extent that racial identities are productive, that is, create differential access to public and private resources, some persons attempt to acculturate, that is, to transgress across racial boundaries.

Self-identification and labeling conventions are social norms that emerge to distinguish social groups and thereby facilitates differential degrees of access to private and social resources within and between social groups. Racial conventions are fashioned to limit entry into the wealthiest social group. When racialized identities exist as a social norm, an obvious convention is, "Persons with light skin color are White; otherwise, the person is Non-White, for example, Black." Over time, this binary descriptor would make "European" synonymous with "White" and "African" synonymous with "Black." But, both actual and perceived skin shade and other physical differences are imprecise and subjective, meaning that racial categorization by other-group persons will also be imprecise and subjective.

3

Mechanisms of Stratification

Insecurities and Inequities of Capitalist Competition

Structural racism arose with European exploration, enslavement, and colonization of Africans, triangular trade, and the historical development of capitalism as a world system (Williams, 1994; Mason, 2013). Structural racism is far more than personal racial prejudice, that is, racially biased decisions based on incomplete, incorrect, or imprecise information. It is also far more than personal racial bigotry, that is, racially hostile behavior, attitudes, or values based on irrational opposition toward those perceived as different. Structural racism consists of public policies and institutional practices with persistently racially disparate outcomes, cultural representations that continuously encourage invidious comparisons across racial groups, and norms of social interactions that encourage the reproduction of racialized social identities. Structural racism allows "privileges associated with 'Whiteness' and disadvantages associated with 'color' to endure and adapt over time. … [I]t has been a feature of the social, economic and political systems in which we all exist" (The Aspen Institute, 2004: 1). Racism is multi-dimensional and deeply rooted within American society. However, those facts do not imply that racism is a naturally occurring social phenomena due to some immutable characteristic of "human nature" and will therefore always be with us.

In addition to the formation of racial identity as a social norm, wealth inequality, involuntary unemployment, and the exploitation of labor are economic mechanisms that create the conditions for permanent structural racism. Racial differences in wealth, initially created by chattel and servitude capitalisms, reproduce racial disparities in economic, political, and social outcomes. These disparities embed a disproportionately large fraction of Whites in positions of power and authority within hiring institutions.

Involuntary unemployment creates the possibility for the use of racial identity as a job allocation mechanism. In particular, African Americans will have less access to employment than otherwise identical White workers. Inter-

and intra-industry differences in competitive structure and managerial strategy indicate that persons of identical skill (and market-functional behaviors) will not necessarily receive identical treatment within the labor market: the competitive pursuit of profit creates differentiation and inequality. Persistent racial discrimination is consistent with market competition and the accumulation of profits. Within this framework, "race" is an economic strategy for determining access to resources and opportunities; racial identity is strongly related to inequality in wealth (Darity, Mason, and Stewart, 2006). Historically, the slave trade, enslavement, and Jim Crow created both racial identities and enormous racial inequalities in wealth. The privileges of wealth reproduce both wealth inequalities and racial identities. Racialized competition within the labor market and persistent wealth inequality combine to reproduce structural racism.

3.1 PERSISTENT PRIVILEGE: WEALTH

Chattel and servitude capitalism were social systems designed to transfer wealth from persons of African descent to persons of European descent. Both systems worked as planned, creating enormous wealth inequality between Blacks and Whites. Hence, racialized managerial capitalism originates with this racial disparity and transfers it into the future by means of bequests and inheritances, in vivo transfers, intra-family contributions of time and information, and the social privileges and differential access to opportunities associated with wealth. Past racial wealth inequality establishes the material basis for persistent intergenerational racial wealth inequality and the continuous reproduction of racialized identities. Neither the First Reconstruction of 1865–1877, after the demise of chattel capitalism, nor the Second Reconstruction of 1955–1968, which ended servitude capitalism, provided reparations to African Americans to compensate for past and ongoing racist processes that were responsible for unjust enrichment.

For pre-school children in 2002, African American parents had three cents of wealth relative to each dollar of wealth of White parents; African American grandparents had eleven cents of wealth relative to each dollar of wealth of White grandparents (Chiteji, 2010). Thirty-four percent and 10 percent of African American parents and grandparents, respectively, had no wealth versus 9% and 4% of White parents and grandparents, respectively. The interracial differences in family wealth were a direct reflection of the legacy of slavery, Jim Crow, and continuing racial discrimination in American society. Racial disparity in socioeconomic outcomes will persist as long as there is a racial wealth gap. Consider Table 3.1, which demonstrates the hypothetical wealth effects for four generations of an extended family over a period of 40 years. Initially, the family consists of grandparents (G1) who are 54 years of age, young adult parents (G2) who are 30 years of age, and grandchildren (G3) who are 6 years of age. The grandparents are at their peak earnings years. Net worth is the difference between the market value of a family's assets (things owned by the

TABLE 3.1. *Wealth and intergenerational mobility: The nature and significance of "inheritances"*

	Grandparents	Young Adult Parents	Grandchildren	Great Grandchildren
	G1	G2	G3	G4
Age	54	30	6	
	Peek Income Years No Debt Many Assets	Peek Debt Years Few Assets Modest Income		
		Down Payment Help From G1	Tuition Assistance From G1	
Age	75	51	27	3
	Nursing Home? Sick? Financial Assistance from G2 Time Assistance from G2, G3	Peek Income Years No Debt Many Assets	Peek Debt Years Few Assets Modest Income Down Payment Help from G1 G2	Tuition Assistance from G1, G2, G3
Age	94	70	46	22
	Heaven or Elsewhere	Bequest from G1 Social Capital from G1 Cultural Capital from G1	Bequest from G1 Social Capital from G1, G2 Cultural Capital from G1, G2	Bequest from G1 Social Capital from G1, G2, G3 Cultural Capital from G1, G2, G3

family) and the market value of a family's liabilities (debts owed to others). In our example, grandparents have very high net worth because they have no debt, many assets, and high savings out of current income.

Young adult parents have few assets, are accumulating debt, and have only modest income. Hence, they may not have the cash to make the 20 percent down payment on a home with a conventional mortgage. However, grandparents have the wealth to provide an in vivo transfer (gift) to the young adult parents. Rather than renting, the intra-family transfer will permit young adult parents to accumulate equity in their own home. Also, with sufficient wealth, the grandparents can make in vivo transfers to their grandchildren. For example, the grandparents purchase higher quality education for their grandchildren. Accordingly, during the initial period, grandparents use in vivo transfers to increase the net worth of young adult parents and to increase the human capital (or skill) of grandchildren.

During the next period, the family consists of grandparents who are 75 years of age, young adult parents who are 51 years of age, grandchildren who are 27 years of age, and there are now 3-year-old great grandchildren (G4). G2, who were young adult parents but who are now grandparents, can provide financial assistance to G1, who are now elderly and may have rising health care needs. Further, G2 and G3 (the original grandchildren who are now young adult parents) can provide time resources to G1. If G1 does not require financial assistance, then both G1 and G2 will be able to assist G3 in obtaining a home, purchasing income producing assets, or obtaining an advanced educational degree. Similarly, G1, G2, and G3 may be in a position to provide high quality pre-school education to the great grandchildren (G4).

Social capital is a family's set of embedded relationships. These relationships provide sources of information, access to persons with control over resources, and access to decision-making authority. Cultural capital is an accumulation of alternative ways of knowing, the ability to successfully communicate in alternative social milieus, the ability to successfully act in different cultural scenarios, and the capacity to understand the symbols of various social groups; it is knowledge that is largely accumulated outside of formal academic training.

During the final time-period, G1 has expired at 94 years of age, leaving bequests for G2, G3, and G4. G1 has also transferred social and cultural capital to all the other generations. Note that G4 enters adulthood with financial wealth, skill advantages, social capital advantages, and cultural capital advantages.

The discussion has focused on a virtuous cycle of wealth accumulation across generations of an extended family. Note, however, that a vicious cycle of wealth non-accumulation across generations of an extended family is also possible. If G1 does not have wealth or has great debt, then there will be no wealth, or social and cultural advantages to transfer to young generations. Median White family wealth is 25 and 10 times median Black family wealth for the Non-South and South, respectively.[1] Comparatively speaking, White families have a virtuous cycle of wealth creation, while African American families have a vicious cycle of wealth accumulation. Even if there were no contemporary differences in savings behavior, income, or education, the interracial differences in wealth are sufficiently vast so as to continuously reproduce intergenerational disparity in wealth for African American and White families.

[1] See Table 8.1.

3.2 PERSISTENT ECONOMIC POWER: RACE–GENDER COMPOSITION OF MANAGERIAL OCCUPATIONS

Managers are the locus of power within firms, organizations, and institutions. Among many other tasks, they are responsible for recruiting, training, supervising, and evaluating workers. Managers have discretionary authority over resources, information, and decision-making. It is important then to examine the race–gender composition of occupations, as the manager–worker identity match may not yield an identical flow of managerial time, information, supervisory support, and other resources for intra- and intergroup matches.

White men are 31.6 percent of the population of US persons 25–64 years-old, but they are 47.5 of managers (Table 3.2). This indicates that White men are 50 percent overrepresented among managers. Except for Non-Latinx Other men, that is, American Indians, Pacific Islander Americans, and Asian Americans, all other groups are underrepresented among managers. African American and Latinx women are the most underrepresented, 46 percent and 53.4 percent, respectively. African American men and Latinx men are 5.6 percent and 8.3 percent of the population, respectively, but 3.5 percent and 5.3 percent of managers, yielding underrepresentation rates of 37.8 percent and 35.9 percent, respectively. White women have an underrepresentation rate of 8.7 percent.

White men have extreme overrepresentation among most of the 15 highest paid managerial occupations; for example, they are 63 percent of chief executives, 72 percent of engineering managers, 65 percent of industrial managers as well as funeral directors, 57 percent of general and operations managers, and 51 percent of computer and information systems managers (Table 3.3). White men are underrepresented among human resources managers, representing 19–24.6 percent of this group; White women are overrepresented among these managers, about 53–57 percent of human resources managers. White women are also overrepresented among medical and health services managers (52.2 percent), another managerial occupation where White males are underrepresented (21 percent). Lodging managers and food service managers, two of the four lowest paid managers, are the only managerial occupations where White persons are not overrepresented. Together, White men and women are 61 percent of lodging managers and 62 percent of food service managers.

3.3 PERSISTENT INSECURITY: INVOLUNTARY JOBLESSNESS

Involuntary joblessness creates room for racial employment discrimination without sacrificing productive efficiency, that is, the possibility that individual productive capacity is not the only factor determining who works and who does not work – jobs may be allocated according to factors other than the productivity related characteristics of workers. A long and varied list of economists have argued that capitalist economies (such as the economy of the

TABLE 3.2. *Race–gender composition of managerial occupations and population: Workers 25–64 years-old, 2009–2019*

	Men				Women			
	White	African	Other	Latinx	White	African	Other	Latinx
Managers	0.475	0.035	0.040	0.053	0.295	0.037	0.028	0.037
Population	0.316	0.056	0.036	0.083	0.323	0.068	0.040	0.079
Representation	50.3%	−37.8%	13.2%	−35.9%	−8.7%	−46.0%	−29.9%	−53.4%

Occupations are for job worked during previous week. Occupational codes for human resources managers, funeral directors, farm, ranch, and other agricultural managers, and farmers and ranchers are determined by 2003–2010 census classification codes. All other classification codes are for 2011 and later years. Latinx are treated as a mutually exclusive racial category.
Source: Author's calculations, ASEC CPS, 2009–2019

TABLE 3.3. *Race–gender composition and mean weekly wage of managerial occupations: Workers 25–64 years-old, 2009–2019*

Men				Women					
White	African	Other	Latinx	White	African	Other	Latinx	Wage	Management Occupation
0.632	0.024	0.040	0.033	0.221	0.012	0.020	0.018	$3,060	Chief executives
0.719	0.049	0.102	0.041	0.075	0.006	0.004	0.004	$2,338	Engineering managers
0.513	0.042	0.116	0.034	0.220	0.025	0.035	0.015	$2,072	Computer and information systems managers
0.409	0.029	0.012	0.057	0.376	0.058	0.037	0.022	$1,929	Natural sciences managers
0.461	0.029	0.031	0.038	0.349	0.026	0.031	0.035	$1,769	Marketing and sales managers
0.339	0.030	0.039	0.042	0.407	0.049	0.043	0.051	$1,746	Financial managers
0.570	0.036	0.037	0.058	0.228	0.024	0.018	0.030	$1,682	General and operations managers
0.339	0.023	0.019	0.025	0.491	0.061	0.016	0.025	$1,633	Public relations managers
0.354	0.019	0.026	0.029	0.440	0.029	0.048	0.054	$1,587	Advertising and promotions managers
0.246	0.015	0.010	0.029	0.571	0.062	0.032	0.034	$1,579	Human resources managers*
0.471	0.041	0.000	0.000	0.306	0.106	0.018	0.058	$1,577	Emergency management directors
0.654	0.037	0.034	0.083	0.146	0.010	0.019	0.017	$1,534	Industrial production managers
0.504	0.039	0.043	0.059	0.263	0.031	0.027	0.033	$1,513	Managers, all other
0.190	0.024	0.017	0.029	0.528	0.104	0.037	0.071	$1,508	Human resources managers
0.210	0.028	0.023	0.026	0.522	0.092	0.040	0.060	$1,457	Medical and health services managers
0.374	0.046	0.030	0.045	0.365	0.055	0.031	0.055	$1,447	Purchasing managers
0.190	0.020	0.028	0.008	0.583	0.080	0.040	0.052	$1,367	Compensation and benefits managers
0.757	0.033	0.030	0.099	0.062	0.007	0.004	0.009	$1,366	Construction managers
0.267	0.039	0.016	0.026	0.481	0.086	0.026	0.058	$1,346	Education administrators
0.447	0.061	0.033	0.065	0.302	0.029	0.022	0.040	$1,335	Administrative services managers
0.337	0.060	0.020	0.050	0.432	0.030	0.021	0.050	$1,321	Training and development managers
0.370	0.046	0.025	0.056	0.357	0.053	0.028	0.066	$1,178	Property, real estate, and community association managers

(continued)

TABLE 3.3. *(continued)*

Men				Women					
White	African	Other	Latinx	White	African	Other	Latinx	Wage	Management Occupation
0.606	0.070	0.039	0.108	0.122	0.020	0.009	0.025	$1,175	Transportation, storage, and distribution managers
0.209	0.044	0.015	0.028	0.513	0.090	0.042	0.058	$1,174	Social and community service managers
0.734	0.005	0.013	0.074	0.146	0.000	0.004	0.024	$1,110	Farm, ranch, and other agricultural managers*
0.409	0.066	0.103	0.026	0.263	0.057	0.049	0.027	$1,029	Gaming managers
0.298	0.042	0.093	0.065	0.313	0.052	0.085	0.052	$928	Lodging managers
0.332	0.043	0.076	0.093	0.286	0.045	0.057	0.068	$868	Food service managers
0.692	0.013	0.010	0.016	0.251	0.001	0.005	0.012	$808	Farmers and ranchers*
0.658	0.008	0.017	0.051	0.245	0.003	0.007	0.011	$623	Farmers, ranchers, and other agricultural managers

Occupations are for job worked during previous week.

* Census classification code for 2003–2010. All other classification codes are for 2011 and later years. Latinx are treated as a mutually exclusive racial category.

Source: Author's calculations, ASEC CPS, 2009–2019

United States) cannot provide employment to every person who is willing and able to work (Malthus, 1820; Keynes, 1936; Gordon, Edwards, and Reich, 1982; Minsky, 1992; Galbraith and Darity, 1994; Stiglitz and Bilmes, 2008; Kalecki, 2009; Shaikh, 2016). Involuntary joblessness, that is, chronic unemployment and underemployment, is a labor market norm. It is a characteristic of the economic system itself; some persons will be unemployed regardless of their education, family background, intelligence, personal initiative, motivation, achievement orientation, delayed gratification, family values, group culture, family functioning, family structure, or other individual characteristics.

Business cycles represent periodic changes in the macroeconomic activity, for example, the total level of output, total employment, total national income, the average price level for all goods and services, and the rate of interest on the most secure loans. A complete business cycle consists of the following stages: trough (bottom of downturn), recovery (boom), peak, and recession (downturn). A *recession* is a sustained period of decline in national economic activity, while the *trough* is the low point of a recession. Typically, there is a decline in national income, national production of goods and services, and national employment. A *recovery* marks the end of a recession. Economic production and employment begin to expand. National income, national production of goods and services, and national employment begin a period of sustained increase. Eventually, this expansion in activity (also called a boom) reaches a *peak*, that is, a high point in employment, output, and earnings. Involuntary unemployment is likely to exist even at the peak of the business cycle. The economy declines from the peak at the onset of a recession.

Macroeconomic expansions encourage growth in the supply of and demand for workers. Labor supply grows because expansions encourage labor force participation. As workers find work and wages rise, new workers are encouraged to enter the market. Labor demand grows because expansions increase the capacity utilization of existing businesses and encourage entry into the market by new businesses. Eventually, during booms labor demand grows faster than labor supply and thereby expansions increase the probability of employment. During macroeconomic contractions the growth of the demand for laborers slows or even declines sharply, while the growth of the supply of laborers also declines: joblessness increases as labor force participation declines and unemployment increases during recessions. The ebbs and flows of involuntary unemployment over the course of the business cycle create the opportunity for racial identity to be used as a mechanism for rationing employment.

The ability to fight wars is the ultimate government policy. The US Civil War – not slowly evolving market forces – destroyed chattel capitalism. For the 12 years that followed, the federal government was committed to improving the socioeconomic circumstances of freedmen. During the middle of Reconstruction, the financial crisis of 1873 initiated the Depression of 1873–1897. This depression, also called the Long Depression, was a series of six recessions, with four recessions initiated by a financial crisis ("panic")

TABLE 3.4. *Recessions covering the Nadir: 1873–1927*

Peak	Trough	Months
Depression of 1873–1896 (aka "Long Depression")		
October 1873	March 1879	65 Panic of 1873
March 1882	May 1885	38 Panic of 1884
March 1887	April 1888	13
July 1890	May 1891	10
January 1893	June 1894	17 Panic of 1893
December 1895	June 1897	18 Panic of 1896
June 1899	December 1900	18
September 1902	August 1904	23
May 1907	June 1908	13 Panic of 1907
January 1910	January 1912	24 Panic of 1910
January 1913	December 1914	23
August 1918	March 1919	7 Post-WWI recession
January 1920	July 1921	18 Depression of 1920–1921
May 1923	July 1924	14
October 1926	November 1927	13

Source: National Bureau of Economic Research. www.nber.org/cycles.html. Last accessed December 13, 2022

(see Table 3.4). Two of the most severe recessions in American history occurred during the Long Depression. According to the National Bureau of Economic Research, the economy peaked in October 1973 and thereafter entered 65 months of decline, bottoming out in March 1879. By comparison, the Great Depression of the 1930s had 43 months of decline, from August 1929 to March 1933. According to the National Bureau of Economic Research, the third longest American recession of the nineteenth, twentieth, and twenty-first centuries occurred during the 38 months from March 1882 to May 1885. Hence, the 1880s created additional economic incentives for a White backlash. The economy was in depression for a combined 161 months during the years of the Long Depression, that is nearly 57 percent of the 284 months from October 1873 to June 1897. The period from October 1873 to March 1919 (four months after the end of World War I) represents nearly one-half century of persistent economic insecurity. There were 269 months of recession, representing about 49 percent of the five decades.

Given an economic decline of this magnitude, the rise in economic insecurity was such that both elite and nonelite Whites in the North and South were increasingly disinterested in racial justice for formerly enslaved Africans. The slowdown and reversal in racial progress occasioned by the Long Depression established a pattern that remains with us today: severe recessions undermine positive trends in racial progress and may usher in a period of intense anti-Black

TABLE 3.5. *Recessions from the Great Depression to the Great Recession: 1929–2009*

Peak	Trough	Months
August 1929	March 1933	43 *Great Depression*
May 1937	June 1938	13
February 1945	October 1945	8
November 1948	October 1949	11
July 1953	May 1954	10
August 1957	April 1958	8
April 1960	February 1961	10
December 1969	November 1970	11
November 1973	March 1975	16 *Stagflation*
January 1980	July 1980	6
July 1981	November 1982	16
July 1990	March 1991	8
March 2001	November 2001	8
December 2007	June 2009	18 *Great Recession*

Source: National Bureau of Economic Research. www.nber.org/cycles.html. Last accessed December 13, 2022

racism. The state-sponsored Black codes, laws initiated by Southern governments to undermine Reconstruction, gave way to the Nadir and servitude capitalism. Starting in 1877, the Nadir lasted until 1917, the start of the US involvement in World War I. This 40-year epoch of injustice is the low point of the African American struggle to obtain political economic equality and basic human rights within in the United States. The Nadir is the formative period of servitude capitalism, which ushered in a set of political economic policies designed to maintain the racial subjugation and economic exploitation of African Americans. The decline of servitude capitalism began in 1941, the start of direct United States involvement in World War II.

The Great Depression of 1929–1933 was another period of immense economic insecurity (Table 3.5). The unemployment rate was 25 percent during the trough of this economic downturn. The presidential administration of Franklin D. Roosevelt responded with a set of programs that became known as "The New Deal." These programs provided direct employment creation by the federal government, regulation of the banking and finance, and less racial discrimination in federal employment among private employers with government contracts and within the military. The social security system was created in 1935 and major pieces of legislation made it easier for workers to organize unions and bargain collectively for wages, hours, and working conditions. Federal fiscal and monetary policy were used aggressively to fight unemployment. Tax policy deliberately sought to redistribute income and wealth. The unions themselves became less discriminatory and, eventually, important allies in the struggle against racial discrimination in the labor market and the successful battle to end Jim Crow. President Harry Truman's "Fair Deal" (1945–1953) continued many of the core accomplishments of the Roosevelt administration. Importantly, the New Deal and the Fair Deal succeeded in reducing the impact of recessions. America still had a capitalist economy and recessions continued to occur. However, the recessions from 1945 to 1973 were comparatively mild in intensity and duration, with the average recession lasting 9–10 months. Given that it takes about 6–9 months to determine if the economy is in recession, these recessions were nearly over before economists could say with certainty the economy was in recession.

Starting in the mid-1970s there was an increase in the intensity and duration of recessions and a decrease in the federal government's commitment to keeping unemployment low. In addition to the 11-month minor contraction in economic activity between December 1969 and November 1970, there was a 16-month major inflationary recession from November 1973 to March 1975. There was a minor 6-month recession from January 1980 to July 1980, with a one-year recovery from July 1980 to July 1981. The next major recession occurred over the 16 months of July 1981–November 1982. The one-year "recovery" of 1980–81 – the shortest recovery of the post–World War II era – was only a brief respite in a long period of stagnation from December 31, 1979 to December 31, 1982. A third major recession occurred from July 1990 to March 1991. A 10-year expansion followed this recession. The fourth major post-1965 recession lasted just eight months, starting in March 2001 and reaching its trough in November 2001.

The Federal Reserve System (the "FED") reacted to the stagflation of 1974–1975 and the following years of inflation by making a fundamental change in macroeconomic policy, viz., it became more concerned with fighting inflation than fighting unemployment. The African American employment–population ratio is more sensitive to restrictive monetary policy than the White employment–population ratio (Carpenter and Rodgers, 2005). This is so because interest rate increases by the FED increase African American unemployment (especially among teenage African Americans) more so than White unemployment. In particular, African Americans are not necessarily disproportionately employed in interest rate sensitive industries, but African Americans have a relatively more difficult time finding employment during recessions. Importantly, Carpenter and Rodgers also find that contractionary monetary policy does not decrease labor force participation rates; hence, the fall in employment–population ratio is due entirely to the rise in unemployment.

Prior to 1991 the average recession lasted just 11 months while the average boom lasted 43 months. Excluding the 1973–1975 and 1981–1982 recessions, the two most severe post–World War II recessions prior to the onset of the Great Recession, the average recession lasted just 9 months. Hence, the 1973–1975 stagflation and 1980–1982 stagnation represent periods of exceptional trauma for the American economy.

"The Great Recession" started in December 2007 and ended in June 2009; it was the nation's most severe recession since the Great Depression of the 1930s. GDP declined by 5.1 percent. The civilian noninstitutional employment–population ratio shows the fraction of working age persons (that is, individuals 16–64 years of age), who were not in the military and who were not institutionalized, but who were employed either full-time or part-time during the survey period. At the start of the Great Recession, December 2007, the employment–population ratio for working age African American males was 69.3 percent. By December 2009, this ratio was 63.2 percent – representing one of the largest two-year increases in African American joblessness since 1965. Americans today are still grappling with the social and economic consequences of the Great Recession of 2007–2009, which lasted 18 months. By contrast, there were eight recessions during 1873–1921 that were equal to or longer than the Great Recession of 2007–2009. Severe recessions intensify racial job competition, racial competition for public resources and political support, and magnify existing racial tensions. The COVID-19 pandemic recession lasted two months, February 2020–April 2020, though the impact of COVID-19 on national and international economic activity is continuing through 2022.

Persistent involuntary joblessness in a competitive capitalist economy creates the possibility for differential treatment by race within the labor market, that is, the possibility that individual productive capacity is not the only factor determining who works and who does not work – jobs may be allocated according to factors other than the productivity related characteristics of workers. The manager–worker identity match disfavors African American workers: a disproportionate number of managers are White (and male) and these managers are racialized agents, that is, they are more likely to share managerial resources (time, financial resources, information and knowledge, managerial supervision) in intragroup manager–worker identity matches than in intergroup manager–worker identity matches. The productivity of workers is determined by the characteristics of workers (for example, experience and education), as well as the manger–worker identity match and the characteristics of the organization. Accordingly, multiple mechanisms present opportunities for racially differential outcomes.

- [I]n the presence of chronic unemployment, discrimination plays an active and determining role in *rationing* the available total of employment and unemployment (Harris, 1972: 11).
- But, given the total amount of employment, the mechanism also operates to channel Blacks into low-paid unskilled jobs (Harris, 1972: 26).
- [D]iscrimination and unemployment are causally related (Harris, 1972: 26). [In this respect, discrimination is not an *independent*, but a *dependent*, variable of the problem (Harris, 1972: 32)].
- [I]n addition, because of the structural division in the working class which discrimination implies, it serves also to weaken the position of the working class as a whole (Harris, 1972: 27).

- The struggle against discrimination and "racism" in employment is, in part, a struggle for *equalizing the distribution of employment and unemployment.* It is in part also a struggle for strengthening the position of workers as a class and their ability to make demands upon the system (Harris, 1972: 27–28).

Persistent full employment is an important first step for eradicating structural racism. But there are racial differences in the effects of counter-cyclical employment policies. For example, after the stagflation of 1974–1975 and following years of inflation, the Federal Reserve System became much more concerned with fighting inflation than fighting unemployment. Carpenter and Rodgers (2004) show that the African American employment–population ratio is more sensitive to restrictive monetary policy than the White employment–population ratio. This is so because interest rate increases by the FED increase African American unemployment (especially among teenage African Americans) more so than White unemployment. In particular, they find that African Americans are not necessarily disproportionately employed in interest rate sensitive industries, but that African Americans have a relatively more difficult time finding employment during recessions. Importantly, they also find that contractionary monetary policy does not decrease labor force participation rates; hence, the fall in employment–population ratio is due entirely to the rise in unemployment.

3.4 PERSISTENT EXPLOITATION: WAGES, PROFIT, AND RACIAL DISPARITY

Competition generates differential pay for workers of equal productive ability. Compensation depends on a firm's ability to pay, the competitive strategy for determining compensation, the manager–worker identity match, and the ability of workers to make firms pay. For example, some firms may opt for a high supervision strategy: low pay, high turnover (bad working conditions), and intense supervisions, while other firms may opt for a high motivation strategy: high pay, lower turnover (excellent working conditions), and moderate supervision. Workers of identical characteristics will receive differential pay and working conditions according to their firm of employment. If managers are disproportionately White, Black workers may not have an equal opportunity to obtain employment at high motivation firms or equal opportunity to obtain better jobs and more training within firms; thereby, we will observe racial disparity in wages and workers that is unrelated to worker characteristics.

3.4.1 Exploitation and Inequality

Competition creates differentiation, which works against equality of opportunity, equality of treatment, or establishing a racially unbiased meritocracy. Competitive processes consist of rivalry and strategic interactions: firms strategically compete with other firms within the same industry (by lowering the unit cost of production), firms strategically interact with other firms in different industries (by entering and exiting industries in response to profitability), the owners of firms compete with their workforce over control of the labor process and distribution of the fruits of production (by struggling over the wage rate, working conditions, and the effort level of workers), and individuals and social groups of workers compete with other individuals and social groups of workers. Within this competitive process, economic power does not necessarily imply the absence of competition but may be a necessary requirement to successfully compete.

Diversity and heterogeneity are inherent elements of the competitive process. Individuals of identical productive characteristics may not receive identical treatment in the market, that is, otherwise identical workers may receive differential wages, access to employment, promotion, and training, and working conditions.

3.4.2 Exploitation and Conflict

Production for profit is the driving force of capitalist firms. The source of a firm's profits is the difference between the income created by workers and the compensation (wages, benefits, and quality working conditions) received by workers. Property income (profit, interest, rent, capital gains, and dividends) is a form of unpaid labor time. Managers constantly seek to raise the rate of profit, thereby creating constant pressure for workers to work longer, harder, faster, and smarter without necessarily receiving an equivalent increase in compensation: higher productivity does not automatically support higher worker compensation.

Suppose, for example, it costs $1,200 dollars per week for the standard American family to obtain the median standard of living, the normal workweek is 40 hours, each hour of labor a worker creates $60 of output, and there is only one adult worker per family. If the average wage is equal to the cost of maintaining the average worker's family at the median standard of living, then the average worker will earn $1,200/40 = $30 per hour and create $480 of output during the course of an 8 hour workday.

Paid labor time (wage or value of productive capacity)	$240
Unpaid labor time (Profit)	$240
Total value created by worker per day	$480

In this example, the worker provides $240 per day of unpaid labor time. This unpaid labor time is the source of profit (and all other property income). Exploitation does not occur because each worker is paid less than the value of her/his productive capacity. On the contrary, each worker is paid a wage exactly equal to the value of her/his productive capacity, that is, $30 per hour.

Exploitation occurs because workers are not hired to produce a specific amount of work. Rather, they are hired for a specific period of time. During this time, managers try to extract an increasing amount of output. Each worker creates $60 output per hour of laboring activity – an amount greater than the wage paid to the average worker. Hence, exploitation occurs because each worker creates total value ($480) that is greater than the value of productive capacity ($240). Necessary labor time is just 4 hours per day or 20 hours per week. This is the necessary amount of time used to produce the income required to maintain a working family at the average standard of living. Surplus labor time is also 4 hours per day or 20 hours per week. So, the wage-productivity ratio = $240/$480 = 50 percent.

All profit (the market value of unpaid labor time) goes to the owners of capital, that is, the property owners. But it does not go to the property owners because they have contributed to the production of goods and services. It goes to them as an ownership right. Property owners are constantly trying to get workers to work longer, harder, faster, or smarter. If they are successful, output per hour of labor – productivity – will increase. Increases in productivity imply that the proportion of the day that is allocated to unpaid labor time will also increase. For example, suppose the owners of capital are able to get workers to work faster, "to speed-up" their labor activity. This might be done by eliminating breaks, eliminating a paid lunch hour, and making sure that workers start to work at exactly 8:00 a.m. and do not quit one minute before 5:00 p.m.

As a result of this speed-up, productivity goes up by 25%. Each worker now creates $75 of income per hour of the workday = $600 of value per day = $3,000 of value per week. The value of productive capacity is $1,200 per week or 30 per hour.

Paid labor time (wage or value of productive capacity)	*$240*
Unpaid labor time (Profit)	*$360*
Total value created by worker per day	*$600*

The wage-productivity ratio = $240/$600 = 40 percent. The speed-up raised daily productivity per worker by $120 = $600 – $480. If workers are organized and strong, they will be able to get some of the greater value they have produced. Otherwise, it will all go towards extra profit for the company owner or lower price per unit of output.

The wage–productivity ratio is a contested outcome, varying according to the bargaining power of workers and the monitoring power of executives. Workers and executives have differing economic identities. Also, racial identities are an important element of the work process. Altruism within racial groups and antagonism between social groups affects income distribution: if racial disparity contributes to the reproduction of racialized social identities and thereby weakens worker cooperation and bargaining power or strengthens the monitoring power of managers, firms have a strong incentive to engage in discriminatory labor practices.

3.4.3 Exploitation and Competitive Rivalry

Competitive rivalry implies that firms move into and out of industries in pursuit of higher rates of profit. It also implies that firms constantly look for ways to slash costs, lower prices, and thereby secure an increasing share of the market. This ceaseless pursuit of higher profit leads to a wide variety of technologies and managerial practices within and between industries. The technical conditions and the social relations of production between and within industries establish differential rates of productivity and profit between and within industries (Shaikh, 2016).

The processes of competitive rivalry and labor exploitation yields at least two important results: (1) a tendency toward equal rates of profit between and within industries by regulating firms; and (2) technical and managerial diversity, product differentiation, and wage inequality are the expected norms of operation by firms within and between industries. Regulating firms are those firms using the best generally available technologies of production. The tendency toward the equalization of profit rates is not something that happens instantly; at any given point-in-time regulating firms will have different rates of profit. But, if we consider a period of time long enough for capital and labor to move into or out of an industry in response to changes in profitability, to adjust their marketing strategies, to alter managerial practices, and to change labor and other contracts – say, a complete business cycle – there will be a tendency for regulating firms to obtain roughly equal rates of profit. Wage inequality will persist because identically skilled workers may not be employed at firms with identical technologies, managerial strategies, manager–worker identity matches, or market position. For workers at any given skill level, remuneration will differ between and within industries in accordance with the limits to wage differentials derived from the competition of firms and the class struggle between labor and capital.

3.5 TRENDS IN THE WAGE–PRODUCTIVITY NEXUS AND RACIAL DISPARITY

The competitive struggle between workers and managers creates the possibility that workers will not automatically share in productivity gains. Technically, the hourly wage–hourly productivity ratio, $0 < \left(\frac{wage}{productivity}\right) \leq 1$, is variable across firms, industries, and time. Among other factors, this ratio is proportional to the relative strength of worker bargaining power. From the end of World War II until the 1974–1975 recession, wages and productivity (real GDP per capita) grew at the same rate (Figure 3.1). However, between the 1974–1975 and 1981–1982 recessions, productivity grew as the average wage stagnated and the median wage was falling. From 1980 to 2014 productivity grew by about 80 percent while real wages showed lower growth (average real wage, GDP

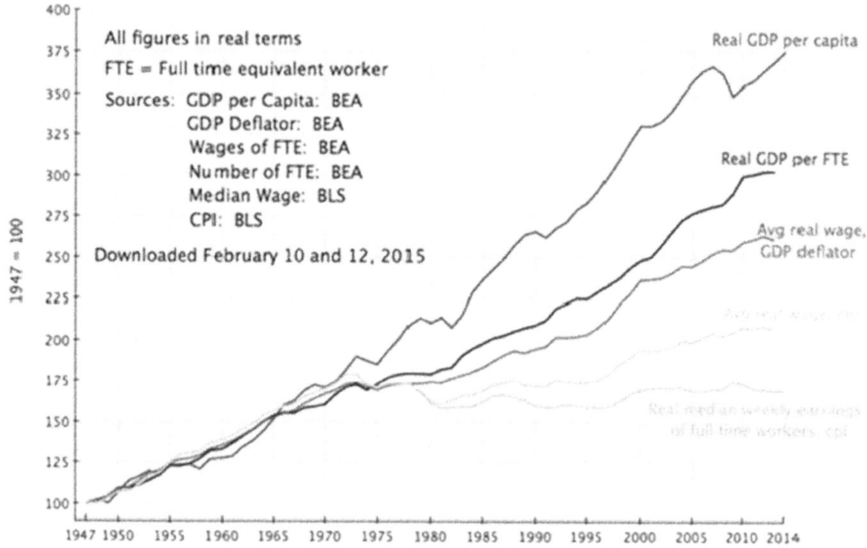

FIGURE 3.1. Productivity and real wage indices: 1947–2014, 1947 = 100
Source: Frank J. Lysy. "Why Wages Have Stagnated While GDP Has Grown: The Proximate Factors." An Economic Sense. February 13, 2015. https://aneconomicsense.org/2015/02/13/why-wages-have-stagnated-while-gdp-has-grown-the-proximate-factors/. Last accessed December 13, 2022

deflator), dramatically lower growth (average real wage, consumer price index), or declined for most of the period (real median weekly earnings of full-time workers, consumer price index). Companies had the ability to pay higher wages between 1975 and 2014, but workers lost the ability to make them pay – especially workers below the highest wage levels.

The 1974–1975 and 1981–1982 recessions were turning points in the struggle against racial discrimination within the labor market; discrimination also increased during 1975–2016 (Figure 3.2). Figure 3.2 shows the differential in mean years of education for African American and White males. During 1966 White male workers aged 16–64 had an advantage of 2.57 years of education. This advantage was 1.95 years in 1975, 1.29 years in 1982, 0.95 years in 1992, 0.68 years in 2007, and 0.76 years in 2016. Hence, the racial difference in this measure of skill declined between the mid-1960s and the mid-1970s and continued to decline from the mid-1970s to the present.

The decline in the racial gap in years of education more or less tracks well with the decline in the racial wage differential during 1960–1980; thereafter, this skills gap continues to decline while the racial wage gap increases for a few years before settling back down. There has been virtually no progress in closing the racial wage gap during 1980–2018. The racial wage gap was 0.25 log points (22 percent) in 1980 and 0.25 log points in 2015.

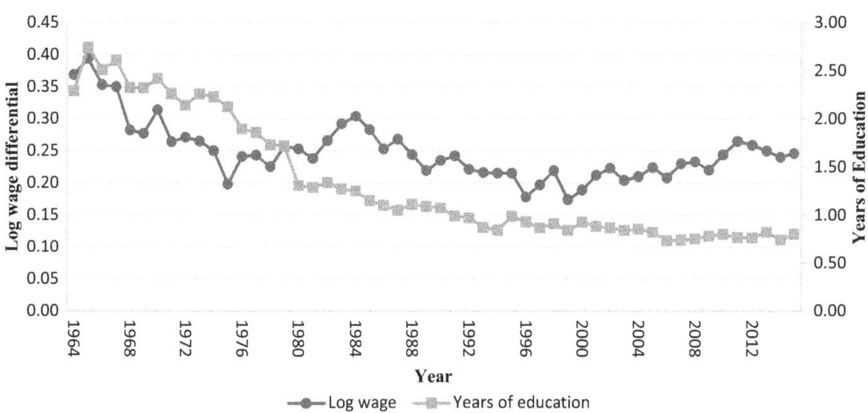

FIGURE 3.2. Male racial years of education and log wage differential: 1964–2015
Source: Author's calculations, Current Population Survey Annual Social and Economic Supplement, 1965–2016. Sample includes Non-Latinx White and African American males 16–64 years of age, not self-employed, not institutionalized, and labor force participants

Collectively, Figures 3.1 and 3.2 are consistent with the stratification perspective that bargaining power and racial identity are important factors for determining the distribution of income in competitive markets; all workers lost bargaining power relative to management between 1980 and 2016 and Black workers lost bargaining power relative to White workers. As a result, median wages stagnated during a period when productivity was increasing and racial wage inequality stagnated during a period when racial skill inequality was declining.

3.6 JOB COMPETITION AND RACIAL DISCRIMINATION IN THE LABOR MARKET

Racial discrimination can be profit-increasing and, therefore, an element of competitive managerial strategies by firms (Mason, 1995, 1999). Compensation is determined by the ability of firms to pay (productivity, competitive structure, and managerial strategy), the ability of workers to make firms pay (bargaining power), and the manager–worker identity match. Competition for profit forces firms to innovate, cut unit cost, create product diversity, and expand market share. But competition does not ensure that wages are a fixed and just percentage of productivity and it will not ensure that equally skilled workers will have equal labor market treatment. Labor–capital bargaining over the share of output as well as differential compensation for otherwise identical workers is the competitive norm, not the exception.

Firm managers are in a continuous competitive rivalry with their workforce. Competitive survival and profit-increasing behavior establishes constant pressure to increase work effort, to hold down pay (reduce the wage–productivity ratio), to trade lower firm wages for the promise of a higher social wage, and to use managerial discretion regarding labor allocation. Within an industry, the competition between workers and managers is most intense at high cost firms. Between industries, the competition between workers and managers is most intense among industries with the least resistance to entry by potential rivals. Each firm selects a managerial strategy consistent with its competitive rivalry with other firms and its internal competition with workers. The average wage rate paid by firms to otherwise identical workers will differ because firms have differing competitive structures and differing managerial strategies, within and between industries.

Interracial job competition is a source of persistent discrimination (Darity and Williams, 1985; Williams, 1987, 1991; Darity, 1989; Mason, 1995, 1999). Racial identity is a coalescing force among workers and between workers and managers. Racial groups have unequal access to managers, that is, persons with control over resources who are embedded into positions of power and authority. With less power in manager–worker interactions, African American workers have a more difficult time than Whites in gaining access to the most desirable jobs.

Suppose we have a group of racially different but otherwise identical workers. These otherwise identical workers may receive different pay for doing the same work because they are employed at firms that are differentiated by the capacity to pay, by the capacity of workers to make firms pay, and by the manager–worker identity match. Workers who perform similar jobs at the same firm may receive similar pay. However, otherwise identical workers who perform similar jobs at firms with less competitive characteristics or who are part of workforces with lower bargaining power may receive lower pay. Competing racial identities and different pay for equal work is the competitive norm as each firm utilizes the technology, managerial strategy, and marketing strategy that provides the strongest competitive advantage.

The bargaining power of workers is strongly related to the fraction of the workforce that is organized, the quality of worker organization, and the form, scope, ideology, and structure of worker organization. Worker inequality lowers bargaining power, which in turn reduces the firm's average wage rate. Movements away from egalitarian wages, hours, working conditions, on-the-job training, hiring, layoff, and promotion opportunities disrupt bargaining cohesion among workers. Racial conflict outside of the workplace also limits coalition building within the workplace; hence, a socially homogeneous workforce may be more easily organized and more cohesive than a socially heterogeneous workforce. Also, the racial composition of the workforce is an important economic variable if the social identity match of journeyman and incoming workers is an important factor in the relative efficiency of on-the-job training. These considerations suggest that neither managers nor workers are indifferent to the identity composition of the workforce and the nature and extent of inequalities among workers. The actual social composition of the labor force, that is, its racial–ethnic, gender, or other diversity, depends on the contending interests between and among workers and managers.

Differences in pay for otherwise identical workers will encourage intense competition among workers for the highest paying jobs and greater labor effort among those workers who are able to obtain employment. Workers will participate in strategic identity coalitions that seek to limit competition from other social groups. Race and gender are two of the more salient ascriptive characteristics for establishing coalitions. Racial identity matters because it is a cultural coalescing force used by workers to improve their relative positions in the labor queue (Darity, 1989). White male employment density has a positive correlation with the wage differential; regardless of race, individual remuneration increases with the White male employment density of a job (Mason, 1995).

Notably, also, there is nothing within the stratification perspective which provides an automatic link between changes in the racial skills gap and changes in the racial wage or employment gap. Measured over time or across regions, the racial skills gap may decline even as the racial wage and employment gaps are increasing. Hence, the stratification perspective is consistent with 1974–present stagnation in racial disparity (among males), while considerable improvement took place in the relative educational attainment of Blacks (especially between 1974 and 1990). Similarly, during the Nadir (1877–1914) the racial skills gap decreased while the racial gap in occupational status increased (Darity, Guilkey, and Winfrey, 1996; Darity, Dietrich, and Guilkey, 2001).

3.7 SUMMARY AND DISCUSSION

Immense and longstanding interracial differences in wealth will produce interracial differences in socioeconomic outcomes, even in the absence of racial discrimination. Involuntary joblessness creates room for racial identity as an employment sorting mechanism. The over-representation of White (male) workers in managerial positions means that African American workers will have less power to influence manager–worker identity matches and, thereby, less access to managerial resources. The wage rate and wage–productivity ratio and conditions of employment vary across firms for otherwise identical workers; job competition for the best jobs will sustain interracial competition for employment.

4

Regimes of Racial Stratification

1865–Present

The US has experienced three racial stratification regimes: chattel capitalism (1619–1865), servitude capitalism (1865–1965), and racialized managerial capitalism (1933–present).

A unique racial norm limits Black access to public and private resources during each of these regimes. Specifically, during chattel capitalism African life was a commodity. People of African descent were intermediate capital goods on for-profit plantation economies. Or, they were consumer goods in the homes of Whites. The profit calculations of plantation owners governed the reproduction of African life and labor, that is, Black family formation and fertility and Black skill accumulation. The family plans, expectations, and occupational hopes of African men and women were not issues of primary concern for enslavers.

The Civil War established a decisive end to chattel capitalism; it did not end structural racism. Instead, federal, state, and local governments expropriated and monopolized African American citizenship during the regime of servitude capitalism. Servitude capitalism did not have an abrupt end. African American migration and urbanization during 1917–1964, when more than six million African Americans left the South for life in the urban North, and the political victories of the Civil Rights and Black Power movements of 1941–1973 were important self-help strategies for resisting and undermining servitude capitalism. Correspondingly, the New Deal (President Franklin D. Roosevelt), Fair Deal (President Harry S. Truman), New Frontier (President John F. Kennedy), and Great Society (President Lyndon B. Johnson) domestic programs provided a second Reconstruction of the South by the federal government. President Eisenhower's decision to send federal troops to Little Rock, Arkansas to enforce school racial desegregation during the 1957–1958 school year was the first time federal troops were used in the South since 1877. These political events contributed to the end of servitude capitalism and to the establishment of racialized managerial capitalism.

Racialized managerial capitalism is characterized by greatly unequal racial access to wealth and managerial resources. First, the regimes of chattel capitalism and servitude capitalism lasted from 1619 to 1965 and collectively established massive racial wealth inequality between African Americans and Whites. Wealth creates social, economic, political, educational, and cultural privileges. Second, an army of managers with discretion over the allocation of public and private resources is an outcome of the rise of modern corporations and the rise of the state as an activist agent concerned with the protection of individual rights and the promotion of socioeconomic well-being of citizens. Third, manager–subordinate and manager–citizen racial identity matches govern access to managerial resources, which affect worker productivity and government accountability, respectively. Fourth, the racial wealth gap yields a disproportionate number of White managers, who are also disproportionately located in positions of control over public and private resources. The African American–White wealth gap is so large that, even if all racism was eliminated from American society, the privileges of wealth will yield racial disparities in socioeconomic outcomes in perpetuity. Simultaneously, racial income and wealth gaps will be reproduced persistently because of the structural racism embedded in manager–subordinate and manager–citizen racial identity matches.

4.1 CHATTEL CAPITALISM

Chattel capitalism arose out of European exploration and colonization, encompassing the period of the transatlantic slave trade and African enslavement in the United States. During this regime Africans were commodities, capital goods that were bought and sold as inputs into the plantation production process. Chattel capitalism existed for 246 years, from 1619 to 1865, and it continues to influence contemporary racial disparities. First, today's racial disparity in wealth is directly attributable to chattel capitalism. Just prior to the start of the US civil war and the abolition of chattel capitalism, the White–Black wealth per person ratio was 56:1 in 1860. This ratio declined rapidly to 20:1 in 1870, 10:1 in 1900, 7:1 in 1950, and settled at 5.6:1 in 1970, and remains at that level today (Derenoncourt et al., 2021: 11). Two and a half centuries of enslavement have contributed to one and a half centuries of racial wealth disparity after the abolition of chattel capitalism.

Second, Black enslavement was an instrumental affair: Whites enslaved Africans because slave labor was a fruitful mechanism for increasing White wealth. No African was enslaved because (s)he was raised in a pathological family, had dysfunctional values, had ruinous behavior, or had inferior skills. Further, neither the federal, state, nor local government required anyone to be an enslaver, rather enslavement was allowed by federal, state, and local governments; White persons selected enslaver status because it was a wealth-increasing identity action. Finally, enslavers might have had anti-Black racial prejudice or bigotry. But, the instrumental nature of chattel capitalism did not require either of these subjective dispositions, it required only persons with sufficient financial capital who were willing to increase their wealth by purchasing and exploiting human commodities.

Third, chattel capitalism established American racial categories. "Black" persons were persons whose lives could be converted into commodities, while "White" persons were not eligible for commodification and were citizens entitled to have access to public resources. Whereas the enslaver–overseer identity match paired two White males separated by class, it was nevertheless possible for an unlucky, lazy, or prodigal planter to fall to the status of an overseer or for a lucky, hardworking, and frugal overseer to become an enslaver. But, enslaver–enslaved and overseer–enslaved identity matches paired racial groups separated by class; it was not possible for any White enslaver or overseer to become either enslaved or Black and it was not possible for any Black enslaved person to become an enslaver or overseer of Whites or White. The enslaver–enslaved and overseer–enslaved identity matches paired specific individuals, but these individuals had a class status that was defined by their racial group affiliation. Racialized manager–worker identity matches remain a defining feature of contemporary American capitalism.

Fourth, full employment is necessary but not sufficient to eliminate racial disparities in wages, occupations, and well-being.

> Some estimates placed the average longevity of Blacks at 21.4 years of age in 1850, with the average longevity for Whites at age 25.5. The combination of lower living standards, greater exposure, heavier labor, and poorer medical care gave slaves a higher mortality rate than whites. In 1860, 3.5 percent of the slaves and 4.4 percent of the Whites were over sixty. The death rate was 1.8 percent for the slaves and 1.2 percent for Whites. (Stampp, 1965: 77, quoted in Stanford School of Medicine, 2021: 1)

In addition to racial disparities in life expectancy, White workers were also free and in control of their marriage decisions, fertility decisions, family stability, and sexual activity. Commoditized Africans existed in the plantation labor process, where all these decisions were removed from their control; instead, these decisions were economic strategies under the control of enslavers. Further, enslaved Africans worked harder than free White workers and the maintenance cost of enslaved persons was lower than the wage of free workers (Fogel, 1989, ch. 3). The 2020 labor value of a person enslaved in 1850 is $114,000 (Williamson and Cain, 2021). Absent enslavement, this money would have accrued to the enslaved African.

Finally, market competition did not eliminate enslavement of Africans. Chattel capitalism allowed persistently lower wages and worst working conditions for enslaved Africans relative to otherwise identical free White workers. War – the most dramatic of government policies, abolished chattel capitalism.

It did not, however, end racism or abolish the mechanisms of racial stratification. Racial identity remained an important norm for determining access to public and private resources. Freedmen did not receive reparations; the massive racial disparity in wealth created by enslavement was not addressed.

4.2 SERVITUDE CAPITALISM (BLACK CODES AND JIM CROW)

Servitude capitalism occurred during 1865–1965, with 1877–1941 being the core years. Collective White expropriation and monopolization of Black citizenship was the foundation of servitude capitalism. The monopoly was maintained through racial coercion, both the institutional injustice of the criminal legal system and personal violence. During the core years, Whites used state tolerated and state-sponsored violence and the criminal legal system to keep African Americans in the South and in agricultural and extractive production. White employers had control over the labor process and over federal, state, and local government; from 1877 to 1941 the federal government allowed Southern governments to deny human rights to African Americans. Open discrimination in market transactions was legal: racial discrimination in housing, employment, credit, etc. was permitted by the law and not undermined by market competition. De jure racial segregation occurred throughout the South; it was expressed in anti-Black discrimination in access to public resources and opportunities in education, military service, public sector employment, burials, parks and public facilities, etc.

African Americans entered the labor market without physical capital or financial wealth or other forms of economic power, without political power and protection of the rule of law, without formal education, without favorable relations with entrepreneurs and managers embedded in public and private positions of power, and without organized institutions and resources to provide armed self-defense against violent coercion despite living in a society where they were hated.

4.2.1 Black Codes and Reconstruction: 1865–1877

For the two major periods after chattel capitalism, Reconstruction (1865–1877) and Jim Crow (1877–1965), the South continued to differ dramatically from the rest of the country. The immense technological change of this period, competitive markets, and African American self-help were not sufficient to dislodge widespread racial discrimination throughout the economy.

The 13th, 14th, and 15th amendments were added to the American constitution during Reconstruction. The 13th amendment (1865) abolished and prohibited slavery and involuntary servitude – except for criminal punishment. The 13th amendment became the law of the land after it was ratified by 27 of the 36 states (3/4) in existence in 1865. Three of those 36 states did not ratify the 13th amendment until the twentieth century: Delaware (1901), Kentucky

(1976), Mississippi (1995). The 14th amendment (1868) established the right of citizenship for formerly enslaved persons. All persons were entitled to equal protection of the laws of the land and no person could be deprived of their property or freedom without due process of law. The 15th amendment (1870) granted the right to vote to Black males. These constitutional amendments were given force with the additional passage of important pieces of enabling federal civil rights legislation.

At the start of servitude capitalism, control over the working time, working conditions, and life of Africans became a contested issue. The Reconstruction amendments ensured that freedmen would not be deported, but these amendments did not create paid employment or business ownership for African Americans. There was neither 40 acres nor mules for farming. The old plantations were not broken up and given to the freedmen, though the labor-time and ability forcibly extracted from enslaved Africans paid for the plantations and created the wealth of the plantations.

Aggressive public policy rather than the unfettered operation of competitive markets created the conditions for structural change in the economic opportunities confronting African Americans. Federal public policy outlawed racial discrimination within the labor market, housing market, and public accommodations. The housing market and public accommodations are social arenas that nurture the accumulation of social capital, that is, a set of skills, information, and socioeconomic connections that are not efficiently provided (if at all) by market processes but which enhance the income and life chances of individuals and families.

Just as federal legislation was passed to bring African Americans into formal equality with Whites, all Southern states passed Black codes during the 1860s. These state codes were designed to establish second class citizenship for Freedmen, by making it very difficult to vote, own property, attain fair wages, and so forth. Second class citizenship had labor market consequences: (1) it reduced Black worker bargaining power in manager–worker and entrepreneur–worker racial identity matches; and, (2) it lowered Black bargaining power relative to White workers. Black workers could be forced into jobs with the lowest pay and worst working conditions. Second class citizenship also put African Americans at a disadvantage in access to public resources.

The federal government countered the Southern Black codes strategy with the Civil Rights Acts of 1866 and 1875. The former act enabled African Americans to sue, make contracts, bear witness in court, and own private property. Section 1981 of the 1866 Act made it illegal to engage in employment discrimination. Effectively, also, the ability to make contracts and sue also made it illegal to engage in housing discrimination. However, the 1866 Act provided no federal remedies and each person had to obtain his own legal counsel to bring charges under the Act. The 1875 Act guaranteed to all persons equal treatment in public accommodations. The Civil Rights of 1875 desegregated public accommodations, that is, all privately and publicly owned facilities used by the public, and public transportation. It also ended exclusion of African Americans from jury service.

Despite the first set of Black codes, the elimination of slavery and the passage of important pieces of federal legislation made it possible for African Americans to make substantial political and economic progress during 1865–1877. Even so, African American progress was inconsistent across states and erratic across time; reactionary Whites within the Southern states achieved varying degrees of resistance to the amelioration of persistent racial discrimination against African Americans.

If racial discrimination impedes the operation of competitive markets and harms profitability, one would expect to see the Southern elites fighting against discriminatory practices and social policies. Instead, we observe the opposite. The Hayes-Tilden electoral compromise of 1877, the civil rights cases of 1882–1883, and the *Plessy* v. *Ferguson* Supreme Court case of 1896 were major setbacks for African American political and economic progress.

As a compromise between the Republican and Democratic parties over the disputed presidential election of 1876, Rutherford B. Hayes (Republican) became President and Union troops were pulled out of the South (clearing the way for White Democrats to return to power and drive out Black Republicans and their political allies). With the removal of the Union army, Reconstruction was brought to an end. The Long Depression (1873–1897) heightened White economic insecurity, which decreased White support for racial justice and equality. Libertarian federal economic policy reduced the power of workers relative to capital and decreased the power of Black workers relative to White workers. During 1882–1883 the Supreme Court declared unconstitutional the Civil Rights Act of 1875, stating that it interfered with the property rights of individual (White) citizens. Notably, political conservatives of today also wish to eliminate federal civil rights laws because such laws (they claim) infringe on the property rights of Whites. Finally, in the infamous *Plessy* v. *Ferguson* case of 1896 the Supreme Court enshrined "separate but equal" as the law of the land. The Court declared that it was acceptable for public and private entities to provide racially separate but equal facilities and, thereby, the Court provided legal cover for decades of political, legal, and economic exclusion, inequality, and persistent discrimination within both markets and extra-market social processes.[1] Also, the force of the court's opinion was to collapse distinctions among African Americans: Blacks (Negroes), mulattoes, quadroons, octaroons, and persons with "any known black ancestry" were all Black – regardless of physical appearance, education, or economic status.

[1] During his famous "Atlanta Exposition" speech of 1895, Booker T. Washington had argued that African Americans should forsake political rights and social inclusion. Rather, he argued African Americans should concentrate on obtaining an industrial education (skilled crafts and trades) valued by Whites and accept racial segregation.

4.2.2 Jim Crow: 1877–1965

4.2.2.1 *The Nadir: 1877–1917*

Historians refer to the years from 1877 to 1917 (the start of American participation in World War I) as "the Nadir," the low point of the African American post-Civil War struggle for racial equality. The Equal Justice Institute (2017) indicates that there were 4,075 lynchings of African Americans during 1877–1950 in Alabama, Arkansas, Florida, Georgia, Kentucky, Louisiana, Mississippi, North Carolina, South Carolina, Tennessee, Texas, and Virginia. At least one African American man, woman, or child was lynched every week during 1882–1930 (Tolnay and Beck, 1992). Most of these lynching were in Southern states (Work, 1922). On January 13, 2000, the *New York Times* reported that 4,742 African Americans were lynched between 1882 and 1968, a rate of about one lynching every 6.6 days. But, most of these lynching occurred prior to 1955. It has been estimated that 127 Blacks were lynched every year between 1889 and 1899, a rate of nearly 2.5 African Americans per week (Woodward, 1951: 351–352). Lynchings of African Americans were not mere chance events related to idiosyncratic acts by bigots. Lynchings were a joint venture, an essential element of the public–private campaign of anti-Black terrorism. In 1892, Ida B. Wells Barnett wrote that lynching was "an excuse to get rid of Negroes who were acquiring wealth and property and thus keep the race terrorized" (quoted in Jones, 1998: 333). Lynchings were designed to stifle African American political and economic competition with Whites, most especially the political and economic competition arising from independent Black males (Olzak, 1990).[2] Williams, Logan, and Hardy (2021) inform us that,

> tax increases, which support the provision of public infrastructure and public goods, are associated with increased violent attacks on Black officeholders. Black lynchings are also associated with increased segregation during the 1880s and with reduced Black voter registration both before and after the [Voting Rights Act of 1965]. This reduction in participation, via racialized violence, can be traced to a series of depressed modern-day state economic and policy outcomes, including higher poverty and unemployment and lowered economic policy generosity ... Black lynchings ... are strongly associated with both historical and contemporary political economy outcomes. (104)

CONVICT LEASING. Convict leasing was private for-profit imprisonment; it was a capitalist criminal legal system. It began in the 1860s shortly after the end of the Civil War and continued through World War I. Prior to the end of slavery, plantation owners were the legal system for enslaved Africans; they

[2] King (2005) argues that violence can be used to defend and to challenge property rights in Whiteness. In particular, Black rioting during the 1960s is correlated with Black economic improvement during that era. Black riots and willingness to use violence for self-defense encouraged employers and policy makers to create more economic and social opportunities for African Americans. King does not claim she has demonstrated a causal connection between Black violence and African American social progress.

determined what was acceptable or unacceptable behavior, the guilt or innocence of those charged, and the necessity and extent of punishment. Under convict leasing prisoners are convicted of a crime by a public court and sentenced to some period of imprisonment. The sentence may include only a period of imprisonment or, more often, a period of imprisonment combined with a financial penalty that the alleged criminal was unable to pay. The state leased convicted persons to a labor contractor who then subleased the prisoner to a farm, railroad, mine, or other business willing and able to pay the leasing fee. Ninety percent of leased convicts were Black (Mancini, 1978).

The state received fees for the leased convicts, without having to provide for a prisoner's food, clothing, housing, medical care, and supervision. Over time, the fees increased (convicts were productive), convicts became younger, and sentences increased. Prisoners were a source of extra-normal profitability for the leasing company or farm. Private companies had discretionary power to do whatever they wanted with convicts, as state oversight was virtually nonexistent. Convicts frequently had sub-human working conditions and death rates might approach 30–40 percent per year. Labor disputes and food costs were minimized. Arguably, convict leasing was worse than de jure slavery. Enslaved persons were a long-term capital investment, convicts were nearly inexhaustible short-term production possibilities. Convicts were cheap to replace; therefore, they could be abused more than slaves. Convict miners cost 50–80 percent less than free miners.

Convict leasing contributed to massive growth in Southern prison populations. In 1890, Blacks were 30 percent of the prison inmates, but 12 percent of the population. This process criminalized "Blackness." From this perspective, Blacks were a criminal race and, therefore, freedom was a mistake; Blacks needed to be under the control of Whites. Across the South, voting rights were reduced. The processes of racialized imprisonment for state and private profit, reduced voting rights, and economic exploitation combined to remind all that Blacks have a place in American society and that place is fully subordinate to Whites.

DEBT PEONAGE. Peonage is crypto-enslavement based on alleged debt owed to an entrepreneur. The debt might be directly owed to the entrepreneur or the businessman may have purchased the debt by paying a legal fine or fee imposed on convicted persons by a sheriff or other legal official. The indebted person would then sign a so-called contract (which illiterate persons were unable to read or understand) agreeing to work off their debt at the entrepreneur's place of business. There is an obvious similarity with convict leasing. When a convicted person worked beyond the original length of time required by the contract, which was often the case, they became debt peons. Debt servitude was outlawed by the federal government in Anti-Peonage Law of 1867. The federal government made peonage illegal as a result of the US acquisition of New Mexico. In particular, the federal government did not want to incorporate

Mexican peonage into US law. Nevertheless, debt peonage was incorporated in the "Black codes" of Southern states as early as 1865 (Carper, 1976).

Workers were not usually allowed to work off their debt to the company. The initial charges were frequently false, motivated more by an employer's desire for supra-exploitable workers than criminal behavior. Freedmen were taken to court, fined, and charged court fees. Once convicted, Freedmen were turned over to White businessmen who could sell them to anyone they wanted to. So-called contracts gave owners the right to beat or trade workers as long as the debt was not paid. The local and state criminal and civil legal systems were corrupt. Justices of the Peace and other legal officials were often paid off by White businessmen. Death was a frequent punishment to keep Black workers in line under debt peonage and convict leasing.

CHAIN GANGS. Chain gangs were groups of imprisoned individuals forced to work together on public agricultural projects as well as roads, ditches, and other infrastructure projects. This work activity, especially road-building and other infrastructure projects, made it profitable for private businesses to locate in certain areas or to expand their operations. Rural areas were able to connect to urban markets. The cost of guarding prisoners in an un-enclosed area was minimized by having prisoners wear heavy ankle shackles and by having them shackled to each other. Chain gangs started in the first decade of the twentieth century and lasted to about the end of World War II. As convict leasing and debt peonage began to wane, Southern states wanted to find ways to reduce the cost of housing prisoners and to directly profit from prison labor. States began to use prisoners on state-controlled enterprises, especially roads and other transportation infrastructure. Chain gangs were a mechanism to improve the state economy without raising taxes. Local and state convictions for real or imagined crimes were strongly related to the government's need for workers.

SHARECROPPING. Convict leasing, debt peonage, and chain gangs were crypto-enslavement institutions that interacted with the criminal legal system. Sharecropping was also aided and abetted by corrupt local and state legal systems, but more as enforcers of private economic arrangements than as direct participants in the laboring process. Sharecropping was a form of debt peonage, but without the intervention of an alleged criminal act.

The economics of sharecropping as a system of de facto slavery are straightforward. At the start of planting season, a family borrows seed, fertilizer, or agricultural items from a larger farmer. The sharecropper rented a portion of the landlord's property to farm and lived in rental housing provided by the landlord. The housing rent, land rent, plus the cost of seeds and other farm items were paid after the harvest. The pay was a portion of the crop. All the risks of farming – which included crop-destroying pests, disease, drought, flood, excessive cold, excessive heat, wild and domestic animals eating plants and livestock, swings in the market price of agricultural products, etc. – were borne by the sharecropper, not the landlord.

The landlord kept the financial records and determined the terms of the trade. Usually, the sharecropper paid 50 percent or more of the crop to the landlord (Mandle, 1983). Upward mobility was unlikely as it was difficult for the sharecropper to pay off debt. Sharecroppers were legally tied to the land. If they left, the Sheriff would find the sharecropper and return him or her and the family to the farm. Sharecropping began in the years immediately following the end of de jure slavery and came to an end during World War II.

4.2.2.2 *Racial Ideology and Public Policy*

Racism during servitude capitalism was not solely a Southern phenomenon. America was infested with social Darwinism, an ideology which justified socioeconomic inequalities by appealing to competition, survival of the fittest, and natural hierarchies among persons and groups. Among evolutionary biologists, Darwinian fitness refers only to attributes that contribute to fertility. For example, the sickle trait protects individuals from becoming infected with malaria, a disease common to tropical countries. Persons with the sickle cell trait are less likely to contract malaria than those who do not have the trait. Hence, persons with the sickle cell trait are more likely to live to adulthood and have children. The sickle cell trait is inherited. Relatively greater fertility among those with the trait means that it will be present in a large portion of society.

Fitness among social Darwinists was different from fitness in evolutionary biology. For social Darwinists, fitness is related to the absence or presence of "feeble-mindedness." According to social Darwinists, feeble-minded persons lack the intellect, ambition, discipline, and future orientation to compete with the intelligent persons of society. Poverty, poor health, low education, sterile thinking, etc. will predominate among the feeble-minded, while affluence, better health, higher education, and creativity will predominate among the intelligent. From this perspective, inequality is produced by nature and heredity, and there is nothing government can or should do to reduce inequalities between the feeble-minded and the intelligent. Morally, social Darwinists made the case that the rich, powerful, and affluent deserved their elite positions and the poor, powerless, unhealthy, and less educated deserved their low-status positions. Rather than limit the ambition and talent of the intelligent, government should limit the spread of the feeble-minded.

In addition to justifying intra-group inequality among native-born White Americans, social Darwinism was also used to justify inter-group inequality between Whites and African Americans and between natives and immigrants. "Discussions of race have always been tied up with perceptions of morality, intelligence, and civilization" (The Royal Society, 2022). Social Darwinists accepted the evolutionary biology finding that all humans have a common ancestral origin, but they argued that evolution created a hierarchy of four racial groups: (1) Whites (Aryans, Caucasians, Occidentals, etc.) are the most intelligent, virtuous, and attractive; (2) Yellows (Asians, Orientals, etc.) were closes to Whites; (3) Reds (Amerindians); and (4) Blacks (Sub-Saharan

Africans) were the least intelligent, least moral, and least civilized.[3] Social Darwinists argued that Blacks have the least evolutionary development and, therefore, are the closest to primates, the common ancestors of humanity. Social Darwinists saw Africans as beast-like men, while apes are men-like beasts (Jordan, 1968). Within social Darwinism's hierarchy of racial groups, Blacks were a "missing link," that is, humans that are very near relatives of apes and far less evolved than Whites with respect to intelligence, virtue, attractiveness, or other desirable attributes of humans. Social Darwinists also claimed that all knew their place: individuals of each racial group are cognizant of the group's position in the racial hierarchy.

Among its many odious implications, simianization, that is, closeness to apes, also has implications for sex, reproduction, and rape (Mills, 2015). In particular, simianization implies that White women need protection from rape by Black men and that the racial purity of the White race needs protection from mixed-race children. Within social Darwinist thought, apes (especially males) were characterized as creatures of ravenous and uncontrolled libido. Apes, too, are creatures of great physical strength. Hence, Black males – near relatives of apes – were also stereotyped as creatures of ravenous and uncontrolled libido, and a physical threat to White women. White women need protection from these ape-like men. "From the racist's point of view, inferior races, cognizant of their inferiority "desire upwards" not only in terms of ascending the rungs of the social ladder but in clambering up the links" of the racial hierarchy (Mills, 2015: 32). If successful, the sexual desire for White women by ape-like Black men would lift up the social position of the Black male (by intimate association) and raise the children of Black men to a higher status (by the blood infusion of the superior White woman). Because the White woman is the vessel of reproduction of the White race, White female sexual relations with a Black male is racial pollution that will eventually bring about the destruction of the White race. The superior race (Whites) must forcefully oppose (with violence, if necessary) interracial sexual demands of the males of the inferior race (Blacks). Notably, within the context of simianization, all sexual activity between White women and Black men was rape. From this perspective, Blacks are near relatives of apes "and thus a separate species from Whites so that *inter*-racial sex ... could be declared against the biological laws of Nature" (Mills, 2015: 34). Any White woman having consensual sex with a Black man was engaging in bestiality, an act of an insane person. So, Black male–White female sex is always force. It is important to note that rape was the primary rationalization given for lynching Black males.

Francis Amasa Walker, founder and first president of the American Economic Association, statistician, and President, Massachusetts Institute of Technology, is the social Darwinist credited with propagating "the

[3] Nott and Gliddon (1854) argued that humans do not have a common ancestral origin.

disappearance hypothesis" (Darity, 1994). But it was Frederick Hoffman who provided the clearest statement of the disappearance hypothesis: Blacks would disappear from America in a few generations because they are inherently inferior to Anglo-Saxons. For Hoffman, slavery protected Blacks and allowed people of African descent to increase in population. He argued that, without White protection, the inability of Blacks to compete as free people in an industrial society would cause African Americans to die out.

The racism of social Darwinism had a strong influence on immigration policy. For example, the Chinese Exclusion Act 1882 cut off all immigration from China to the United States. The Gentlemen's Agreement of 1907 put a halt to Japanese immigration. The Immigration Act of 1917 (Literacy Act also known as the Asiatic Barred Zone Act) cut off all immigration from all of Asia.[4] Finally, with the Immigration Act of 1924 (Johnson–Reed Act): annual number of immigrants from any country is limited to 2% of the number of people from that country who were already living in the United States as of the 1890 census (revised Emergency Quota of 1921 limited immigration to 3% from any country and Census of 1910); banned immigration of Arabs and Asians; restricted immigration of Southern Europeans and Eastern Europeans, especially Italians, Slavs and Eastern European Jews; and, severely restricted the immigration of Africans and banned the immigration of Arabs and Asians.

How did the racist ideology (social Darwinism) benefit White owners and workers? Negative stereotypes of African Americans and racial minority immigrants reduced their bargaining power relative to White business owners and provided a rationale to exclude them from participation in democratic representation and the provision of public services. Cutting off African American and racial minority immigrant competition provided White workers with relatively greater access to land, employment and better jobs in manufacturing, better public goods (schools, parks, etc.), and the opportunity for European immigrants to enter America (even if they were also discriminated against in the United States).

4.2.2.3 *African American Self-Help: Moving up despite Negative Incentives*

Amid the public–private joint venture which produced the multi-decade reign of terror that characterized the Nadir and, therefore, despite economic incentives to the contrary, African Americans closed the literacy gap with Whites, experienced exceptional entrepreneurial development, and inaugurated an impressive period of institution building. Except for the years of Reconstruction (1865–1877), all federal, state, and local governments of the South were explicitly aligned against African Americans achieving political, economic, and social equality and independence; instead, White businesses,

[4] *Dow* v. *United States* 1914 and 1915. Indian Citizenship Act of 1924.

governments, and institutions operating during servitude capitalism sought to kept African Americans in a servile position, thoroughly subordinate to and dependent on Whites. Even during Reconstruction, Black striving for upward mobility was often met with White hostility and violence through the actions of local and state governments and White civic organizations and businesses. Black progress during the Nadir occurred despite negative market incentives and despite negative public policy and public–private racial terrorism joint venture. Progress during this era was governed by the strengths of African American cultural identity, not by the individualistic calculus of costs and benefits of skill acquisition. Both the National Association for the Advancement of Colored People (1905, 1909) and the National Urban League (1910) were brought into existence during the Nadir. Hence, despite widespread negative economic incentives and public policies, African Americans engaged in individual and collective self-help that would raise the economic standing of future generations.

In 1866, nearly 4.5 million African Americans owned 12,000 homes, that is 2.67 homes per 1,000 people (see Table 4.1). This number rose to 264,288 by 1890, an increase of 2,100%. There were 10.5 million African Americans in 1922 and they owned 650,000 homes, that is 61.9 homes per 1,000 people. African Americans operated 20,000 farms in 1866 and 1,000,00 farms in 1922, increasing from 4.44 farms per 100 African Americans to 95.24 farms per 1,000 African Americans. Businesses owned by African Americans increased from 0.47 businesses per 1,000 citizens to 5.71 businesses per 1,000 African Americans, as the total number of Black owned businesses rose from 2,100 to 60,000. Finally, the aggregate wealth of African Americans rose from $20,000,000 to $1,500,000,000, that is, from $4,444.44 per 1,000 African Americans to $142,857.14 per 1,000 African Americans.

No other emancipated people have made so great a progress in so short a time.

The Russian serfs were emancipated in 1861. Fifty years after it was found that 14,000,000 of them had accumulated $500,000,000 worth of property or about $36 per capita, an average of about $200 per family. Fifty years after their emancipation only about 30 percent of the Russian peasants were able to read and write. After fifty years of freedom the eleven million Negroes in the United States have accumulated over $1,500,000,000 worth of property, or over $100 per capita, which is an average of $350 per family. After 50 years of freedom 80 per cent of them have some education in books. (Work, 1922: 440)

At the end of chattel capitalism, just 10 percent of African Americans were literate. By 1922, 80 percent of African Americans were literate.[5] There were 100,000 Black students in 1866 and 2,000,000 Black students in 1922, while African American teachers rose from 600 to 44,000. Pupils studied reading,

[5] Collins and Margo (2003) show that illiteracy rates among African Americans declined from 81 percent in 1870 to 34 percent by 1910. The illiteracy rates are for persons 10–69 years of age. During this same period of time, White illiteracy declined from 13 percent to 5 percent.

TABLE 4.1. *Socioeconomic contribution of Black culture, self-help, and personal responsibility during Nadir*

Some Lines of Progress	1866	1867	1890	1910	1922	Gain in 56 Years
Economic Progress						
Homes owned	12,000		264,288	506,590	650,000	638,000
Farms operated	20,000				1,000,000	980,000
Businesses Conducted	2,100				60,000	57,900
Wealth Accumulated	$20,000,000				$1,500,000,000	$1,480,000,000
Educational Progress						
Schools for freedmen		1,839				
All Teachers		2,087				
Percent Literate	10				80	70
Colleges and Normal Schools	15				500	485
Students in Public Schools	100,000	111,442			2,000,000	1,900,000
Studying alphabet		18,758				
Studying spelling & easy reading		55,163				
Studying writing		42,879				
Studying arithmetic		40,454				
Studying higher branches of math		4,661				
Students in industrial schools		2,124				
Negro Teachers in All Schools	600	699			44,000	43,400
Property for Higher Education	$60,000				$30,000,000	$29,940,000
Annual Expenditures for Education	$700,000				$28,000,000	$27,300,000
Raised by Negroes	80,000				2,000,000	1,920,000
Religious Progress						
Number of Churches	700				45,000	44,300
Number of Communicants	600,000				4,800,000	4,200,000
Number of Sunday Schools	1,000				46,000	45,000
Sunday School Pupils	50,000				2,250,000	2,200,000
Value of Church Property	$1,500,000				$90,000,000	$88,500,000

Source: All statistics in this table are taken from Work (1922)

writing, and arithmetic, though students in industrial school also studied sewing, knitting, straw braiding, repairing and making garments. Of the more than 100 Historically Black Colleges and Universities in existence today, many were founded during the Nadir.[6]

The national and international institutionalization of the Black Church also occurred during this era (Lincoln and Mamiya, 1990). Eight percent of African American wealth was in churches (Work, 1922: 432). Churches were schools, social centers, and sites for worship service. "This would appear to be a new and distinct advance in the development of church work by Negroes ... Not much difference between Sunday Schools and day schools, both had to teach "the rudiments of learning" (Work, 1922: 432). The total number of African American churches increased from 700 in 1866 to 45,000 in 1922, while membership increased from 600,000 to 4,800,000. There were 46,000 Sunday Schools in 1922 versus just 1,000 in 1866, with students rising from 50,000 to 2,250,000.

In 1880 the labor market characteristics (skill) of African American men reduced their occupational status by 29.7 percent relative to the average American male (see Table 4.2). On the other hand, differential treatment in the market, that is, discrimination in the rate of return to African American skill, lowered African American occupational status by 31.2 percent. By 1910 the reduction in occupational status due to deficient skill was just 18.5 percent, despite the rise and consolidation of Jim Crow during 1880–1910. Yet, the impact of market discrimination increased from 31 to 44 percent during this same period.

> Decreasing losses associated with deficient characteristics tracks well with the sharp rise in black male literacy, while increasing losses attributable to disadvantageous returns to characteristics track well with the hardening of Jim Crow practices in the US South. This may suggest evidence of a simple pattern of endogenous discrimination: as blacks became harder to exclude from preferential employment and status positions on grounds of qualifications, outright exclusion intensified. (Darity, Dietrich, and Guilkey, 1997: 304)

Darity, Dietrich, and Guilkey (2001) then assess whether group occupational status in 1880, 1900, and 1910 had an impact on individual occupational status in 1980 and 1990. At the turn of the century African American men attained lower occupational status because of market discrimination and lower skill characteristics. Lower labor market characteristics among African American males were directly caused by slavery and the formation of Jim Crow in the South. Darity, Dietrich, and Guilkey show that the effect of both market discrimination and skill deficits continued to have a negative impact on the occupational status of African American males 100 years later. Of course, some

[6] See https://en.wikipedia.org/wiki/List_of_historically_black_colleges_and_universities. Last accessed December 13, 2022.

TABLE 4.2. *Duncan Index of Occupational Status for African American Men, 1880–1990*

	1880		1900		1910		1980		1990	
	Diff.	%	Diff.	%	Diff.	%	Diff.	%	Diff.	%
Characteristics	−0.297	48.77%	−0.224	36.78%	−0.185	29.65%	−0.148	47.28%	−0.11	44.18%
Rate of return	−0.312	51.23%	−0.385	63.22%	−0.439	70.35%	−0.165	52.72%	−0.139	55.82%
Total	−0.609	100%	−0.609	100%	−0.624	100%	−0.313	100%	−0.249	100%

Source: Modification of table 2, Darity, Dietrich, and Guilkey (1997)

White men had skill characteristics similar to those of African Americans at the turn of the century; however, they also received market premiums that they were able to pass on to their ethnic descendants four generations later. Current generations of Whites continue to benefit from past racism, while current generations of African Americans are harmed by past racism.

Theodore "Teddy" Roosevelt was president during 1901–1909. His domestic program was called the "Square Deal." The Square Deal of this progressive Republican included the right of workers to organize and form unions, with restrictions on the power of monopolies. President Theodore Roosevelt (1910) declared that:

> Practical equality of opportunity for all citizens, when we achieve it, will have two great results. First, every man will have a fair chance to make of himself all that in him lies; to reach the highest point to which his capacities, unassisted by special privilege of his own and unhampered by the special privilege of others, can carry him, and to get for himself and his family substantially what he has earned. Second, equality of opportunity means that the commonwealth will get from every citizen the highest service of which he is capable. No man who carries the burden of the special privileges of another can give to the commonwealth that service to which it is fairly entitled.
>
> I stand for the square deal. But when I say that I am for the square deal, I mean not merely that I stand for fair play under the present rules of the game, but that I stand for having those rules changed so as to work for a more substantial equality of opportunity and of reward for equally good service … When I say I want a square deal for the poor man, I do not mean that I want a square deal for the man who remains poor because he has not got the energy to work for himself. If a man who has had a chance will not make good, then he has got to quit … (p. 1)

Progressives did not fight for racial equality or racial justice. As shown in Table 4.2, discrimination increased during the Roosevelt years. Within hours of becoming president, on October 16, 1901, President Roosevelt invited Booker T. Washington for dinner at the White House. Also, a friend of Roosevelt would be in attendance. White women were present. Roosevelt wanted Washington's advice on cabinet appointments. The dinner invitation implied social equality between Blacks and Whites. A national furor ensued.[7] No other African American was asked to dine at the White House. When Alabama farmers were convicted of offering public bribes and debt peonage, they were given light sentences, before being pardoned by Roosevelt (*New York Times*, 1903).

4.2.2.4 *World War II*

The process of crypto-slavery ended as the United States entered World War II. The US port of Pearl Harbor, Hawaii was bombed by Japan on December 7,

[7] See www.pbs.org/video/roosevelts-booker-t-washington-white-house/. Last accessed December 13, 2022.

1941. One unintended consequence of the bombing of Pearl Harbor was that President Franklin Delano Roosevelt became worried about issues the Japanese would use to embarrass America in other countries around the world. A cabinet officer explained to Roosevelt, "the condition of the Negro" would be an issue (Blackmon, 2012). So, as a national defense priority, Roosevelt set out to end all forms of involuntary servitude. Ironically, during this same period, Japanese Americans were sent to concentration camps and had their property taken without just compensation.

World War II and its aftermath made the status of African Americans an international issue. Foreign policy, domestic policy, war, economics, racism, crime, and inequality all interact in very powerful ways – often with unintended consequences. During the war, the US government was worried that Nazi Germany and Japan would use American racial problems to embarrass the United States in the international court of public opinion. So, just five days after the bombing of Pearl Harbor, on December 12, 1941, the Attorney General Francis Biddle issued Circular No. 3591.[8] Henceforth, federal prosecutors were to aggressively prosecute any case of involuntary servitude or slavery. Effectively speaking, crypto-slavery came to an end in 1942 when a federal court in Corpus Christi, Texas convicted and imprisoned Alex L. Skrobarczyk and his daughter Susie – a White family – for holding Alfred Irvin (an African America) in slavery.[9] After the war, the federal government was worried that the Soviet Union, "the Communists," would use American racial problems to embarrass the United States in the international court of public opinion. By 1954 the federal government had decided to re-intervene in the South via the school desegregation case of *Brown* v. *Topeka Board of Education.*

4.3 RACIALIZED MANAGERIAL CAPITALISM: 1933–1973

The initial years of racialized managerial capitalism (1933–1968) were also the final years of servitude capitalism. Servitude capitalism was not eliminated by the competitive forces of the market; it was eliminated by government policy, starting with the presidency of Franklin D. Roosevelt (1933–1945) and reaching completion with President Lyndon B. Johnson (1963–1968). Chattel and servitude capitalisms bequeathed to racial managerial capitalism a racist political economic legacy: massive racial wealth disparity, racialized manager–worker identity matches, a racially segregated society where separate usually means unequal, and racial disparities in a range of socioeconomic outcomes. De jure racism was eliminated, but the legacy of chattel and servitude capitalisms created structures and racial identity norms insuring that racial disparities would be endemic to American society in perpetuity.

[8] See https://en.wikisource.org/wiki/Circular_No._3591. Last accessed December 13, 2022.

[9] See www.newspapers.com/clip/2387500/skrobarczyks_convicted_of_peonage/. Last accessed December 13, 2022.

Under racialized managerial capitalism, White managers dominate control over public and private sources. Managers use discretionary authority to ration access to opportunity and resources. Managerial discretion has a racial and class bias; implementation of organizational rules and procedures depend on the manager–worker and manager–citizen racial identity match, managerial discretion is biased toward Whites and biased toward the economic elite. Intellectual and political managers produce and distribute theories of Black deficiency to justify persistent racial disparity in the distribution of wealth and other socioeconomic outcomes.

Chattel and servitude capitalisms were political economies of a racist state and an economy where the state was fully subservient to corporate interests. Racialized managerial capitalism is characterized by substantial public sector regulation and oversight of banking and capital markets, labor markets, education, health care, housing, international trade, etc. The federal government is also committed to using monetary and fiscal policy to fight recessions and inflation. The federal government developed a commitment to end de jure racism. Racialized managerial capitalism is characterized by a formal commitment to equality of opportunity, but hostility to interracial redistribution of wealth that would make opportunities equal; racialized managerial capitalism has eschewed equality of racial power and socioeconomic status. Racialized managerial capitalism is characterized by adherence to race neutral standards that reproduce anti-Black racial exclusion and persistent subordination of African Americans.

4.3.1 Migration and Urbanization: 1917–1965

American entry into World War I in 1917, the Red Scare of 1919–1920, and the Immigration Restriction Act of 1921 effectively ended large-scale European immigration to America. Northern and Eastern manufacturers had to draw on America's internal labor pool to satisfy their employment needs. The rise of racialized managerial capitalism coincided with African American migration and urbanization. The period from World War I to 1965 was characterized by Black migration out of the South, urbanization of African Americans within the South and other regions, and, ultimately, "The Movement."

The African American tradition of self-help found significant expression in the rise of the Black women's social clubs and the increasing prominence of Historically Black Colleges and Universities.[10] For example, the 1930s and 1940s are celebrated as the golden age of Howard University, whose liberal

[10] Giddings (1984) establishes the Black women's club movement began in the mid- to late-nineteenth century and has extended into the present era. Black women's clubs were distinctive in that they were neither the female appendages of Black men's organizations nor were they minority members or caucuses of White women's organizations. These were organizations formed and led by African American women.

arts faculty of that period was a competitive challenge to any university in the country (Table 4.3). After receiving his Ph.D. in mathematics (at 22 years of age) from the University of Illinois–Urbana Champaign in 1941, David H. Blackwell received a post-doctoral fellowship at Princeton's Institute of Advanced Study, taught briefly at Southern University and Clark College (currently called the Clark Atlanta University), before teaching at Howard during 1944–1954, where he also chaired the mathematics department during 1947–1954. Blackwell went on to become one of the world's most celebrated statisticians. Abram Harris obtained his Ph.D. in economics from Columbia in 1930 and taught at Howard for many years before moving on to the University of Chicago. Frank Knight, godfather of the Chicago School of Economics, declared that Harris was the smartest man on campus.[11] Ralphe J. Bunche, who received his BA and MA from UCLA and his doctorate from Harvard, was a professor of political science at Howard. He chaired the department from 1928 to 1950. Bunche authored the United Nations Convention on the Decolonization of Africa and received the 1950 Nobel Prize for negotiating the 1949 Arab–Israeli armistice agreements.[12] Emmet E. Dorsey, Bunche's brilliant colleague at Howard, was also responsible for building the political science department. Renowned literary figure, Sterling A. Brown was born on the campus of Howard University, where his father (former slave and prominent minister Sterling N. Brown) was a member of the Divinity School. Brown was a Howard professor from 1929 to 1969.[13] E. Franklin Frazier was a professor of sociology at Howard and went on to become President of the American Sociology Association.[14]

Howard's history department included William Leo Hansberry and Eric Williams. Williams published several impressive works, including *Capitalism and Slavery*, and went on to become President, Trinidad and Tobago. Alain Locke, Rhodes Scholar and Professor of Philosophy, was an architect of the "The New Negro" movement, similar in spirit to Leopold Senghor's (author and President of Senegal) "Negritude" movement, both of which emphasized

[11] Darity (1987).

[12] Bunche and Harris were both Marxists at Howard, but later moved to the right. During the 1950s, the McCarthyites falsely labeled Bunche a Communist. See Urquhart (1988) for a biography of Bunche.

[13] Among others, Brown's students included Kwame Ture (Stokely Carmichael), Kwame Nkrumah (first President of Ghana and prominent proponent of Pan-Africanism), Thomas Sowell (who claimed to be a Marxist at Howard but who is now identified as a black conservative), Ossie Davis (famous actor, social activist, and eulogist of Malcolm X), and the author and activist Amiri Baraka (Leroi Jones).

[14] Dubois labeled Sterling Brown, E. Franklin Frazier, Abram Harris, and Emmet Dorsey "Young Turks" because their ideas seemed to suggest the primacy of class over race. Both Dubois and the Young Turks of the 1930s were strongly influenced by Marx; however, Dubois strongly insisted that race remain a distinct analytical and descriptive category. Harris criticized Dubois for being a racialist.

TABLE 4.3. *Prominent faculty members of Howard University*

Blackwell, David H.	Mathematics	1944–1954
Brown, Sterling A.	Literature	1929–1969
Bunche, Ralphe J.	Political Science	Chair, 1928–1950
Childers, Lulu Vere	Fine Arts	1905–1942
Dorsey, Emmet E.	Political Science	1929–1965*
Franklin, John Hope	History	1947–1956
Frazier, E. Franklin	Sociology	1934–1962
Hansberry, William Leo	History	1922–1959
Harris, Abram	Economics	1927–1945
Hastie, William H.	Law	Dean, 1939–1946
Houston, Charles Hamilton	Law	1924–1935
Julian, Percy	Chemistry	1927–1929, 1931–1932
Just, Ernest Everett	Biology	1907–1941
Locke, Alain	Literature and Philosophy	1912–1916, 1918–1925, 1928–1953
Logan, Rayford	History	1938–1965
Mays, Benjamin	Religion	Chair, 1934–1940
Snowden, Frank	Literature (classics)	1940–1976
Thurmond, Howard	Religion	1932–1944
Williams, Eric	Social & Political Science	1939–1952

* These dates may not be correct. It is difficult to find the exact dates of Dorsey's affiliation with Howard University.

the cultural autonomy, intellectual independence, and complete cultural and intellectual equality of people of African descent with all others. The Pan-Africanist "New Negro" and "Negritude" cultural movements for-shadowed the post-1965 Black Power Movement and the Black Arts Movement of the 1960s and 1970s. William H. Hastie graduated at the top of his class at Amherst College, received a law degree from Harvard, and subsequently taught Thurgood Marshall. Hastie, Dean of Howard Law School from 1939 to 1946. Hastie, Charles Hamilton Houston ("The man who killed Jim Crow"), and other members of Howard Law School led the legal fight to destroy servitude capitalism.

E. Franklin Frazier witnessed the first decades of the massive migration and urbanization of African Americans, persons who were either born during slavery or born during the years of formation and consolidation of Jim Crow. Frazier viewed the migration and urbanization of African Americans as analogous to the experience of contemporary Europeans assimilating into American society. This was an inviting comparison, since the period of 1877–1910 witnessed massive Irish and Eastern and Southern European immigration to the United States. Robert E. Park and his colleagues at the University of Chicago argued that America was a giant melting pot: immigrants quickly leave behind their old country culture once they set foot on the shores of America and after a short period of adjustment they take on American culture and values and become productive citizens willing to work hard and take advantage of the opportunities presented to them in America. The short period of cultural adjustment by ethnic immigrants might be characterized by above average criminality and family instability, but these problems eventually decline as groups fully acculturate into American life. Similarly, Frazier argued that African Americans abandoned their African culture at the shores of America. From this perspective, slavery further destroyed the African-based family without permitting compensating opportunities for acculturation, assimilation, and integration. Thus, from Frazier's perspective, the migration and urbanization of African Americans presented an opportunity for Black migrants to acculturate, assimilate, and integrate in precisely the same manner (and at the precisely the same time) as European immigrants. There would be a short period of adjustment to life in urban areas within and outside of the South and to life in the North, but African Americans would more or less quickly integrate into the American melting pot.

For Frazier and Park, the melting pot analogy was a racially and ethnically inclusive policy approach. Other scholars of the late nineteenth and early twentieth century argued that Irish, Italian, Jews (especially Eastern European Jews), and other immigrants of that era were too different to ever assimilate into America. These groups, it was argued, pollute the White race because they are biologically and culturally inferior. The Eugenics movement and cultural Darwinism arose as a reaction to the presence of these new ersatz-White immigrants.[15] At the same, it was argued that African Americans were so genetically inferior that they would die out by the mid-twentieth century.[16] Frazier and Park argued against the racism and ethnocentrism of their era.

4.3.2 Second Reconstruction: 1941–1973

The US economy recovered during the 1940s as World War II and President Franklin D. Roosevelt's "New Deal" economic agenda brought the Great Depression to an end. The late 1940s was a period of declining racial disparity in wage income, high employment and low unemployment, and a rising standard of living for African Americans and all others. The New Deal reshaped America's economy and began the second Reconstruction of the South. It was,

[15] White racial identity was not immediately granted to some of these new immigrants. See, for example, several of the founding texts on Whiteness studies, i.e., Ignatiev (1995), Brodkin (1998), and Roediger (1991, 2005).

[16] Robert Cherry (1976) and William A. Darity, Jr. (1994) analyze the racial views of US neoclassical economics from the end of the nineteenth through early twentieth century. Levy (2001) builds a more positive case for the racial views of mid-eighteenth British classical economists, especially John Stuart Mill. See also Levy and Peart (2000, 2003). Peart and Levy (2001) explore British and American economists' connections to the Eugenics movement.

however, an imperfect beginning. For example, the original version (later amended) of the 1935 Social Security Act did not provide old-age pensions for farm and domestic workers. These were the major occupations of African American men and women, respectively. Also, the GI Bill was a strong force for expanding the White middle class, but African Americans did not benefit to the same extent because Black veterans were often excluded; the GI Bill was a federal program but controlled by state governments who systematically excluded African Americans.

Going into World War II, the federal government was segregated, including the armed forces charged with defending the country. It was also difficult for Black workers to find employment in lucrative jobs among companies with military and other government contracts. In response, on January 25, 1941 Asa Philip Randolph, founder and first President of the Brotherhood of Sleeping Car Porters (BSCP), proposed that African Americans organize a March on Washington (Kindig, 2007). The BSCP had 18,000 members, mostly Black men. It was expected that 100,000 African Americans would participate in the March on Washington, scheduled for July 1. March on Washington committees were set up across the country. One June 25, President Roosevelt issued Executive Order 8802, which prohibited discrimination in the Defense Industry (Executive Order 8802, 1941).

The details of Executive Order 8802 state the following.

1. All departments and agencies of the Government of the United States concerned with vocational and training programs for defense production shall take special measures appropriate to assure that such programs are administered without discrimination because of race, creed, color, or national origin;
2. All contracting agencies of the Government of the United States shall include in all defense contracts hereafter negotiated by them a provision obligating the contractor not to discriminate against any worker because of race, creed, color, or national origin;
3. There is established in the Office of Production Management a Committee on Fair Employment Practice, which shall consist of a chairman and four other members to be appointed by the President. ... The Committee shall receive and investigate complaints of discrimination in violation of the provisions of this order and shall take appropriate steps to redress grievances which it finds to be valid. The Committee shall also recommend to the several departments and agencies of the Government of the United States and to the President all measures which may be deemed by it necessary or proper to effectuate the provisions of this order.

Generals Dwight D. Eisenhower and John C. H. Lee racially integrated the US Army during the Battle of the Bulge, December 16, 1944–January 25, 1945 (Andrews, 2019). Black soldiers fought alongside White soldiers to liberate

Europe from fascism. President Harry S. Truman racially integrated the armed services in law when he issued Executive Order 9981, on July 26, 1948, establishing the President's Committee on Equality of Treatment and Opportunity in the Armed Services. At the same time, Truman issued Executive Order 9980, which desegregated the federal civilian workforce. Executive Orders 9980 and 9981 ended President's Woodrow Wilson's 35 years-old policy of racially segregating the federal workforce.[17]

During the next two decades several other major federal laws would be passed eliminating segregation in government agencies and private companies, within and outside of the Southern states of the United States.

- 1954. *Brown* v. *Board of Education of Topeka, Kansas*. Supreme Court declared that public school segregation is unconstitutional. This court decision was a major step in overturning *Plessy* v. *Ferguson*. Racially separate public education systems were inherently unequal, as White controlled school boards would not adequately fund African American schools. This decision helped increase the quantity and quality of African American education.
- 1955. Montgomery bus boycott begins. Led to elimination of segregated seating in public transportation.
- 1964. Twenty-fourth Amendment abolished poll tax. Also, the Civil rights Act of 1964 prohibited racial discrimination in all public accommodations (both privately owned organizations and publicly owned) and gave the federal government the power to enforce desegregation.
- The Voting Rights Act of 1965 eliminated literacy tests, poll taxes, and similar impediments to voting.
- Executive Order 11246 (September 24, 1965) required federal government contractors to take affirmative action with respect to minority employees in decisions related to hiring and employment.
- 1965. Immigration Reform Act of 1965. Immigration policy would no longer be a tool to Whiten the country's population. Entry into the United States was governed by three categories: (1) refugees – persons who are unable or unwilling to return to their country of origin because of a "well-founded fear of persecution" due to race, membership in a particular social group, political opinion, religion, or national origin; (2) unique skill – persons able to fill a job for which there were an insufficient number of qualified Americans; and (3) family reunification.

[17] Harry S. Truman, Executive Order 9980 – Regulations Governing Fair Employment Practices within the Federal Establishment Online by Gerhard Peters and John T. Woolley, The American Presidency Project; www.presidency.ucsb.edu/node/278504. Last accessed December 13, 2022. Harry S. Truman, Executive Order 9981 – Establishing the President's Committee on Equality of Treatment and Opportunity in the Armed Services Online by Gerhard Peters and John T. Woolley, The American Presidency Project; www.presidency.ucsb.edu/node/231614. Last accessed December 13, 2022.

- 1967 Supreme Court declared that laws prohibiting interracial marriage are unconstitutional.
- 1967 Stokely Carmichael coined the phrase "black power," signaling a major change in African American advocacy for political and economic equality.
- Civil Rights Act of 1968 prohibited discrimination in the sale, rental, and financing of housing.

"Affirmative action" entered American public consciousness on March 6, 1961 when President John F. Kennedy signed Executive Order 10925, creating the Committee on Equal Employment Opportunity. Executive Order 10925 mandated that projects financed with federal funds "take affirmative action" to ensure that hiring and employment practices are free of racial bias. The Civil Rights Act of 1964 (July 2) established the Equal Employment Opportunity Commission and made it illegal to "fail or refuse to hire or to discharge any individual, or otherwise to discriminate against any individual with respect to his compensation, terms, conditions or privileges or employment, because of such individual's race, color, religion, sex, or national origin."

Table 4.4 presents a sample of help wanted advertisements from selected major newspapers from 1950 to 1960. The advertisements are clear: prior to the Civil Rights Act of 1964 competitive employers openly engaged in racial, gender, marital, and age discrimination within their labor market practices. Executive Order 11246 (September 24, 1965) required federal contractors to develop a written affirmative action plan. The plan did not force contractors to hire, train, or promote anyone. Rather, the plan requirements were designed to help the contractor take the necessary steps to remove impediments (if any) to the hiring, training, and promotion of women and racial and ethnic minorities by the contractor. Affirmative action included aggressive steps in outreach, recruitment, training, and other activities that would help women and racial and ethnic minorities compete on a level playing field. Over time, the concept of affirmative action spread from federal contractors to other private companies, state agencies, and universities. Yet, by 1978 this modest effort to breakdown discrimination was under full assault.[18] That year, the Supreme Court declared that the University of California–Davis Medical School's affirmative action plan had discriminated against Alan Bakke, a White male applicant. Thereafter, a series of court challenges have considerably reduced the intensity and scope of affirmative action.

The Second Reconstruction were a set of government policies that were the outcomes of the Civil Rights Movement of 1941–1965 and the Black Power Movement of 1965–1973. African American absolute and relative progress during 1941–1973 was an outcome achieved by government policies and political action, not the competitive forces of the market breaking down racism

[18] For an interesting contrast, see Katznelson (2005).

TABLE 4.4. *Examples of racial preferences in help wanted advertisements: Selected newspapers and years, 1950–1960*

CHICAGO TRIBUNE	LOS ANGELES TIMES	NEW YORK TIMES	WASHINGTON POST
January 6, 1950 COMPANION-HOUSEKEEPER – For elderly lady; small apt., N.W. side; private bedrm.; salary \$20–\$25 week; white only. Phone Mon., RO dney 3-9460 cook and 2d maid or cpl., cook and houseman – must be exp.; white Swedish or German pref. Call Andover 3-2345. Mr. Rolfson	**January 1, 1950** CPL. WHITE DOM. FOR 1 PERSON. S&M Agency, 660 S. Vint, Du.73368	**January 3, 1950** COOK, white experienced, sleep in. 15 W81 SE (13B), call 11-3	**January 1, 1950** WAITRESSES, WHITE OPENINGS ON ALL SHIFTS EXCELLENT EARNINGS APPLY TO HEADWAITER AMBASSADOR HOTEL 14th and K 818 NW
COOK and General Housework – colored own rm.; stay; other help; \$30 to start. IRving 8-2420	COOK, WHITE, EXPERIENCED. Apply 4226 E. OLYMPIC BLVD	HOUSEWORKER – cook, white, sleep out, A-1 worker, city refs. AT 9-0307	Waitresses, white. Experienced; meals and uniforms furnished; good pay and tips; openings 4PM to 12 midnight, and 12 to 8 a.m. Apply GREYHOUND GRILL (Bus Terminal) 12th and NY Ave NW
January 25, 1956 WANTED – steady cpl.; white: Lake Geneva, Wisc. Cook and houseman bet. 40–50 years. Good salary. Recent references required. Write MAV 462, Tribune	**January 2, 1955** HSKPR., wht., gd. cook, under 60. Stay. No wash. Disabled bus. man & father. West Side Drive, Refs. Box B-221 Times	**January 2, 1955** COOK-HOUSEKEEPER White; thoroughly experienced and qualified; capable of handling all household details in connection with this type of	**January 2, 1955** MAIL CLERK (white) Age 20–30. Neat appearance. Hotel front-desk experienced helpful. Must be able to work 7 a.m. to 3:30 p.m. one week and 3:30 p.m. to 11:30 p.m.

(*continued*)

TABLE 4.4. (*continued*)

CHICAGO TRIBUNE	LOS ANGELES TIMES	NEW YORK TIMES	WASHINGTON POST
		work; own room; location Old Westbury; other help; recent references; salary $65, Y6175 Times	the following week. Permanent position, with employees' benefits, after 3 months employment. APPLY PERSONNEL OFFICE MAYFLOWER HOTEL CONN. & DESALES ST NW
HOUSEKEEPER – White; stay; 5 1/2 day wk: nice home. La Grange: no children. Phone Sun. Fleetwood 2-1367 or Monday WHitehall 4-1842	MAID WHITE HSKPR Good refs., prvt. rm., ba: WH 2221	COOK-houseworker, Negro, and 40 years, just be good cook & baker, 2 year. city ref. 2 adults. No laun: 5 days, 12 till after dinner, $40. K 50's MU 8-1350	
January 3, 1960 LABORATORY TECHNICIAN Experienced, Modern southside medical center. White. Salary open. Call Vincennes 6-3401	**January 2, 1960** COMPANION. White. Lite hswk. for single lady. Must drive. Local refers. CR 1-7704	**January 3, 1960** COOK, housekeeper, Negro preferred, experience essential, prominent family, permanent position, high salary, MA 7-5369	**January 3, 1960** NURSE (practical) white, for small nursing home, Silver Spring area. Car nec. Good salary. EV 4-6161

and creating a level playing field for all racial groups and individuals. Migration and urbanization, sharp declines in the racial gap in the quantity and quality of education, and the anti-discrimination policies of the second Reconstruction led to a substantial reduction in the Black–White wage gap during 1940–1980 (Smith and Welch, 1989; Donohue and Heckman, 1991). By the early 1970s, African Americans of 25–36 years of age had achieved nearly equal years of education with their White cohorts (Bernstein, 1995). For the nation as a whole, 1941–1973 was a period of declining unemployment, stable prices, and raising real wages for all workers; hence, this sustained macroeconomic boom, combined with public policy and self-help by African Americans and the demands of Black social movements, created an economic environment which pushed the Black wage distribution rightward toward the White wage distribution.

4.4 THE GREAT DEBATE: FAMILY, CULTURE, IDENTITY, AND PERSISTENT RACIAL DISPARITY

Servitude capitalism was destroyed during 1965–1973. Nonetheless, large racial gaps in income and wealth remained even after African Americans were able to reclaim their citizenship from federal, state, and local governments under the control of White managers. Despite the fact that the state had expropriated African American citizenship for a century, no reparations were paid after the termination of servitude capitalism – just as reparations were not paid to African Africans after the end of chattel capitalism.

Individualist thinking on racial inequality in the labor market ignored the racial norms of chattel and servitude capitalisms and ignored readily available data from want ads. Instead, individualist orthodoxy argued that competition will eliminate racial differences in wages and employment that are unrelated to racial differences in productivity (Becker, 1957). From this perspective, racial disparity in labor market outcomes occur because of racial differences in productive ability. Because the eugenics movement, biological theories of race, and social Darwinism were championed by Nazi Germany and other fascists, the link between these ideas and the genocidal massacre of European Jews reduced the appeal of using biological theories of race to explain racial disparity.

Daniel P. Moynihan, Harvard Sociologist and US Senator (Democrat, New York) established a new individualist social science racist orthodoxy. His 1965 study asserted that Black family pathology and culture are the primary mechanisms responsibility for persistent racial income and wealth inequality (Moynihan, 1965). This new intellectual orthodoxy was the start of the second reversal, policies and actions designed to undo the second Reconstruction. The relationship between income and wealth, on the one hand, and culture, family structure, and family functioning, on the other hand, is an important issue. Prior to Moynihan, the debate among African American and other scholars was defined by adherents to the historically developmental approach to understanding African American families versus the culturally emulative perspective on the African American family.[19]

4.4.1 Du Bois and the Black Family

Du Bois presented the first scientific analysis of the African American family and thereby "established the agenda for studying the African family as a unique cultural population" (McDaniel, 1994: 59). Du Bois proposed that slavery did not destroy the African family but rather created political, social, and economic conditions that lead to the transformation of the African family to the African American family. Among others, Herskovitz (1942) provided anthropological validation of Du Bois' claim. Internal family functioning remained nurturing, though the African-origin family structure was adaptive in its response to the material circumstances of American life. The cultural prerogatives that Africans brought to America – child centered families, consanguine rather than conjugal kinship systems, extended versus nuclear families, marriage as a merger of families rather than simply the joining of individuals – conditioned the manner in which enslaved Africans responded to the political economy of slavery and the abusive power of the enslaver.[20] The unique cultural heritage of African Americans suggests that African American family structure and marital stability would differ from Whites, even if there were no interracial differences in social and economic circumstances or the quality of family functioning. But African American families have been additionally confronted with social and economic circumstances of a qualitatively and quantitatively different character than those confronting White families.

From the historically developmental perspective, changes in family structure are responses to income and wealth opportunities. Family functioning, culture, and behavior are shaped by racial identity to increase wealth accumulation and to maintain family stability. Contemporary research and public policy analysis within the tradition of Du Bois' historical developmental approach to understanding of the interrelationships among culture, family functioning, and family economic well-being emphasizes mate availability, an understanding of socioeconomic classes, persistent discrimination, and the unique cultural heritage of African Americans.

Within the Du Bois historically developmental approach, racial disparity in wealth, income, and civil liberties, combined with cultural prerogatives that Africans brought to America, are used to explain interracial differences in family structure and intraracial changes in family structure over time.

19 The roots of the historically developmental approach as found in W. E. B. Du Bois (1908) and Melvin J. Herskovitz (1942). Frazier (1939) established the foundations of the culturally emulative perspective.

20 Robert B. Hill (1972, 1993); Antonio McDaniel (1990); Andrew Billingsley (1992).

Moreover, for this approach, family structure and family functioning are not the same thing: families may function well, despite differences in structure. The Du Bois approach is embedded within the stratification perspective.

4.4.2 Moynihan Thesis: Intellectual Foundations for Reversing the Second Reconstruction

Many contemporary activists, social scientists, and policymakers have been influenced by a sociological tradition which asserts that African American family life is "pathological" (Moynihan, 1965). This is an individualist explanation on the relationship between families and racial inequality. Moynihan's thesis that Black families are pathological is a bastardization of E. Franklin Frazier's cultural emulative analysis of the African American family. Moynihan's analysis supported the racism of his era.

Moynihan's report was constructed on the basis of four unquestioned axioms. First, both Moynihan and his followers assume that family structure determines economic well-being. For example, Moynihan argued that, "At the heart of the deterioration of the fabric of Negro society is the deterioration of the Negro family. It is *the fundamental source of the weakness* of the Negro community at the present time" (Moynihan, 1965: 5, emphasis added).

On the other hand, Moynihan strongly suggests that the impact of past and contemporary economic circumstances on family structure is minimal. For Moynihan and many of today's social scientists, family structure is determined by the cultural practices of social groups. Loury (1989) refines this line of argument by focusing on the importance of household values and the social capital of neighborhoods, where social capital refers to market functional values, attitudes, and behaviors. Austen-Smith and Fryer (2005) argue that African American identity is anti-intellectual. Murray (1984) and Mead (1992) extend the logic of this approach one step further when they argue that public assistance to the needy and targeted employment programs ultimately reduce social capital. Therefore, they assert that these programs create more unstable families and marriages which then worsen problems of poverty, joblessness, crime, and welfare dependency. Herrnstein and Murray (1994) pushed the issue back to the late nineteenth century, arguing that genetic ability (which for them differs by race and by class to the disadvantage of Blacks and low income Whites) is a more powerful determinant of family structure and stability than culture.

For Moynihan, African American families are pathological because they are matriarchal. He argues that matriarchy developed because slavery destroyed the African-based family and did not allow African Americans to perfectly emulate Whites. This alleged matriarchal structure is equated with family functioning: "female-head families" and "unstable families" are synonyms, while "male-headed families," that is, two-parent families, and "stable families" are interchangeable terms. Therefore, according to the Moynihan perspective, the increasing number of children born to unmarried women is a major indicator of pathology.

> In essence, the *Negro community has been forced into a matriarchal structure* which, because it is to (sic) out of line with the rest of the American society, seriously retards the progress of the group as a whole, and imposes a crushing burden on the Negro male and, in consequence, on a great many Negro women as well.
>
> There is, presumably, no special reason why a society in which males are dominant in family relationships is to be preferred to a matriarchal arrangement. However, *it is clearly a disadvantage for a minority group to be operating on one principle, while the great majority of the population*, and the one with the most advantages to begin with, is operating on another. This is the present situation of the Negro. *Ours is a society which presumes male leadership in private and public affairs. The arrangements of society facilitate such leadership and reward it.* A subculture, such as that of the Negro American, in which this is not the pattern, is placed at a distinct disadvantage. (Moynihan, 1965: 23, emphasis added)
>
> There is no one Negro community. There is no one Negro problem. There is no one solution. Nonetheless, at the center of the tangle of pathology is the weakness of the family structure. Once or twice removed, it will be found to be the principal source of most of the aberrant, inadequate, or antisocial behavior that did not establish, but now serves to perpetuate the cycle of poverty and deprivation.
>
> *It was by destroying the Negro family under slavery that white America broke the will of the Negro people.* Although that will has reasserted itself in our time, it is a resurgence doomed to frustration unless the viability of the Negro family is restored. (Moynihan, 1965: 24–25, emphasis added)

Third, the Moynihan perspective assumes that African Americans do not possess a unique or distinctive culture of their own. Allegedly, African American culture is emulative. After arriving in America, Africans shed all of their cultural past and begin to imperfectly emulate the values, customs, traditions, and (to the extent possible) the family structure of Whites. Thereby, all differences between African American and White families indicate pathology in African American families, rather than competitive innovation or efficient adaption.

Moynihan accepted the axiom that American society is meritocratic: equal opportunity for upward mobility and full employment are the norms of the economy. It is argued that the market is a great equalizer. Left to its own devices, a competitive economy will eliminate racial discrimination in market outcomes (Becker, 1957). Just as White ethnic groups were able to overcome discrimination through stable families, deferred gratification, hard work, the pursuit of education, and the avoidance of crime – or so the argument goes – African Americans can overcome social and economic barriers confronting them once they have learned to sufficiently emulate White or "mainstream" cultural values. From the Moynihan perspective, interracial differences in the economic well-being of families are ultimately related to interracial differences in family values; differences in social class and the pervasive impact of racism are irrelevant.

Racial chauvinism of the type embodied in the Moynihan Report continues to limit, indeed is the normative assumption embodied within today's research on racial inequality. For example, when discussing the general phenomenon of increasing inequality among Whites the major economic explanations usually focus on the relative importance of technological change, globalization, institutional changes such as the decline in the minimum wage rate and decrease in the extent of unionization, deregulation of industries, or changes in the organization of work. But, when discussing analysis of the problem of increasing racial inequality, inferior "family and neighborhood" backgrounds, dysfunctional "values," and "cultural" problems dominate the discussion. It is always African Americans who are presumed to have a deficit of the requisite behavioral attributes. A large chorus of economists insists that racial inequality has remained a social issue because African American families and neighborhoods do not encourage the necessary skill accumulation required to obtain the high wage jobs available in today's economy. Critics of this perspective argue that once again African American family values, functioning, and structure have become the scapegoat for racial discrimination rather than the class structure and institutional racism of American society.

4.4.3 Black Power Economic Agendas

Table 4.5 summarizes the differences between the historically developmental and culturally emulative approaches to understanding African American families. The public policy agenda of most African American organizations incorporated the Du Bois approach to understanding Black families.

The Moynihan Report was brought to the attention of the American public during the early stages of the Black Power Movement of 1965–1973. Jim Crow was a Southern institution. African Americans in the North also faced economic exploitation and political oppression, but much less de jure racial segregation than that experienced by Southern African Americans. After the Civil Rights gains of 1941–1965, the Southern and Northern African American experiences began to converge. Black power proponents placed emphasis on attaining complete economic and political equality. Black power advocates wanted immediate equality, de-emphasized the primacy of racial integration as a goal in and for itself, and abandoned the notion that nonviolent civil disobedience is the only appropriate strategy for achieving social change. Further, Black power advocates often sought an immediate end to police brutality and racism within the criminal legal system.

Some Black power advocates aligned themselves with militant Whites who wanted fundamental structural transformation of the American economy. Except for its abandonment of nonviolent civil disobedience as the only appropriate strategy for social change and its de-emphasis on racial integration, this particular group of Black power advocates had a social and economic vision close to that of Martin Luther King, Jr. King also believed that America needed

TABLE 4.5. *Comparative analysis of African American families: Du Bois versus Moynihan*

	Du Bois	Moynihan
Methodology	Historically developmental: Black families have African heritage and norms that adapt to political economic circumstances in the United States	Culturally emulative: Black families have no African roots, but have not fully acculturated in "American" family norms
Family functioning	Strong	Pathological
Economic causation	Difference in political economic circumstances (family income and wealth) cause differences in family structure	Differences in family structure cause differences in economic circumstances. Political power is de-emphasized
Intergenerational racial disparity	Persistent differences in family structure because of lower political economic resources (and African heritage)	Persistent poverty because of pathological families
Public policy and political action	Racial equality in wealth and income and political power	Help Black families acculturate to "American" values and norms

to be "born again" and "address itself to the question of restructuring the whole of American society." America must have a "revolution of values" of its people and "a broader distribution of wealth."[21] African Americans, insisted King, are not interested in integrating into the then current value system.

The "Black Panther Party for Self Defense," which had party affiliates from New Jersey to California, with bases of support in Newark, Chicago, Detroit, Los Angeles, and Oakland, sought fundamental transformation of the American economy. The Panthers emphasized self-help among African Americans and oppressed people, political equality, a socialist economic system, monitoring the police, armed self-defense, and alliances with militant White leftists (Table 4.6). During January 1969, the Panthers established their Free Breakfast for School Children Program, which spread from Oakland, California across America, eventually feeding 20,000 children per day (Pien, 2010). The contemporary governor of California and future president of the United States, Ronald W. Reagan, was unequivocally hostile to the Panthers.

[21] See King (1968).

TABLE 4.6. *Ten point plan of the Black Panther Party for Self-Defense*

1	WE WANT FREEDOM. WE WANT POWER TO DETERMINE THE DESTINY OF OUR BLACK AND OPPRESSED COMMUNITIES. We believe that Black and oppressed people will not be free until we are able to determine our destinies in our own communities ourselves, by fully controlling all the institutions which exist in our communities.
2	WE WANT FULL EMPLOYMENT FOR OUR PEOPLE. We believe that the federal government is responsible and obligated to give every person employment or a guaranteed income. We believe that if the American businessmen will not give full employment, then the technology and means of production should be taken from the businessmen and placed in the community so that the people of the community can organize and employ all of its people and give a high standard of living.
3	WE WANT AN END TO THE ROBBERY BY THE CAPITALISTS OF OUR BLACK AND OPPRESSED COMMUNITIES. We believe that this racist government has robbed us and now we are demanding the overdue debt of 40 acres and 2 mules. Forty acres and two mules were promised 100 years ago as restitution for slave labor and mass murder of Black people. We will accept the payment in currency which will be distributed to our many communities. The American racist has taken part in the slaughter of our 50 million Black people. Therefore, we feel this is a modest demand that we make.
4	WE WANT DECENT HOUSING, FIT FOR THE SHELTER OF HUMAN BEINGS. We believe that if the landlords will not give decent housing to our Black and oppressed communities, then housing and the land should be made into cooperatives so that the people in our communities, with government aid, can build and make decent housing for the people.
5	WE WANT DECENT EDUCATION FOR OUR PEOPLE THAT EXPOSES THE TRUE NATURE OF THIS DECADENT AMERICAN SOCIETY. WE WANT EDUCATION THAT TEACHES US OUR TRUE HISTORY AND OUR ROLE IN THE PRESENT-DAY SOCIETY. We believe in an educational system that will give to our people a knowledge of the self. If you do not have knowledge of yourself and your position in the society and in the world, then you will have little chance to know anything else.
6	WE WANT COMPLETELY FREE HEALTH CARE FOR ALL BLACK AND OPPRESSED PEOPLE. We believe that the government must provide, free of charge, for the people, health facilities which will not only treat our illnesses, most of which have come about as a result of our oppression, but which will also develop preventive medical programs to guarantee our future survival. We believe that mass health education and research programs must be developed to give all Black and oppressed people access to advanced scientific and medical information, so we may provide ourselves with proper medical attention and care.
7	WE WANT AN IMMEDIATE END TO POLICE BRUTALITY AND MURDER OF BLACK PEOPLE, OTHER PEOPLE OF COLOR, ALL OPPRESSED PEOPLE INSIDE THE UNITED STATES. We believe that the racist and fascist government of the United States uses its domestic enforcement agencies to carry out its program of oppression against black people, other people of color and poor people inside the United States. We believe it is our right, therefore, to defend ourselves against such armed forces and that all Black and oppressed people should be armed for self-defense of our homes and communities against these fascist police forces.

8 WE WANT AN IMMEDIATE END TO ALL WARS OF AGGRESSION. We believe that the various conflicts which exist around the world stem directly from the aggressive desire of the United States ruling circle and government to force its domination upon the oppressed people of the world. We believe that if the United States government or its lackeys do not cease these aggressive wars it is the right of the people to defend themselves by any means necessary against their aggressors.

9 WE WANT FREEDOM FOR ALL BLACK AND OPPRESSED PEOPLE NOW HELD IN US FEDERAL, STATE, COUNTY, CITY, AND MILITARY PRISONS AND JAILS. WE WANT TRIALS BY A JURY OF PEERS FOR ALL PERSONS CHARGED WITH SO-CALLED CRIMES UNDER THE LAWS OF THIS COUNTRY. We believe that the many Black and poor oppressed people now held in United States prisons and jails have not received fair and impartial trials under a racist and fascist judicial system and should be free from incarceration. We believe in the ultimate elimination of all wretched, inhuman penal institutions, because the masses of men and women imprisoned inside the United States or by the United States military are the victims of oppressive conditions which are the real cause of their imprisonment. We believe that when persons are brought to trial they must be guaranteed, by the United States, juries of their peers, attorneys of their choice, and freedom from imprisonment while awaiting trial.

10 WE WANT LAND, BREAD, HOUSING, EDUCATION, CLOTHING, JUSTICE, PEACE, AND PEOPLE'S COMMUNITY CONTROL OF MODERN TECHNOLOGY. When, in the course of human events, it becomes necessary for one people to dissolve the political bonds which have connected them with another, and to assume, among the powers of the earth, the separate and equal station to which the laws of nature and nature's God entitle them, a decent respect to the opinions of mankind requires that they should declare the causes which impel them to the separation.

We hold these truths to be self-evident, that all men are created equal; that they are endowed by their Creator with certain unalienable rights; that among these are life, liberty, and the pursuit of happiness. That to secure these rights, governments are instituted among men, deriving their just powers from the consent of the governed; that, whenever any form of government becomes destructive of these ends, it is the right of the people to alter or to abolish it, and to institute a new government, laying its foundation on such principles, and organizing its powers in such form as to them shall seem most likely to effect their safety and happiness. Prudence, indeed, will dictate that governments long established should not be changed for light and transient causes; and, accordingly, all experience hath shown that mankind are most disposed to suffer, while evils are sufferable, than to right themselves by abolishing the forms to which they are accustomed. But, when a long train of abuses and usurpation, pursuing invariably the same object, evinces a design to reduce them under absolute despotism, it is their right, it is their duty, to throw off such government, and to provide new guards for their future security.

Source: www.blackpast.org/african-american-history/primary-documents-african-american-history/black-panther-party-ten-point-program-1966/. Last accessed December 13, 2022

FBI Director J. Edgar Hoover declared that the Panthers were the "greatest threat to the internal security of the country."

The "Nation of Islam," popularly referred to as "Black Muslims," emphasized religious asceticism, economic self-help, the primacy of male authority within the family, moral transformation of persons currently leading immoral lives, modest dress and behavior, obedience to religious authority, and education as a source of liberation. The Nation also emphasized complete racial separatism, advocating for the creation of a Black nation in the South (out of five states) or elsewhere. The Nation taught that Whites are devils created by an insanely evil scientist. The Nation refrained from participating in the "integrationist" Civil Rights Movement; after all, members of The Nation had no interest in integrating with Whites. Malcolm X, assassinated in February 1965, is the most famous member of The Nation, where he was a member during 1952–1963. The Nation advocated cooperative Black capitalism, an integrated set of mutually dependent Black businesses, workers, and consumers.

The "Republic of New Afrika" (RNA) was a secular Black Nationalist organization created in 1969, whose political and economic policy focused on creating a separate Black nation in the "subjugated lands" of the Deep South, viz., South Carolina, Georgia, Alabama, Mississippi, and Louisiana. The RNA also demanded $400 billion in reparations for slavery and Jim Crow. The RNA wanted an economic system based on the African Socialism ideas of Julius K. Nyerere (ujamaa), that is, a system of cooperative economics and community self-sufficiency.

Chokwe Lumumba was sworn in as the newly-elected mayor of Jackson, Mississippi on July 1, 2013. He died on February 25, 2014. Lumumba was former President of the Republic of New Afrika, founder of Black United Front, and a co-founder of the National Coalition of Blacks for Reparations in America. Martin Luther King Jr. was assassinated on April 4, 1968. The next day Lumumba and a group of students occupied a university building at Western Michigan University. The students protested the lack of African American faculty and made other academic demands. His son, Choke Antar Lumumba, was elected mayor in 2017. The younger Lumumba was endorsed by Our Revolution and the Working Families Party. Our Revolution includes Nina Turner, Bernie Sanders, Ben Jealous, James Hightower, and James Zogby.

Prior to his death, Martin King teamed with A. Philip Randolph and Bayard Rustin to draft a "Freedom Budget for all Americans" (Rustin, 1966). The Freedom Budget had an ambitious goal: abolish poverty within 10 years. Accomplishing this goal required meeting several objectives:

1. To provide full employment for all who are willing and able to work, including those who need education or training to make them willing and able.
   Guaranteed full employment. With full employment a major cause for poverty and racial discrimination will be eliminated. Full production and high economic growth.

2. To assure decent and adequate wages to all who work.
   A $2.00/hour minimum wage by 1968. This would be $14.88/hour during 2020.[22]
3. To assure a decent living standard to those who cannot or should not work.
   Guaranteed minimum income for families unable to work and equitable tax and money policies.
   Updated social security and welfare programs. Farm income parity.
4. To wipe out slum ghettos and provide decent homes for all Americans.
5. To provide decent medical care and adequate educational opportunities to all Americans, at a cost they can afford.
6. To purify our air and water and develop our transportation and natural resources on a scale suitable to our growing needs.
7. To unite sustained full employment with sustained full production and high economic growth.

Black capitalism and Operation COINTELPRO. The rise of the "Black capitalism" movement epitomized yet another strand of Black nationalism, which, like The Nation of Islam, had its roots in the teachings of Booker T. Washington, Du Bois' great political rival. Washington consistently advocated Black alliances with the White elite. The regime of Republican President Richard M. Nixon (1969–1974) was heavily influenced by the ideas of Moynihan and the advocates of Black capitalism (Kotlowski, 1998; Weems and Randolph, 2001). Nixon appointed Benjamin Hooks to head the Federal Communications Commission. Hooks, who would later become president of the NAACP, saw to it that African Americans had access to radio and television licenses – a historic first. Nixon carried out a number of other initiatives to expand Black access to capital and thereby increase the numbers of Black entrepreneurs. Simultaneously, entrepreneurs such as television journalist Tony Brown (who later became an ardent supporter of conservative Republican President Ronald Reagan) made strategic alliances with large corporations. Specifically, the Pepsi-Cola Company was the longtime sponsor of the television show, "Tony Brown's Journal." Future Republican President George Herbert Walker Bush was CIA Director and UN Ambassador during the Nixon regime. Bush also began a long-term relationship with the United Negro College Fund (UNCF), an organization started by Dr. Frederick Patterson, Booker T. Washington disciple and third president of Tuskegee University. For many years David Rockefeller, President of Chase-Manhattan

[22] The minimum wage was $1.25/hour in 1966 and $1.60/hour in 1968. The 1966 minimum wage would be $9.96/hour in 2020, while the 1968 minimum wage would be $11.90/hour in 2020. The Freedom Budget was proposing that the 1968 minimum should have been 25 percent higher than the actual 1968 minimum wage.

Bank, then the largest bank in the world, was Chairman of the Board of UNCF. As a Congressman, Bush had opposed major civil rights legislation of the 1960s. However, UNCF was the safe harbor for politically conservative White elites who wished to participate in fighting racial inequality.

Simultaneous with its expansion of affirmative action to include women and others and its advocacy of Black capitalism, the Nixon regime also intensified Operation COINTELPRO, an acronym for "Counter-Intelligence Program" (United States Senate, 1976; Churchill and Wall, 1990). COINTELPRO was initiated in 1956 and lasted until 1971. It was a program of domestic spying, harassment, and violence against American citizens and organizations, especially Civil Rights and Black Power organizations and individuals. For the FBI, "Black militants" and other social radicals included Martin and Coretta King, the Southern Christian Leadership Conference (SCLC), Cesar Chavez, the NAACP, the National Lawyer's Guild, American Friends Service Committee ("Quakers"), and many others who were not criminals. During Nixon's COINTELPRO era African Americans and others deemed too militant were systematically jailed or otherwise had their civil rights severely abused, ran out of the country, or killed. Those who accepted the Nixon regime's promise of Black capitalism were sometimes the beneficiaries of substantial public and private largesse.

Despite Operation COINTELPRO, African Americans made dramatic progress during 1965–1973. This progress was a testament to African American self-help, perseverance, and struggle for equality, the elimination of Jim Crow, the extremely low rates of unemployment and inflation during this period, along with a number of governmental policies designed to increase economic opportunities for African Americans. Nevertheless, Operation COINTELPRO did play an important role in ending the Black Power Movement and weakening the Civil Rights Movement.

4.5 THE SECOND REVERSAL: 1973–1990

Among women, the Black–White median income ratio rose from 0.57 to 0.86 between 1960 and 1970 (Freeman, 1973). The male median income ratio rose from 0.58 to 0.64. Among 20–24 year-old young men, the Black–White median income ratio rose from 0.67 to 0.82. After observing this trend, preeminent sociologist William J. Wilson concluded that economic class had become more important than race in determining the life chances of individual African Americans (Wilson, 1978). Despite this optimism, racial wage and employment inequality increased from the mid-1970s through the 1980s, leading John Bound and Richard Freeman to query, "What went wrong?" (Bound and Freeman, 1992).

4.5.1 Impact of Recessions

Just as the Long Depression of 1873–1896 brought an end to Reconstruction and established the conditions for Jim Crow, the recessions of November

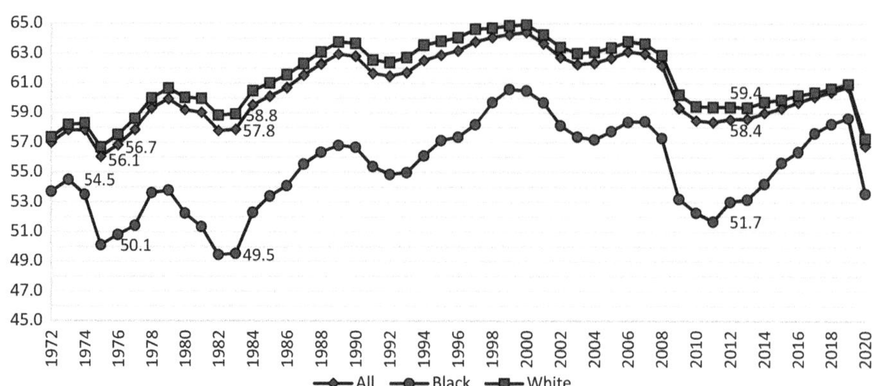

FIGURE 4.1. Employment–population ratio by race: 1972–2020
Source: US Bureau of Labor Statistics, Employment-Population Ratio – White [LNS12300003]. FRED, Federal Reserve Bank of St. Louis; https://fred.stlouisfed.org/series/LNS12300003. Last accessed November 4, 2021

1973–March 1975 and July 1981–November 1982 brought an end to the Second Reconstruction and created the incentives for policies that have had a negative effect on African Americans for two generations.

The 1973–1975 recession was the deepest recession since the Great Depression of the 1930s. The national employment–population ratio bottomed out at 56.1 percent, while the White and African American employment rates were 56.7 percent and 50.1 percent, respectively (see Figure 4.1). Conspicuously, the White employment–population ratio during this substantial recession remained higher than the 1973 "full employment" year Black employment–population ratio of 54.5 percent. The White employment–population ratio declined 2.2 percentage points from the 1973 peak of 58.3 percent to the 1975 trough of 56.1 percent. The African American employment–population ratio declined 4.4 percentage points from 54.5 percent to 50.1 percent.

The 1974–1975 recession was accompanied by unusually high inflation. Between 1972 and 1974 inflation increased from 3 percent to 11.1 percent, before declining to 5.7 percent in 1976 (see Figure 4.2). The White employment–population ratio grew to 60.7 percent by 1979 – higher than the 1973 peak. The Black employment–population ratio reached 53.8 percent – lower than the 1973 peak. Simultaneously, inflation increased to 13.5 percent during 1979.

4.5.2 Change in Monetary Policy

From the New Deal to 1979, the Federal Reserve System used monetary policy to fight unemployment. But, on October 6, 1979, Paul Volker, Chair, Board of Governors, Federal Reserve System ("Fed"), announced major policy change:

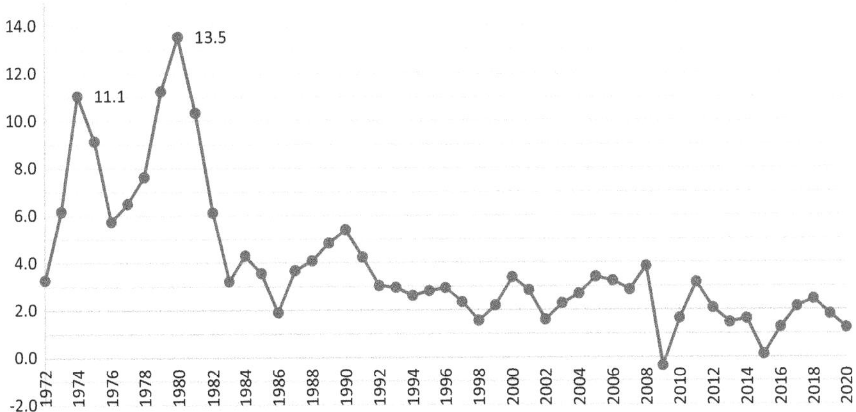

FIGURE 4.2. Inflation rate: 1972–2020
Source: www.macrotrends.net/countries/USA/united-states/inflation-rate-cpi; US Inflation Rate 1960–2021. www.macrotrends.net. Last accessed November 4, 2021

the Fed would no longer use monetary policy to fight unemployment; henceforth, the Fed would use monetary policy to fight inflation. The Fed reduced the nation's supply of money in circulation, causing interest rates to increase and national spending on goods and services to decrease. Inflation was brought to a halt as the Fed policy change contributed to a small recession in 1980 and a major recession in 1981–1982.

The high interest rates and high unemployment had a devastating impact on Midwestern industries, for example, auto, steel, glass, rubber, meatpacking. These industries employed a disproportionate number of Black (male) workers. By 1982 the African American employment–population ratio had declined to a new low, 49.5 percent.

4.5.3 Loss of Worker Bargaining Power

On August 3, 1981, 13,000 members of the Professional Air Traffic Controllers Organization (PATCO) went on strike (Houlihan, 2021). PATCO workers were disproportionately White, male, and highly paid. During the presidential campaign, candidate Reagan supported the union and its bargaining goals; the union supported Reagan in the 1980 election. Nevertheless, on August 5, 1981, President Reagan fired 11,345 PATCO workers and the union was decertified on October 22, 1981.

Unions raise the median wage rate, decrease wage inequality, improve benefits and improve working conditions, and decrease racial discrimination in hiring, promotion, and firing/layoffs. A decrease in union coverage rates is a metric of decline in the bargaining power of workers. For 1973–1980, about

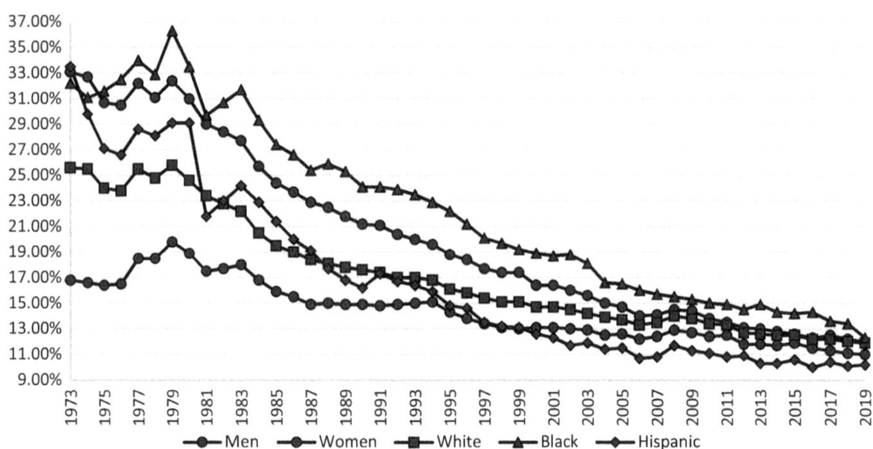

FIGURE 4.3. Union membership rate by race and sex: 1973–2020
Source: Economic Policy Institute, State of Working America Data Library, "Union Coverage," 2021

26 percent of workers were members of or covered by a union (Economic Policy Institute, 2021). American unions lost power and membership after the 1981–1982 recession and Reagan's destruction of PATCO sent union membership on a permanent downward decline: employers attacked unions with the assistance of the federal government. By 2020, just 12 percent of workers were members of or covered by unions: the union membership rate was 34.8 percent for the public sector and 6.3 percent for the private sector (United States Bureau of Labor Statistics, 2021).

Black workers have lost the greatest amount of bargaining power, 36.3 percent were covered by unions in 1979 and 13.6 percent were covered by unions in 2020 (Figure 4.3). White worker union coverage declined from 25.8 percent to 12.3 percent during this same period. Similarly, men lost more bargaining power than women, as union coverage for men and women declined from 32.4 percent to 12.3 percent and from 19.8 percent to 11 percent, respectively.

Workers with 12 or fewer years of education (dropout) had a dramatic reduction in bargaining power, as their union coverage rate declined from 27 percent to 6 percent during 1979–2020 (Figure 4.4). Persons with exactly 12 years of education (High School) and persons with 13–15 years of education (Some College) also had sharp declines in unionization, from 30 percent to 11 percent and from 23 percent to 12 percent, respectively. Persons with 16 years of education (Bachelor's Degree) had similar decreases in union coverage, falling from 23 percent to 11.5 percent. Persons with the highest level of education (Graduate Degree) had the least decline in bargaining power and now have the highest level of union coverage, with representation from 30 percent in 1979 to 17.6 percent in 2020.

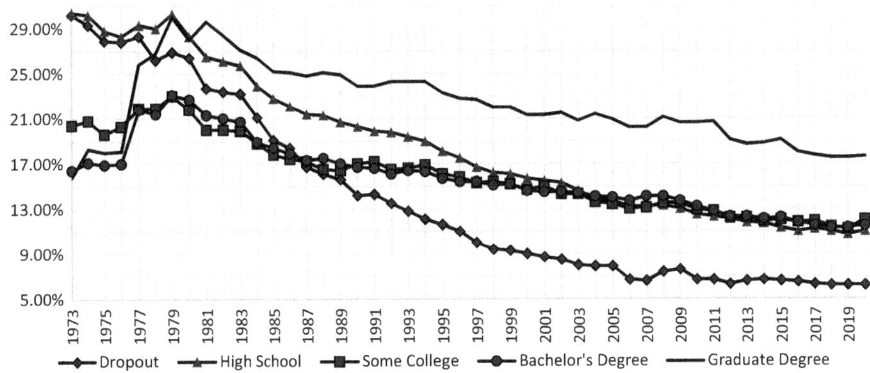

FIGURE 4.4. Union membership rate by educational status: 1973–2020
Source: Economic Policy Institute, State of Working America Data Library, "Union Coverage," 2021

4.5.4 1981–1989 Policy Changes

The stagnation in economic activity during the early-1980s is correlated with changes in federal anti-discrimination policy. James Chaney, Andrew Goodman, and Michael Schwerner, three young civil rights workers, were murdered in Philadelphia, Neshoba County, Mississippi, on June 21, 1964. During August 1980, conservative Republican presidential candidate Ronald Reagan announced his vision to undo the Great Society.

> [O]ne of the great tragedies of welfare in America today, and I don't believe stereotype after what we did, of people in need who are there simply because they prefer to be there. We found the overwhelming majority would like nothing better than to be out, with jobs for the future, and out here in the society with the rest of us. The trouble is, again, that bureaucracy has them so economically trapped that there is no way they can get away. And they're trapped because that bureaucracy needs them as a clientele to preserve the jobs of the bureaucrats themselves.
>
> I believe that there are programs like … education and others, that should be turned back to the states and the local communities with the tax sources to fund them …
>
> *I believe in states' rights*; I believe in people doing as much as they can for themselves at the community level and at the private level. And I believe that we've distorted the balance of our government today by giving powers that were never intended in the constitution to that federal establishment. And if I do get the job I'm looking for, I'm going to devote myself to trying to reorder those priorities and to restore to the states and local communities those functions which properly belong there.
>
> I'm going to try also to change federal regulations in the tax structure that has made this once-powerful industrial giant in this land and in the world now with a lower rate of productivity than any of the other industrial nations, with a lower rate of savings and investment on the part of our people and put us back where we belong. (*The Neshoba Democrat*, 2021, emphasis added)

After winning the election and ascending to office in 1981, President Reagan followed through with his anti-Great Society agenda: public assistance was cut, federal support for education was weakened, and federal taxes were cut, especially for the most affluent Americans.

"States' rights" was the shibboleth of supporters of the racial norms of chattel and servitude capitalisms. Candidate Reagan's supports of states' rights was widely viewed as a signal that Mr. Reagan was hostile to African American civil rights.

The Reagan administration quickly confirmed the conservative President's animosity to the civil rights of African Americans. Among other actions, the list of hostile acts include: the Civil Rights division of the Justice Department abruptly changed sides in several cases; Reagan fired several members of the United States Commission on Civil Rights and stacked it conservatives opposed to civil rights as understood by African Americans; the administration opposed the 1982 amendment of the Voting Rights Act; and Reagan vetoed the Civil Rights Restoration Act (Crenshaw, 1988).

Affirmative action was gutted by the Reagan administration. "Affirmative action under the contract compliance program virtually ceased to exist in all but name after the 1980s" (Leonard, 1991: 105). Leonard provides evidence that the federal government gutted the Office of Federal Contract Compliance Program, the enforcement vehicle for affirmative action within the federal government. Leonard writes that, by the mid-1980s, affirmative action "no longer aided blacks." Other economists also found that federal enforcement activities declined substantially in the 1980s (Anderson, 1996; Leonard, 1996; Rodgers and Spriggs, 1996). Accordingly, they found that contractor status made a greater contribution to firms' relative employment of Non-White workers during the 1990s than contractor status made during 1980s when there were major changes in the nature and behavior of the federal anti-discrimination and affirmative action machinery.

Crenshaw (1988: 1341) notes that Reagan conservatives held a restrictive view of Civil Rights, while their critics held an expansive view. The expansive view emphasizes equality of outcomes, looks to real consequences for African Americans, seeks to eradicate African American subordination, and seeks to use the courts for the national goal of eliminating racial oppression. The restrictive view of Civil Rights emphasizes equality of process for individuals, does not worry about actual outcomes, believes competitive markets create a level playing field for all groups, and ignores claims of past injustice. "Moreover, even when injustice is found, efforts to redress it must be balanced against, and limited by, competing interests of white workers – even when those interests were actually created by the subordination of Blacks" (Crenshaw, 1988: 1342). The Reagan administration succeeded in institutionalizing the restrictive view of Civil Rights for the courts, as well as federal, state, and local governmental agencies.

A return to Moynihanism is another element of the Reagan legacy. The restrictive view of civil rights accepts the reality of racial equality but denies the materiality of structural racism. Proponents of this civil rights perspective link racial inequality to alleged deficiencies within African American culture. Advocates of the Reagan–Moynihan perspective argue that public assistance turns Black women into "welfare queens" and turns Black men into "dysfunctional dads." These dysfunctional families produce children who are less proficient at skill accumulation and do not have the behaviors to compete successfully in the labor market (Cammett, 2014). Ultimately, the Reagan view of public assistance found its policy expression in President William J. Clinton's Personal Responsibility and Work Opportunity Reconciliation Act of 1996, which gutted the public safety net without having much positive impact on poor families (Boushey, 2002). Reagan era hostility to African American culture, in combination with structural racism, would continue to guide US public policy into the most recent years.

4.5.5 Post-racialism, 1989–Present

In November 2008, Barack Hussein Obama was elected President of the United States of America. Mr. Obama's father was a Black Kenyan immigrant and his mother was a White woman from Kansas. He had only limited ties to the Black political and economic establishment and almost no personal experience of living, working, or visiting the South. During his youth Mr. Obama was raised in Hawaii, Indonesia, and Kansas. He attended the very best academic institutions and made his way to the presidency on the strength of a stirring patriotic keynote speech at the 2004 Democratic Convention that declared,

> Now even as we speak, there are those who are preparing to divide us, the spin masters and negative ad peddlers who embrace the politics of anything goes. Well, I say to them tonight, there's not a liberal America and a conservative America; there's the United States of America. There's not a black American and white America and Latino America and Asian America; there's the United States of America. The pundits, the pundits like to slice and dice our country into red states and blue states: red states for Republicans, blue States for Democrats … We are one people, all of us pledging allegiance to the stars and stripes, all of us defending the United States of America. (*New York Times*, 2004)

During his nationally televised speech the charismatic young senator also said,

> Go into any inner city neighborhood, and folks will tell you that government alone can't teach our kids to learn – they know that parents have to teach, that children can't achieve unless we raise their expectations and turn off the television sets and eradicate the slander that says a black youth with a book is acting white. They know those things. (*New York Times*, 2004)

This is Mr. Obama's explicit endorsement of the false belief that an anti-intellectual bias in African American culture limits educational achievement and, therefore, contributes to persistent racial inequality (Austen-Smith and Fryer, 2005).

Shortly thereafter, Mr. Obama was increasingly referred to as a post-racial leader. When he was elected President four years later many declared that the construction of a post-racial society was well on its way. Notably, President Obama never declared that the United States is a post-racial society and he always self-identified as Black as opposed to "mixed-race." Post-racial – like "underclass" in the 1980s and 1990s – became a popularly used but ill-defined concept. By and large, post-racial was used to indicate a society whereby issues of race and racism were not substantively relevant in discussions of American social and economic problems. On the other hand, it was argued that class, as defined by values, behaviors, or family culture, does matter and will continue to be important for understanding American social problems.

Racial discrimination may exist in a post-racial society, but it is individualistic discrimination consistent with the Reagan restrictive civil rights perspective. From this perspective, discrimination is caused by individual acts of bigotry or prejudice, not structural racism. By the late-1990s, James Heckman (1998), Nobel Laureate and one of the world's best known empirical economists, claimed that "... [T]he disparity in earnings between Blacks and Whites in the labor market of the 1990s is due to the differences in skills they bring to the market, and not to discrimination within the market ... [L]abor market discrimination is no longer a first-order quantitative problem in American society." Heckman (2011: 72–73) repeats this assertion, "a substantial body of evidence that shows that discrimination in the labor market is no longer a first-order cause of racial disparity." From this perspective, racial inequalities in wages, employment, occupational achievement, and work hours are caused by racial inequalities in skill. Further, racial inequalities in skills are not caused by racial differences in schools but by racial differences in the quality of parenting (Heckman, 2011).

4.5.6 Mass Incarceration

Mass incarceration means simply that the United States is the world's incarceration leader, with respect to both the total number of persons incarcerated and the rate of incarceration. Moreover, the American criminal legal system's "approach to punishment often lacks a public safety rationale, disproportionately affects minorities, and inflicts overly harsh sentences" (Cullen, 2018: 1). Roughly 650 persons per 100,000 Americans are incarcerated in federal prisons, state prisons, or local jails (see Figure 4.5). There was no trend in the incarceration rate during 1950–1970. Each year during this period, less than 190 Americans are incarcerated per 100,000 persons.[23] The era of mass

[23] For the five decades from 1925 to the late 1970s, the annual rate of imprisonment was relatively constant, about 100–110 state and federal prisoners per 100,000 Americans (Raphael and Stoll, 2013). Persons incarcerated in local jails are excluded, but follow the same trend. Persons on probation (not sent to prison or jail) and parole (have spent some time in prison or jail) are also excluded.

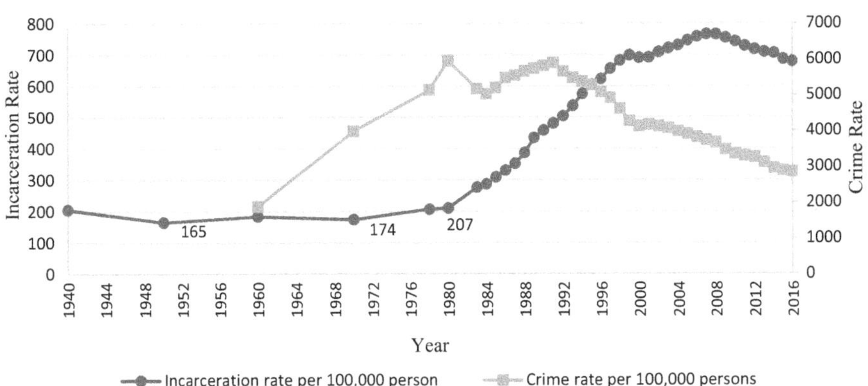

FIGURE 4.5. US crime rate, 1978–2016, and incarceration rate for federal, state, and local institutions

Source: Crime rate data are extracted from www.disastercenter.com/crime/uscrime.htm. Last accessed December 13, 2022. "United States Crime Rates 1960–2019." Crime data include both violent and property crimes. Incarceration rate data extracted from "Incarceration counts and rates, 1925–2016," compiled by the Prison Policy Initiative www.prisonpolicy.org/data/. Last accessed December 13, 2022. Both crime and incarcerations are per 100,000 Americans of all ages

incarceration started after 1970, when the incarceration rate was 174 inmates per 100,000 persons, elevated to 207 prisoners per 100,000 persons in 1978, and hit its peak in 2007, when the rate of imprisonment was more than 765 federal, state, and local prisoners per 100,000 Americans. The 2007 rate was more than 3.8 times higher than the historic norm of 1950–1970, with the Southern states leading the way. Incarcerated persons are primarily in state institutions (90 percent), male (93 percent), not high school graduates (66.2), racial or ethnic minorities (Latinx – 18.1 percent, African American – 43.8 percent, Other race – 8.6 percent), and young (Raphael and Stoll, 2013: table 1.2).

During 1974, 3.6 percent of men and 0.3 percent of women were at risk of going to prison during their lifetime (see Table 4.7). After the onset of mass incarceration, 11.3 percent of men and 1.8 percent of women had a lifetime risk of going to prison in 2001 as the incarceration rate was nearing its peak. Mass incarceration increased the risk of incarceration for all racial and ethnic groups; for example, White male risk increased from 2.2 percent to 5.9 percent (a 123% increase) African American male risk rose from 13.4 percent to 32.2 percent (140% increase), and Latinx male risk rose from 4 percent to 17.2 percent.

Mass incarceration commenced with President Richard M. Nixon's June 18, 1971 announcement of a war on drugs. The prison population began to grow shortly thereafter, but the most explosive growth was during the 1980s. Between 1980 and 1988 the prison population increased by more than

TABLE 4.7. *Lifetime risk of a child serving time in Federal or State prison by year of birth*

	1974	2001
Male	0.036	0.113
White	0.022	0.059
Black	0.134	0.322
Latinx	0.040	0.172
Female	0.003	0.018
White	0.002	0.009
Black	0.011	0.056
Latinx	0.004	0.022

Source: Bonczar (2003)

90 percent (Greenfeld, 1989). Public policy leaders and managers initiated the war on drugs with racist intent. According to John Ehrlichman, domestic policy advisor to President Nixon,

> The Nixon campaign in 1968, and the Nixon White House after that, had two enemies: the antiwar left and black people ... You understand what I'm saying? We knew we couldn't make it illegal to be either against the war or black, but by getting the public to associate the hippies with marijuana and blacks with heroin. And then criminalizing both heavily, we could disrupt those communities ... We could arrest their leaders, raid their homes, break up their meetings, and vilify them night after night on the evening news. Did we know we were lying about the drugs? Of course *we did*. (Baum, 2016: 1).

Massive incarceration and other racial disparities within the criminal legal system have had major negative effects on African American families, labor market outcomes, and police interactions. Moreover, the racialized criminal legal system is accompanied by persistent anti-Black crimes. These public and private devaluations of Black life are constitutive elements of racialized managerial capitalism.

4.6 SUMMARY AND DISCUSSION

Africans were commodities in chattel capitalism. This racial stratification regime was brought to an end by the US Civil War. Enslaved laborers had been the financial assets of many Southern White families, one of the world's wealthiest aristocracies. Fifty percent of the capital in the Deep South was in enslaved persons. The newly-freed Africans did not receive reparations. Consequently, emancipation caused a massive destruction of the financial wealth of White enslavers, without transferring financial assets to African Americans. Before emancipation, White elites owned the full laboring capacity of enslaved Africans – all skill, all natural ability, all effort, all laboring and non-laboring time.

After slavery, during servitude capitalism each African American owned his life – his productive capacity, time, and effort, though, the racist libertarian state expropriated and publicly monopolized Black citizenship and provided no legal protection for freedman. Both chattel and servitude capitalisms depended on the economic exploitation of Black labor and political oppression of Black lives. Servitude capitalism created a cryto-slave political economy in the South. Involuntary servitude of African Americans was not hidden from public authorities or society in general; rather, it was a form of enslavement hidden under the libertarian pretense of individual freedom of choice. Elite White Southerners wanted to restore their economic fortunes, which required re-intensified domination of their lost capital. Many Southern Whites did not own slaves and one-third were illiterate. But, working class Whites saw Freedmen as job competitors; hence, common Whites aligned with the White elite to deprive Freedmen of their political and economic rights and social standing. Government power (controlled by White elites), force, and brutality were the mechanisms of economic exploitation and political oppression. Death was a frequent punishment to keep all Blacks in line during servitude capitalism.

Formerly enslaved Africans wanted individual and collective independence. They wanted to own businesses, farms, churches, schools, homes, etc. They wanted paid employment, the ability to move to opportunity, and control over their own work hours. Freedmen were willing to work hard. They were committed to reaffirming marriages formed under enslavement and without the protection of law. They sought to reconstitute their families. African Americans wanted freedom and they were willing to integrate into American society to achieve it. Free people were entitled to equal respect, ownership of their own labor, equal protection under the law, the ability to own guns for personal protection, etc. Emancipation brought a change in identity for Blacks and Whites. African Americans wanted to transition from being embodiments of financial capital to being owners of their own labor (and lives) and owners of economic resources. As such, the post-slavery Black identity was not consistent with the desire of Whites to re-intensify domination of their former capital.

In addition to repeated and massive recessions after 1873, creating employment instability for Blacks and common Whites until the start of World War II, the US economy of this era was also characterized by tremendous technological change, the rise of modern corporations, major increases in income and wealth inequality, major immigration into the Northeast and Midwest, so-called small libertarian government, that is, limited federal, state, and local protection of the rights and property of Freedmen, combined with active governmental assistance to the Whites in denying African American civil rights, economic opportunity, the ability to sell goods and services, and access to financial capital. The federal government had no child labor protection, no labor protection, no protection of voting rights, limited oversight of local and state courts, no oversight of local and state police, and no oversight of educational standards and access. With the economy in depression, support for Reconstruction waning in the North, and conservative (Democratic party) conquest of the House of Representatives in 1874, there was no sustained federal presence in the South during 1874–1954. The Post-Reconstruction era was a period of reintensified domination by Southern Whites. Amid the depression of 1873–1879, Northern Whites decided there was not much the federal government can or should do to assist African Americans in their quest for racial justice and political and economic equality. In today's parlance, Northern Whites were willing to allow Southern White elites to steal the opportunity for the "American Dream" from all Southern Blacks – regardless of individual values, family structure and functioning, work and school effort, skill, and any of the other characteristics that are often linked with individual and family success in the labor market and society.

Racialized managerial capitalism developed during 1933–1965 as servitude capitalism was dying. African Americans gained ownership of their own citizenship. But, racialized managerial capitalism is an economy where Whites have preserved pre-existing advantages created under chattel and servitude capitalism: no reparations were paid for enslavement or Jim Crow, leaving in place the enormous racial wealth disparity created under these regimes; the rules of operation and institutions governing access to public and private resources were established with little Black representation; and Whites enjoy a near monopoly of managerial discretion in implementing the rules of the economy, government, and society. Also, racialized managerial capitalism came into existence with entrenched racial identity norms.

The discussion of regimes of structural racism alert us to several themes that we will discuss in the remaining chapters of this text:

- The economy has difficulty providing a job (with a livable wage) to every individual who is willing and able to work; racism plays an important role in determining access to employment.
- Competition and racial discrimination in the labor market are not antithetical. Otherwise identical individuals may receive different pay because of differences in where they work and differences in bargaining power. Racial discrimination persists because of racial differences in access to employment, access to better paying jobs, and differences in bargaining power.
- Major periods of change in racial equality and racial discrimination in the market are often ushered in by government policy rather than the unfettered operation of competitive markets. The national attempts to fight unemployment and inflation have a disproportionate impact on African American labor market outcomes.
- There is a sustained tradition of African American self-help, which manifests itself in entrepreneurial activity, educational achievement, institutional building, and collective efforts in the struggle for social and economic justice.
- Family structure and family functioning are separate issues. Transitions in family structure are responses to market outcomes. Differences in family

functioning cannot explain interracial differences in income and employment but may explain some intraracial differences in income and employment.

- Race is a social construction that is not synonymous with class (socioeconomic status), dysfunctional behavior, family structure, poverty status, or educational status. As such, an economic theory of racial identity as a social construction is a necessary element of our understanding of the political economy of race.
- The rules of operation of society, economy, and government are racially biased in favor of White Americans.
- White Americans have disproportion control over managerial decision-making.
- The White wealth advantage is so large that, even if all racism were to immediately end, racial disparity in social and economic outcomes would be reproduced in perpetuity.

PART II

AFRICAN AMERICAN EDUCATIONAL PROGRESS AND TRANSFORMATIONS IN FAMILY STRUCTURE, 1965–PRESENT

5

African American Educational Progress

1965–Present

This chapter documents racial trends in the quantity and quality of education since the demise of servitude capitalism during the mid-1960s. There is also a limited discussion of the causes of differences in racial trends. Except for college graduation rates, there has been substantial progress in eliminating racial differences in education. There is no evidence that African American identity is anti-intellectual. Finally, the trends in the racial gaps in employment, wages, and wealth (Chapters 6–9) have exhibited less progress than the trend in the racial gap in education.

The quantity and quality of education are important personal and social attributes. Better education increases the quality of problem solving and communication skills in the market, at home, in social institutions, and in social interactions. The skill content associated with higher levels of education provides a causal explanation for a common empirical observation: on average, persons with higher levels of education have higher wealth, earnings, and other material accomplishments. For example, individual employment productivity increases as an individual's education increases. Employment productivity will increase because a more highly educated worker can produce more output per hour or a higher quality of hourly output. There is an increase in the worker's ability to receive more or better on-the-job training; it is cheaper to train workers with more education; increases in education reduce the amount of direct supervision required for a worker; increases in education increase a worker's occupational versatility. Finally, more highly educated workers increase the productivity of other workers they are matched with in the employment process.

In addition to providing complex employment skills for individuals, education also provides a mechanism for reproduction of parental social status. As parental education increases, parents have more money, time, materials, and social resources to devote to the education of their children. For example, more highly educated parents provide a higher quality of educational assistance to their school-age children, and they have more income to purchase tutorial assistance or other market resources to assist school-age children. More highly educated parents have greater knowledge of the educational process and better contacts with managers with control over resources and decision-making. Wealthier parents have the means to pay for their children's education. As a result of these advantages, children of highly educated and wealthier parents tend to obtain higher levels of education.

Higher education increases a person's homework productivity for many of the same reasons it increases a worker's productivity in market work. Management of family finances, negotiating family contracts, childrearing, dispute resolution, proper cleaning, etc. are all activities whereby productivity increases with increases in education.

There are also important social benefits associated with increasing an individual's education. More highly educated persons have a higher probability of finding a marriage partner and are less likely to engage in violent crime. Individuals who have attained diplomas, degrees, professional certifications, and so forth present objective evidence that they are achievement oriented, goal-persistent, and efficacious in their utilization of time. The voluntary time contributions of individuals with higher education increases the quality of schools, fraternal organizations, citizen's public welfare organizations, churches, governmental agencies, and interpersonal flows of complex information and ideas. Less educated persons living near or belonging to the same social organizations as more highly educated persons benefit from these social effects.

There are racial identity benefits to education. Lacking sufficient economic, political, and coercive power to compete effectively with dominant groups, subaltern racial groups may seek to compete with dominant groups by raising the relative educational status of the group. The subaltern group will be better off materially if its members are embedded in occupations that provide some degree of control over employment resources. Subaltern groups teach their children an important rule regarding the relationship between racism and effort: to be equal, you must be better.

In addition to the employment, intergenerational mobility, household, social, and racial identity effects associated with an individual's education, there are mandatory school attendance requirements for individuals, substantial public expenditures on education from pre-school through doctoral degrees, and racial and class competitions over the allocation of resources and control of the educational process.

A mandatory minimum age of school attendance, for example, requiring students to remain in school until they are at least 16 years of age, means that a large portion of educational attainment is determined by public policy. After the mandatory age of attendance, years of schooling for young adults is heavily weighted by parental choices, parental information, parental resources, and parental control. Completing high school is mostly determined by parental discretion, while post-secondary options are strongly influenced by parental discretion and financial resources.

The skill acquisition process is strongly influenced by interactions between public policy, parental concerns regarding intergenerational mobility, and racial identity. Parents seek to transmit their own or a higher level of social status to their children. Similarly, children seek to obtain the parent's or a higher level of social status. Racial groups, too, are interested in the relative education of the group. For example, racial groups with below average income and wealth might encourage supra-normal educational effort as an element of a strategy to achieve equality (Mason, 1997, 2007; Coleman, 2003; Tyson, Darity, and Castellino, 2005; Mangino, 2010, 2012; Diamond and Huguley, 2014; Rangel, 2015). Educational norms are established via group institutions, for example, social clubs and churches, and through intragroup social interactions. For example, most African Americans understand persistent racial discrimination in the labor market as a reality of American life and, on average, African American families have less wealth than White families. Hence, African American adults teach African American children and young adults that they must work harder and achieve a higher level of education than a White child of similar ability and resources if they wish to obtain an equal level of income.

5.1 EDUCATION, INCOME, AND WEALTH

Consider the following simple relationship between the natural logarithm of individual weekly wages (lnwage) and individual years of education (E). The average individual weekly wage increases with individual years of education (E), such that

(1) $\text{lnwage} = \beta_0 + \beta_1 \times E,$

where $\beta_0 > 0$ is the average wage for persons with no education ($E = 0$) and $\beta_1 > 0$ is the percentage increase in wages when individual education increases by 1 year and may be referred to as the rate return to education.

Consider any two groups: a "high" wage group, *h*, and a "low" wage group, *l*. There are persons with wages above or below the average in each group, but the average wage for group *h* is greater than the average wage for group *l*. For example, persons with 16 years of education (college graduates) are a high wage group, while persons with 12 years of education are a low wage group. Suppose persons in these two groups are identical, except one group has four years more education than the other. The wage differential for college graduates and high school graduates is (lnwageleducation = 16) – (lnwagel education = 12) = $\beta_1 \times 4$, that is,

(2) Wage gap between groups *h* and *l* = 4× Education gap between groups *h* and *l*.

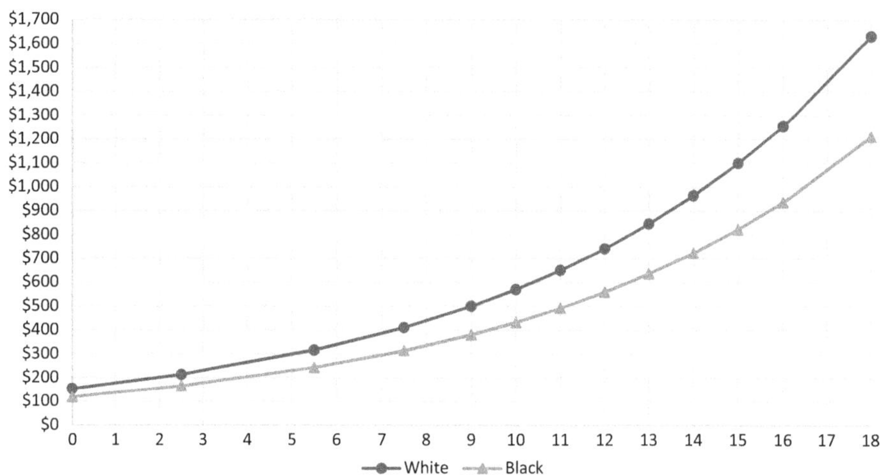

FIGURE 5.1. Weekly wages by years of education: White and Black males, 2008–2015

This equation yields four predictions: all other things equal,

i. $\beta_1 > 0$ and is the same for both groups, there is an equal rate of return to education, regardless of group affiliation;
ii. individual wages increase with increases in individual years of education;
iii. for any two groups, if the education gap decreases, the earnings gap will decrease; and
iv. if the education of both groups is increasing over a period of years, but the education of the low wage group (l) is increasing faster than the education of the high wage group (h), we should also observe that the wage gap is decreasing over that same period of years.

Applying this model to a sample of White (w) and Black (b) males, statistical analysis reveals that

$$\text{lnwage} = 5.0313 + 0.1315 \times E \quad \text{(White males) and}$$
$$\text{lnwage} = 4.7807 + 0.1289 \times E \quad \text{(Black males).}$$

Figure 5.1 is a graphical presentation of these two equations.[1] As predicted, regardless of race, the average weekly wage rate increases with years of education. But, for each year of education the mean weekly wage of African American males is lower than the mean weekly wage of White males. An African American male needs 14.19 years of education (Associate of Arts degree) to achieve the same weekly wage as a White male with 12 years of

[1] The sample is taken from 2009 to 2016 March Current Population Surveys. All individuals are 25–54 years of age.

education (high school diploma). An African American male with a Master of Arts degree (18 years of education) earns less than a White male with a Bachelor of Arts degree (16 years of education), \$1,211 versus \$1,255. Ending the racial gap in years of education is a necessary and important goal (related to all the reasons individuals, families, groups, and society value education), but it is not sufficient to eliminate the racial wage gap.

This very simple model of wage determination can also help us understand important issues related to wealth inequality. Suppose the proportion of income saved is $s \equiv$ saving rate. The racial wealth gap between groups Whites (w) and Blacks (b) is related to racial differences in saving behavior, racial differences in education (or, more broadly, skill), and racial differences in inheritances. Given the saving rates, the wealth gap is

$$\text{(3) Wealth gap} = s^{h} \times \text{racial wage difference due to education gap} + (s^{w} - s^{b}) \times \text{average wage of Blacks} + \text{inheritance gap}$$

Once again, this simple theory yields two predictions:

i. if the racial gap in education decreases, racial wealth disparity will decrease; and
ii. if the rate gap in savings rates ($s^{w} - s^{b}$) decreases, the racial wealth gap will decrease.

If the education of both groups is increasing over a period of years but the education of African Americans is increasing faster than the education of Whites, we should also observe that the racial wealth gap is decreasing over that same period of years. Finally, if there is a large racial gap in inheritances and in vivo transfers ($\text{inheritance}^{w} - \text{inheritance}^{b}$), then the racial wealth gap may not change even when the education and savings gaps are decreasing.

Currently existing discrimination (racial differences regarding the rate of return to education) and the persistent impact of past discrimination (racial inheritance gap) will cause the racial wealth gap to increase even if African Americans have a savings rate equal to or higher than White Americans. The best evidence is that $s^{w} - s^{b} = 0$, and the education gap is relatively small. Hence, ending the racial gap in years of education is a necessary and important goal, but it is not sufficient to eliminate the racial wealth gap; the racial gap in inheritances (due to enslavement, Jim Crow, and continuing racism) is the primary mechanism responsible for the large and persistent wealth gap.

Individualist economists emphasize racial differences in culture, values, and behaviors as an explanation for persistent racial wealth disparity. In particular, the individualist argument is African American culture discourages education and savings. From this perspective, persistent racial wealth disparity is caused by persistent racial differences in education and savings, but the persistent racial differences in education and savings are caused by African American culture, which is not as proficient as White culture in encouraging education and savings. Stratification economists argue that the empirical evidence refutes this belief.

Closing the racial gap in education will reduce some of the racial earnings and wealth gaps. Yet, it is possible that a very large proportion of the racial earnings gap (say, 50 percent or more) and an even greater proportion of the wealth gap may remain after closing the racial gap in education. Within racial groups, high earning persons have a higher savings rate than low earning persons. However, after controlling for income, African Americans may have an equal or higher savings rate than Whites. Similarly, the racial gap in education is not large enough to cause the racial wealth gap. From the stratification perspective, the persistent racial wealth gap is caused by current discrimination (racial differences the rate of return to education) and the persistent effects of past discrimination (racial inheritance gap). We will examine the veracity of the stratification and individualist perspectives in this chapter and Chapters 7–11.

5.2 EDUCATIONAL INEQUALITY: PUBLIC POLICY, FAMILY, AND RACIAL IDENTITY

A state's policies on education have a major effect on the quantity of education obtained by children residing within the state (Diffey and Steffes, 2017). Racial differences in years of education may be affected by these policies if there are racial differences in states of residence. For example, depending on the state, children are required to remain in school until they are 16–18 years of age. But the mandatory age of attendance is not always a binding constraint. For example, Alaskan students are required to attend school until they are 16 years of age or they have completed 12th grade. In Arizona and Wyoming, its 16 years of age or completing 10th grade. Missouri students must attend school until they are 17 years of age or they have completed 16 credits toward high school graduation. Montana students may leave school before age 16 if they have completed 8th grade. In New York, state law maintains that students must attend school until age 16. However, local school boards have the option of requiring jobless 16- and 17-year-old students to attend school. Rhode Island students must remain in school until age 18, though the compulsory age of attendance is 16 if the student has an alternative learning plan for obtaining a high school diploma or its equivalent. South Dakota students cannot leave school before age 18. However, the child is not required to attend beyond age 16 "if a child enrolls in a general education development test preparation program that is school-based or for which a school contracts, and the child successfully completes the test ..."

States also vary according to the minimum age they are required to start offering free education, ranging from age 4 to age 6. Each state determines its mandatory age to start school, ranging from 5 to 7 years old. States vary, too, according to the maximum age they will offer free education, ranging from 17 to 22 years of age.

Individual years of education will differ because individuals reside in states with differences in mandatory attendance and other policies. Let $E_{min}|state$

TABLE 5.1. *The marginal effect of an additional year of mandatory schooling on mean education*

	African American	White	Latinx	
Female	0.0395***	0.0385***	0.0263*	Years of Education
	(0.0150)	(0.0065)	(0.0145)	
Male	0.0699***	0.0457***	0.0528***	
	(0.0162)	(0.0063)	(0.0146)	
Female	−0.0098**	−0.0089***	−0.0133***	Dropout
	(0.0042)	(0.0017)	(0.0040)	
Male	−0.0129***	−0.0102***	−0.0119***	
	(0.0046)	(0.0017)	(0.0041)	
Female	0.0166*	−0.0015	−0.0095	High School Graduate Exactly 12 years of education or GED
	(0.0094)	(0.0037)	(0.0080)	
Male	−0.0020	−0.0083**	−0.0046	
	(0.0097)	(0.0038)	(0.0084)	
Female	0.0057	0.0137***	0.0065	Post-secondary education
	(0.0052)	(0.0021)	(0.0050)	
Male	0.0159***	0.0138***	0.0157***	
	(0.0053)	(0.0021)	(0.0048)	

All persons <22 years of age, not currently enrolled in school, and native-born, adult civilians. African Americans and Whites are Non-Latinx. The marginal effects are from an education regression that includes mandatory years of education, age, and region. Standard errors of the estimates are included in parentheses. *** 0.01 significance. ** 0.05 significance. * 0.10 significance.

Source: Author's calculations. Current Population Survey Annual Social and Economic Supplement, 2002–2016

equal the mean level of education obtained by individuals who do not remain in school beyond the compulsory age of attendance, conditional on the state of residence, that is, the mandatory years of education = years of education associated with mandatory age of attendance – mandatory starting age. For example, if a state requires that all children remain in school until age 16 and that all children start preschool by age 5, then $E_{min}|state = 11$ years of mandatory education.

Estimates of racial differences in the impact of an additional year of mandatory school are presented in Table 5.1.[2] An additional year increase in a state's mandatory years of schooling raises years of education for all groups and reduces racial and ethnic gaps in years of education. For example, a one-year

[2] There is no claim that these estimates provide a causal impact. The estimates illustrate that seemingly race-neutral state polices may have disparate racial effects.

increase in mandatory schooling will reduce the probability that a student will be a dropout by 1.33 percentage points, 0.98 percentage points, and 0.89 percentage points for Latinx, African American, and White women, respectively. The effects for men are 1.29 percentage points, 1.19 percentage points, and 1.02 percentage points for African American, Latinx, and White men, respectively.

An additional year of mandatory schooling has positive effects on the probability an African American woman or Latina will obtain postsecondary education, though these effects are not measured precisely. However, the marginal effects are 1.37 percentage points for White women and 1.38 percentage points for White men. A one-year increase in mandatory schooling is associated with a 1.59 percentage increase in the probability an African American male will obtain post-secondary education, while the marginal effect is 1.57 percentage points for Latinx males.

In addition to differences in mandatory years of schooling, states also differ in the extent of exposure to court ordered racial desegregation within public schools. Racial segregation of public schools was a characteristic feature of the education system during servitude capitalism, especially in Southern states.[3] Court ordered racial desegregation of school districts was one of the public policies that facilitated the transition from servitude capitalism to racialized managerial capitalism. Starting with the 1954 *Brown* v. *Board of Education* Supreme Court decision and continuing into the present, state and federal courts have issued multiple rulings that have paved the way to a racially desegregated educational process. The desegregation decisions affected both Southern and Northern school districts. Even so, desegregation was slow between the 1954 Brown decision and the Civil Rights Act of 1964; thereafter, the desegregation process picked up steam. By 1972, public schools in the South were less segregated than public schools in the North (Farley, 2004).

Desegregation reduced the Baby Boomer racial gap in years of education.[4] Court ordered school desegregation quickly reduced racial segregation of students and teachers within the school district. It also allowed Black students to be exposed to schools with greater amounts of spending per pupil and lower student-to-teacher ratios. As a result, court ordered desegregation of a school

[3] Racial segregation was legal in Alabama, Arkansas, Delaware, Florida, Georgia, Kentucky, Louisiana, Maryland, Mississippi, Missouri, North Carolina, Oklahoma, South Carolina, Tennessee, Texas, Virginia, and West Virginia. Washington, DC allow segregation only for elementary schools. Wyoming permitted but never implemented racially segregation public schools. Segregated schools were permitted in Arizona, Kansas, and New Mexico, but this was never an issue in those states. See Infoplease (2012).

[4] See Johnson (2015). The sample in this paper included persons born during 1945–1958 and their adult attainments were analyzed subject to desegregation during 1954–1990. Baby boomers are persons born during 1945–1964. Early boomers were born during 1945–1954 (from the end of World War II to *Broad* v. *Topeka Board of Education*) and late boomers were born during 1955–1964 (post-Brown era to 1964 Civil Rights Act).

district had several beneficial effects on African American students, with no negative effects on White students; specifically, it led to increases in years of education, the probability of graduating from high school, and the quality of college attended by African American students. Desegregation also increased hourly wages, annual earnings, family income, and occupational attainment, while reducing poverty. Desegregation reduced the annual incarceration rate of African Americans, as well as the likelihood of ever being incarcerated. Finally, desegregation allowed African American students to have more positive health outcomes as adults, that is, it lowered the probability of moderate/problematic health problems and improved health status.

Given the positive correlation of parent–child outcomes, Baby Boomer parental improvements in education, occupation and income, criminal legal outcomes, and health care bore improvements in these outcomes among Baby Boomer children, thereby contributing to close racial gaps in socioeconomic status for decades after the end of court ordered racial desegregation.

5.3 YEARS OF EDUCATION

Consider White–African American inequality, where the African American measure of well-being is smaller than the White measure of well-being. Unambiguous racial progress exists when the average well-being of both groups is increasing, when inequality within both groups is decreasing and when the well-being of the average African American is growing at least as fast as the well-being of the average White.[5] By this definition, African Americans have made unambiguous racial progress in both the quantity and quality of education since 1940. One year before America's entry into World War II (1940), almost 41 percent of African Americans of 25 years of age and above had 4 years of elementary school education or less, 7 percent had completed high school or higher, and just over 1 percent had 4 or more years of college (US Bureau of the Census, 2021). By comparison, 11 percent of Whites of 25 years of age and above had 5 years of elementary school education or less, 26 percent had completed high school or higher, and 5 percent had 4 or more years of college.

A generation later, amid the Black Power movement (1970), the probability of a White person being at the lowest end of the education distribution (5 years of less of elementary school education) was reduced by more than half, falling to just 4 percent. The probabilities of completing high school or higher and completing 4 or more years of college had more than doubled, rising to 57 percent and 12 percent, respectively. The education gains for African Americans were breathtaking: 15 percent had 5 years of elementary school

[5] Of course, it is always possible to have increasing equality with both racial groups experiencing a decreasing well-being – but that is the opposite of the definition put forth here (and the opposite of what is desired by most Americans).

education or less (nearly a third of the 1940 rate), 36 percent had completed high school or higher (4.5 times higher than in 1940), and 6 percent had 4 or more years of college (about 5 times higher than 1940).

Figures 5.2 and 5.3 present average mean years of education for African American and White women and men, ages 25–65, for the years 1965–2019. We use this age range because most Americans have finished their formal education by age 25 and many leave the labor market after age 65. Also, at about 25 years of age many Americans start their families, have relatively

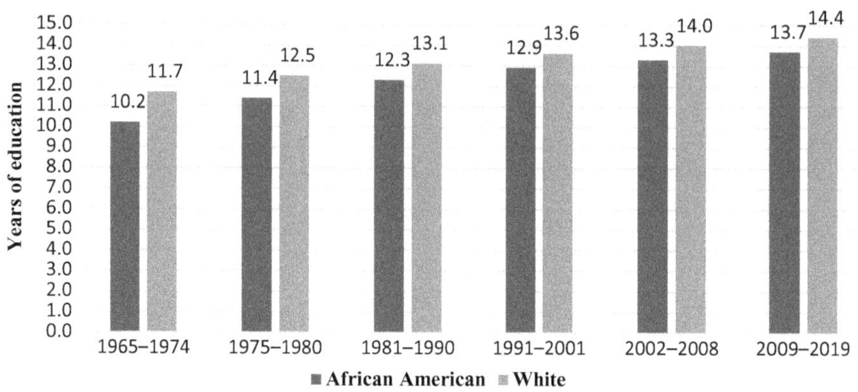

FIGURE 5.2. Years of education, women
Source: Author's calculations, Current Population Survey Annual Social and Demographic Supplement, 1966–2019

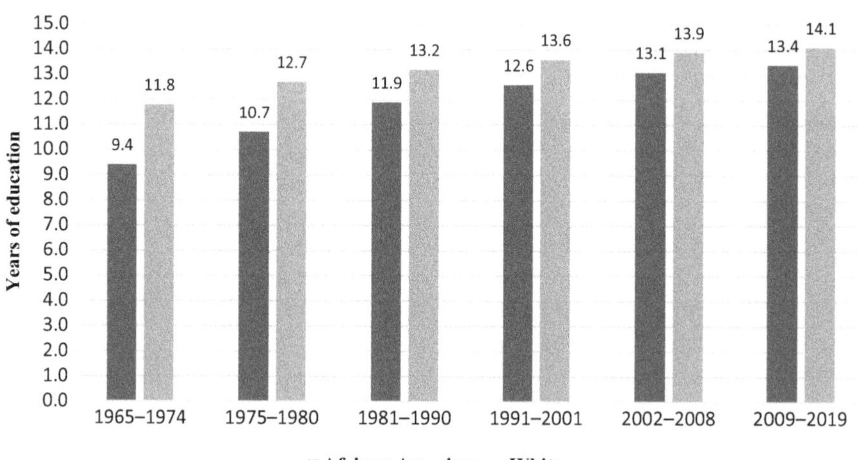

FIGURE 5.3. Years of education, men
Source: Author's calculations, Current Population Survey Annual Social and Demographic Supplement, 1966–2019

young children, or begin giving serious consideration to forming a household independent of their parents.

During 1965–1974, the first decade after the end of servitude capitalism, African American men and women had 9.4 and 10.2 years of education, respectively. The means for White men and women were 11.8 and 11.7 years of education, respectively. Thus, the racial gaps were 2.4 and 1.5 years of education for men and women, respectively, and –0.8 and 0.01 years for the gender gaps among African Americans and Whites, respectively.

African American women and men achieved unambiguous educational progress in each on the next five periods, eventually reducing the racial gap to 0.7 years and witnessing a 0.3 year gender advantage for African American women. Consider 1981–1990, one generation after the end of servitude capitalism. Mean years of education for African American men and women was 11.9 and 12.3, respectively. There was an increase of 2.5 years for African American men and 2.1 years for African American women relative to 1965–1974. Mean years of education for White men and women was 13.2 and 13.1, respectively. There was an increase of 1. 5 and 1.3 years for White men and women relative to 1965–1974. The racial gap had declined to 0.8 years for women and 1.3 years for men.

The women's racial wage differential expanded during a period (1979–2019) when the racial differential in women's years of education was declining or constant (Figure 5.4). Specifically, the women's racial gap in years of education declined from a high of 1.92 years in 1966 to 0.66 years in 1986 and remained constant between 1986 and 2019. As expected, the racial gap in weekly wages declined from 0.65 log points (95 percent) in 1965 to 0.03 log points (3 percent) in 1979. Thereafter, the wage differential rose to 0.17 log points (18.5 percent) by 2019.

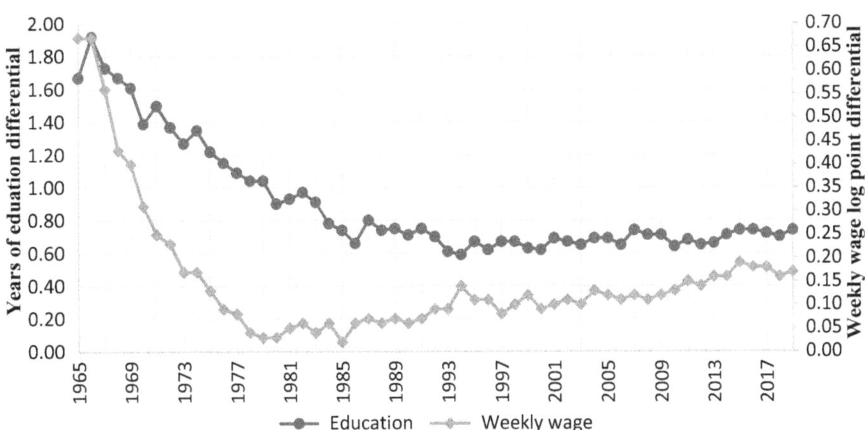

FIGURE 5.4. Racial years of education and weekly wage differential, women

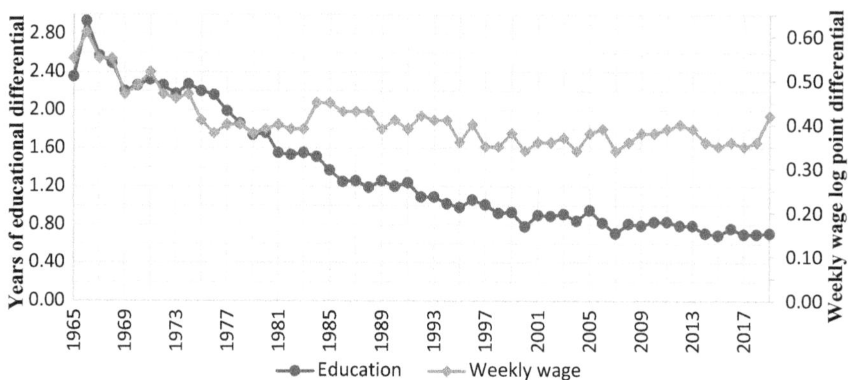

FIGURE 5.5. Racial years of education and weekly wage differential, men

Similarly, the men's racial wage differential was constant during a period (1974–2019) when the years of education differential was continuing to decline (Figure 5.5). The racial gap in years of education declined from a high of 2.93 years in 1966 to about 0.70 years between 2014 and 2019. As expected, the racial gap in weekly wages declined from 0.61 log points (84 percent) in 1966 to 0.41 log points (51 percent) in 1975 and, thereafter, remained constant.

The counter-intuitive movements of the weekly wage and years of education racial gaps for women during 1979–2019 and for men during 1974–2019 are not unique historical events. As we have discussed previously (see Table 4.2), the racial gap in occupational prestige rose from 61 percent to 63 during 1880–1910. During 1880 the racial gap in skill differences accounted for 30 percentage points of the occupational prestige gap and discrimination accounted for 31 percentage points. By 1910, racial differences in skills accounted for 19 percentage points of the gap in occupational prestige, while discrimination accounted for 44 percentage points. For both 1880–1910 and 1974–2019 racial discrimination in the labor market increased as African Americans became more competitive in the labor market.

Why would African Americans continue to increase their relative level of skill competitiveness, even though the labor market incentive (weekly wages relative to Whites) was declining or otherwise not a positive inducement to accumulate skill? This is a racial identity response among African Americans: as the challenges to the group increase, persons within the group become more identified with the well-being of the group and increase the intensity of their actions that will benefit the group. From this perspective, African Americans will accumulate more years of education than otherwise similar Whites (Mason, 1997; Mangino, 2013, 2014, 2019). Families are embedded into racial identity groups. Racial groups, like families, work to achieve expanded reproduction, that is, racial groups seek to preserve or increase the group's social

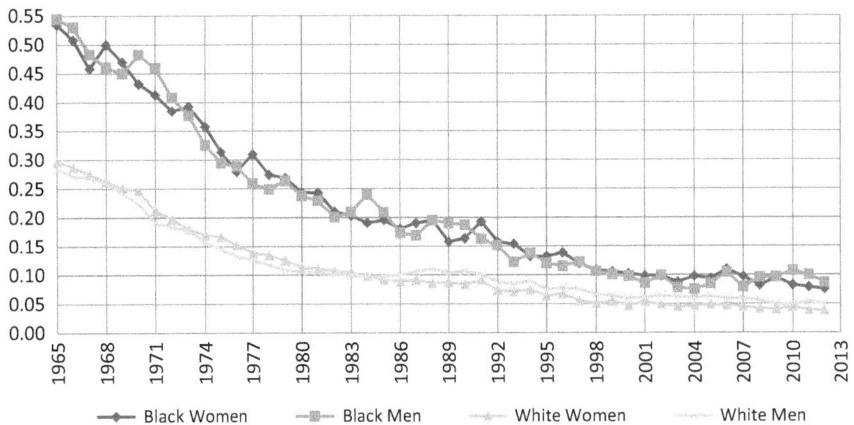

FIGURE 5.6. Fraction of dropouts, 25–34 years of age
Source: Author's calculations, Unicon CPS data

status across generations. The leaders and institutions of the subaltern group pursue a dynastic strategy emphasizing relatively greater achievement by the next generation in comparison to the dominant group's higher quality-of-life. To the extent that the subaltern family has a greater or lesser identification with the group, the achievement strategies of the group will have a positive effect on the achievement strategy of the family.

This identity response appears to have been particularly strong among the least educated. African Americans made exceptional progress in reducing the fraction of persons with 11 or fewer years of education, that is, "dropouts" (see Figure 5.6). In 1965 more than half of African American women (0.53) and men (0.54) aged 25–34 were dropouts. Three of every 10 White persons in this age group were dropouts, 0.30 women and 0.28 men. By 1990, the fractions were 0.16 and 0.19 for African American women and men and 0.08 for White women and men. By 2019, 8 percent of African American men and women, 4 percent of White women, and 6 percent of White men aged 25–34 were dropouts.

Similar patterns of unambiguous progress in years of education are shown in Figure 5.7. Just under half of African Americans 25–34 years of age and more 70 percent of Whites had attained 12 or more years of education during 1965 (Figure 5.7). Eighteen percent of White males and 10 percent of White females in this age group had obtained 16 or more years of education, while the percentages for African American men and women were 8 percent and 7 percent, respectively (Figure 5.8). Thus, at the high point of the Civil Rights Movement college educated individuals were an intellectual elite – especially among women and among African Americans.

A generation later, in 1990, the fraction of young African American adults with 12 or more years of education was 0.84 (women) and 0.81 (men), while

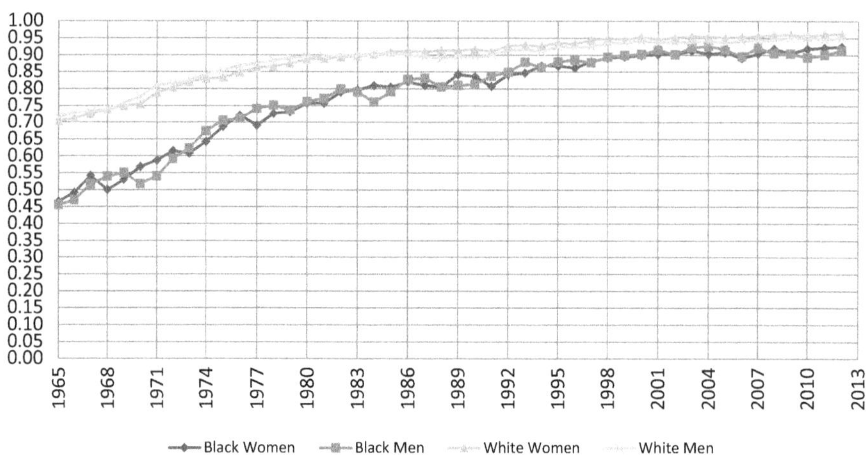

FIGURE 5.7. Fraction of persons with 12 or more years of education, 25–34 years of age
Source: Author's calculations, Unicon CPS data

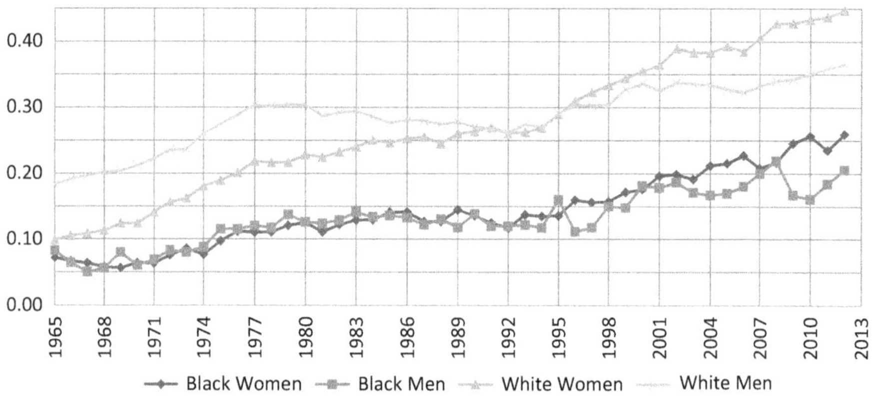

FIGURE 5.8. Fraction of persons with 16 years or more education, 25–34 years of age
Source: Author's calculations, Unicon CPS data

14 percent had 16 or more years of education. Among Whites, the fraction of persons aged 25–34 with 12 or more years of education was 0.92 (women) and 0.89 (men), while 26 percent of White women and 27 percent of White men had 16 or more years of education. The Civil Rights, Black Power, and Women's Movements had equalizing effects on educational attainment. As of 2007, 90 percent, 92 percent, 96 percent, and 94 percent of African women and men and White women and men, respectively, 25–34 years of age, had attained 12 or more years of education. During this same year, 1 of every 5 African

American young adults, 4 of every 10 White female young adults, and 1 of every 3 White males 25–34 years of age had attained 16 or more years of education.

Nevertheless, African American males have not kept pace with White males at the highest levels of education. The racial gap in advanced education was 10 percentage points during 1965 (Figure 5.8). Eight percent of African Americans and 18 percent of Whites had bachelor's or graduate degrees. The advanced education gap rose to 17 points during 1980, when 13 percent and 30 percent of African Americans and Whites, respectively, had college degrees.

During the 1980s the advanced education gap closed to as little as 14 percentage points. During the final year of our sample, 21 percent of African Americans males of 25–34 years of age had attained college degrees in 2019, which is equal to the fraction of White males of 25–34 years of age who had attained college degrees in 1970. Thirty-seven percent of White males in this age group had obtained college degrees in 2019; hence, the racial gap was 16 percentage points.

African American women have lost ground relative to White women at the highest levels of education. The racial gap in advanced education was 3 percentage points during 1965 (Figure 5.8). Seven percent of African Americans and 10 percent of Whites had bachelor's or graduate degrees. The advanced education gap rose to 10 points during 1980, when 13 percent and 23 percent of African Americans and Whites, respectively, had college degrees. By 1992, the female racial gap in advanced education for individuals 25–34 years of age was 14 percentage points: 12 percent for African Americans and 26 percent for Whites. During the final year of our sample, 26 percent of African American females of 25–34 years of age had attained college degrees in 2019, which is equal to the fraction of White females of 25–34 years of age who had attained college degrees in 1987–1993. Forty-five percent of White females in this age group had obtained college degrees in 2019; hence, the racial gap was 19 percentage points.

The South experienced dramatic educational progress relative to other regions of the country (see Table 5.2). In 1965, more than half of African American Southerners, aged 25–34, were dropouts. Less than 1 of every 10 had obtained a bachelor's or graduate degree. Among White Southerners of the same age group, 30 percent were dropouts, 12 percent of women were college graduates, and 20 percent of White men were college graduates. Among African Americans, Westerners had the fewest fraction of dropouts: 25 percent of African American women and 21 percent of African American men. Also, White Westerners had the fewest fraction of dropouts: 21 percent of women and 17 percent of men and the highest fractions of persons with college degrees, 14 percent and 23 percent of women and men, respectively.

By 1975–1980, the South had a dropout rate of 32 percent for African American women and men and college graduate rates of 0.12 and 0.10, respectively. African American women and men in the West had dropout rates

TABLE 5.2. *Educational attainment by race, gender, region, ages 25–34*

		South				Northcentral			
		African American		White		African American		White	
Year	Education	Women	Men	Women	Men	Women	Men	Women	Men
1965–1974	Dropout	0.52	0.55	0.30	0.28	0.39	0.40	0.22	0.22
	High school	0.32	0.31	0.46	0.38	0.44	0.43	0.53	0.44
	Some college	0.07	0.08	0.12	0.15	0.12	0.10	0.13	0.14
	Bachelor's degree	0.07	0.04	0.10	0.12	0.03	0.05	0.09	0.11
	Graduate degree	0.02	0.02	0.02	0.08	0.01	0.02	0.03	0.09
1975–1980	Dropout	0.32	0.32	0.18	0.16	0.26	0.24	0.13	0.11
	High school	0.42	0.42	0.45	0.35	0.44	0.42	0.49	0.40
	Some college	0.14	0.16	0.18	0.21	0.20	0.21	0.17	0.21
	Bachelor's degree	0.09	0.07	0.14	0.16	0.08	0.09	0.14	0.17
	Graduate degree	0.03	0.03	0.06	0.11	0.03	0.04	0.06	0.11
1981–1990	Dropout	0.20	0.23	0.13	0.14	0.21	0.18	0.09	0.09
	High school	0.46	0.48	0.43	0.39	0.46	0.42	0.48	0.45
	Some college	0.20	0.18	0.21	0.20	0.23	0.24	0.21	0.20
	Bachelor's degree	0.10	0.08	0.16	0.17	0.07	0.11	0.15	0.16
	Graduate degree	0.04	0.03	0.08	0.10	0.03	0.05	0.06	0.09
1991–2001	Dropout	0.13	0.13	0.08	0.11	0.14	0.13	0.06	0.07
	High school	0.40	0.49	0.34	0.36	0.39	0.44	0.35	0.38
	Some college	0.31	0.26	0.29	0.26	0.33	0.29	0.30	0.27
	Bachelor's degree	0.13	0.10	0.23	0.21	0.11	0.12	0.23	0.22
	Graduate degree	0.02	0.02	0.06	0.07	0.02	0.03	0.05	0.06

2002–2008	Dropout	0.09	0.10	0.06	0.08	0.11	0.10	0.04	0.06
	High school	0.35	0.44	0.26	0.33	0.36	0.42	0.27	0.34
	Some college	0.34	0.28	0.31	0.28	0.37	0.32	0.32	0.30
	Bachelor's degree	0.16	0.14	0.28	0.24	0.12	0.13	0.28	0.24
	Graduate degree	0.05	0.03	0.09	0.07	0.04	0.03	0.09	0.06
2009–2019	Dropout	0.07	0.09	0.04	0.05	0.07	0.09	0.04	0.05
	High school	0.30	0.40	0.22	0.31	0.32	0.43	0.21	0.30
	Some college	0.36	0.31	0.30	0.28	0.39	0.29	0.32	0.31
	Bachelor's degree	0.19	0.16	0.30	0.26	0.15	0.16	0.31	0.27
	Graduate degree	0.08	0.04	0.13	0.10	0.06	0.04	0.13	0.08

		Northeast				West			
		African American		White		African American		White	
Year	Education	Women	Men	Women	Men	Women	Men	Women	Men
1965–1974	Dropout	0.42	0.39	0.22	0.22	0.25	0.21	0.21	0.17
	High school	0.44	0.41	0.52	0.41	0.46	0.46	0.45	0.36
	Some college	0.08	0.11	0.12	0.14	0.21	0.24	0.19	0.23
	Bachelor's degree	0.04	0.06	0.10	0.13	0.05	0.06	0.10	0.13
	Graduate degree	0.01	0.03	0.04	0.11	0.03	0.03	0.04	0.10
1975–1980	Dropout	0.28	0.23	0.12	0.12	0.13	0.12	0.10	0.07
	High school	0.49	0.43	0.47	0.36	0.41	0.40	0.39	0.30
	Some college	0.14	0.20	0.18	0.20	0.35	0.33	0.28	0.30
	Bachelor's degree	0.06	0.09	0.15	0.17	0.07	0.08	0.15	0.18
	Graduate degree	0.03	0.05	0.08	0.14	0.05	0.08	0.09	0.15

(continued)

(*continued*)

		Northeast				West			
		African American		White		African American		White	
Year	Education	Women	Men	Women	Men	Women	Men	Women	Men
1981–1990	Dropout	0.20	0.19	0.07	0.09	0.09	0.10	0.07	0.07
	High school	0.44	0.44	0.43	0.40	0.42	0.39	0.38	0.35
	Some college	0.23	0.22	0.20	0.19	0.35	0.36	0.30	0.29
	Bachelor's degree	0.10	0.11	0.19	0.20	0.11	0.10	0.17	0.18
	Graduate degree	0.04	0.05	0.10	0.12	0.04	0.05	0.09	0.12
1991–2001	Dropout	0.14	0.12	0.05	0.07	0.07	0.05	0.05	0.06
	High school	0.40	0.44	0.35	0.37	0.33	0.40	0.29	0.32
	Some college	0.30	0.27	0.26	0.22	0.44	0.39	0.35	0.32
	Bachelor's degree	0.12	0.14	0.26	0.25	0.13	0.13	0.24	0.23
	Graduate degree	0.03	0.03	0.09	0.08	0.04	0.03	0.07	0.07
2002–2008	Dropout	0.11	0.08	0.04	0.05	0.07	0.04	0.04	0.04
	High school	0.36	0.41	0.25	0.32	0.31	0.37	0.21	0.27
	Some college	0.30	0.29	0.25	0.23	0.40	0.38	0.35	0.33
	Bachelor's degree	0.17	0.17	0.31	0.29	0.18	0.18	0.30	0.27
	Graduate degree	0.06	0.04	0.15	0.10	0.05	0.03	0.10	0.09
2009–2019	Dropout	0.06	0.05	0.03	0.04	0.06	0.04	0.02	0.03
	High school	0.33	0.36	0.19	0.28	0.26	0.31	0.19	0.26
	Some college	0.32	0.33	0.22	0.22	0.42	0.40	0.32	0.32
	Bachelor's degree	0.20	0.20	0.35	0.34	0.19	0.19	0.33	0.29
	Graduate degree	0.09	0.05	0.20	0.13	0.08	0.06	0.13	0.10

Source: Author's calculations, Unicon CPS data

and college graduate rates of 0.13 and 0.12 and 0.12 and 0.16, respectively. Southern Whites made similar progress. The Southern dropout rates were 18 percent and 16 percent for White women and men, respectively, with college graduation rates of 20 percent and 27 percent. White women and men in the West had dropout rates and college graduate rates of 0.10 and 0.07 and 0.24 and 0.33, respectively.

For the most recent period (2009–2019), Southern and Northcentral African American dropout rates for men and women 25–34 years of age were 0.07 and 0.09, respectively, while the Northeast and West had a dropout rate of 6 percent for women and 5 percent and 4 percent, respectively, for African American men. Similarly, among Southern and Northcentral Whites 25–34 years of age, the dropout rates were 0.04 and 0.05 for White women and men, respectively. The White dropout rates were 3 percent and 4 percent for women and men in the Northeast and 2 percent and 3 percent for women and men, respectively, residing in the West.

The 2009–2019 college degree attainment rates show similarly remarkable progress for African Americans and Southerners. Twenty-seven percent and 20 percent of Southern African American women and men 25–34 years of age had obtained college degrees. This is similar to the Northcentral states, where the rates for women and men are 21 percent and 20 percent, respectively. In the Northeast and West, 29 and 27 percent of African American women 25–34 years of age had attained college degrees, while 25 percent of young adult African American men residing in these two regions had attained college degrees.

By 2009–2019, 43 percent of Southern White women and 36 percent of Southern White men, 25–34 years of age, had attained bachelor's and graduate degrees. These numbers were about the same as the college graduation rates of White women and men of Northcentral states, 44 percent and 35 percent, respectively. Fifty-five and 47 percent of young Northeastern White women and men, along with 46 percent of Western White women and 39 percent of Western White men had obtained college degrees.

Years of education by race, gender, age group, and time period are presented in Table 5.3. Among new entrants to the labor market, that is, among workers 16–25 years of age, mean African American male education rose from 10.92 years to 12.37 years during 1965–2019. Mean White male education rose from 12.04 years to 12.81 years. For this age group, the male racial education gap declined from 1.12 years in 1965–1974 to 0.44 years in 2009–2019. Among new African American female entrants to the labor market, mean years of education rose from 11.42 to 12.70 during 1965–2019. Mean White female years of education rose from 12.21 years to 13.17 years. For this age group, the female racial education gap declined from 0.79 years in 1965–1974 to 0.47 years in 2009–2019. Hence, the male racial gap declined at a faster pace than the female racial gap in years of education.

For both Blacks and Whites, educational inequality between the youngest and oldest cohorts declined, but inequality declined faster among African

TABLE 5.3. *Years of education, by race and by age group: 1965–2019*

Age group	1965–1974	1975–1980	1981–1990	1991–2001	2002–2008	2009–2019
African American Women						
16–25	**11.42**	11.94	12.25	12.43	12.54	12.70
26–35	11.34	**12.30**	12.85	13.05	13.38	13.59
36–45	10.37	11.51	**12.47**	13.12	13.37	13.65
46–55	9.11	10.50	11.77	**12.84**	13.31	13.50
56–65	8.06	9.08	10.58	12.08	**12.98**	13.28
African American Men						
16–25	**10.92**	11.53	11.86	12.10	12.24	12.37
26–35	10.80	**12.07**	12.56	12.81	13.15	13.11
36–45	9.50	10.85	**12.23**	12.80	13.06	13.33
46–55	8.44	9.47	10.99	**12.40**	13.03	13.13
56–65	6.92	8.11	9.70	11.35	**12.68**	13.13
White Women						
16–25	**12.21**	12.47	12.63	13.01	13.01	13.17
26–35	12.28	**13.13**	13.51	14.28	14.26	14.51
36–45	11.69	12.42	**13.24**	13.95	13.93	14.29
46–55	11.42	11.98	12.67	**13.96**	13.97	14.00
56–65	10.94	11.57	12.24	13.65	**13.63**	14.02
White Men						
16–25	**12.04**	12.35	12.38	12.56	12.66	12.81
26–35	12.52	**13.42**	13.51	13.55	13.83	13.94
36–45	11.96	12.75	**13.58**	13.71	13.84	14.01
46–55	11.27	12.07	12.86	**13.77**	13.97	13.85
56–65	10.45	11.38	12.32	13.17	**13.98**	14.19

Americans (Table 5.3). During the period immediately after the elimination of Jim Crow (1965–1974), the most senior African American male and female workers (persons 56–65 years old) had only a middle school education, averaging 6.92 years and 8.06 years, respectively. By comparison, during 1965–1974 young adult male and female African Americans averaged some years of high school, averaging 10.92 years and 11.42 years, respectively. On average, by 2009–2019 African Americans at all age-groups were high school graduates. But older workers now averaged more years of education than younger workers: 13.28 and 13.13 for 55–65 year-old Black women and men versus 12.70 and 12.37 for 16–25 year-old Black women and men. The senior–new worker years of education gap for Black males moved from –4.0 years to 0.86 years, while the senior–new workers years of education gap for Black women moved from –3.36 years to 0.58 years. By comparison, the senior–new worker years of education gap for White males moved from –1.59 years to 0.38 years, while the senior–new workers years of education gap for White women moved from –1.27 years to 0.85 years.

Controlling for age, gender inequality in years of education declined among African Americans but increased among Whites. Consider persons aged 26–35 years of age. Among Whites, female–male differentials were –0.24 for 1965–1974, –0.29 for 1975–1980, 0.00 for 1981–1990, 0.73 for 1991–2001, 0.43 for 2002–2008, and 0.56 for 2009–2019. Among Blacks, female–male differentials were 0.54 for 1965–1974, 0.23 for 1975–1980, 0.29 for 1981–1990, 0.24 for 1991–2001, 0.23 for 2001–2008, and 0.48 for 2009–2019.

Persons 16–25 years of age during 1981–1990 are 26–35 during the 1990s, 36–45 during the first decade of the 2000s, and members of the 46–55 years old age-group during 2009–2019. During the 1980s 16–25 years old African American women entered the labor market with 12.25 years of education, while White women entered the labor market with 12.63 years of education; hence, the 1980s female racial gap for new entrants was 0.38 years. The gap grew to 1.23 years during the 1990s, 0.56 years during 2001–2008, and 0.50 years during 2009–2019. So, for a given cohort, White women tend to accumulate slightly more years of education after 25 years of age. During the 1980s 16–25 years old African American men entered the labor market with 11.86 years of education, while White men entered the labor market with 12.38 years of education; hence, the 1980s male racial gap for new entrants was 0.52 years. The gap grew to 0.74 years during the 1990s, 0.78 years during 2001–2008, and 0.72 years during 2009–2019. So, for a given cohort, White men tend to accumulate slightly more years of education after 25 years of age.

Accordingly, the educational attainment of new entrants will tend to reduce racial disparity in labor market outcomes while the continuing education of older workers will tend to mildly expand racial disparity in labor market outcomes. As older workers are increasingly replaced by younger workers, labor market inequality should decline rather than increase.

5.4 QUALITY OF EDUCATION

Between the early 1970s and the late 1980s there is evidence of a decline in the White–African American differential in the quality of education among new cohorts. But there is evidence that the gap may not have closed much further for new cohorts during the 1990s and 2000s.

A select group of students take the Scholastic Aptitude Test (SAT), viz., students considering college matriculation. Between 1976 and 1995 the White–African American SAT mathematics gap declined by more than 21 percent, while the White–African American SAT verbal gap declined by 25 percent (Bowen and Bok, 1998). During 1987–2016, African Americans and Whites had similar growth in SAT verbal and mathematics scores (College Entrance Examination Board, 2016).

The National Assessment of Educational Progress (NAEP) is a broader assessment of educational progress than the SAT, it's "the largest nationally representative and continuing assessment of what America's students know and can do in various subject areas".[6] Mathematics, reading, and science are common subject areas used to assess educational quality. All areas of the country use the same NAEP examinations, with limited year-to-year changes in content. For the long-term trend assessments, NAEP results are based on representative samples of 9, 13, and 17 years old. All age groups are not assessed each time. During 1975–2020, reading scores grew faster among African American students than White students of the same age (Table 5.4). For example, the reading scores of African American students grew by 13 percent, 8 percent, and 12 percent for ages 9, 13, and 17, respectively, but 5 percent, 3 percent, and 1 percent for White students of the same age. The NAEP scores of African American children grew as faster or faster than the scores of all other groups.

During 1978–2020, NAEP mathematics scores grew slower among African American 9 years old students than among White students of the same age (2 percent versus 5 percent), though 13 years old for both groups had similar growth (2 percent). Among 17 years old White students, scores grew by 6 percent, while African American scores increased by 2 percent.

During 1975–1990, the African American–White gap in NAEP reading scores for 17 years old declined by 34, 42, 49, and 22 percent in the Northeast, Midwest, South, and West, respectively (Bernstein, 1995). During 1978–1990 the African American–White gap in NAEP math scores for 17 years old increased by 3 percent in the Northeast, but declined by 35 percent in the Midwest, 61 percent in the South, and 31 percent in the West. During 1977–1990, the African American–White gap in NAEP science scores for 17 years old increased by 15 percent in the Northeast, but declined by 18 percent in the Midwest, 22 percent in the South, and 48 percent in the West. Even

[6] See https://nces.ed.gov/nationsreportcard/. Last accessed December 14, 2022.

TABLE 5.4. *Growth of average scale scores for ages 9, 13, and 17 long-term trend reading, by race/ethnicity, selected years, 1975–2020*

Reading					Mathematics				
Year	Black	Latinx	Other	White	Year	Black	Latinx	Other	White
9 years old									
2020	1.13	1.15	1.10	1.05	2020	1.02	1.05	1.11	1.05
2012	1.14	1.14	1.11	1.06	2012	1.01	1.06	1.10	1.05
2008	1.13	1.13	1.11	1.05	2008	1.01	1.05	1.09	1.06
2004	1.09	1.09	1.08	1.03	2004	1.01	1.01	1.05	1.03
2004	1.10	1.12	1.11	1.04	2004	1.01	1.03	1.08	1.05
1999	1.03	1.05	1.03	1.02	1999	1.01	0.96	1.02	0.98
1996	1.06	1.07	1.03	1.01	1996	1.01	0.98	1.03	0.98
1994	1.02	1.02	1.01	1.00	1994	1.00	0.95	0.98	0.97
1992	1.02	1.05	1.00	1.00	1992	1.00	0.95	1.01	0.95
1990	1.01	1.03	0.99	1.00	1990	1.00	0.94	1.00	0.94
1986	1.04	1.06	1.10	1.00	1986	1.00	0.97	1.02	1.04
1982	1.03	1.02	1.07	1.00	1982	1.00	0.96	0.99	1.02
1978	1.04	1.04	1.05	1.02	1978	1.00	1.00	1.00	1.00
1975	1.00	1.00	1.00	1.00					
13 years old									
2020	1.08	1.08	1.07	1.03	2020	1.02	1.03	1.04	1.02
2012	1.09	1.07	1.09	1.03	2012	1.02	1.05	1.03	1.04
2008	1.09	1.04	1.05	1.02	2008	1.02	1.05	1.00	1.01
2004	1.06	1.04	1.03	1.01	2004	1.01	1.01	1.00	0.98
2004	1.08	1.04	1.04	1.02	2004	1.01	1.03	1.00	0.99
1999	1.05	1.05	1.01	1.02	1999	1.01	1.01	1.01	0.96

(continued)

TABLE 5.4. (*continued*)

Reading					Mathematics				
Year	Black	Latinx	Other	White	Year	Black	Latinx	Other	White
1996	1.04	1.03	0.99	1.02	1996	1.01	0.99	0.99	0.94
1994	1.04	1.01	1.00	1.01	1994	1.01	0.99	0.98	0.96
1992	1.05	1.03	1.05	1.02	1992	1.01	1.01	0.99	1.00
1990	1.07	1.03	0.99	1.00	1990	1.01	1.02	0.99	0.94
1986	1.08	1.03	1.05	1.00	1986	1.00	1.03	1.00	1.00
1982	1.04	1.03	1.02	1.00	1982	1.00	1.00	1.00	0.97
1978	1.03	1.02	0.99	1.01	1978	1.00	1.00	1.00	1.00
1975	1.00	1.00	1.00	1.00					
17 years old									
2012	1.12	1.09	1.08	1.01	2012	1.02	1.11	1.05	1.06
2008	1.10	1.07	1.07	1.01	2008	1.02	1.09	1.03	1.04
2004	1.09	1.06	1.06	0.99	2004	1.01	1.08	1.02	1.04
2004	1.10	1.05	1.04	1.00	2004	1.01	1.09	1.01	1.02
1999	1.10	1.08	1.06	1.01	1999	1.01	1.09	1.04	1.04
1996	1.10	1.05	1.03	1.01	1996	1.01	1.09	1.02	1.00
1994	1.10	1.04	1.05	1.01	1994	1.01	1.09	1.01	1.03
1992	1.08	1.08	1.05	1.01	1992	1.01	1.07	1.04	1.03
1990	1.11	1.09	1.06	1.01	1990	1.01	1.10	1.05	1.04
1986	1.14	1.08	1.06	1.01	1986	1.00	1.13	1.04	1.04
1982	1.10	1.06	1.04	1.01	1982	1.00	1.09	1.03	1.01
1978	1.01	1.04	1.02	1.00	1978	1.00	1.00	1.00	1.00
1975	1.00	1.00	1.00	1.00					

Scores for 1975–2004 are for original assessment format, while 2004–2020 are for modified assessment format.
Source: US Department of Education, Institute of Education Sciences, National Center for Education Statistics, National Assessment of Educational Progress (NAEP), selected year, 1975–2020 Long-Term Trend Reading and Mathematics Assessments, for ages 9, 13, and 17

if there was no progress in closing the gap after (say) 1990, the overall African American–White skills gap would have continued to decline throughout the 1990s and 2000s as older cohorts with wider racial gaps in both the quality and quantity of education left the market and newer cohorts with smaller gaps in the quantity and quality of education entered the labor market.

5.5 WEALTH AND RACE EFFECTS

There are wealth and racial identify effects associated with educational attainment. Children of wealthy parents obtain more years of education than children whose parents do not have much wealth. Most states require children to be enrolled in school between 6 and 16 years of age. As parental wealth increases, children are more likely to be enrolled in high quality daycare and pre-school; thus, they will have better academic performance in school and will have a greater attachment to school. Further, as parental wealth increases, children 16 years of age and above are more likely to graduate from high school, more likely to attend college, and more likely to obtain a college degree. Also, there is some statistical evidence that suggests African American children are able to translate a given amount of family resources into greater years of education (Mason, 1997; Mangino, 2013, 2014, 2019).

Consider an additional $100,000 of parental wealth during a child's pre-school years, that is, between a child's birth and age 5. This increase in family wealth will increase educational achievement by more than 4 weeks for White young adults (persons 25–36 years of age) and about 11 weeks for African American young adults, assuming 39 weeks of schooling per year.[7] The average wealth of Southern White families is $300,000 greater than the average wealth of Southern Black families, while Non-Southern White families have average wealth that is $400,000 greater than the average wealth of Non-Southern Black families.[8] On average, young adult White men and women have 0.83 and 0.92 more years of education than young adult African American men and women, respectively, that is, racial disparities of 32.4 and 35.9 weeks of education for men and women, respectively.[9] If African American families had the same wealth as White families, then the average years of education for African American young adults would rise by 32.8–43.7 weeks, nearly eliminating or completely reversing the racial disparity in years of education.

Among potential college applicants, for students of the same race, nativity, psychological traits (motivation, effort, and locus of control), and other characteristics, a 10 percent increase in wealth during a student's senior year in high school will increase years of education by 4 percent, measured 8 years after high school (Dimarche, 2020). White family wealth is at least five times greater than

[7] Burgin (2021), chapter 2, table 2.5. [8] See Table 8.1. Net worth with home equity.
[9] See Table 5.3. Years of education, by race and by age group: 1965–2019.

Black family wealth.[10] Hence, raising the family wealth of Black high school seniors considering attending college to the level of family wealth of a similar group of White students will increase average years of education by 200 percent for African American students. Importantly, Dimarche also shows that young Black men and women obtain 11 percent and 28 percent more education than otherwise identical young White men and women, though the male differential is not measured with sufficient precision.

5.6 IDENTITY EFFECTS ON THE QUANTITY AND QUALITY OF INSTRUCTION TIME

Teachers are the production managers of the educational process, exercising considerable discretion over the allocation of education resources to students; these resources include the teacher's time, information, materials, connections, and other resources. Student scores on standardized tests increase with access to higher quantity and quality of instruction time (Marcotte, 2007; Goodman, 2014; Halloran et al., 2021). The teacher–student racial identity configuration influences the productivity of the educational production process, in particular, same-race and other-race identity matches may yield differences in student educational outcomes.

White teachers allocate fewer managerial resources to Black students because they view Black students as less disciplined and less likely to graduate from college. Exclusionary discipline, that is, out-of-school suspensions, in-school suspensions, and expulsions, reduce the quantity and quality of instruction time available to students. For elementary, middle, and high school students, for boys and girls, and for students who receive or who do not receive free or reduced price lunch, own-race teacher–student identity matches reduce the probability a Black student receives exclusionary discipline (Lindsay and Hart, 2017). Office referrals for "willful defiance" decline with own-race teacher–student identity matches. Teacher discretion plays a role in determining these results.

Non-Black teachers have lower expectations of Black students than Black teachers (Gershenson, Holt, and Papageorge, 2016). Specifically, Non-Black (White, Asian, and Hispanic) teachers were 12 percent less likely than Black teachers to expect Black 10th grade students to graduate from college. Non-Black teachers of the opposite sex are 17 percent less likely than Black teachers of the same sex to expect Black 10 grade students to graduate from college. These racially differential expectations will lead to racial differences in the allocation of educational resources.

[10] Using Table 8.1, mean White family wealth is 5.09 and 6.73 times mean African American family wealth in the South and Non-South, respectively, while the ratios at the medians are 8.07 and 22.14.

Consider children with Black-identified names versus their siblings with traditional White-identified names, for example, Dwayne (Black-identified) versus Drew (White-identified). Compared to their siblings, children with Black-identified names have lower mathematics scores, lower reading scores, and are less likely to be enrolled in gifted courses (Figlio, 2005). The negative effect of a Black-identified name on the quality of education are amplified when the Black-identified name is also associated with low socioeconomic status; the production of educational outcomes declines when teachers are matched with children whose names signify that they are low-income African Americans. However, as the share of Black teachers within the school rises from 10 percent to 90 percent – and Black students are matched with Black teachers, the African American identity penalty disappears.

African American students matched with at least one African American teacher between kindergarten and third grade are 9 percentage points (13%) more likely to graduate high school and 6 percentage points (19%) more likely to enroll in college than other Black students who are not matched with a Black teacher during these formative years of education (Gershenson et al., 2021). There is no Black teacher effect on White students in these grades. Gershenson et al. report that the results are "concentrated among males and in schools with high proportions of disadvantaged students" (p. 2).

5.7 SUMMARY AND DISCUSSION

African Americans have made unambiguous educational progress since the end of servitude capitalism. Both White and Black years and quality of education have increased since the mid-1960s, but Black education increased at a faster rate. These trends indicate that public policy (school desegregation and increases in years of free public education) can be used to reduce racial disparities in educational outcomes. Further, these trends are inconsistent with the individualist perspective that African American racial identity is antithetical to reducing racial disparities in education.

Racial differences in the college graduation rate are an exception to the overall trend. Racial differences in wealth can explain a large proportion of the racial disparity in mean years of education, suggesting that racial disparity in wealth may be important for explaining racial differences in college graduation rates. Further, the student–teacher racial identity match can account for racial differences in students' educational outcomes.

6

Transformations in Family Structure

Major transformations have occurred in American family structure and economic well-being since the mid-1960s. The fraction of two-parent families has decreased and the fraction of single-parent families has increased. Married-couple families have a higher standard of living than families headed by never-married or previously-married persons (see Chapter 7). Simultaneously, many American families have experienced stagnating or declining incomes since the early 1970s. These changes have become a focal point of scholarly and popular debate, especially as they relate to changes in racial economic income inequality. African American households have experienced greater transformations than White families, from married couple families to single-parent families. From the individualist perspective, "single-parent" often means "female-headed and dysfunctional family," while "stable family" often means "two-parent family." Hence, from the individualist perspective it is argued that changes in economic well-being are caused by changes in family structure, that is, the change from stable (two-parent) families to dysfunctional (female-headed) families has reduced family income. The stratification perspective argues that it is important to distinguish between family structure, family functioning, and family resources. Taking account of these difference, if marital status and family economic well-being are causally related, the primary direction of causation is from economic outcomes to family structure.

6.1 TRANSFORMATIONS IN FAMILY STRUCTURE

Both African Americans and Whites have experienced a movement away from married-couple families toward single parent families, though the change has been less dramatic for White families. From the end of Jim Crow to the period after the Great Recession, the fraction of African American married couples declined by 19 percentage points (Table 6.1). By 2009–2019, married couples constituted only 47 percent of African American families.

TABLE 6.1. *Selected characteristics of families, by race: March 1965–2019*

	1965–1974		1975–1980		1981–1990		1991–2001		2002–2008		2009–2019	
	Black	White	Black	White	Black	White	Black	White	Black	White	Black	White
Family type												
Married Couple	0.66	0.78	0.58	0.75	0.51	0.74	0.48	0.75	0.49	0.75	0.47	0.75
Female Householder, No Spouse	0.18	0.10	0.24	0.12	0.29	0.13	0.32	0.13	0.32	0.13	0.33	0.13
Male Householder, No Spouse	0.16	0.12	0.18	0.13	0.20	0.13	0.20	0.12	0.19	0.12	0.20	0.12
Family type: own children												
All Families												
With no own children <18	0.39	0.41	0.37	0.43	0.41	0.47	0.44	0.48	0.45	0.51	0.50	0.55
With own children <18	0.61	0.59	0.63	0.57	0.59	0.53	0.56	0.52	0.55	0.49	0.50	0.45
Married Couples												
With no own children <18	0.36	0.40	0.35	0.43	0.38	0.45	0.40	0.47	0.43	0.51	0.47	0.53
With own children <18	0.64	0.60	0.65	0.57	0.62	0.55	0.60	0.53	0.57	0.49	0.53	0.47
Female householder, no spouse present												
With no own children <18	0.37	0.43	0.31	0.37	0.34	0.44	0.35	0.43	0.36	0.43	0.41	0.52
With own children <18	0.63	0.57	0.69	0.63	0.66	0.56	0.65	0.57	0.64	0.57	0.59	0.48
Male householder, no spouse present												
With no own children <18	0.49	0.47	0.51	0.47	0.62	0.58	0.65	0.61	0.66	0.61	0.73	0.69
With own children <18	0.51	0.53	0.49	0.53	0.38	0.42	0.35	0.39	0.34	0.39	0.27	0.31
Children under 18 years by presence of parents												
Married	0.68	0.79	0.60	0.74	0.54	0.76	0.51	0.76	0.50	0.75	0.48	0.76
Mother only	0.18	0.10	0.26	0.14	0.33	0.14	0.37	0.15	0.38	0.15	0.40	0.15
Father only	0.13	0.10	0.14	0.12	0.13	0.10	0.12	0.09	0.12	0.09	0.12	0.09

Author's calculations. Current Population Survey, March, 1965–2019. Both African Americans and Whites are Non-Latinx. Cohabitating couples are considered unmarried. Married couples include families where a spouse is absent from the residence.

The fraction of African American female households with no spouse present rose 15 percentage points, from 18 percent of families in 1965–1974 to 33 percent of families in 2009–2019. By contrast, White families headed by married couples declined by three percentage points, from 78 percent in 1965–1974 to 75 percent in 2009–2019. The number of White families headed by a woman with no spouse present increased from 10 percent in 1965–1974 to 13 percent in 2009–2019. Table 6.1 also shows that 1965–1990 was the period of the most dramatic change in the structure of African American families.

The fraction of African American families with own-children present has declined from 61 percent to 50 percent, even as the headship composition of these families has changed. Consider African American male householders with no spouse, who were 16 percent of families in 1965–1974 and 20 percent of families in 2009–2019. The presence of children in male householder families has declined from 51 percent of families in 1965–1974 to 27 percent during the period after the Great Recession (Table 6.1). Similarly, the fraction of childless African American married couples has increased by 11 percentage points.

During the immediate post-Jim Crow years, 68 percent of African American children resided in two-parent families, but today 48 percent of African American children live in two-parent homes. By 2009–2019, 40 percent of African American children lived in families where only their mother was present. From 1965–1974 to 2009–2019, the fraction of White children living in mother-only families increased from 10 percent to 15 percent.

Among African American children living in mother-only families during the post-Great Recession period, 67 percent of the mothers have never-married and less than one-fifth (17.8 percent) of the mothers are divorced (Table 6.2). Among White children living with mothers-only, 40 percent of the mothers have never-married and nearly 4 of every 10 (37.4 percent) of the mothers are divorced. Similarly, the majority (72.9 percent) of African American children living in father-only families do so because the father has never-married. Also, among Whites, never-married is the most common (55.7 percent) path to children living in father-only families.

The causes of the rise of single parent families vary by race and by gender. Thirty-five percent of African American single mothers were never-married in 1965–1974 and 67 percent were never-married in 2009–2019. Divorced parents made up 14.8 percent of White mother-only families in 1965–1974, but 37.4 percent of White mother-only families in 2009–2019. Similarly, divorced caused African American and White male father-only families to increase from 8.2 percent to 16.2 percent and from 11.4 percent to 31.5 percent, respectively. During 1975–1980, 45.7 percent and 74.5 percent of African American single female and single male parents were never-married. Forty-two percent of single White women parents and 80.1 percent of single White men parents were never-married in 1975–1980.

Trends in marital status are presented in Table 6.3. Relatively few African Americans are widowed and widows as a fraction of the 16–39 years old

TABLE 6.2. *Presence and marital status of parents for children under 18 years living with only one parent, by sex and race: 1965–2019*

	1965–1974	1975–1980	1981–1990	1991–2001	2002–2008	2009–2019
African American women						
Widowed	0.25	0.13	0.06	0.04	0.04	0.07
Divorced	0.12	0.17	0.18	0.17	0.17	0.18
Separated	0.29	0.25	0.18	0.14	0.10	0.08
Never-married	0.35	0.46	0.58	0.66	0.69	0.67
White women						
Widowed	0.41	0.22	0.09	0.07	0.06	0.14
Divorced	0.15	0.26	0.37	0.38	0.37	0.37
Separated	0.07	0.10	0.12	0.12	0.09	0.09
Never-married	0.38	0.42	0.42	0.43	0.48	0.40
African American men						
Widowed	0.13	0.06	0.03	0.03	0.03	0.05
Divorced	0.08	0.08	0.08	0.11	0.11	0.16
Separated	0.16	0.11	0.06	0.06	0.05	0.06
Never-married	0.63	0.75	0.84	0.80	0.81	0.73
White men						
Widowed	0.13	0.06	0.03	0.03	0.03	0.07
Divorced	0.11	0.10	0.14	0.21	0.22	0.32
Separated	0.05	0.03	0.04	0.05	0.05	0.06
Never-married	0.71	0.80	0.79	0.71	0.70	0.56

Head of household is at least 18 years of age. Children are less than 18 years of age. All individuals are Non-Latinx. "Family" includes primary family and related subfamily. There is at least one child under 18 years of age and the head of household is currently unmarried.

Source: Author's calculation ASEC of CPS, 1965–2019

TABLE 6.3. *Marital status by race, sex, and age, selected years, 1940–2019 (percent)*

		Black Marital Status				White Marital Status			
				Divor.	Never			Divor.	Never
Age	Year	Marr.	Wid.	/Sep.	Marr.	Marr.	Wid.	/Sep.	Marr.
Men									
Ages 16–19	1940	0.03	0.00	0.01	0.96	0.04	0.00	0.00	0.96
	1950	0.03	0.00	0.02	0.95	0.04	0.00	0.00	0.96
	1960	0.03	0.00	0.02	0.95	0.02	0.00	0.00	0.98
	1965–1974	0.02	0.00	0.00	0.98	0.01	0.00	0.00	0.99
	1975–1980	0.01	0.00	0.00	0.99	0.01	0.00	0.00	0.99
	1981–1990	0.01	0.00	0.00	0.99	0.01	0.00	0.01	0.98
	1991–2001	0.00	0.00	0.00	0.99	0.04	0.00	0.00	0.96
	2002–2008	0.01	0.00	0.01	0.99	0.04	0.00	0.00	0.96
	2009–2019	0.01	0.00	0.01	0.99	0.02	0.00	0.00	0.98
Ages 20–23	1940	0.32	0.01	0.05	0.63	0.21	0.00	0.22	0.77
	1950	0.31	0.00	0.07	0.61	0.29	0.00	0.03	0.68
	1960	0.31	0.00	0.09	0.59	0.38	0.00	0.05	0.57
	1965–1974	0.30	0.00	0.03	0.67	0.39	0.00	0.02	0.59
	1975–1980	0.19	0.00	0.03	0.78	0.29	0.00	0.02	0.68
	1981–1990	0.9.7	0.00	0.01	0.89	0.20	0.00	0.02	0.78
	1991–2001	0.07	0.00	0.01	0.92	0.13	0.00	0.02	0.85
	2002–2008	0.05	0.00	0.01	0.93	0.09	0.00	0.01	0.90
	2009–2019	0.03	0.00	0.02	0.95	0.07	0.00	0.02	0.92
Ages 24–29	1940	0.59	0.01	0.09	0.31	0.56	0.00	0.04	0.40
	1950	0.61	0.01	0.12	0.26	0.68	0.00	0.04	0.27
	1960	0.59	0.01	0.14	0.27	0.72	0.00	0.05	0.22
	1965–1974	0.62	0.00	0.08	0.30	0.76	0.00	0.04	0.21

	1975–1980	0.48	0.00	0.11	0.41	0.64	0.00	0.08	0.29
	1981–1990	0.35	0.00	0.07	0.58	0.51	0.00	0.07	0.41
	1991–2001	0.27	0.00	0.06	0.68	0.43	0.00	0.06	0.51
	2002–2008	0.21	0.00	0.05	0.74	0.39	0.00	0.05	0.56
	2009–2019	0.15	0.00	0.03	0.81	0.30	0.00	0.04	0.66
Ages 30–39	1940	0.69	0.03	0.11	0.17	0.77	0.01	0.05	0.18
	1950	0.77	0.01	0.12	0.10	0.86	0.00	0.04	0.10
	1960	0.69	0.01	0.16	0.14	0.84	0.00	0.05	0.10
	1965–1974	0.73	0.01	0.12	0.14	0.87	0.00	0.04	0.09
	1975–1980	0.64	0.01	0.18	0.18	0.82	0.00	0.08	0.10
	1981–1990	0.51	0.01	0.20	0.29	0.73	0.00	0.11	0.16
	1991–2001	0.42	0.00	0.16	0.42	0.66	0.00	0.12	0.22
	2002–2008	0.45	0.00	0.12	0.43	0.64	0.00	0.11	0.25
	2009–2019	0.38	0.00	0.10	0.51	0.61	0.00	0.10	0.29
Women									
Ages 16–19	1940	0.19	0.01	0.04	0.76	0.12	0.00	0.01	0.86
	1950	0.16	0.00	0.07	0.77	0.14	0.00	0.28	0.83
	1960	0.15	0.00	0.05	0.80	0.17	0.00	0.03	0.80
	1965–1974	0.12	0.00	0.01	0.87	0.14	0.00	0.01	0.85
	1975–1980	0.07	0.00	0.01	0.92	0.11	0.00	0.01	0.88
	1981–1990	0.02	0.00	0.00	0.98	0.07	0.00	0.01	0.92
	1991–2001	0.01	0.00	0.01	0.98	0.04	0.00	0.01	0.96
	2002–2008	0.01	0.00	0.01	0.98	0.02	0.00	0.01	0.97
	2009–2019	0.01	0.00	0.01	0.98	0.02	0.00	0.01	0.97
Ages 20–23	1940	0.51	0.02	0.10	0.37	0.45	0.00	0.03	0.52
	1950	0.46	0.01	0.16	0.37	0.55	0.00	0.06	0.39
	1960	0.46	0.01	0.16	0.38	0.62	0.00	0.07	0.31
	1965–1974	0.43	0.00	0.10	0.47	0.58	0.00	0.04	0.38
	1975–1980	0.25	0.00	0.08	0.67	0.46	0.00	0.06	0.48

(*continued*)

TABLE 6.3. *(continued)*

		Black Marital Status				White Marital Status			
				Divor.	Never			Divor.	Never
Age	Year	Marr.	Wid.	/Sep.	Marr.	Marr.	Wid.	/Sep.	Marr.
	1981–1990	0.17	0.00	0.04	0.79	0.35	0.00	0.05	0.60
	1991–2001	0.10	0.00	0.03	0.87	0.25	0.00	0.04	0.71
	2002–2008	0.08	0.00	0.02	0.90	0.18	0.00	0.03	0.79
	2009–2019	0.05	0.00	0.02	0.94	0.13	0.00	0.03	0.85
Ages 24–29	1940	0.62	0.04	0.14	0.20	0.70	0.01	0.05	0.25
	1950	0.64	0.02	0.19	0.16	0.80	0.01	0.06	0.14
	1960	0.60	0.02	0.21	0.17	0.83	0.01	0.06	0.11
	1965–1974	0.59	0.01	0.20	0.20	0.83	0.00	0.06	0.11
	1975–1980	0.43	0.01	0.21	0.35	0.73	0.00	0.10	0.17
	1981–1990	0.35	0.01	0.15	0.50	0.62	0.00	0.11	0.26
	1991–2001	0.27	0.00	0.10	0.62	0.55	0.00	0.10	0.35
	2002–2008	0.24	0.00	0.07	0.69	0.49	0.00	0.08	0.42
	2009–2019	0.18	0.00	0.05	0.76	0.41	0.00	0.06	0.53
Ages 30–39	1940	0.64	0.11	0.15	0.10	0.78	0.03	0.06	0.13
	1950	0.71	0.06	0.17	0.78	0.87	0.02	0.05	0.07
	1960	0.64	0.04	0.24	0.09	0.86	0.01	0.06	0.06
	1965–1974	0.64	0.04	0.24	0.09	0.88	0.01	0.07	0.05
	1975–1980	0.50	0.03	0.31	0.15	0.82	0.01	0.12	0.06
	1981–1990	0.44	0.02	0.29	0.25	0.75	0.01	0.15	0.09
	1991–2001	0.38	0.01	0.23	0.38	0.72	0.01	0.15	0.13
	2002–2008	0.38	0.01	0.19	0.42	0.70	0.01	0.14	0.15
	2009–2019	0.34	0.01	0.14	0.51	0.66	0.01	0.13	0.21

Source: For 1940–1960, the data are from Winship and Mare (1991): 182–184, table 1, where married denotes married spouse present; divorced/separated includes divorced, separated, and married, spouse absent. For 1965–2019, author's calculations, March CPS, 1965–2019, were married includes both spouse present and spouse absent. Data for 1965–2019 includes Non-Latinx White and Non-Latinx Blacks

population has been declining since 1940; albeit, the probability of widowhood among African Americans is often higher than the probability of widowhood among Whites. The percentage of African American men and women who are currently divorced or separated has tended to decline since 1980. Additionally, except among teens, the current rate of divorced or separated persons is higher among African Americans than among Whites. For all age groups and for both racial groups, there has been a large and mostly continuous rise in the incidence of never-married men and women during 1940–2019. This pattern is particularly pronounced among African Americans. By the late 1970s, marriage was no longer the statistical norm among African American women and men between ages 24 to 29, that is, young adults who have probably finished their formal schooling, have established their own households, and should have settled into stable work situations. Among African American males during 2009–2019, 15 percent were married, versus 62.1 percent during 1965–1974. More than 8 of every 10 of these men (81.1 percent) had never-married during 2009–2019, while nearly 3 of every 10 (29.7 percent) had never-married during 1965–1974. Among 24- to 29-year-old African American women during 2009–2019, 18.1 percent were married versus nearly 58.8 percent during 1965–1974. During the immediate post-Jim Crow era, only 19.9 percent of these women had never-married, but by 2009–2019 a large majority (76.3 percent) had never-married.

Among African American men in their 30s, the fraction currently married plummeted from 72.9 percent in 1965–1974 to 38.4 percent in 2009–2019. Today, by ages 30–39, only 33.5 percent of African American women are currently married and 51.1 percent have never-married. For White women in their 30s, 65.9 percent are currently married and 20.8 percent have never-married. The rise of never-married White women and men is trailing African Americans by about one generation. For example, 52.9 percent of White women aged 24–29 were never-married during 2009–2019, moderately higher than the African American rate of 49.8 percent during the 1980s. Similarly, 20.8 percent of White women aged 30–39 were never-married during 2009–2019, lower than the African American rate of 31.3 percent during the late 1970s.

Among White males aged 24–29, 66.2 percent were never-married during 2009–2019, about the same as the African American rate of 67.5 percent during the 1990s but lower than the African American rate of 73.9 percent during the 2000s. More than 29 percent of White men aged 30–39 were never-married during 2009–2019, the same as the African American rate of 29 percent during the 1980s.

The decline in marriage among African Americans (and Whites) means that the fraction of births to unmarried women would have increased from (say) the mid-1960s onward, even if the average number of births per woman aged 15 to 44 had remained the same. The decline in marriage also would have led to an increase in the fraction of children living in families with only a mother present.

Persons who are not currently married may be co-habiting, that is, sharing a residence for an extended period with a romantic partner but not legally married. Moreover, some currently married persons were previously married. Hence, the fraction of persons currently divorced or separated is not the same as the fraction of persons who were ever divorced, separated, or who have ended co-habitation. The data in Table 6.3 omit entry into or exit from co-habitation. Given that a divorce occurs, Whites are more likely than African Americans to re-partner, that is, to re-marry or to co-habit after divorce (McNamee and Raley, 2011).

Some unmarried mothers are cohabiting, that is, these unmarried mothers live in two-parent families, but the parents are not legally married. Of all the births to unmarried Non-Latinx Black women in 2002, 29 percent were to mothers who were cohabiting at the time of the birth.[1] For 2006–2010 this figure was just under 35 percent. Cohabiting mothers were an even higher percentage of births to unmarried Latinx mothers and Non-Latinx White mothers. Cohabiting mothers were 51 percent and 68 percent of births to unmarried Latinx women in 2002 and 2006–2010, respectively. Cohabiting Non-Latinx White mothers were 40 percent and 68 percent for these two periods, respectively.

6.2 SCHOOLING AND FAMILY STRUCTURE

Trends in marital status for 18–39 years old by race, sex, and years of education are presented Table 6.4. Three patters are evident in the data: the probability of marriage increases with years of education, especially during the most recent period; there is a decline in marriage for men and women in all education groups; and the least educated persons have had the greatest decline in marriage.

Consider 2009–2019. The marriage rates for African American women are: 12 percent (Dropout, 11 or fewer years of education), 14 percent (High School, 12 years of education), 19 percent (Some College, 13–15 years of education), 31 percent (Bachelor's degree), and 42 percent (Graduate degree). The marriage rates for White women are much higher: 23 percent (Dropout), 37 percent (High School), 37 percent (Some College), 53 percent (Bachelor's degree), and 65 percent (Graduate degree).

There is a similar pattern among men. For 2009–2019 the marriage rates for African American men are: 10 percent (Dropout), 14 percent (High School), 20 percent (Some College), 33 percent (Bachelor's degree), and 49 percent (Graduate degree). The marriage rates of White men without college attendance are two times the rate of similarly educated African American men, but this

[1] Child Trends Databank (2015). Births to unmarried women. Available at: www.childtrends.org/?indicators=births-to-unmarried-women. Last accessed August 1, 2019.

TABLE 6.4. *Marital status of persons 18–39 years old, by race, gender, and years of education: 1965–2019*

	African American Women						White Women					
Dropout	1965–1974	1975–1980	1981–1990	1991–2001	2002–2008	2009–2019	1965–1974	1975–1980	1981–1990	1991–2001	2002–2008	2009–2019
Married	0.52	0.32	0.22	0.15	0.13	0.12	0.76	0.65	0.54	0.42	0.30	0.23
Prev. Married	0.23	0.26	0.20	0.14	0.09	0.06	0.09	0.13	0.16	0.16	0.12	0.10
Never Married	0.25	0.42	0.58	0.72	0.78	0.83	0.16	0.22	0.30	0.42	0.58	0.67
N	10,539	5,146	7,103	4,371	3,987	3,808	42,814	19,854	25,637	14,534	12,398	11,342
High School												
Married	0.53	0.40	0.33	0.26	0.23	0.14	0.75	0.68	0.62	0.59	0.50	0.37
Prev. Married	0.16	0.20	0.19	0.16	0.12	0.07	0.05	0.09	0.12	0.14	0.13	0.11
Never Married	0.31	0.40	0.49	0.58	0.65	0.79	0.20	0.23	0.26	0.28	0.37	0.53
N	8,954	7,066	13,962	11,172	11,412	5,600	87,463	58,526	97,634	59,880	46,147	17,057
Some College												
Married	0.45	0.34	0.34	0.29	0.26	0.19	0.59	0.55	0.52	0.49	0.44	0.37
Prev. Married	0.12	0.17	0.17	0.15	0.12	0.09	0.04	0.08	0.10	0.11	0.11	0.10
Never Married	0.42	0.49	0.50	0.56	0.62	0.72	0.37	0.37	0.38	0.40	0.46	0.54
N	2,611	2,886	6,889	9,065	10,786	14,814	28,552	26,376	53,257	58,225	56,523	60,966
Bachelor's Degree												
Married	0.65	0.48	0.45	0.39	0.37	0.31	0.74	0.68	0.61	0.60	0.59	0.53
Prev. Married	0.09	0.13	0.14	0.11	0.12	0.10	0.03	0.06	0.07	0.07	0.06	0.06
Never Married	0.27	0.40	0.41	0.50	0.52	0.60	0.23	0.27	0.32	0.33	0.35	0.41
N	891	972	2,256	2,708	4,033	5,718	13,747	13,184	28,905	32,729	34,063	41,943

(continued)

TABLE 6.4. (*continued*)

	African American Women						White Women					
Graduate Degree												
Married	0.63	0.53	0.52	0.46	0.46	0.42	0.68	0.64	0.62	0.65	0.68	0.65
Prev. Married	0.10	0.13	0.15	0.11	0.10	0.09	0.05	0.09	0.09	0.07	0.06	0.06
Never Married	0.27	0.34	0.34	0.44	0.44	0.49	0.27	0.27	0.29	0.28	0.27	0.29
N	240	383	913	668	1,332	2,574	4,041	5,714	13,853	9,255	11,308	18,449
Drop out	1965–1974	1975–1980	1981–1990	1991–2001	2002–2008	2009–2019	1965–1974	1975–1980	1981–1990	1991–2001	2002–2008	2009–2019
Married	0.49	0.34	0.22	0.13	0.11	0.10	0.66	0.54	0.42	0.34	0.24	0.20
Prev. Married	0.09	0.10	0.10	0.08	0.05	0.04	0.04	0.06	0.09	0.10	0.08	0.06
Never Married	0.43	0.56	0.68	0.79	0.84	0.86	0.31	0.40	0.48	0.57	0.67	0.74
N	8,434	4,159	5,861	3,550	3,357	3,696	40,273	19,119	27,518	16,822	14,840	13,340
High School												
Married	0.53	0.44	0.34	0.28	0.24	0.14	0.67	0.58	0.52	0.47	0.39	0.30
Prev. Married	0.07	0.10	0.10	0.10	0.08	0.05	0.03	0.06	0.09	0.11	0.09	0.08
Never Married	0.40	0.46	0.56	0.62	0.68	0.80	0.30	0.36	0.40	0.42	0.52	0.62
N	6,000	5,066	10,260	9,129	9,852	5,555	65,062	47,764	86,140	61,098	48,962	20,998
Some College												
Married	0.47	0.40	0.35	0.31	0.27	0.20	0.52	0.50	0.46	0.42	0.37	0.32
Prev. Married	0.07	0.10	0.11	0.09	0.07	0.06	0.02	0.06	0.07	0.07	0.06	0.06
Never Married	0.46	0.50	0.54	0.60	0.66	0.74	0.46	0.45	0.47	0.51	0.57	0.62
N	1,959	2,272	4,915	5,822	7,297	10,381	31,562	27,559	50,123	50,617	46,439	51,550

Bachelor's Degree												
Married	0.67	0.50	0.47	0.41	0.41	0.33	0.74	0.64	0.58	0.54	0.54	0.47
Prev. Married	0.05	0.10	0.09	0.07	0.07	0.05	0.02	0.05	0.06	0.05	0.04	0.04
Never Married	0.28	0.41	0.44	0.52	0.52	0.62	0.24	0.31	0.36	0.41	0.42	0.49
N	585	634	1,584	1,924	2,611	3,885	15,226	14,484	29,525	29,052	27,334	33,394
Graduate Degree												
Married	0.71	0.57	0.54	0.43	0.54	0.49	0.77	0.71	0.66	0.67	0.69	0.65
Prev. Married	0.05	0.10	0.10	0.07	0.06	0.07	0.02	0.06	0.06	0.05	0.04	0.03
Never Married	0.24	0.33	0.36	0.50	0.41	0.44	0.20	0.23	0.28	0.28	0.27	0.32
N	235	358	796	480	736	1,304	10,871	10,622	19,262	10,243	9,387	12,852

ratio is lower among men who have attended college. In particular, the marriage rates for White men are: 20 percent (Dropout), 30 percent (High School), 32 percent (Some College), 47 percent (Bachelor's degree), and 65 percent (Graduate degree).

The marital status trend of African American women with some college education is illustrative of the trends in marital status of all African American women. During the first decade after the end of servitude capitalism, 42 percent of Black women with 13–15 years of education were never married. This number increased to 49 percent and 50 percent during 1975–1980 and 1981–1990, respectively. For 1991–2001 and 2002–2008, 56 percent and 62 percent of African American women with some college education were never married. Finally, this number peaked at 72 percent during 2000–2019. White women with some college education experienced the same trend in marital status as African American women, though the levels were lower.

Forty-six percent of Black men with 13–15 years of education were never married in 1965–1974 and this number rose to 74 percent during 2009–2019. For dropouts and high school graduates, the percentage of African American men who were never married rose from 43 percent to 86 percent and from 40 percent to 86 percent, respectively, during 1965–2019. For African American men with bachelor's degrees and graduate degrees, the never married percentage rose from 28 percent to 62 percent and from 24 percent to 44 percent, respectively, between 1965–1974 and 2009–2019. White male changes in marital status were similar to changes in the marital status trends of African American men.

6.3 BIRTHS AND MARITAL STATUS

There has been an increase in the percentage of children born to unmarried women in every American racial and ethnic group. For example, in 1969, 35 percent of African American births were to unmarried women (Figure 6.1). Just seven years later, in 1976, half of African American children were born to unmarried women. During the 1990s the rate of births to unmarried women stalled for African Americans: 71 percent and 72 percent of African American children were born to unmarried women during 1994 and 2019, respectively. Twenty-one percent of White children were born to unmarried women during 1994 and 30 percent of White children were born to unmarried women during 2019. At 30 percent, the rate of children born to unmarried White women is nearly two generations behind African American women but the White rate has been growing rapidly. The White rate increased by a factor of 6 between 1969 and 2019, moving from 5 percent to 30 percent.

Fifty-four percent of American Indian and Native Alaskan children were born to unmarried women during 1990 and 68 percent of American Indian and Native Alaskan children were born to unmarried women during 2019.

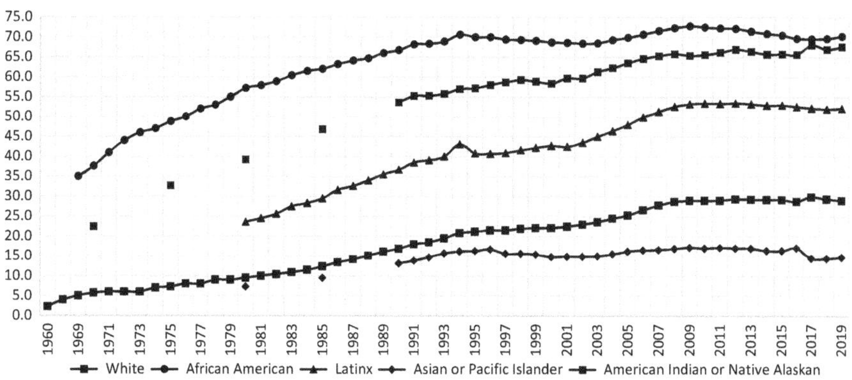

FIGURE 6.1. Percent of births to unmarried women, by race and ethnicity, 1960–2019
Sources: US Dept of Health and Human Services, National Center for Health Statistics, Vital Statistics of the United States, Volume I, Natality, 1993, page 199, for 1960–1980. Data by race and Hispanic origin for 1980–1989: US Department of Health and Human Services, Centers for Disease Control and Prevention, National Center for Health Statistics (2014). Health, United States, 2013 [table 5]. Hyattsville, MD: Author. Retrieved from www.cdc.gov/nchs/hus/previous .htm#tables. Last accessed February 3, 2022. All other data for 1960–1999: Ventura, S. J., and Bachrach, C. A. (2000). Nonmarital childbearing in the United States, 1940-1999 [table 4]. National Vital Statistics Reports, 48(16). Retrieved from www.cdc.gov/nchs/data/nvsr/nvsr48/ nvs48_16.pdf. Last accessed December 14, 2022. Data for 2000–2006: US Department of Health and Human Services, Centers for Disease Control and Prevention, National Center for Health Statistics (2002–2009). Births: Final data for 2000–2006. Hyattsville, MD: Author. Retrieved from www.cdc.gov/nchs/products/nvsr.htm. Last accessed December 14, 2022. Data for 2007–2016: US Department of Health and Human Services, Centers for Disease Control and Prevention, National Center for Health Statistics (2018). CDC WONDER [Data tool]. Hyattsville, MD: Author. Retrieved from http://wonder.cdc.gov/natality-current.html. Last accessed December 14, 2022. Race/ethnicity data for 2016–2019 are calculated using bridged race estimates to remain comparable with previous years. Data for estimates before 1980 are based on the race/ethnicity of the child, from 1980 on estimates are based on the race/ethnicity of the mother. Before 1980 data for the mother's marital status was estimated for the United States from data for registration areas in which marital status of the mother was reported. For 1980 on, data for States in which the mother's marital status was not reported were inferred from other items on the birth certificate and included with data from the reporting States. Latinx exclude data for New Hampshire and Oklahoma which did not report Hispanic origin on the birth certificate

From 1980 to 2008, the percentage of Latinx children born to unmarried mothers rose from 24 percent to 53 percent, where it stabilized through 2019. Thirteen percent of Asian American and Pacific Islander children were born to unmarried mothers in 1990, while 17 percent were born to unmarried mothers in 2017, falling to 15 percent during 2019.

The trends of Figure 6.1 do not tell us whether the secular rise in the rate of children born to unmarried women is due to rising fertility rates among unmarried women or increases in the fraction of unmarried women. From at least the

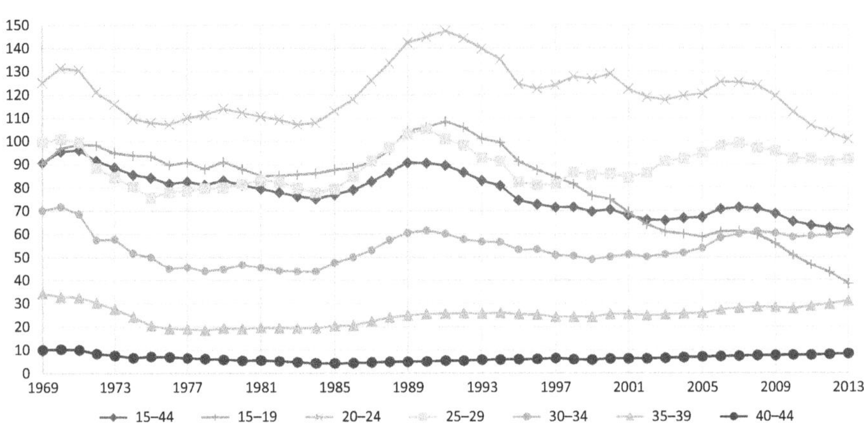

FIGURE 6.2. Birth rates for unmarried women by age of mother: African Americans, 1969–1993 (rates are live births to unmarried women per 1,000 unmarried women in specified group. Beginning 1970 excludes births to nonresidents of the US)
Source: US Dept of Health and Human Services, National Center for Health Statistics, Vital Statistics of the United States, Volume I, Natality, 1993, page 205. See notes accompanying table 6 for additional details. Martin, J. A., Hamilton, B. E., Osterman, M. J. K., et al. Births: Final data for 2013. National vital statistics reports; vol 64, no 1. Hyattsville, MD: National Center for Health Statistics. 2015

late 1950s to the mid-1980s, fertility rates for both African American and White women were on a downward trend.[2] Therefore, *absolute* increases in fertility rates cannot explain the increase in the incidence of births to unmarried African American women. Rather, the increase in the fraction of births to unmarried African American women is due to an increase in their *relative* fertility, that is, their fertility has fallen less than the declining fertility rate among married African American women. In other words, the fertility rates of both married and unmarried African American women have fallen; however, the fertility rate of married women has declined at a faster pace.

For example, in 1970 there were 96 births per 1,000 unmarried African American women aged 15–44 and 130 births per 1,000 married African American women aged 15–44 (see Figure 6.2). By 1986, the fertility rate for both groups of African American women was 79 births per 1,000 women. Indeed, for each year from 1987 to 1993 the fertility rate of unmarried African American women exceeded the rate for married African American women. This is a historic reversal of African American fertility rates by marital status.

The fertility rate of unmarried White women increased from 14 births per 1,000 unmarried women aged 15–44 in 1970 to 25 births per 1,000

[2] See Bianchi and Spain (1986) for data on the years prior to 1969.

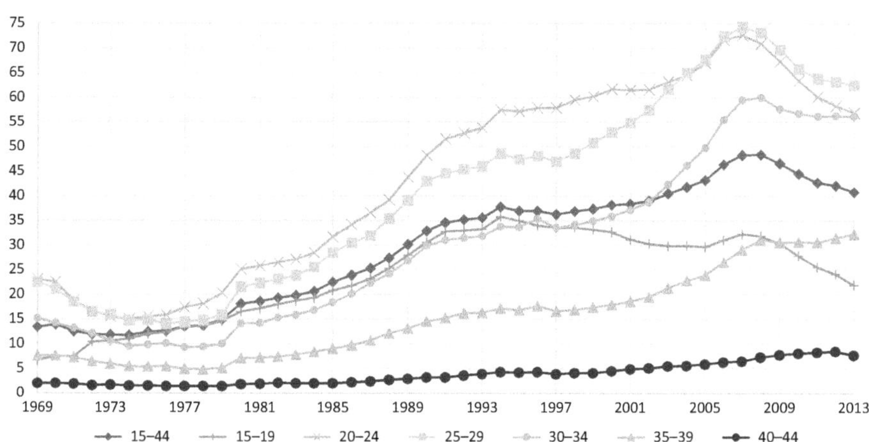

FIGURE 6.3. Birth rates for unmarried women by age of mother: Whites, 1969–2013 (rates are live births to unmarried women per 1,000 unmarried women in specified group. Beginning 1970 excludes births to nonresidents of the US)
Source: US Dept of Health and Human Services, National Center for Health Statistics, Vital Statistics of the United States, Volume I, Natality, 1993, pages 200–201. See notes accompanying table 6 for additional details. Martin, J. A., Hamilton, B. E., Osterman, M. J. K., et al. Births: Final data for 2013. National vital statistics reports; vol 64, no 1. Hyattsville, MD: National Center for Health Statistics. 2015

unmarried women aged 15–44 in 1987 (Figure 6.3). During 1970–1987, the fertility rate of married White women aged 15–44 declined from 120 to 91. Indeed, the fertility rate of married White women had declined to 88 per 1,000 by 1993.

As the fertility rate of unmarried African American women declined by 9 points the fertility rate of unmarried White women increased by 11 points. Also, the considerably more rapid decline in the fertility rate of married African American women, in comparison to married White women, saw the fertility rate of married African American women fall below the fertility rate of married White women from 1979 onward. This, too, is a historic reversal of relative interracial trends (US Department of Health and Human Services, 1993: 203–205, table 6). Summing up, the increase in the proportion of births to unmarried African American women has two sources: the decline in marriage and the fertility rate of married women declined faster than the fertility rate of unmarried women.

6.4 MEASURING MALE MARGINALIZATION

Increasing years of education during 1965–2019 likely explains the decline in marriage among 16–24 year-old men and women during this period. As young people spend more time in school, they delay their entry into marriage. Male marginalization provides an explanation for rise in fraction of never-married persons of 25–39 years of age. To the extent that men are expected to be "providers" or "breadwinners" of families, there is a relatively stronger economic requirement for male marriage eligibility, as women are more likely to be eligible for marriage regardless of employment status. The increases in female-headed households, fraction of never-married African Americans, and formerly married persons are caused by economic marginalization – social unwantedness and economic redundancy – of African American males. This perspective provides an economic explanation of family structure that is conformable with a social-psychological explanation of family functioning, that is, the dissolution of marriages is attributable to male provider role strain due to declining wages and employment for men (Bowman, 1988, 1989; Bowman and Sanders, 1998).

There are multiple measures of mate availability. Cox (1940) emphasized the importance of the sex ratio, a demographic variable that is captured by the total number of unmarried men within an age-group divided by the total number of unmarried women within the same age-group.

$$\text{Sex ratio} = \frac{\text{All unmarried women in age} - \text{group}}{\text{All unmarried women in age} - \text{group}} = \frac{UM}{UW}.$$

As a measure of mate availability, the sex ratio assumes that all unmarried males are marriage-eligible. For example, if there are 900 unmarried men aged 24–29 and 1,000 unmarried women aged 24–29 then the sex ratio $\equiv \frac{UM}{UW} =$ 0.90. For this example, the sex ratio suggests that for persons 24–29 years-old there are only 900 marriageable men for every 1,000 marriageable women. Ten percent of unmarried women will be unable to find a spouse; if these women wish to have children, they will be single parents.

The sex ratio omits economic considerations for determining the pool of marriage-eligible males. Suppose a man is eligible for marriage if he is (1) unmarried and (2) employed full-time or in the military (Wilson and Neckerman, 1986). For a given age-group, this measure of Wilsons' male marriageable pool index (MMPI.1) is the total number of unmarried males in an age-group eligible for marriage divided by the total number of unmarried women within an age-group, that is, $\text{MMPI.1} = \frac{UM(ft+m)}{UW}$, where ft is the fraction of unmarried men employed fulltime and m is the fraction of unmarried men enlisted in the military. In the absence of full employment, Wilsons' male marriageable pool index (MMPI.1) < sex ratio should do a better job of explaining changes in family structure. Suppose, for example, there are 900 unmarried men aged 24–29 and 1,000 unmarried women aged 24–29, the fraction of men with fulltime employment (ft) = 0.62, and the fraction of men in the military (m) = 0.03, then MMPI.1 = 0.585. The male marriageable pool index implies that 585 unmarried 24–29 years old men are marriage-eligible per 1,000 unmarried 24–29 years old women, but 315 men per 1,000 women are marginalized and not eligible for marriage. The demographic shortage combines with the job shortage to cause an increase in the probability of single parent families.

An alternative construction of Wilson's male marriageable pool index focuses on income rather than employment. A person employed fulltime but part-year or part-time but full-year might earn sufficient income to be marriage-eligible. Some individuals employed fulltime and full-year may not have sufficient income to be marriage-eligible. The income-based definition of mate availability is MMPI.2 $= \frac{UM^{*}i}{UW}$, where for unmarried men of a given age-group, *i* is the fraction of men with income at or above a certain level, for example, the fraction of men with income at or above the poverty level for a family of three persons. Suppose, for example, there are 900 unmarried men aged 24–29 and 1,000 unmarried women aged 24–29 and 72 percent of unmarried men earn sufficient income to support a family of three, MMPI.2 = 0.648 and there will be 648 marriage-eligible men for every 1,000 unmarried women.

The Darity-Myers Index (DMI.1) of mate availability adds an education component to the MMPI: DMI.1 = the total number of unmarried men either employed, in the military, or enrolled in school divided by the fraction of unmarried women, that is, DMI.1 $= \frac{UM(ft+m+e)}{UW}$, where *e* is the fraction of unmarried males within a given age-group who are currently enrolled in school. So, MMPI.1 $\leq$ DMI.1 $\leq$ sex ratio. Suppose, for example, for men and women aged 24–29, UM = 900, UW = 1,000, ft = 0.62, m = 0.03, and e = 0.20, then DMI.1 = 0.765 and there are 765 marriage-eligible males per 1,000 unmarried women.

There are additional details associated with the Darity-Myers discussion of male marginalization. In particular, the complete Darity-Myers (DMI.2) discussion of male marginalization emphasizes male institutionalization (involvement with the criminal legal system); premature death and disability; and whether the individual has any children. Marginalized males are clearly unavailable as mates if they have suffered premature death (violent crimes and accidents) or if they are involuntarily institutionalized, for example, jail/prison or hospital. If not involuntarily institutionalized, marginalized males may be economically unsuitable as mates due to insufficient or unstable earnings. Marginalized males may be socially unsuitable as mates because of current participation in illegal activities. Marginalization may also result from insufficient access to health care and information, as well as from over-representation in hazardous work, for example, combat assignment in the military or hazardous industrial employment. Males may also be considered unsuitable for marriage if they have children from a previous relationship. In this case, the Darity-Myers index is:

$$\text{DMI.2} = \frac{\hat{UM}\ x\ (1-a)\ x\ (ft+m+e)\ x\ (1-c)\ x\ (1-k)}{UW},$$

Where, for a given age-group of unmarried males, $\widehat{UM}$ is the number of unmarried that would exist in the absence of premature death, a is the fraction of individuals subject to premature death and disability; c is the fraction of persons in jail, on probation, on parole, or involved in illegal activities; and k is the fraction of men with pre-existing children.

Suppose, for example, for men and women aged 24–29, $\widehat{UM} = 1{,}000$, $UW = 1{,}000$, $a = 0.10$, $ft = 0.62$, $m = 0.03$, $e = 0.20$, $c = 0.25$, $k = 0.25$, then DMI.2 = 0.43 and there are just 430 marriage-eligible males per 1,000 unmarried women.

The complete Darity-Myers Index (DMI.2) has important policy suggestions. To the extent that marriage is a desirable social goal, we can increase marriage by reducing premature deaths and disability, increasing employment and college enrollment, reducing contact with the criminal legal system and reducing incentives for criminal behavior, and reducing premarital births and dissolution of unions when children are present.

Alternative estimates of male marriage-eligibility by age and by race are presented in Table 6.5. By any measure of mate availability, there is a shortage of African American men. On the other hand, the sex ratio shows a surplus of unmarried White men. For all measures of mate availability and for all age-groups, White women have a relatively larger group of marriage-eligible males from which to select a spouse. For example, during 1964–1973 there were 895 unmarried African American males per 1,000 unmarried African American women among 18–24 years old, but 1,199 unmarried White males per 1,000 unmarried White females. The African American sex ratio declines with age, falling to just 544 men per 1,000 women for persons 35–44 years of age. Between 1964–1973 and 1990–2000 and between 1964–1973 and 1974–1979, the African American sex ratio decreased for the youngest and oldest age groups, respectively. For example, in 1964–1973 the African American sex ratio was 0.544, for 35–44 years old, but it was 0.526 during 1974–1979, before rising to 0.672 in the most recent period.

For 1964–1973, if we restrict our attention to the ratio of unmarried and fulltime employed men per unmarried women, there are 791 marriage-eligible men per 1,000 women among 25–34 years old African Americans. Among Whites, this ratio is higher, 849 unmarried and fulltime employed 25–34 years old men per 1,000 unmarried women. After the Great Recession, the ratio of unmarried and fulltime employed men per unmarried woman is 617 marriage-eligible men per 1,000 women among 25–34 years old African Americans and 757 unmarried and fulltime employed 25–34 years old White men per 1,000 unmarried White women. Using an income criterion to determine male mate availability yields a similar pattern. For example, during 1964–1973 if we consider only those males with income above the poverty threshold for a family of four are considered marriage eligible there are 841 marriageable African American males per 1,000 unmarried women at 25–34 years old. This ratio declines to 815 men per 1,000 women by 2008–2018.

TABLE 6.5 *Mate availability by race, 1964–2018*

		African American					
		1964–1973	1974–1979	1981–1989	1990–2000	2001–2007	2008–2018
Age 18–24	Sex ratio	0.895	0.852	0.836	0.821	0.858	0.927
	Fulltime employment	0.560	0.501	0.432	0.398	0.376	0.295
	No children present	0.442	0.515	0.599	0.652	0.697	0.830
	Above poverty income	0.754	0.758	0.724	0.774	0.776	0.754
Age 25–34	Sex ratio	0.570	0.614	0.708	0.710	0.697	0.753
	Fulltime employment	0.791	0.757	0.686	0.714	0.678	0.617
	No children present	0.809	0.845	0.860	0.862	0.853	0.866
	Above poverty income	0.841	0.855	0.796	0.826	0.828	0.815
Age 35–44	Sex ratio	0.544	0.526	0.568	0.646	0.660	0.672
	Fulltime employment	0.801	0.726	0.688	0.673	0.689	0.635
	No children present	0.865	0.871	0.881	0.876	0.866	0.810
	Above poverty income	0.796	0.822	0.771	0.787	0.821	0.791
White							
Age 18–24	Sex ratio	1.199	1.192	1.140	1.086	1.061	1.054
	Fulltime employment	0.550	0.620	0.572	0.525	0.478	0.398
	No children present	0.512	0.584	0.681	0.717	0.728	0.844
	Above poverty income	0.925	0.931	0.910	0.905	0.890	0.868
Age 25–34	Sex ratio	1.170	1.179	1.204	1.198	1.091	1.075
	Fulltime employment	0.849	0.837	0.829	0.837	0.822	0.757
	No children present	0.889	0.911	0.925	0.921	0.912	0.900
	Above poverty income	0.943	0.936	0.922	0.921	0.918	0.899
Age 35–44	Sex ratio	0.819	0.832	0.908	1.080	1.022	1.000
	Fulltime employment	0.864	0.844	0.834	0.816	0.801	0.757
	No children present	0.890	0.888	0.878	0.887	0.873	0.820
	Above poverty income	0.925	0.927	0.903	0.904	0.896	0.880

Source: Author's calculations. Current Population Survey, Annual Demographic Files, Various Years

6.5 FAMILY FUNCTIONING

Family structure is not the same as family functioning (Hill, 1993). Family structure refers to the demographic composition of family members, that is, whether a family has children, whether a family is nuclear or extended, whether a family with children has a single parent or multiple parents, or whether a family is blended or all the children in the family have the same two biological parents. Family functioning refers to the quality of interpersonal relationships within the family and, in particular, whether the quality of interpersonal relationships nurture emotional, social, and economic well-being. Too often in both scholarly and popular discussion "single parent" (a description of family structure) is synonymous with "dysfunctional values, behavior, or family culture" (a description of family functioning).

The Darity-Myers focus on the marginalization of African American males and Bowen's analysis of male provider role strain within families and its ripple effects and wives and children provides important causal explanations for the disproportionate decline of marriage among African Americans. Provider role strain establishes an explanation of the casual link from joblessness to family functioning to transitions in family structure (Bowman, 1988, 1989; Bowman and Sanders, 1998). Male provider role strain occurs when a husband becomes unemployed, underemployed, or otherwise unable to secure sufficient income to function as the primary economic provider for his family. Joblessness and economic isolation create economic insecurity for African American males. This economic insecurity may take the form of an inability to find work or an inability to find stable work at a family-supporting wage. Consequently, African American males subject to the forces of joblessness and economic isolation suffer provider role strain. Provider role strain is likely to be most intense for two groups of men: prime age working class men who have been laid off or who face an insecure employment future; and young working class men facing a future of limited employment opportunities.

Provider role strain suffered by African American men has "ripple effects" within the family. Mothers, who bear the primary responsibility for childcare, are forced to take on additional responsibilities. Teenage children of fathers suffering from provider role strain also feel the pressure to replace the income which the father might normally provide. Male provider role strain then increases the role strain on mothers and teenage children and affects the quality of family life.

6.5.1 Intrafamily Transfers

Married couples, co-habiting couples, and single parent families are constituents of kinship networks, which provide resources for family functioning. This kinship network includes grandparents, parental siblings, and other significant persons. The kinship network is bound together through transfers of information and material resources, intra-family allocation of time and provision of services, and integration into nonfamily networks and persons embedded in strategic occupations.

Slavery and Jim Crow have a contemporary legacy: persistent and massive wealth inequality between African Americans and Whites; persistent racial differences in poverty; and persistent and extraordinary racial differences in the probability of incarceration. Racial differences in family structures are shaped by these differences and racial differences in family functioning respond to the problems caused by this equality. Intra-family transfers of economic and other resources provide familial insurance against adverse life events, support for the socioeconomic aspirations of younger family members, and support to maintain family stability. Between 9 and 16 percent of families provide monetary assistance to other households and 5–33 percent of households receive monetary assistance (Chiteji and Hamilton, 2002). Middle income African American families are more likely to have poor parents than middle income White families (36 percent versus 8 percent) and are more likely to have poor siblings than White families (34 percent versus 8 percent).[3] Because middle income African American families have greater exposure to poverty within their extended families, intrafamily transfers to parents and siblings is correlated with a reduction of Black middle class wealth accumulation by 3.1 percent and 8.5 percent, respectively, relative to middle class White households.[4] On the other hand, middle class White families have wealthier parents than middle class African American families; bequests and other transfers from wealthy parents to middle class households raise White wealth by 3 percent and 13 percent, respectively, relative to middle class Black households.

The wealth of grandparents also affects the well-being of children. Each $100,000 in grandparental wealth increases the probability of young adult college enrollment by 2–3 percent (Chiteji, 2010). Children whose grandparents have no wealth or negative wealth are 8 percent less likely to have a college fund, 16.4 percent less likely to consider attending a private college, 9 percent less likely to consider post-secondary education, and 9 percent less likely to attend a private elementary or secondary school (Chiteji, 2007).

Siblings are altruistic in a well-functioning family. This means that financial assistance to adult siblings is also an important element of intrafamily transfers. Individuals in economic distress turn to affluent siblings. Serious health

[3] Chiteji and Hamilton define middle class families are families with income within the 21st and 80th percentile of the distribution of income.

[4] Chiteji and Hamilton (2005) show that monetary transfers from affluent family members to nonaffluent family members does not necessarily reduce savings (and, hence, wealth accumulation) for the affluent family member. The monetary transfer may lead to lower consumption by the affluent family member, rather than lower savings. Note 14 of Chiteji and Hamilton indicates that poverty in Black family networks does not have a statistically significant effect on either bank account or stock ownership.

conditions are an expensive economic problem. Middle and upper income persons may have the insurance, income, or savings to pay for health care, while lower income persons may not have the resources to cover health care expenses associated with a serious health condition. Affluent siblings may provide financial support for low income siblings with health problems, even if the assistance lowers their own wealth accumulation. Financial assistance to poor siblings with serious health problems lowers wealth accumulation by $14,000, $42,000, and $154,000 among low, middle, and high income families (Heflin and Chiteji, 2014). Middle and high income persons with serious health problems do not have an economic impact on the wealth accumulation of their siblings. The economic impact of sibling health on wealth accumulation is the same for both Black and White families.

6.6 MALE MARGINALIZATION: LABOR MARKET OUTCOMES

Many studies carried out over a long period of time, using alternative definitions of male marriageability, have consistently found that male marginalization has a negative effect on the marriage rate, especially for African American women. For example, Oliver C. Cox (1940) found that a 10 percentage point increase in the sex ratio was associated with a 4 percent increase in marriage for African American women and 2.8 percent increase in marriage for White women. Observing never-married and newly-married persons of 16–39 years old for 1940–1980, Winship and Mare (1991) calculated the determinants of the timing of first marriage. They found that, for African American males a 0.10 increase in the expected probability of employment after marriage increased the odds of marriage by 25 percent for African American men aged 20–23 years old and by 15 percent for African American men aged 30–39.[5] Mare and Winship found that decreases in expected employment account for roughly 20 percent of the decline in the probability of marriage among African American males aged 16–29 and 14 percent of the decline for African American males aged 30–39.

Hoffman and Duncan (1995) examined the economic determinants of divorce for women entering into their first marriage between 1967 and 1983. Regardless of race, husband's earnings had a positive impact on remaining married. For their data, the cumulative baseline divorce rates at 5, 10, and 15 years were 22.50 percent, 31.50 percent, and 39.50 percent. The simulated effect on the baseline divorce rates of a 25 percent increase in husband's earnings show that divorce would decline for all women, roughly 8 percent, with the steepest percentage point declines for marriages of 1–3 years duration:

[5] "A $100 increase in weekly earnings raised the odds of marriage by about 30 percent for Black men age 20–23 and by about 20 percent for those age 30–39. The employment and earnings effects for White men were remarkably similar to those for Black men in every age group. For both races, these effects were large" (Winship and Mare, 1991: 191).

falling to 20.90 percent, 29.40 percent, and 36.90 percent after 5, 10, and 15 years, respectively.

Lichter et al. (1992) focused on women 23–28 years of age who responded affirmatively to the query of whether marriage was anticipated in the next five years and the unmarried male–unmarried female marriageability ratio according the woman's race, age, and labor market area. African American women are 51 percent as likely to enter first marriage as White women if one does not statistically control for male marriageability. However, when one controls for male marriageability, young African American women are 71 percent as likely to enter first marriage as young White women.[6] Similarly, if the sample is restricted to women who expect to marry within five years, the relative probability of marriage increases from 46 percent to 59 percent when the pool of full-time employed men is included as an explanatory factor. These estimates show that 24–41 percent of the interracial difference in entry into first marriage is due to African American male marginality.

Craigie, Myers, and Darity (2018) focus on families headed by never-married women at least 18 years of age and use the Darity-Myers index (DMI.1) to measure mate availability for the labor market area/commuting zone where the woman resides. Analyzing data for 1980–2010, their best estimate shows that a 10 percentage point increase in the marriageability index will reduce African American never-married female headship by 7.88 percentage points.[7]

Ruggles (2021) examines entry into first marriage for Non-Latinx Black and White men during 1960–2019. Marriageability is determined by income decile position, employment status, and institutionalization (employed, not employed but worked last year, did not work last year, and institutional residence), occupation (professional, managerial, skilled; clerical, sales, operative; service and laborers; no occupation in last five years), and age. During 1960 and 1970, Black men in the first–seventh income deciles had higher marriage rates than White males. By 1980, Black men in the first–fourth income deciles had higher rates of entry into marriage than White males and the marriage rates were nearly equal for the fifth and sixth income deciles. During 2008–2010 and 2017–2019 Black males in the second and third deciles had higher rates of entry into marriage.

During 1960 the racial marriage gap was 15.6, in particular, 152.3 African American men per 1,000 entered marriage for the first time and 167.9 White

[6] In fact, when the pool of full-time employed men is included in the model the coefficient on the race variable becomes statistically insignificant.

[7] This estimate is derived from their probit equation with instrumental variable estimation of male marriageability for a woman of 25–29 years old, with one child, some college education, and with controls for median family earnings, maximum public assistance benefits, and the male incarceration rate. For the White equation, a 10 percentage point increase in male marriageability causes a 4.12 percentage point increase in the probability of female headed households.

men entered marriage for the first time. Marriage rates fell for both groups of men over the next 60 years and the marriage gap increased. The African American male marriage rates were 112.4 (1970), 66.5 (1980), 27.4 (2008–2010), and 23.1 (2017–2019) and the marriage gaps were 20.8, 28.0, 20.3, and 23.2, respectively.

The interracial marriage gap is small compared to intraracial differences in marriage rates due to differences in economic circumstances. For example, during 1960 African American men at the eighth income decile were 2.2 times as likely as African American men at the third income decile to enter marriage for the first time and the marriage gap for these two groups of Black males was 134.4. The intraracial marriage rate ratio and gaps for affluent (eighth decile) and low income (third decile) African American were 3.2 and 138.8 for 1970, 3.0 and 38.7 for 1980, 3.4 and 38.5 for 2008–2010, and 2.7 and 27.4 for 2017–2019.

Ruggles analysis shows that if African American men had the same economic composition as White men, viz., the same distributions for income decile, employment status and institutionalization, occupation, and age, then the Black male marriage rate would increase by 48.9 for 1960, 30 for 1970, 25.6 for 1980, 14.1 for 2008–2010, and 12.6 for 2017–2019. The racial differences in the economic circumstances of African American and White men more than explain the racial gap in 1960 and 1970, explain nearly all of the racial gap for 1980, and explain 69.4 percent and 54.3 percent of the racial gaps for 2008–2010 and 2017–2019, respectively.[8]

Nakosteen and Zimmer (2019) also examine entry into first marriage for a sample of African American and White men of 18–40 years-old, for 2002–2010. Marriageability is determined by a man's position in the distribution of annual wage earnings: men at the top of the distribution are more marriageable than men at the bottom of the distribution. The earnings process differs for Black and White men. For a given set of observable characteristics, such as age, education, disability status, occupation, and whether the job is unionized, Black men earn less than White men. Earnings also depend on characteristics that are not observed by analysts though they are observed by employers, workers, and potential marriage partners. These "unobserved" characteristics may include racial differences in bargaining power (which is higher for White men), racial differences in the quality of education, or racial differences in promptness, reliability, ambition, and so forth.

The White male difference between actual and predicted earnings based on their observable characteristics is a measure of latent earnings among White men. The Black male difference between actual and "counterfactual" predicted

[8] These numbers are slightly different if White men are the population standard, rather than Black men.

earnings based on their observable characteristics is a measure of latent earnings among Black men, where "counterfactual" predicted earnings are the wages a Black male would receive if the market treated his observable characteristics the same as it treated a White male's observable characteristics. The mean latent earnings of African American men are lower than the mean latent earnings of White men, placing Black men in the lower half of the White male distribution of annual wage earnings. Nakosteen and Zimmer argue that this earnings difference is responsible for the racial difference in marriage, not a racial difference in the preference for marriage.

Without accounting for racial differences in latent earnings, the African American male rate of entry into first marriage is 5.3 percent and the White male rate is 15.6 percent.[9] Using latent earnings for African American men that fit into the top half of the White male earnings distribution, the racial marriage gap slightly favors African Americans, 7.8 percent for high latent earning Black men versus 6.1 percent for high latent earning White men. If the men with no earnings are excluded, then the marriage rates are 8.5 percent and 7.2 percent, for Black and White men, respectively. Comparing low latent earnings White men with Black men with above average latent earnings, the marriage rates are 7.1 percent and 4.7 percent, for Black and White men, respectively, for the whole sample and 21.9 percent and 15.8 percent, for Black and White men, respectively, when zero-earners are excluded. Comparing low latent earnings White men with Black men with high latent earnings, the marriage rates are 5.1 percent and 5.1 percent, for Black and White men, respectively, for the whole sample and 15.3 percent and 10.5 percent, for Black and White men, respectively, when zero-earners are excluded. Finally, comparing low latent earnings White men to Black males with below average latent earnings, the marriage rates are 12.5 percent and 12.8 percent, for Black and White men, respectively, for the whole sample and 6.4 percent and 6.5 percent, for Black and White men, respectively, when zero-earners are excluded.

Nakosteen and Zimmer also examine the probability of marriage when latent earnings are directly included as an explanatory variable. For the full sample a one standard deviation in latent earnings has no effect on the marriage rate but it increases the marriage rate by 1 percentage point when men with no earnings are excluded from the sample. For the full sample the marriage rates are 12.3 percent and 11.5 percent, for Black and White men, respectively, but 6.2 percent and 5.5 percent, for Black and White men, respectively, when zero-earners are excluded.

[9] These percentages are derived from Nakosteen and Zimmer (2019, table 4), where they use a probit equation to estimate movement from never-married status in year t to married status at year $t + 1$. The control variables assume the man is 25 years-old, does not have health limitations on the type or amount of work, has 14 years of education, is not a homeowner, and is never-married in 2009 but possibly entering into marriage in 2010.

6.7 SUMMARY AND DISCUSSION

From 1890 to 1960 and 1970, African American men and women, respectively, were more likely to be married than White men and women (Elliott et al., 2012). Median age at first marriage declined for all four race–gender groups from the end of the nineteenth century through the middle of the twentieth century.[10] African American male median age at first marriage fell from 25 in 1890 to less than 23 in 1950 before leveling out at over 23 in 1960 and 1970. Median age at first marriage was higher for White men, but followed the same trend, from almost 27 in 1890 to 24 in 1970. During 1890–1950, median age at first marriage declined from 23.5 to 21.5 and from 22 to 21 for White and African American women, respectively. After 1950, age at first marriage rose to 26.5 and 30 during 2010 for White and African American women and to 31 and 30 for White and African American men, respectively.

Similarly, the percent never married by age 35 was less than 10 percent for African Americans during 1890–1980 but rose to more than 25 percent by 2010. The percent never married by age 35 was roughly 5 percent during 1890–1950, but rose to more than 25 percent by 2010.[11] The percent never-married by age 35 was lower among African American men than White men during 1890–1950, but increasingly higher during 1960–2010. The percent never-married by age 35 was lower among African American women than White women during 1890–1960, but increasingly higher during 1970–2010.

Interracial economic inequality explains interracial differences in family structure and certain aspects of family functioning. In particular, the male marginalization hypothesis indicates that increases in economic potential among males yield increases in the African American marriage rate, while decreasing the probability of divorce. Simultaneously, an increase in legitimate economic outcomes among males reduces the probability of involvement in illegal economic activities, increasing the ratio of marriageable males and, thereby, raising the probability of marriage.

More employment, better jobs, and greater compensation, especially among African American men with a high school diploma or less, must be at the core of any strategy to increase the likelihood and the stability of marriage among African Americans. Concomitantly, both the scope and the economic attractiveness of illegal activities must be reduced.

[10] See Elliot et al. (2012, graph 4).

[11] See Elliot et al. (2012, graph 4).

PART III

AFRICAN AMERICAN INCOME AND WEALTH, 1965–PRESENT

7

Family Income Growth and Inequality

1965–Present

The Post–World War II Civil Rights Movement (1945–1965) forced the federal government to eliminate legalized racial segregation in public institutions and commercial enterprises within American society, especially among the former Confederate States of America ("the South"). The Black Power Movement (1965–1973) served notice that, after centuries of racism, mere equality of opportunity was not sufficient to satisfy African American demands for racial justice. These revolutionary social movements were characterized by a stunning series of courtroom triumphs by the National Association for the Advancement of Colored People (NAACP) and hosts of other individual activists and organizations, along with a continuing series of economic boycotts, mass protests, monitoring of police and organizing of the urban dispossessed by the Black Panther Party for Self-Defense, and other forms of direct action by countless numbers of individuals and organizations. Actual racial equality in political, economic, social, and cultural affairs was an important goal for "the movement."

Many believed that the rise of new laws forbidding discrimination in the labor, housing, and financial markets, the rise of new legal changes that promoted increased educational opportunities for African Americans, and a series of other important social and economic activities would inexorably and quickly produce a Black middle class and Black elite similar to White America.

7.1 CHANGES IN FAMILY INCOME AND EARNINGS

A family is two or more individuals living in the same household and who are related by blood, marriage, or adoption.[1] Earnings refer to labor market

[1] This is the federal definition of a family used by the Current Population Survey. See Unicon Research Corporation (2007: glossary).

compensation, that is, wages and salaries. Income refers to labor market compensation plus property income (interest, rent, dividends, capital gains) plus public and private transfer payments (unemployment compensation, workers compensation, social security, supplemental security, public assistance and welfare, veteran's benefits, survivor's benefits, disability income, retirement payments, child support, alimony, income from education, financial assistance from friends, and other family income).[2]

Table 7.1 shows that the deep recessions of 1974–1975 and 1981–1982 brought African American economic progress to a standstill; hence, 1974–1989 stands out as a period of relative and absolute reversal for African American economic progress. Similarly, the prolonged boom of the 1990s, when the national unemployment rate dropped from 7.5 percent in 1992 to 4.0 percent in 2000, created the macroeconomic environment for exceptional relative and absolute improvement for African American families.[3] Mean family earnings of African Americans were slightly higher during the 1970s ($37,215) and slightly lower during 1980s ($36,243) than during the late 1960s ($36,922), though median family earnings were nearly $4,000 lower – declining from $31,007 to $26,999 during 1964–1989. African American mean family income also shows a decline between 1973–1979 and 1980–1989. In comparison to the median, the mean places greater weight on extreme values. Therefore, if the mean is higher (lower) than the median it implies that the distribution of income is skewed toward high (low) income families. Whether we examine family earnings or family income, racial equality has shown very little progress since the elimination of Jim Crow. During the late 1970s African American mean family income was 64 percent of White mean family income. During the 2000s African American mean family income was 64 percent of White mean family income. The median African American family earned nearly 57 cents for each dollar of median White family earnings during 1967–1973. This ratio "improved" to

[2] Family earnings include all income from wages and salaries (1963–2019), non-farm self-employment (1963–2019), or farm self-employment from all family members (1963–2019). Public transfer payments include: unemployment compensation (1988–2019), worker compensation (1988–2019), social security and railroad retirement (1976–2019), supplemental security income (1976–2019), public assistance and welfare (1976–2019), veteran pay (1988–2019), survivors benefits (1988–2019), and disability (1988–2019). Property income includes: retirement (1976–2019), interest (1976–2019), dividends (1988–2019), rents (1988–2019), income from education (1988–2019), child support (1988–2019), alimony (1988–2019), financial assistance from private sources (1988–2019), and family income from other sources (1963–2019). Private transfer payments include: income from education (1988–2019), child support (1988–2019), alimony (1988–2019), and financial assistance from private sources (1988–2019). Residual income includes family income from other sources (1963–2019).

[3] The national employment-to-population ratio increased from 61.2 in 1991 to 64.6 in 2000, indicating that the decrease in the unemployment occurred because more Americans were working and not because of a decline in labor force participation. See "Economic Research," Federal Reserve Bank of St. Louis, available at: https://fred.stlouisfed.org/series/EMRATIO. Last accessed December 14, 2022.

TABLE 7.1. *Family earnings and income, by race, 1967–2018*

	White		African American		Ratios	
Earnings	Mean	Median	Mean	Median	Mean	Median
1967–1973	$59,211	$54,582	$36,922	$31,007	0.624	0.568
1974–1979	$59,256	$54,821	$37,215	$29,501	0.628	0.538
1980–1989	$56,434	$49,168	$36,243	$26,999	0.642	0.549
1990–2000	$61,748	$49,488	$40,562	$29,484	0.657	0.596
2001–2007	$69,903	$52,098	$45,234	$32,340	0.647	0.621
2008–2018	$68,984	$49,181	$45,603	$30,405	0.661	0.618
Income					Mean	Median
1967–1973	$63,152	$55,729	$39,181	$31,981	0.620	0.574
1974–1979	$69,155	$61,227	$44,387	$35,709	0.642	0.583
1980–1989	$69,049	$58,427	$43,522	$33,337	0.630	0.571
1990–2000	$75,938	$60,459	$48,698	$36,356	0.641	0.601
2001–2007	$84,303	$63,631	$53,697	$39,031	0.637	0.613
2008–2018	$84,195	$62,276	$54,161	$37,532	0.643	0.603

Income figures are inflation-adjusted using the consumer price index, all urban consumers (March $2011). All families are Non-Latinx. Families include all age-groups. The earnings sample is limited to persons with non-negative earnings and the initial period is for the 1967–1972 work-years.
Source: Author's calculations. Data are from the March Current Population Survey, Annual Social & Economic Supplement, 1965–2019

62 cents per dollar during 2008–2018. This was perverse progress; median White family earnings went down by $4,500, while median African American family earnings declined by $600 – creating downward equalization among median Black and White families but increasing racial inequality among high income families with rising income.

Median African American and White family earnings declined outside the South between 1967–1973 and 2008–2018 (Table 7.2). Specifically, median income on Non-Southern African American families declined for most of the period, falling from $38,807 in 1967–1973 to $30,432 during 2008–2018. For African American families outside of the South, mean family earnings declined from $42,858 during 1967–1973 to $38,897 during the 1980s, before reaching $46,275 in 2008–2018.

African American family earnings were also lower in the South than outside of the South during the 1960s and 1970s. Southern African American families experienced rapid median earnings growth, from $25,602 during 1967–1973 to $27,177 during 1974–1979. The income of Southern African American families declined during the 1980s, before rising to $32,038 and $30,360 during 2001–2007 and 2008–2018, respectively.

Regional inequality in family earnings was eliminated during 1964–2018. In 1964–1973 Southern African American mean earnings were 35 percent lower

TABLE 7.2. *Family earnings by region, 1967–2018*

	African American		White		Racial Ratio	
	Mean	Median	Mean	Median	Mean	Median
Non-South						
1967–1973	$42,858	$38,807	$61,261	$56,936	0.700	0.682
1974–1979	$40,657	$33,188	$61,030	$56,660	0.666	0.586
1980–1989	$38,897	$29,076	$57,883	$51,003	0.672	0.570
1990–2000	$42,435	$30,631	$63,554	$51,597	0.668	0.594
2001–2007	$46,657	$32,807	$71,932	$54,315	0.649	0.604
2008–2018	$46,275	$30,432	$71,252	$51,586	0.649	0.590
South						
1967–1973	$31,640	$25,602	$54,020	$48,712	0.586	0.526
1974–1979	$34,098	$27,177	$55,075	$49,543	0.619	0.549
1980–1989	$33,997	$25,119	$53,328	$45,167	0.638	0.556
1990–2000	$39,078	$28,670	$58,065	$45,576	0.673	0.629
2001–2007	$44,083	$32,038	$65,919	$48,454	0.669	0.661
2008–2018	$45,094	$30,360	$64,753	$45,583	0.696	0.666
Regional Ratio						
1967–1973	1.35	1.52	1.13	1.17		
1974–1979	1.19	1.22	1.11	1.14		
1980–1989	1.14	1.16	1.09	1.13		
1990–2000	1.09	1.07	1.09	1.13		
2001–2007	1.06	1.02	1.09	1.12		
2008–2018	1.03	1.00	1.10	1.13		

Income figures are inflation-adjusted using consumer price index, all urban consumers (March $2011). All families are Non-Latinx. Families include all age-groups. The earnings sample is limited to persons with non-negative earnings and the initial period is for the 1967–1972 work-years.
Source: Author's calculations. Data are March Current Population Survey, Annual Social & Economic Supplement, 1965–2019

than the mean income of African Americans outside of the South. By 2008–2018 the South/Non-South ratio had nearly reached parity, at 103 percent. The median earnings of White Southern families also showed growth relative to Non-Southern White families, moving from 17 percent lower income to 13 percent lower income. So, both White and African American Southern families experienced an increase in their standard of living relative to families outside of the South, but Southern African American families posted the most dramatic gains.

The Post-Civil Rights era has witnessed an increase in racial disparity in family earnings outside of the South. The mean and median earnings of all families decreased, but there was a greater decrease in African American family earnings. In 1964–1973 the Non-Southern African American family–White family mean earnings ratio was 0.70, that is, outside of the South at the height of "the movement," the mean income of African American families was $70 for every $100 in mean earnings obtained by White families. In 2008–2018 this ratio had declined to about 0.65. The median family racial income ratio for Non-Southerners dropped 9 percentage points, from 0.68 in 1964–1973 to 0.59 in 2008–2018. Measuring by median earnings, the White family standard of living fell by $5,500 during 1964–2018, but African American standard of living dropped by $8,500.

There has been moderate progress in reducing racial disparity in family earnings within the South. During 1964–1973 the Southern African American–White family median earnings ratio was 0.53. By 2008–2018 the Southern ratio was 0.67. The median earnings of Southern African American families increased from $25,602 to $30,360 during 1964–2018, but the median earnings of Southern White families fell from $48,712 to $45,583. Using mean income, there was moderate progress in the South as the racial equality ratio increased from 0.59 in 1964–1973 to 0.70 in 2008–2018. This is just an 11 percentage point increase in equality in 5 decades. At this pace, racial equality in mean family earnings in the South will be achieved about 2170, that is, about 205 years after the end of Jim Crow and 305 years after the end of slavery. Summing up, there is now greater racial equality in family earnings in the South than outside of the South, racial disparity in family earnings is increasing outside the South, and the pace of racial progress in family income equality is woefully slow within the South.

7.2 POVERTY STATUS OF FAMILIES

At the end of Jim Crow, 29 of every 100 African American families were impoverished. By contrast, only 9 of every 100 White families were impoverished during this era (Table 7.3). The years 1974–1989 were a period of stagnation in the goal to reduce poverty. Twenty-seven of every 100 African American families were impoverished during the 1970s, with the rate returning to 29 of every 100 African American families during the next decade. However, by 2008–2018 the African American poverty rate declined to 23 percent. By comparison, the White poverty rate has remained more or less unchanged at 9 percent from the end of Jim Crow to the decade after the Great Recession.

Regional and racial changes in poverty mirrored regional and racial changes in family income. Southern African American families experienced the greatest reduction in poverty, falling from 0.36 in 1967–1973 to 0.21 during the most recent years. Non-Southern African American families experienced an increase in poverty, from 20 percent in 1967–1973 to 26 percent during 1980–1989, dropping back to 22 percent during 2008–2018. Today, neither African American nor White Southerners are more likely to be impoverished than African American and White Non-Southerners. Within and outside the South there are 11 and 14 percentage point gaps, respectively, in the racial incidence

TABLE 7.3. *Poverty rate by race and region, 1967–2018*

	African American	White	Racial Difference
1967–1973	0.29	0.09	0.20
1974–1979	0.27	0.08	0.19
1980–1989	0.29	0.09	0.20
1990–2000	0.24	0.08	0.16
2001–2007	0.21	0.08	0.13
2008–2018	0.22	0.09	0.13
Non-South			
1967–1973	0.20	0.08	0.12
1974–1979	0.24	0.07	0.17
1980–1989	0.26	0.08	0.18
1990–2000	0.24	0.08	0.16
2001–2007	0.21	0.07	0.14
2008–2018	0.22	0.08	0.14
South			
1967–1973	0.36	0.10	0.26
1974–1979	0.31	0.09	0.22
1980–1989	0.31	0.10	0.21
1990–2000	0.24	0.09	0.15
2001–2007	0.20	0.09	0.11
2008–2018	0.21	0.10	0.11
Regional Difference			
1967–1973	0.16	0.02	
1974–1979	0.07	0.02	
1980–1989	0.05	0.02	
1990–2000	0.00	0.01	
2001–2007	-0.01	0.02	
2008–2018	-0.01	0.02	

Income figures are inflation-adjusted using consumer price index, all urban consumers (March $2011). All families are Non-Latinx. Families include all age-groups. The initial period is for the 1967–1972 work-years.

Source: Author's calculations. Data are March Current Population Survey, Annual Social & Economic Supplement, 1965–2018

of poverty, down from the 25 percentage point difference in the South during 1967–1973 but up slightly from the initial 12 percentage point racial gap in Non-Southern states.

7.3 EDUCATION AND FAMILY ECONOMIC STATUS

Family poverty declines impressively with increases in education for the family's head of household (Table 7.4). Poverty is severe among African American families where heads of household are dropouts (less than 12 years

TABLE 7.4. *Black family income and poverty status, by head's education, 1964–2018*

				Growth		High School Ratio	
	Poverty	Earnings	Income	Earnings	Income	Earnings	Income
Dropout							
1964–1973	0.361	$30,150	$33,410			0.67	0.71
1974–1979	0.362	$28,069	$36,417	−6.90%	9.00%	0.64	0.74
1980–1989	0.414	$23,602	$32,241	−15.91%	−11.47%	0.61	0.72
1990–2000	0.391	$24,196	$33,439	2.52%	3.72%	0.66	0.76
2001–2007	0.342	$28,638	$37,382	18.36%	11.79%	0.78	0.84
2008–2018	0.361	$30,654	$38,934	7.04%	4.15%	0.89	0.92
High School							
1964–1973	0.165	$45,334	$47,037				
1974–1979	0.193	$43,638	$49,241	−3.74%	4.69%		
1980–1989	0.245	$38,848	$44,744	−10.98%	−9.13%		
1990–2000	0.239	$36,887	$43,917	−5.05%	−1.85%		
2001–2007	0.229	$36,860	$44,428	−0.07%	1.16%		
2008–2018	0.261	$34,569	$42,329	−6.22%	−4.72%		
Some College							
1964–1973	0.128	$52,270	$54,252			1.15	1.15
1974–1979	0.143	$49,766	$55,644	−4.79%	2.57%	1.14	1.13
1980–1989	0.159	$48,648	$54,943	−2.25%	−1.26%	1.25	1.23
1990–2000	0.144	$49,529	$56,956	1.81%	3.66%	1.34	1.30
2001–2007	0.139	$50,633	$58,756	2.23%	3.16%	1.37	1.32
2008–2018	0.174	$46,606	$54,647	−7.95%	−6.99%	1.35	1.29

(continued)

TABLE 7.4. *(continued)*

				Growth		High School Ratio	
	Poverty	Earnings	Income	Earnings	Income	Earnings	Income
Bachelor's Degree							
1964–1973	0.060	$65,909	$66,192			1.45	1.41
1974–1979	0.068	$63,999	$69,818	−2.90%	5.48%	1.47	1.42
1980–1989	0.072	$62,932	$69,552	−1.67%	−0.38%	1.62	1.55
1990–2000	0.058	$70,064	$78,882	11.33%	13.41%	1.90	1.80
2001–2007	0.064	$74,156	$83,198	5.84%	5.47%	2.01	1.87
2008–2018	0.079	$69,103	$78,574	−6.81%	−5.56%	2.00	1.86
Graduate Degree							
1964–1973	0.042	$84,847	$85,475			1.87	1.82
1974–1979	0.045	$80,666	$87,176	−4.93%	1.99%	1.85	1.77
1980–1989	0.051	$75,960	$85,513	−5.83%	−1.91%	1.96	1.91
1990–2000	0.043	$86,572	$100,118	13.97%	17.08%	2.35	2.28
2001–2007	0.046	$95,533	$110,088	10.35%	9.96%	2.59	2.48
2008–2018	0.056	$91,110	$104,983	−4.63%	−4.64%	2.64	2.48

Income figures are inflation-adjusted using consumer price index, all urban consumers (March $2011). All families are Non-Latinx. Families include all age-groups.
Source: Author's calculations. Data are March Current Population Survey, Annual Social & Economic Supplement, 1965–2018

of education). For the most recent years, 36 of every 100 of these families have incomes below the poverty level, the same level of poverty as 1964–1973. Worst, the mean earnings of these families have declined sharply during 1964–1989, falling by 6.9 percent from 1964–1973 to 1974–1979 and by 15.9 percent from 1974–1979 to 1980–1989. For families headed by dropouts, mean earnings were $30,150 during the late 1960s and $30,650 during the 2010s.

During 1964–2018, mean family earnings declined for families where the head has exactly 12 years of education (high school), as well as for families where the head has some college education (but no degree). Relative to African American families where the head of household has 12 years of education, inequality among African American families fell slightly between 1964–1973 and 1974–1979 but rose sharply during 1974–2018. In the earliest period Black families whose heads were dropouts earned $67 for each $100 of earnings of African American families where the head is a high school graduate. By the 1980s families whose head was a dropout obtained $61 for each $100 of income of families whose head was a high school graduate. During the mid- to late-1970s, for African American families whose head had some college education, mean family earnings were 13 percent greater than the mean family earnings of African American families headed by a high school graduate; this differential grew to 34 percent during the 1990s and has remained at that level or higher since that time.

During the years immediately following the end of Jim Crow, African American families whose head had a graduate degree had mean family earnings more 1.87 times greater than the earnings of African American families where the head was a high school graduate. During 2008–2018 this ratio increased to 2.64. All of this increase was ushered in by the recession of 1981–1982, as inequality actually declined between the first two periods. By 2008–2018, African American families headed by a person with a graduate degree had $91,110 in family earnings versus $34,569 family earnings for families headed by a high school graduate. The Great Recession (December 2007–June 2009) reduced mean family income and earnings by 4.72 percent and 6.22 percent, respectively, for families headed by a high school graduate, but income and earnings declined by 4.64 percent and 4.63 percent, respectively, for African American families headed by a person with a graduate degree.

7.4 MARITAL STATUS AND FAMILY ECONOMIC STATUS

The Great Recession impeded growth in family earnings and income. Family income grew slowly between 2001–2007 and 2008–2018 for both African Americans and Whites and for all family types. For example, the mean family earnings of married African Americans grew from $45,303 in 1964–1973 to $65,995 during the Great Recession years (Table 7.5). The mean family earnings of never-married African American women fell from $34,678 in the late

TABLE 7.5. *Family income and poverty status, by race and marital status, 1964–2018*

	White			African American				
	Poverty			Poverty			Ratios	
	Rate	Earnings	Income	Rate	Earnings	Income	Earn.	Inc.
Married								
1964–1973	0.057	$62,163	$65,356	0.180	$45,303	$44,854	0.729	0.686
1974–1979	0.046	$63,498	$73,245	0.137	$49,359	$55,496	0.777	0.758
1980–1989	0.054	$62,684	$76,022	0.139	$50,154	$57,689	0.800	0.759
1990–2000	0.042	$72,011	$87,937	0.101	$59,044	$68,697	0.820	0.781
2001–2007	0.037	$83,699	$100,349	0.089	$65,758	$76,116	0.786	0.759
2008–2018	0.041	$82,725	$102,352	0.091	$65,995	$78,604	0.798	0.768
Prior Marriage Men								
1964–1973	0.156	$38,107	$46,007	0.297	$25,739	$29,467	0.675	0.640
1974–1979	0.114	$39,384	$50,197	0.241	$27,418	$34,349	0.696	0.684
1980–1989	0.115	$38,919	$50,716	0.269	$25,300	$32,966	0.650	0.650
1990–2000	0.105	$39,152	$52,447	0.241	$28,008	$36,664	0.715	0.699
2001–2007	0.108	$40,226	$54,018	0.212	$30,036	$39,826	0.747	0.737
2008–2018	0.119	$39,708	$53,517	0.230	$28,883	$39,052	0.727	0.730
Prior Marriage Women								
1964–1973	0.275	$22,734	$33,548	0.476	$17,277	$23,607	0.760	0.704
1974–1979	0.215	$20,709	$34,727	0.459	$17,262	$26,080	0.834	0.751
1980–1989	0.215	$20,565	$35,648	0.445	$18,608	$26,930	0.905	0.755
1990–2000	0.185	$23,034	$38,131	0.349	$22,756	$32,085	0.988	0.841
2001–2007	0.164	$26,550	$41,496	0.274	$26,703	$36,504	1.006	0.880
2008–2018	0.171	$27,630	$41,836	0.260	$27,074	$37,559	0.980	0.898

Never Married Men								
1964–1973	0.086	$69,033	$71,751	0.317	$38,173	$41,126	0.553	0.573
1974–1979	0.079	$69,162	$77,354	0.295	$38,342	$45,732	0.554	0.591
1980–1989	0.095	$63,172	$72,657	0.294	$37,188	$43,740	0.589	0.602
1990–2000	0.098	$63,596	$73,212	0.246	$39,211	$45,856	0.617	0.626
2001–2007	0.108	$68,673	$77,671	0.231	$41,110	$47,855	0.599	0.616
2008–2018	0.127	$68,139	$75,382	0.255	$42,947	$48,604	0.630	0.645
Never Married Women								
1964–1973	0.101	$65,615	$68,477	0.378	$34,678	$38,444	0.528	0.561
1974–1979	0.097	$65,182	$73,893	0.389	$32,036	$39,763	0.491	0.538
1980–1989	0.124	$59,030	$68,907	0.438	$28,395	$34,756	0.481	0.504
1990–2000	0.136	$58,652	$67,992	0.367	$29,988	$35,904	0.511	0.528
2001–2007	0.141	$64,280	$73,100	0.310	$34,919	$40,698	0.543	0.557
2008–2018	0.165	$64,857	$70,290	0.313	$36,736	$40,972	0.566	0.583

Income figures are inflation-adjusted using consumer price index, all urban consumers (March $2011). All families are Non-Latinx. Families include all age-groups.

Source: Author's calculations. Data are March Current Population Survey, Annual Social & Economic Supplement, 1965–2018

1960s to $28,395 in the 1980s. The mean family income of never-married African American men fell from $38,173 during 1964–1973 to $37,188 during the 1980s.

Mean family earnings of previously married African Americans, that is, families with divorced, widowed, and separated heads of household, exhibited a pattern similar to never-married families, falling between 1964–1973 and 1980–1989, before recovering during 1990–2018. Median earnings of previously married African American women increased from $18,608 in the 1980s to $27,074 in 2008–2018. The family earnings of previously married men increased from $25,300 in the 1980s to $28,883 in the 2010s.

Considering the entire two generations since the end of Jim Crow, African American families experienced superior increases (or less decline) than White families of the same type. For previously married Black men and women, mean earnings grew by 5 percentage points and 22 percentage points, respectively, relative to their White counterparts. Mean earnings for African American married families increased by 7 percentage points relative to White families during 1964–2018. Mean earnings of never-married White men declined by about $1,000, while the earnings of African American men grew by nearly $5,000. The mean earnings of never-married African American women increased by $2,000, while the means earnings of White women was stagnant. The 1980s was a particularly bad decade for families headed by never-married persons: mean earnings of families headed by African American and White women fell $4,000 and $6,000, respectively, while mean earnings of families headed by never-married African American and White men declined by $1,000 and $6,000, respectively.

Regardless of family structure, earnings growth of Southern African American families outpaced earnings growth of Non-Southern African American families in every period (Table 7.6). Sometimes earnings of Southern African American families increased, while earnings of Non-Southern African American families declined. For example, for 1964–2018 mean and median earnings of never-married Southern males increased by 26.7 percent and 8.4 percent, respectively, while the mean and median earnings of their Non-Southern counterparts declined by 0.4 percent and 23 percent, respectively. The mean earnings of never-married Southern African American increased by 16 percent for women, while median earnings increased by 1.1 percent. But the mean and median earnings of their Non-Southern counterparts declined by 3.7 percent and 24.8 percent, respectively. Mean and median earnings of married Southern African American families grew rapidly between the end of Jim Crow and the Great Recession, by 71 percent and 57 percent, respectively, but mean and median earnings Non-Southern married African American families increased by 28 percent and 5 percent, respectively. Among families of previously married African American women, median earnings of Southern families grew four times as much as incomes of Non-Southern families; and, among families of previously married African American men, the

TABLE 7.6. *Family earnings growth by marital status, 1964–2018*

	White				African American			
	Non-South		South		Non-South		South	
	Mean	Median	Mean	Median	Mean	Median	Mean	Median
Married								
1964–2018	33.5%	15.3%	36.9%	17.7%	27.6%	5.3%	70.7%	56.9%
1974–1979	1.7%	3.6%	3.4%	5.8%	4.1%	5.5%	15.7%	19.0%
1980–1989	−1.8%	−4.4%	0.7%	−3.4%	−1.0%	−4.9%	5.7%	4.2%
1990–2000	16.1%	9.5%	13.7%	7.7%	14.0%	9.3%	21.7%	20.3%
2001–2007	16.0%	9.6%	17.2%	11.0%	10.4%	4.5%	12.1%	8.8%
2008–2018	−0.8%	−3.0%	−1.3%	−3.6%	−1.6%	−8.0%	2.3%	−3.3%
Prior Married Men								
1964–2018	5.1%	−25.7%	6.8%	−13.9%	−2.7%	−48.1%	33.5%	5.5%
1974–1979	3.0%	1.5%	4.8%	13.7%	1.0%	−9.4%	13.1%	15.0%
1980–1989	−1.4%	−3.9%	0.1%	−3.7%	−9.4%	−18.9%	−4.8%	−16.0%
1990–2000	0.8%	−7.5%	1.3%	−3.8%	5.3%	−1.1%	17.9%	37.7%
2001–2007	3.6%	−0.9%	1.7%	−2.9%	3.0%	4.0%	10.2%	8.2%
2008–2018	−0.9%	−16.9%	−1.1%	−15.8%	−1.9%	−31.5%	−4.6%	−26.7%
Prior Married Women								
1964–2018	21.8%	0.9%	25.2%	−8.9%	41.4%	32.5%	77.1%	132.6%
1974–1979	−9.4%	−30.4%	−7.4%	−28.6%	−1.4%	−25.7%	1.2%	−8.5%
1980–1989	−1.2%	−14.3%	1.4%	8.7%	6.9%	12.5%	10.6%	12.8%
1990–2000	12.9%	66.5%	10.8%	24.9%	18.2%	55.9%	27.5%	87.5%
2001–2007	15.4%	34.5%	15.1%	34.3%	12.4%	26.7%	21.7%	36.1%
2008–2018	4.3%	−24.4%	4.4%	−30.1%	0.9%	−19.8%	2.0%	−11.8%

(*continued*)

TABLE 7.6. *(continued)*

	White				African American			
	Non-South		South		Non-South		South	
	Mean	Median	Mean	Median	Mean	Median	Mean	Median
Never Married Men								
1964–2018	−1.6%	−26.1%	2.4%	−21.0%	−0.4%	−23.0%	26.7%	8.4%
1974–1979	−0.5%	−2.3%	1.8%	0.1%	−9.0%	−19.2%	10.1%	6.4%
1980–1989	−8.8%	−14.9%	−7.5%	−11.8%	−1.8%	−5.4%	−4.0%	−7.0%
1990–2000	0.5%	−8.5%	2.4%	−7.5%	4.5%	2.0%	6.9%	6.0%
2001–2007	8.6%	0.1%	6.7%	−0.9%	3.9%	3.2%	5.5%	8.6%
2008–2018	−0.6%	−3.1%	−0.4%	−2.4%	2.7%	−4.2%	6.3%	−4.8%
Never Married Women								
1964–2018	−1.4%	−27.9%	2.5%	−22.4%	−3.7%	−24.8%	16.0%	1.1%
1974–1979	−1.9%	−4.7%	2.9%	1.7%	−11.9%	−27.0%	−4.0%	−6.1%
1980–1989	−9.5%	−18.9%	−8.5%	−17.2%	−12.6%	−26.9%	−9.7%	−23.7%
1990–2000	−0.6%	−7.8%	0.0%	−6.8%	5.3%	16.1%	5.9%	12.1%
2001–2007	10.2%	0.3%	8.4%	−1.4%	15.7%	22.3%	17.0%	21.2%
2008–2018	1.3%	0.9%	0.4%	0.2%	2.5%	−0.7%	7.8%	3.8%

Income figures are inflation-adjusted using consumer price index, all urban consumers (March $2011). All families are Non-Latinx. Families include all age-groups.
Author's calculations. Data are March Current Population Survey, Annual Social & Economic Supplement, 1965–2019

earnings of Southern families grew by 5.5 percent, while family earnings declined by 48.1 percent for Non-Southern families.

There have been substantial declines in both regional and racial disparity during the Post-Civil Rights era (Table 7.7). In 2008–2018 Southern African American families have median and mean earnings that are 96–127 percent and 94–100 percent as large as the earnings of Non-Southern African Americans families, respectively, an impressive increase from 1964 to 1973 when Southern families' earnings were only 62–74 percent (median) or 70–83 percent (mean) as large as Non-Southern families.

Controlling for family structure, Southern racial disparity declined during the five decades under observation. Never-married Southern African American women had median earnings of $44 per $100 of earnings of never-married White women in 1964–1973. This ratio declined to 0.41 during 1974–1979 and further declined to 0.38 during 1980–1989, before recovering to 0.58 during 2008–2018. Married Southern African American families had median earnings of $63 per $100 of earnings of married White families in 1964–1973. This ratio rose to $84 per $100 during 2001–2018. Married Non-Southern African American families had median earnings of $84 per $100 of earnings of married White families in 1964–1973. This ratio changed to $77 per $100 during 2001–2018. Never-married Non-Southern African American women had median earnings of $52 per $100 of earnings of never-married White women in 1964–1973. This ratio declined to 0.40 during 1974–1979 and further declined to 0.36 during 1980–1989, before recovering to 0.54 during 2008–2018.

7.5 EXPANSION OF THE BLACK MIDDLE CLASS

The African American population was numbered about 21 million persons during the middle-1960s and rose to 45 million persons by 2020. As a result of this population growth, the total number of African Americans employed as doctors, lawyers, college professors, engineers, and other high income professionals has increased. It is important to know, however, whether the *fraction* of African Americans living in affluence has expanded.

Intertemporal changes in the socioeconomic status of families are presented in Table 7.8. Families are divided into five groups: elite (families whose income places them in the 91st percentile or higher), upper income (families with an income between the 76th and 90th percentile), middle income (families with an income between the 26th and 75th percentile), lower income (families whose income places them within the 11th and 15th percentile), and the very poor (families with an income at or below the 10th percentile). During 1964–1973, elite families had an income greater than $99,189.52. Upper income families had an income greater than $71,132.44 but no more than $99,189.52, while middle income families had an income greater than $27,136.35 but no more than $71,132.44. Lower income families had an income greater than

TABLE 7.7 *Family earnings inequality by marital status, 1964–2018*

	Racial Disparity				Regional Inequality			
	Non-South		South		White		African Amer.	
	Mean	Median	Mean	Median	Mean	Median	Mean	Median
Married								
1964–1973	0.84	0.84	0.67	0.63	0.88	0.86	0.70	0.64
1974–1979	0.86	0.86	0.75	0.71	0.89	0.88	0.78	0.72
1980–1989	0.86	0.85	0.78	0.77	0.91	0.88	0.83	0.79
1990–2000	0.85	0.85	0.84	0.86	0.90	0.87	0.89	0.87
2001–2007	0.81	0.81	0.80	0.84	0.90	0.88	0.90	0.91
2008–2018	0.80	0.77	0.83	0.84	0.90	0.88	0.94	0.96
Prior Married Men								
1964–1973	0.79	0.78	0.60	0.60	0.91	0.81	0.70	0.62
1974–1979	0.77	0.69	0.65	0.61	0.93	0.91	0.78	0.79
1980–1989	0.71	0.59	0.62	0.53	0.94	0.91	0.82	0.82
1990–2000	0.74	0.63	0.72	0.76	0.94	0.94	0.92	1.14
2001–2007	0.74	0.66	0.78	0.84	0.93	0.92	0.98	1.19
2008–2018	0.73	0.54	0.75	0.73	0.92	0.94	0.95	1.27
Prior Married Women								
1964–1973	0.84	1.14	0.72	0.84	0.89	0.91	0.76	0.67
1974–1979	0.91	1.21	0.79	1.07	0.91	0.93	0.79	0.82
1980–1989	0.99	1.59	0.86	1.11	0.93	1.18	0.81	0.83
1990–2000	1.03	1.49	0.99	1.67	0.92	0.88	0.88	0.99
2001–2007	1.01	1.41	1.04	1.70	0.91	0.88	0.95	1.07
2008–2018	0.97	1.49	1.02	2.14	0.92	0.82	0.96	1.17

Never Married Men								
1964–1973	0.62	0.59	0.52	0.47	0.90	0.87	0.76	0.69
1974–1979	0.57	0.49	0.57	0.50	0.92	0.89	0.92	0.91
1980–1989	0.61	0.54	0.59	0.53	0.93	0.92	0.90	0.89
1990–2000	0.64	0.61	0.61	0.60	0.95	0.93	0.92	0.93
2001–2007	0.61	0.63	0.61	0.66	0.93	0.92	0.93	0.98
2008–2018	0.63	0.62	0.65	0.64	0.94	0.93	0.97	0.97
Never Married Women								
1964–1973	0.57	0.52	0.52	0.44	0.90	0.87	0.83	0.74
1974–1979	0.51	0.40	0.49	0.41	0.94	0.92	0.90	0.96
1980–1989	0.49	0.36	0.48	0.38	0.95	0.94	0.93	1.00
1990–2000	0.52	0.45	0.51	0.45	0.96	0.95	0.94	0.97
2001–2007	0.55	0.55	0.55	0.56	0.94	0.94	0.95	0.96
2008–2018	0.56	0.54	0.59	0.58	0.93	0.93	1.00	1.00

Income figures are inflation-adjusted using consumer price index, all urban consumers (March $2011). All families are Non-Latinx. Families include all age-groups.

Source: Author's calculations. Data are March Current Population Survey, Annual Social & Economic Supplement, 1965–2019

TABLE 7.8 *Socioeconomic status of families, by race and region, 1964–2018*

	All					
	1964–1973	1974–1979	1980–1989	1990–2000	2001–2007	2008–2018
Very Poor⁺	11.8	10.9	12.6	12.1	11.2	12.0
Lower Income⁺	16.9	17.2	18.1	17.8	15.7	15.5
Middle Income⁺	50.0	45.6	43.3	40.7	38.0	34.1
Upper Income⁺	13.1	15.3	14.1	14.2	15.5	13.4
Elite⁺	8.2	11.0	12.0	15.1	19.5	25.0
African American						
Very Poor⁺	24.3	22.9	26.7	24.7	22.0	22.1
Lower Income⁺	28.9	25.8	24.4	23.3	22.4	21.7
Middle Income⁺	39.0	39.6	36.3	36.3	36.9	33.1
Upper Income⁺	5.7	8.3	8.0	8.8	9.9	8.8
Elite⁺	2.0	3.4	4.5	6.9	8.8	14.3
African, Non-South						
Very Poor⁺	16.9	19.5	24.9	24.0	21.8	21.8
Lower Income⁺	24.6	24.7	22.7	21.6	21.4	21.2
Middle Income⁺	47.5	40.5	37.2	36.1	36.6	33.1
Upper Income⁺	8.2	10.6	9.5	9.8	10.7	9.1
Elite⁺	2.8	4.7	5.7	8.5	9.5	14.8
African, South						
Very Poor⁺	30.4	25.7	28.0	25.4	22.2	22.4
Lower Income⁺	32.5	26.7	25.8	24.8	23.2	22.0
Middle Income⁺	32.1	38.8	35.7	36.5	37.2	33.0
Upper Income⁺	3.7	6.4	6.9	7.8	9.3	8.7
Elite⁺	1.3	2.4	3.6	5.5	8.2	14.0

White						
Very Poor⁺	10.4	9.6	10.9	10.6	9.4	10.0
Lower Income⁺	15.5	16.2	17.3	17.2	14.6	14.3
Middle Income⁺	51.3	46.3	44.1	41.3	38.2	34.3
Upper Income⁺	13.9	16.1	14.8	14.9	16.5	14.3
Elite⁺	8.8	11.9	12.8	16.1	21.3	27.1
White, Non-South						
Very Poor⁺	9.4	9.1	10.5	10.2	9.1	9.5
Lower Income⁺	14.3	15.6	16.7	16.6	14.2	13.9
Middle Income⁺	51.8	46.1	44.1	41.0	38.0	34.3
Upper Income⁺	15.1	16.8	15.3	15.4	16.9	14.8
Elite⁺	9.4	12.5	13.3	16.9	21.8	27.6
White, South						
Very Poor⁺	13.1	11.0	11.9	11.6	10.4	11.2
Lower Income⁺	18.8	17.9	18.9	18.6	15.9	15.3
Middle Income⁺	49.8	46.8	43.9	41.9	38.6	34.4
Upper Income⁺	11.1	14.1	13.6	13.8	15.4	13.2
Elite⁺	7.3	10.3	11.7	14.1	19.7	26.0

⁺ Classes are adjusted to maintain 1964–1973 income levels for all time periods. Author's calculations. Data are from the March Current Population Survey, Annual Social & Economic Supplement, 1965–2018. Income figures are inflation-adjusted using the consumer price index, all urban consumers (March $2011). All families are Non-Latinx. Families include all age-groups.

$12,733.21 but no more than $27,136.35, and very poor families had an income no more than $12,733.21. For each of the following periods, after adjusting for inflation, we use the same income range for each status category and then determine the fraction of families within those categories. For each of the other periods, family socioeconomic status is defined by 1964–1973 income levels; hence, socioeconomic status is income-constant across time periods.

Using 1964–1973 income levels and adjusting for inflation, the Post-Civil Rights era has seen considerable growth in the Black elite, that is, the fraction of families in the top 10 percent of national income (as measured by 1964–1973 standards of income). Two percent of African American families were in the extreme right tail of the national income distribution during 1964–1973. Elite families are 14 percent of African Americans families during 2008–2018. A similar but less impressive pattern holds for upper income families, those families with income between the 76th and 90th percentiles. Between 1964–1973 and 2008–2018 upper income families rose from 5.7 percent to 8.8 percent of African American families, though none of this increase occurred after 2000. The fraction of affluent African American families, that is, elite plus upper income families, in 2008–2018 (23 percent) is equal to the fraction of affluent White families in 1964–1973.

African American middle income status (fraction of families between the 26th and 75th percentiles of the national income distribution) declined from 39 percent of African American families in 1964–1973 to 33 percent in 2008–2018. The fraction of lower income families declined from 28.9 percent to 21.7 percent, and the fraction of very poor families decreased from 24.3 percent to 22.1 percent. Nearly all of the decrease in very poor families occurred between 1964–1973 and 1974–1979. Note also that struggling families, that is, lower income plus very poor families, account for 43.8 percent of African American families in 2008–2018, far above the fraction of struggling White families in 1964–1973 (25.9 percent).

There are substantial regional differences in the distribution of income. The fraction of Non-South African American struggling families increased from 41.5 percent to 43 percent, with the fraction of very poor families rising by 5 percentage points. The fraction of affluent (upper income and elite) Non-South African American families rose from 11 percent to 23.9 percent, with nearly all of this increase caused by a rise in the fraction of elite families (especially during 1974–2018). So, outside of the South, the fraction of families in the middle class declined because of a 5 percentage point increase in the very poor and an 11 percentage point increase in the elite.

Notice, however, that 23.7 percent of Non-South White families were struggling families in 1964–1973 and, during 2008–2018, 23.4 percent of Non-South White families had incomes that would have placed them among struggling families in 1964–1973. So, during 1964–2018 economic well-being did not improve for Non-Southern White families at the bottom; but during 2008–2018 the probability (43 percent) that a Non-South Black family was at the bottom of the national distribution of income was nearly twice the probability of a Non-South White family in 1964–1973 (23.1 percent).

African American progress in the South was impressive but not unequivocal. The fraction of struggling African American families declined from 62.9 percent to 44.4 percent, while the fraction of affluent African American families grew from 5 percent to 22.7 percent. One-third of African American families remained within the middle class, indicating that some struggling families moved into the middle of the income distribution and replaced middle income families who were moving upward into the affluent tail of the distribution of income.

Two full generations after the end of Jim Crow, Southern African Americans in 2008–2018 had not established an income distribution that compared favorably to Southern Whites in 1964–1973. Struggling and affluent African American families were 63 percent and 5 percent, respectively, of Southern Black families in 1964–1973 and 44 percent and 23 percent, respectively, during 2008–2018. By comparison, struggling and affluent White families were 32 percent and 18 percent, respectively, of Southern White families in 1964–1973 and 27 percent and 39 percent, respectively, during 2008–2018. So, Black families in the South in 2008–2018 had a less favorable distribution of income than White families in the South during 1964–1973.

7.6 SUMMARY AND DISCUSSION

The post-Jim Crow period has seen important changes in intra- and interracial inequality. Despite unambiguous progress in the quality and quantity of African American education (Chapter 5), we have witnessed stagnation in the size of the Black middle class during the 1970s, 1980s, and 1990s, with only slight progress thereafter. Using the mid-1960s income brackets, the percentage of elite and upper income African American families (those in the top 25 percent of the national income distribution) increased from 8 percent in 1964–1973 to 23 percent during 2008–2018. The recessions of 1974–1975, 1981–1982, and 2007–2009 have hampered and sometimes undermined African American relative and absolute progress since 1964–1973.

African American economic progress has been concentrated in the South. Specifically,

a. Outside of the South, median family income stagnated and declined during 1967–2018;
b. Within the South, median family income rose during 1967–2018, though median income stagnated for a generation during 1974–2000;
c. Outside of the South, the poverty rate increased during 1967–2018, especially for a generation during 1967–1989; and,
d. Within the South, the poverty rate fell by 42 percent over 1967–2018, even though there was stagnation during 1974–1989.

The African American–White mean family earnings ratio rose from 0.62 in the late-1960s to 0.66 during the early 1990s and remained at 0.66 during 2008–2018; the median ratio rose from 0.57 to 0.62. Expanding the future size and well-being of the African American middle income families depends on whether the national unemployment rate remains under 4 percent and the employment–population ratio above 90 percent – the rates of the very early 1970s. Even with a national unemployment rate of 4 percent, moving the employment–population rate to 90 percent may require a jobs program for young adults from lower income and very poor African American families. Changes in African American socioeconomic well-being have been periodic, that is, characterized by alternating intervals of progress and regress. Increases (decreases) in the extent of racial disparity and discrimination are frequently induced by a severe recession (prolonged economic booms) and changes in the nature of government policy.

8

Family Wealth Inequality

Pensions, Homeownership, and Property Income

Income is the amount of money accruing to a family or individual during a given time period, a flow of money per week, per month, or per year. Wealth is a stock, the net market value of accumulated assets. Assets are items owned by a family that have market value. Liabilities are outstanding financial obligations to other persons or institutions. Net worth is the difference between assets and liabilities.

Transfer payments provide the difference between income and earnings for struggling families, but property income provides the difference between income and earnings for elite families. Racial differences in net worth produce racial differences in property income, which includes capital gains, increases in home equity, dividends, interest, rent on real property, pension payments, and other sources of income that reflect a market return on financial assets, as well as self-employment income, and inheritances or extra-family lump-sum payments. Some forms of property income are more liquid than others; also, there are differences in the availability of assets for discretionary spending, for example, rental income is immediately received as cash and may be utilized without selling off one's rental property, while increases in home equity represent paper increases in income that cannot be converted into cash without selling one's residence. Similarly, increases in the value of one's pension is an increase in net worth but there may be limited access to pensions and pension wealth is needed as a source of income during retirement.

All forms of property income represent current returns on the accumulation of past savings. Property income increases with wealth accumulation. By examining property income, we have an indicator of an individual's cumulative economic and social opportunities. Interracial differences in property income will occur if there are interracial differences in savings behavior, annual income during curious and previous periods, inheritances and other extra-family lump-sum transfers, rate of return on assets, pension annuities, and the type of assets owned by individuals and families.

8.1 RACIAL DISPARITY IN NET WORTH

There is a strong relationship between racial wealth inequality and all other forms of racial disparity in social and economic outcomes. Wealth passes on social and economic advantages within families across generations (see Table 3.1). Racial disparity in wealth transmits the economic consequences of racial injustice across generations. Slavery and Jim Crow were instituted to create and maintain White economic and political privilege. The racialized political economic systems worked as planned. At the end of Jim Crow, White wealth and earnings were substantially greater than African American wealth and earnings (Myrdal, 1944).

Tables 8.1–8.3 show a persistent and substantial wealth gap between African American and White families during 1984–2017. Mean net worth for African American families during 2017 was $32,000 (South) and $35,000 (Non-South) when we do not consider home equity and $59,000 (South) and $61,000 (Non-South) when we add in home equity. Median net worth for African American families during 2017 was $2,700 (Non-South) and $3,600 (South) when we do not consider home equity and $4,600 (Non-South) and $10,000 (South) when we add in home equity.

The wealth of White families is 5–35 times higher than the wealth of African American families, depending on the region, inclusion of home equity, and use of the mean or median. Mean net worth for White families during 2017 was about $262,000 (South) to $348,000 (Non-South) when we do not consider home equity and $357,000 (South) to $474,000 (Non-South) when we add in home equity. Median net worth for White families during 2017 was about $26,000 (South) to $35,000 (Non-South) when we do not consider home equity and $91,000 (South) to $108,000 (Non-South) when we add in home equity.

Taking account of home equity, during 1984–2017 the median wealth of Southern African American families is often more than twice as high as the median wealth of Non-Southern African American families. Ignoring home equity, during 1984–2017 the median wealth of Southern African American families is about 33 percent higher than the median wealth of Non-Southern African American families.

Mean family wealth is lower among Southern African American families than it is among Non-Southern African American families. Taking account of home equity, during 1984–2017 the mean wealth of Non-Southern African American families is 13 percentage points (or more) higher than the mean wealth of Southern African American families. Ignoring home equity, during 1984–2017 the mean wealth of Non-Southern African American families is usually 30 percentage points higher than the mean wealth of Southern African American families.

The White–African American family wealth ratio is lowest for mean net worth with home equity. During 2017 this ratio was 7.7 (Non-South) – 6.1 (South), moderately higher than in 1984, when the ratios were 6.1 (Non-South)

TABLE 8.1. *Net worth by race, 1984–2017*

	Net Worth without Home Equity				Net Worth with Home Equity			
	Mean		Median		Mean		Median	
Year	Non-South	South	Non-South	South	Non-South	South	Non-South	South
African American								
2017	$34,820	$31,775	$2,734	$3,647	$61,289	$58,641	$4,649	$10,028
2015	$37,667	$19,672	$1,509	$2,828	$61,748	$46,318	$4,714	$8,014
2013	$27,158	$23,216	$863	$3,357	$48,127	$49,619	$2,806	$7,674
2011	$31,639	$23,421	$2,000	$2,200	$51,426	$45,591	$3,000	$6,000
2009	$84,355	$45,036	$1,094	$2,083	$107,395	$73,708	$3,125	$8,333
2007	$41,663	$56,718	$2,694	$3,341	$75,290	$93,780	$5,928	$13,580
2005	$47,670	$43,844	$1,945	$3,433	$80,232	$75,376	$7,666	$13,731
2003	$66,526	$39,830	$3,650	$4,251	$91,804	$64,126	$6,075	$15,910
2001	$56,015	$42,889	$2,726	$3,794	$79,095	$71,718	$6,561	$20,189
1999	$23,920	$29,008	$2,012	$4,024	$51,576	$55,987	$4,024	$16,096
1994	$34,716	$26,653	$4,222	$2,413	$58,517	$50,657	$12,063	$13,571
1989	$38,296	$21,180	$2,163	$1,865	$65,421	$44,473	$5,677	$11,471
1984	$16,035	$21,633	$1,290	$1,721	$36,966	$44,561	$3,334	$8,603
White								
2017	$347,732	$262,033	$34,643	$26,438	$473,999	$357,068	$107,576	$90,984
2015	$342,937	$273,557	$33,188	$27,625	$460,240	$361,145	$107,058	$73,729
2013	$302,067	$223,780	$33,574	$26,859	$408,541	$306,092	$96,886	$83,072
2011	$297,323	$242,594	$33,700	$28,820	$407,646	$324,543	$94,000	$84,700
2009	$340,418	$309,976	$36,457	$32,290	$462,702	$432,256	$110,340	$95,829

(*continued*)

TABLE 8.1. (*continued*)

	Net Worth without Home Equity				Net Worth with Home Equity			
	Mean		Median		Mean		Median	
Year	Non-South	South	Non-South	South	Non-South	South	Non-South	South
2007	$362,519	$280,841	$42,033	$38,431	$510,965	$391,278	$138,493	$114,244
2005	$297,010	$274,937	$45,769	$33,411	$442,092	$374,284	$141,884	$102,981
2003	$288,018	$222,527	$45,786	$40,078	$405,854	$305,393	$129,951	$100,499
2001	$282,654	$223,889	$47,949	$37,854	$385,946	$298,627	$128,894	$96,907
1999	$303,935	$205,598	$46,947	$34,875	$396,860	$276,012	$124,744	$88,750
1994	$194,258	$167,548	$40,713	$35,586	$273,669	$230,143	$101,028	$85,949
1989	$182,115	$169,795	$37,845	$27,032	$273,936	$227,485	$98,217	$71,726
1984	$154,291	$190,006	$29,036	$28,175	$225,428	$249,551	$87,107	$77,536

African American outliers for 2009, 2005, and 2003 were dropped from the sample. White outliers for 2009 were dropped from the sample. Outliers increased the means but had no effect on medians.

Source: Author's calculations, Panel Study of Income Dynamics, 1984–2017

TABLE 8.2. *Net worth by region, 1984–2017*

	Without Equity		With Equity		Without Equity		With Equity	
Year	Mean	Median	Mean	Median	Mean	Median	Mean	Median
	African American Regional Ratios				White Regional Ratios			
2017	1.10	0.75	1.05	0.46	1.33	1.31	1.33	1.18
2015	1.91	0.53	1.33	0.59	1.25	1.20	1.27	1.45
2013	1.17	0.26	0.97	0.37	1.35	1.25	1.33	1.17
2011	1.35	0.91	1.13	0.50	1.23	1.17	1.26	1.11
2009	1.87	0.53	1.46	0.38	1.10	1.13	1.07	1.15
2007	0.73	0.81	0.80	0.44	1.29	1.09	1.31	1.21
2005	1.09	0.57	1.06	0.56	1.08	1.37	1.18	1.38
2003	1.67	0.86	1.43	0.38	1.29	1.14	1.33	1.29
2001	1.31	0.72	1.10	0.32	1.26	1.27	1.29	1.33
1999	0.82	0.50	0.92	0.25	1.48	1.35	1.44	1.41
1994	1.30	1.75	1.16	0.89	1.16	1.14	1.19	1.18
1989	1.81	1.16	1.47	0.49	1.07	1.40	1.20	1.37
1984	0.74	0.75	0.83	0.39	0.81	1.03	0.90	1.12

African American outliers for 2009, 2005, and 2003 were dropped from the sample. White outliers for 2009 were dropped from the sample. Outliers increased the means but had no effect on medians.
Source: Author's calculations, Panel Study of Income Dynamics, 1984–2017

TABLE 8.3. *Racial ratios, 1984–2017*

	Without Home Equity				With Home Equity			
	Mean		Median		Mean		Median	
Year	Non-South	South	Non-South	South	Non-South	South	Non-South	South
2017	10.0	8.2	12.7	7.2	7.7	6.1	23.1	9.1
2015	9.1	13.9	22.0	9.8	7.5	7.8	22.7	9.2
2013	11.1	9.6	38.9	8.0	8.5	6.2	34.5	10.8
2011	9.4	10.4	16.9	13.1	7.9	7.1	31.3	14.1
2009	4.0	6.9	33.3	15.5	4.3	5.9	35.3	11.5
2007	8.7	5.0	15.6	11.5	6.8	4.2	23.4	8.4
2005	6.2	6.3	23.5	9.7	5.5	5.0	18.5	7.5
2003	4.3	5.6	12.5	9.4	4.4	4.8	21.4	6.3
2001	5.0	5.2	17.6	10.0	4.9	4.2	19.6	4.8
1999	12.7	7.1	23.3	8.7	7.7	4.9	31.0	5.5
1994	5.6	6.3	9.6	14.7	4.7	4.5	8.4	6.3
1989	4.8	8.0	17.5	14.5	4.2	5.1	17.3	6.3
1984	9.6	8.8	22.5	16.4	6.1	5.6	26.1	9.0

African American outliers for 2009, 2005, and 2003 were dropped from the sample. White outliers for 2009 were dropped from the sample. Outliers increased the means but had no effect on medians.
Source: Author's calculations, Panel Study of Income Dynamics, 1984–2017

and 5.6 (South). The White–African American family wealth ratio is highest for median net worth of Non-South families. During 2017 this ratio was 23.1 (with home equity) – 12.7 (without home equity), versus 1984, when these ratios were 26.1 and 22.5, respectively. Observing all the racial wealth ratios there is no clear pattern of improvement or decline during 1984–2017.

Median White household net worth was $115,005 for 2009, while median African American and Latinx household wealth was $5,770 and $6,429, respectively.[1] The Great Recession lowered the wealth of all groups. Average White wealth declined 16 percent from 2005, when it was $150,721. But, from 2005 to 2009, African American and Latinx wealth declined by 53 percent and 66 percent, respectively, that is, from $13,537 for Blacks and from $20,498 for Latinx. Mostly, depreciating home values and home foreclosures are responsible for these reductions in African American and Latinx wealth. Historically, White wealth is 10–12 times Black wealth and 7–10 times Latinx wealth. The Great Recession pushed these ratios to 20 and 18, respectively.

The median African American family has $0 home equity during 1984–2017, indicating a lack of ownership and homes that are "under water," that is, the mortgage exceeded the home value (Table 8.4). There is not much difference in mean home equity by region. Mean homeowner wealth was near $21,000 (Non-South) – $23,000 (South) in 1984 and $34,000 (Non-South) – $37,000 (South) in 2007. After the Great Recession of 2008–2009, mean African American homeowner wealth declined to $26,470 (Non-South) and $26,866 (South).

During the 1980s and 1990s, mean African American home equity was 30 percent of mean White home equity outside of the South and 40 percent of home equity within the South. African American home equity grew rapidly during 2001–2007, but not as rapidly as White home equity. During 2001 African American home equity was $23,080 (Non-South) and $28,830 (South), before growing into $33,627 (Non-South) and $37,063 (South) during 2007. Mean White home equity rose from $103,292 to $148,446 (Non-South) and $74,738 to $110,436 (South). Because of the faster growth in home equity among White families during 2001–2007, the racial ratios were 0.23 (Non-South) and 0.34 (South). During the period after the Great Recession, 2009–2017, mean African American family home equity had a greater percentage decline than the mean White family home equity. The home equity racial ratios were 0.21 (Non-South) and 0.28 (South), much lower than the racial ratios of the 1980s and 1990s.

Bankrupt families have zero or negative net worth. Roughly 30 percent of African American families were bankrupt during the late 1990s, with 8 percent

[1] These numbers are inflation adjusted for $2011. Kochbar, Fry, and Taylor (2011) report their findings in $2009. Hence, their reported numbers for 2009 are: $113,149 (Whites), $6,325 (Latinx), and $5,677 (Blacks). The 2005 figures are: $134,992 (Whites), $18,359 (Latinx), and $12,124 (Blacks).

TABLE 8.4. *Homeowner equity by race and region, 1984-2017*

		Mean		Median	
		Non-South	South	Non-South	South
African American	2017	$26,470	$26,866	$0	$0
	2015	$24,081	$26,646	$0	$0
	2013	$20,969	$26,403	$0	$0
	2011	$19,787	$22,170	$0	$0
	2009	$23,040	$28,673	$0	$0
	2007	$33,627	$37,063	$0	$0
	2005	$32,775	$31,532	$0	$0
	2003	$25,278	$24,913	$0	$0
	2001	$23,080	$28,830	$0	$2,524
	1999	$27,655	$26,979	$0	$0
	1994	$23,802	$24,004	$0	$0
	1989	$27,125	$23,293	$0	$0
	1984	$20,930	$22,929	$0	$0
White	2017	$126,267	$95,034	$50,142	$41,025
	2015	$117,303	$87,589	$45,256	$36,582
	2013	$106,475	$82,311	$34,533	$28,778
	2011	$110,323	$81,949	$34,000	$28,984
	2009	$122,284	$92,688	$44,582	$40,623
	2007	$148,446	$110,436	$64,666	$51,733
	2005	$145,083	$99,347	$62,932	$45,769
	2003	$117,836	$82,866	$60,725	$40,078
	2001	$103,292	$74,738	$56,782	$40,378
	1999	$92,925	$70,414	$51,984	$38,899
	1994	$79,410	$62,595	$38,451	$30,157
	1989	$91,820	$57,690	$40,548	$28,834
	1984	$71,137	$59,545	$43,016	$34,413
Racial Ratios	2017	0.21	0.28		
	2015	0.21	0.30		
	2013	0.20	0.32		
	2011	0.18	0.27		
	2009	0.19	0.31		
	2007	0.23	0.34		
	2005	0.23	0.32		
	2003	0.21	0.30		
	2001	0.22	0.39		
	1999	0.30	0.38		
	1994	0.30	0.38		
	1989	0.30	0.40		
	1984	0.29	0.39		

Source: Author's calculations, Panel Study of Income Dynamics, 1984–2017

TABLE 8.5. *Families with zero or negative net worth*

	African American				White			
	Wealth w/o Equity		Wealth with Equity		Wealth w/o Equity		Wealth with Equity	
	Non-South	South	Non-South	South	Non-South	South	Non-South	South
2017	0.354	0.362	0.312	0.304	0.185	0.174	0.140	0.124
2015	0.433	0.390	0.379	0.327	0.192	0.187	0.154	0.142
2013	0.475	0.366	0.435	0.322	0.188	0.201	0.159	0.164
2011	0.420	0.373	0.412	0.331	0.187	0.193	0.156	0.162
2009	0.406	0.404	0.379	0.337	0.185	0.177	0.153	0.145
2007	0.356	0.343	0.313	0.271	0.165	0.179	0.117	0.135
2005	0.369	0.359	0.307	0.271	0.152	0.162	0.112	0.108
2003	0.362	0.310	0.318	0.237	0.147	0.151	0.105	0.110
2001	0.373	0.352	0.335	0.244	0.139	0.154	0.101	0.107
1999	0.390	0.318	0.357	0.225	0.130	0.136	0.101	0.106
1994	0.378	0.390	0.319	0.288	0.130	0.141	0.104	0.101
1989	0.396	0.378	0.342	0.292	0.110	0.138	0.085	0.110
1984	0.401	0.405	0.347	0.312	0.101	0.096	0.077	0.073

Source: Author's calculations, Panel Study of Income Dynamics, 1984–2017

of White families in a similar position (Hurst, Stafford, and Luoh, 1998). From 2005 to 2009 the fraction of bankrupt African American households increased from 29 percent to 35 percent, the fraction of bankrupt White households grew from 11 percent to 15 percent, and the fraction of bankrupt Latinx families rose from 23 percent to 31 percent.[2]

Family bankruptcy rates by race and region are presented in Table 8.5. The African American bankruptcy rate is usually highest for Non-South families. When net worth does not include home equity, 47.5 percent of Non-Southern African American families had zero or negative net worth in 2013, versus 36.6 percent of Southern African American families. When net worth does include home equity, 43.5 percent of Non-Southern African American families had zero or negative net worth versus 32.2 percent of Southern African American families. There were fewer bankrupt African American families in 2017 than 1984, despite the rise in bankruptcy during 2009–2015 after the Great Recession. When home equity is not included, 40 percent of Non-Southern and Southern African American families did not have positive net worth during 1984; 35 percent (Non-Southern) and 36 percent (Southern) of these families

[2] Kochbar, Fry, and Taylor (2011). About one in four African American and Latinx households owned no asset other than an automobile.

did not have positive net worth in 2017. When home equity is not included, 35 percent of Non-Southern and 31 percent of Southern African American families did not have positive net worth during 1984, while 31 percent (Non-Southern) and 30 percent (Southern) of these families did not have positive net worth in 2017.

There was a large increase in the fraction of White families with $0 or negative net worth during 1984–2017. The bankruptcy rate increased from about 10 percent for Non-Southern and Southern White families to about 19 percent and 17 percent, respectively, when home equity is not included. When home equity is included, the White family bankruptcy rose from 0.077 to 0.14 (Non-South) and from 0.073 to 0.12 (South).

Class inequality increased within each racial group (Kochbar, Fry, and Taylor, 2011). Class inequality started at a higher level among African Americans and Latinx and increased by greater percentage points during the Great Recession. In 2005 the top 10 percent of wealthiest families owned 46 percent (White), 56 percent (Latinx), and 59 percent (African American) of own-group wealth. By 2009 these figures were 51 percent (White), 72 percent (Latinx), and African Americans (67 percent). The increase in class inequality did not occur because the rich got richer, but because the Great Recession hurt the rich less than it hurt the poor. White household wealth at the 90th percentile was $803,894 in 2005 and $714,467 in 2009, while Latinx and African American household wealth at the 90th percentile was $441,766 and $324,341, respectively, in 2005 but $240,044 and $238,090, respectively, in 2009.

8.2 PENSION PLAN ACCESS AND PARTICIPATION

Household wealth consists of a variety of financial and physical assets. Financial assets include checking, savings, and money market accounts; certificates of deposit (CDs); savings and corporate and municipal bonds; stocks ("equities") and pooled investment funds ("mutual funds"); cash value of life insurance; retirement accounts ("pensions"); and other financial assets. Physical assets include vehicles, primary and other residences, equity in non-residential properties, business equity, and other physical assets. A pension is the primary financial asset and the family residence is the primary physical asset for most American families.

Pensions increase a family's net worth and provide income during retirement. Social security is a public pension system. Although workers cannot receive a lump-sum social security payment at retirement, it does provide economic security during retirement. Many private pensions offer lump-sum payments at retirement and they may also allow individuals to borrow from the pension prior to retirement. Employment allows participation in social security and private pensions (and it is the major source of health insurance). Participation in private pensions is often voluntary or conditional upon

TABLE 8.6. *Participation in employer pension plans: 1978–2018, workers aged 25–64*

	1979	1980–1989	1990–2000	2001–2007	2008–2018
African American women					
Existence of Pension Plan	0.539	0.562	0.604	0.585	0.505
Inclusion in Pension Plan	0.305	0.320	0.348	0.346	0.322
African American men					
Existence of Pension Plan	0.573	0.567	0.579	0.565	0.481
Inclusion in Pension Plan	0.439	0.401	0.384	0.359	0.325
White women					
Existence of Pension Plan	0.513	0.524	0.600	0.614	0.539
Inclusion in Pension Plan	0.280	0.297	0.368	0.385	0.377
White men					
Existence of Pension Plan	0.634	0.597	0.618	0.617	0.531
Inclusion in Pension Plan	0.544	0.493	0.493	0.479	0.422

Source: Author's calculations. Current Population Survey, Annual Social and Economic (ASEC) Supplement, March 1980–2018

employment tenure. Accordingly, African American joblessness reduces current income, pension participation, home ownership, and health status.

Information on whether a pension plan exists at a person's place of employment and whether the worker is included in an employer's pension plan is provided in Table 8.6. African American male access to a pension plan was stable at 57–58 percent during 1979–2007, but eventually dropped to 48 percent after the Great Recession. African American female access to a pension plan rose from 54 percent to 59 percent during 1979–2007 but declined to 51 percent during 2008–2018. There was a 6 percentage point racial difference among men in 1979, as 57 percent of African American men were employed at organizations that provided a pension plan, while 63 percent of White men were so employed; the gap was 5 percentage points during 2008–2018. During the late 1970s, 54 percent and 51 percent of African American and White women, respectively, had access to an employer provided pension. By 2008–2018, 51 percent and 54 percent of African American and White women were employed at establishments offering a pension plan.

There are race–gender differences in the fraction of employees who participate in employer pension plans. Male participation in their employer's pension plan declined strongly during 1979–2018, while female participation increased during 1979–2007, before falling back after the Great Recession. In 1979, 44 percent of African American men were included in employer pension plans. By 2008–2018, the African American male participation rate had decreased to 33 percent. The White male pension participation rate declined from 0.544 to

0.422 during 1979–2018. The female racial gap in participation is less than half of the male racial gap. Among African American and White women, the pension participation rates were 31 percent and 28 percent, respectively, during 1979 but 35 percent and 39 percent, respectively, during the 2000s. The Great Recession reduced African American female pension participation to 0.322 – about the same rate as the 1980s, while the White female pension participation rate declined to 0.377 – the same as their rate in the 1990s.

Both access to and participation in employer provided pension plans varies by region (Table 8.7). African American men living in the Non-South had the largest relative and absolute decreases in access to and participation in pension plans. Black male access to a pension declined from 65 percent to 49 percent during 1979–2018, while participation fell from 49 percent to 33 percent. The Non-Southern White–Black male racial gap in access increased from 1 percentage point to 6 percentage points and the participation gap increased from 8 percentage points to 12 percentage points.

Southern Black male access to a pension declined from 50 percent to 47 percent during 1979–2018, while participation fell from 38 percent to 32 percent. The Southern White–Black male racial gap in access decreased from 7 percentage points to 3 percentage points and the participation gap decreased from 10 percentage points to 7 percentage points.

Among Southern African American women, both access to and participation in employment-based pensions increased throughout 1979–2007 but declined with the onset of the Great Recession during 2008–2018. Even so, access to and participation in pensions by Southern African American women increased from 0.48 and 0.28, respectively, during 1979, to 0.499 and 0.32, respectively, during 2008–2018. For African American women outside of the South, access to and participation in pensions decreased from 0.60 to 0.51 during 1979–2018, while participation remained constant at 33 percent.

The Non-Southern Black–White female racial gap in pension access favors Black women by 8 percentage points in 1979 but favors White women by 4 percentage points during 2008–2018. Non-Southern African Americans went from being 5 percentage points more likely to participate in a pension to being about 6 percentage points less likely to participate than Non-Southern White women.

The Southern Black–White female racial gap in pension access was 2 percentage points in 1979 and 1 percentage points during 2008–2018. Southern African Americans went from being 2 percentage points more likely to participate in a pension to being about 3 percentage points less likely to participate than Southern White women.

Affluent and upper income African American families have greater access to employer pension plans and are more likely to be participants in such plans than middle income and struggling families (Table 8.8). Prior to the Great Recession, struggling and middle-income Non-Southern African American families had greater access to employer pension plans and were more likely to

TABLE 8.7. *Participation in employer pension plans by region: 1978–2018, ages 25–64*

	1979	1980–1989	1990–2000	2001–2007	2008–2018
South					
African American women					
Existence of Pension Plan	0.480	0.531	0.590	0.583	0.499
Inclusion in Pension Plan	0.278	0.312	0.342	0.345	0.320
African American men					
Existence of Pension Plan	0.503	0.522	0.565	0.554	0.474
Inclusion in Pension Plan	0.384	0.377	0.378	0.352	0.322
White women					
Existence of Pension Plan	0.502	0.516	0.585	0.595	0.507
Inclusion in Pension Plan	0.272	0.291	0.350	0.358	0.346
White men					
Existence of Pension Plan	0.575	0.556	0.589	0.589	0.502
Inclusion in Pension Plan	0.476	0.450	0.460	0.447	0.392
Non-South					
African American women					
Existence of Pension Plan	0.600	0.600	0.623	0.588	0.513
Inclusion in Pension Plan	0.331	0.330	0.356	0.348	0.326
African American men					
Existence of Pension Plan	0.646	0.622	0.598	0.578	0.492
Inclusion in Pension Plan	0.493	0.429	0.390	0.367	0.328
White women					
Existence of Pension Plan	0.518	0.527	0.607	0.624	0.555
Inclusion in Pension Plan	0.283	0.300	0.377	0.398	0.393
White men					
Existence of Pension Plan	0.659	0.616	0.632	0.630	0.547
Inclusion in Pension Plan	0.574	0.512	0.510	0.495	0.438

Source: Author's calculations. Current Population Survey, Annual Social and Economic (ASEC) Supplement, March 1979–2019

participate in these plans than Southern African American families of similar status.[3] Regardless of region or socioeconomic status, male access to and participation in employer pension plans decreased during 1979–2018, while White women had greater access to and participation in employer pensions and there were mixed changes in access and participation for African American women.

[3] The regional numbers are not shown in the table.

TABLE 8.8. *Participation in employer pension plans by family's economic status: 1979–2018, workers 25–64 years of age*

	African American Women					African American Men					
	1979	1980–1989	1990–2000	2001–2007	2008–2018	1979	1980–1989	1990–2000	2001–2007	2008–2018	
Very poor	0.435	0.402	0.507	0.504	0.461	0.502	0.423	0.511	0.509	0.461	Existence
	0.187	0.164	0.213	0.235	0.203	0.334	0.261	0.280	0.266	0.224	Inclusion
Lower income	0.432	0.428	0.490	0.490	0.410	0.393	0.311	0.381	0.380	0.311	Existence
	0.226	0.220	0.223	0.223	0.184	0.261	0.180	0.169	0.142	0.125	Inclusion
Middle income	0.575	0.591	0.659	0.634	0.592	0.586	0.577	0.605	0.584	0.532	Existence
	0.372	0.417	0.452	0.435	0.401	0.483	0.449	0.441	0.413	0.363	Inclusion
Upper income	0.765	0.760	0.770	0.731	0.688	0.771	0.737	0.733	0.703	0.657	Existence
	0.580	0.634	0.639	0.600	0.564	0.673	0.654	0.634	0.593	0.553	Inclusion
Elite	0.772	0.834	0.804	0.758	0.702	0.795	0.754	0.756	0.717	0.680	Existence
	0.578	0.746	0.686	0.637	0.570	0.740	0.686	0.657	0.636	0.592	Inclusion
	White Women					White Men					
Very poor	0.543	0.512	0.591	0.586	0.544	0.511	0.458	0.539	0.539	0.502	Existence
	0.300	0.274	0.341	0.339	0.303	0.383	0.320	0.368	0.351	0.317	Inclusion
Lower income	0.349	0.322	0.387	0.419	0.368	0.317	0.258	0.321	0.336	0.295	Existence
	0.122	0.118	0.136	0.151	0.136	0.187	0.149	0.157	0.154	0.121	Inclusion
Middle income	0.477	0.488	0.573	0.598	0.561	0.646	0.552	0.610	0.613	0.556	Existence
	0.249	0.271	0.341	0.368	0.360	0.560	0.452	0.493	0.484	0.431	Inclusion
Upper income	0.579	0.618	0.681	0.695	0.651	0.742	0.698	0.732	0.720	0.668	Existence
	0.373	0.415	0.499	0.516	0.509	0.697	0.632	0.663	0.649	0.597	Inclusion
Elite	0.587	0.615	0.691	0.694	0.667	0.706	0.682	0.735	0.719	0.673	Existence
	0.352	0.389	0.494	0.504	0.514	0.670	0.630	0.680	0.665	0.619	Inclusion

Source: Author's calculations. Current Population Survey, Annual Social and Economic (ASEC) Supplement, March 1979–2019

During 1979–1989, pension plan participation grew from 52 percent to 75 percent and from 68 percent to 69 percent of women and men, respectively, of elite Southern African American families. By 2008–2018 elite family participants in employer pension plans include 58 percent of women and 61 percent of men. There were similar patterns for Southern African American men and women in each of the other status groups. For Non-Southern African American men and women, pension plan participation declined during 1979–2018 for all status groups.

The Great Recession worsened a pre-existing trend; regardless of race or status, male pension participation declined sharply between 1979 and 2001–2007 – even as pension access did not change very much and sometimes increased. For example, middle income African American males saw their pension participation decline from 48.3 percent in 1979 to 41.3 percent in 2001–2007 even though pension access increased from 58.6 percent to 60.5 percent. Middle income White males had pension access and participation rates of 64.6 percent and 56.0 percent during 1979 and 61.3 percent and 48.3 percent in 2001–2007. Observing all of 1979–2018, pension participation by middle income African American males declined 12 percentage points and White male pension participation declined by 13 percentage points. Pension participation by elite African American males declined by 15 percentage points, while elite White male pension participation declined by 5 percentage points.

Struggling White women had constant or very small increases in pension access and participation. Pension access and participation for middle income White women increased from 48 percent and 25 percent, respectively, during 1979 to 56 percent and 36 percent, respectively, during 2008–2018. Pension access and participation for upper income White women increased by 7 percentage points and 14 percentage points, respectively, during 2008–2018. Pension access and participation for elite White women increased from 59 percent and 35 percent, respectively, during 1979, to 67 percent and 51 percent, respectively, during 2008–2018.

Except for women in very poor families, African American women have higher pension participation rates than White women with the same economic status. However, the Great Recession had a negative effect on the pension participation rates of African Americans of all status groups. For very poor and lower income African American women, pension participation rates declined from 23.5 percent to 20.3 percent and from 22.3 percent to 18.4 percent, respectively, between 2001–2007 and 2008–2018. Middle income, upper income, and elite African American women saw their pension participation rates decline by 3.4 percent, 3.6 percent, and 6.3 percent, respectively, between 2001–2007 and 2008–2018.

Regardless of race, there is no private pension income for the median individual or family for any period during 1979–2018 (see Table 8.9). For those receiving a pension, the mean has grown sharply – especially among African Americans. Mean pension income for African American individuals

TABLE 8.9. *Mean and median pension income for persons >65 years of age*

		Individual		Family		Racial Ratio	
		White	African American	White	African American	Individual	Family
1979	Mean	$3,127	$1,305	$4,956	$2,089	0.417	0.422
	Median	$0	$0	$0	$0		
1980–1989	Mean	$3,868	$1,963	$6,227	$3,132	0.507	0.503
	Median	$0	$0	$0	$0		
1990–2000	Mean	$4,934	$3,014	$7,969	$4,527	0.611	0.568
	Median	$0	$0	$0	$0		
2001–2007	Mean	$5,417	$3,840	$8,630	$5,640	0.709	0.654
	Median	$0	$0	$0	$0		
2008–2018	Mean	$6,439	$4,424	$10,404	$6,457	0.687	0.621
	Median	$0	$0	$0	$0		
	Pension Growth						
1979		1.000	1.000	1.000	1.000		
1980–1989		1.237	1.504	1.256	1.499		
1990–2000		1.578	2.310	1.608	2.167		
2001–2007		1.732	2.943	1.741	2.700		
2008–2018		2.059	3.390	2.099	3.091		

Source: Author's calculations. Social security and VA pensions are not included

and families is 3.39 times and 3.091 times higher, respectively, during 2008–2018 than during 1979. Among Whites, pension income is 2.059 higher for individuals and 2.099 times higher for families during the most recent period than during the late 1970s.

Racial disparity among those receiving pensions has declined. Since the median individual and family has $0 pension, this is equalizing among the more affluent members of each group. In 1979, African American pension income was just $0.42 on the dollar relative to White family pension income. This ratio is now $0.62 on the dollar. For individuals, the pension ratio of racial disparity increased from about 0.42 to nearly 0.69.

Women's pensions are lower than men's pensions, much more so among Whites than among African Americans (Table 8.10). For 2008–2018, the mean pension income for Non-Southern African American women is 64.4 percent of Non-Southern African American men ($4,179 versus $6,520), while this ratio is 56 percent for Southern African American women and men ($3,070 versus $5,050). For 1979 these percentages were 25 percent and 40 percent, respectively.

The Non-South African American–White mean pension ratio was 0.608 in the late 1970s and 0.755 after the Great Recession, while it was 0.288 and 0.665 in the South during these two periods. Non-South African American males have $6,520 mean pension; this is about $543 per month and represents the highest private pension income for African American men and women. Southern African American males have a mean annual pension income of $5,050 – just under $421 per month. Both numbers represent considerable improvement over 1979, when Non-South African American males annual private pension income was $3,148 (a little more than $250 per month) and Southern African American males had pension income of $1,517 (about $125 per month).

8.3 HOMEOWNERSHIP

Both the fraction of families owning a home and the growth in the value of a family's home contributed to racial wealth inequality during 1974–2018. African American homeownership was higher in 1974–1979 at 0.54 than it was during 1990–2000, when it had fallen to 0.52 (see Table 8.11). Throughout this period, the African American home ownership rate was 22–24 percentage points lower than the White homeownership rate. African American homeownership rose to 55 percent during 2001–2007, but was just 50 percent during 2008–2018, bringing the racial gap in home ownership to 26.7 percentage points in 2008–2018 versus 21.4 percentage points in 1974–1979.

The mean return on home equity, that is, the increase in the value of a family's home, is consistently lower among African Americans than Whites; the racial ratio was 0.62 in 1974–1979 ($2,547 versus $4,091) and declined to 0.60

		Individual							
		White				African American			
		Female		Male		Female		Male	
		Non-South	South	Non-South	South	Non-South	South	Non-South	South
1979	Mean	$1,753	$1,773	$5,063	$5,207	$733	$600	$3,148	$1,517
	Median	$0	$0	$0	$0	$0	$0	$0	$0
1980–1989	Mean	$1,821	$1,888	$6,615	$7,087	$1,407	$936	$4,456	$2,319
	Median	$0	$0	$0	$0	$0	$0	$0	$0
1990–2000	Mean	$2,202	$2,182	$8,636	$8,795	$2,346	$1,582	$5,588	$3,989
	Median	$0	$0	$1,026	$0	$0	$0	$0	$0
2001–2007	Mean	$2,675	$2,480	$9,359	$8,776	$3,407	$2,345	$6,199	$4,735
	Median	$0	$0	$0	$0	$0	$0	$0	$0
2008–2018	Mean	$4,122	$3,532	$9,955	$8,769	$4,179	$3,070	$6,520	$5,050
	Median	$0	$0	$0	$0	$0	$0	$0	$0
		Family							
		White				African American			
		Non-South	South			Non-South	South		
1979	Mean	$4,819	$5,268			$2,928	$1,515		
	Median	$0	$0			$0	$0		
1980–1989	Mean	$6,051	$6,599			$4,352	$2,288		
	Median	$0	$0			$0	$0		
1990–2000	Mean	$7,838	$8,228			$5,302	$3,924		
	Median	$0	$0			$0	$0		
2001–2007	Mean	$8,759	$8,394			$6,471	$4,926		
	Median	$0	$0			$0	$0		
2008–2018	Mean	$10,818	$9,667			$7,333	$5,764		
	Median	$0	$0			$0	$0		

Source: Author's calculations. Social security and VA pensions are not included

TABLE 8.11. *Home ownership rates and return to equity, by region: 1976–2018*

		African American			White		
		Ownership	Return to Equity		Ownership	Return to Equity	
		Rate	Mean	Median	Rate	Mean	Median
1974–1979		0.541	$2,547	$1,557	0.755	$4,091	$3,857
1980–1989		0.524	$3,965	$434	0.746	$6,601	$5,663
1990–2000		0.520	$3,069	$296	0.760	$5,228	$3,426
2001–2007		0.553	$2,217	$0	0.792	$3,726	$2,040
2008–2018		0.500	$2,264	$0	0.767	$3,801	$1,911
1974–1979	Non-South	0.541	$2,547	$1,557	0.755	$4,091	$3,857
1980–1989		0.524	$3,965	$434	0.746	$6,601	$5,663
1990–2000		0.520	$3,069	$296	0.760	$5,228	$3,426
2001–2007		0.553	$2,217	$0	0.792	$3,726	$2,040
2008–2018		0.500	$2,264	$0	0.767	$3,801	$1,911
1974–1979	South	0.580	$2,477	$1,770	0.767	$3,565	$3,272
1980–1989		0.568	$3,854	$1,951	0.762	$5,698	$5,089
1990–2000		0.565	$2,774	$803	0.775	$4,197	$2,851
2001–2007		0.600	$1,998	$171	0.809	$3,014	$1,758
2008–2018		0.547	$2,193	$0	0.782	$3,393	$1,843

Source: Author's calculations. Homeownership rates are for 1974–2019, while return to home equity is for 1979–2018

in 2008–2018 ($2,264 versus $3,801). The median ratio declined from 0.40 to 0.00. The African American median return on home equity declined from $1,557 in 1975–1979 to $434 during 1980–1989, while the mean increased from $2,547 to $3,965. This is a clear indication of a large decline in home equity among the poorest families, while affluent families experienced an increase in wealth. Median African American return to equity was $0 for 2001–2018.

The homeownership rate of Southern African Americans is 5 percentage points greater than the home ownership rate of Non-Southern African Americans, 0.55 versus 0.50, respectively. Further, both rates were lower during 2008–2018 than during 1975–1980, with the largest decline occurring among Non-Southern African Americans. The mean value of return on home equity was slightly larger among Non-Southern families than Southern families. However, the median return on home equity was $0 for Non-Southern African American families from 2001 to 2018 and always lower than the median return on equity for Southern African American families. The Black–White median home equity ratio was 0.541 during 1974–1979 and declined steadily to $0 during 2008–2018. Home equity declined for Whites during the 1980s, 1990s, and 2000s, but it decreased much more for African Americans.

Home ownership increases with economic status (Table 8.12). The Southern African American home ownership rate usually exceeds the Non-Southern African American rate. During 2008–2018, 37 percent of very poor families in the South owned their own home, compared to just 27 percent of Non-Southern poor families. Forty-four percent of lower income Southern families owned their home versus 31 percent of lower income Non-Southern families. There is also a 12 percentage point gap between Southern and Non-Southern middle income families, 62.1 and 49.6 percent, respectively. The regional gap is 6.5 percentage points for upper income families and 3.4 percentage points for elite families. Eighty-one percent of Southern upper income families own their homes and 74.4 percent of Non-Southern families own their homes. Eighty-five percent of elite Southerners are homeowners, while 81.6 percent of elite Non-Southerners are homeowners.

Between 2001–2007 and 2008–2018 homeownership among very poor Non-South African Americans declined by 4 percentage points and homeownership among lower income Non-Southern African Americans declined by 6 percentage points. Similarly, middle income Non-Southern African Americans saw their homeownership rates drop by 10 percentage points. There was a 4 percentage point decline among upper income Non-Southern African Americans. By comparison, the 4.6 percentage point loss of home ownership among Non-Southern elite African American families appears to be a small reduction.

Except for a 3 percentage point decline among low-income Non-Southern Whites, there was no homeownership decline among Non-Southern White families during 1976–2018. The homeownership rate of Southern Whites

TABLE 8.12. *African American home ownership by economic status and by region, 1976–2018*

African American					
All	1976–1980	1981–1990	1991–2001	2002–2008	2009–2019
Very poor	0.373	0.347	0.335	0.385	0.327
Low income	0.450	0.460	0.461	0.478	0.388
Middle income	0.653	0.639	0.633	0.665	0.568
Upper income	0.811	0.812	0.815	0.838	0.780
Elite	0.870	0.862	0.872	0.887	0.834
South					
Very poor	0.423	0.403	0.385	0.432	0.372
Low income	0.516	0.512	0.531	0.539	0.444
Middle income	0.695	0.684	0.675	0.718	0.621
Upper income	0.853	0.854	0.834	0.856	0.810
Elite	0.884	0.898	0.894	0.908	0.850
Non-South					
Very poor	0.314	0.280	0.276	0.329	0.270
Low income	0.368	0.384	0.354	0.391	0.307
Middle income	0.604	0.584	0.575	0.597	0.496
Upper income	0.781	0.774	0.795	0.818	0.744
Elite	0.862	0.839	0.855	0.866	0.816
White					
All	1976–1980	1981–1990	1991–2001	2002–2008	2009–2019
Very poor	0.510	0.500	0.531	0.581	0.558
Low income	0.666	0.674	0.698	0.741	0.649
Middle income	0.790	0.792	0.816	0.857	0.799
Upper income	0.907	0.900	0.913	0.939	0.908
Elite	0.941	0.943	0.944	0.955	0.934
South					
Very poor	0.567	0.553	0.577	0.625	0.604
Low income	0.687	0.698	0.734	0.774	0.694
Middle income	0.805	0.801	0.823	0.864	0.810
Upper income	0.912	0.908	0.916	0.944	0.911
Elite	0.950	0.949	0.949	0.964	0.938
Non-South					
Very poor	0.484	0.476	0.510	0.559	0.532
Low income	0.654	0.660	0.675	0.720	0.620
Middle income	0.784	0.788	0.813	0.853	0.794
Upper income	0.905	0.897	0.911	0.937	0.907
Elite	0.937	0.940	0.942	0.951	0.932

increased or remained constant. Very poor Southern White families own homes at about the same rate as middle income Southern African American families, 60.4 percent and 62.1 percent, respectively. Very poor Non-Southern White families have a homeownership rate exceeding the rate of ownership for Non-Southern middle income African American families, 53.2 percent and 49.6 percent, respectively.

Between 1991–2001 and 2002–2008 African American home ownership increased for both South and Non-South, with the most rapid growth in the Non-South and among the lowest income groups. For example, among very poor African Americans living in Non-Southern States home ownership increased by 5.3 percentage points, from 27.6 percent to 32.9 percent. Among lower income and middle income families in that same region home ownership grew by 3.7 and 2.2 percentage points, respectively. Homeownership growth for very poor, lower income, and middle income African American families in the South was 4.5 percent, 1 percent, and 5.43 percent, respectively.

The extraordinary growth in home ownership among African American families outside of the South during the first decade of the new century was very fragile. The best evidence shows that this growth was financed by predatory leading, in particular, so-called sub-prime ("very high interest") loans, with high fees, large pre-payment penalties, adjustable interest rates, and other highly unattractive features (McArthur and Edelman, 2017). These mortgages were far too expensive and had ruinous terms of repayment. They worked against homeowners accumulating equity in their most valuable asset. Predictably, unemployment severed the ability to pay. The Great Recession wiped out nearly all of the 1991–2008 growth in African American home ownership, in both the South and the Non-South.

Married or previously married families have higher ownership rates than never-married families (Table 8.13). Married or previously married families also realize a higher return on home equity (Table 8.14). Regardless of marital status, the largest racial disparity in homeownership and home equity occurs for Non-Southern families.

Seventy percent of Southern married African Americans own their own homes and 60 percent of Non-Southern married African Americans own their own homes. Southern married families increased their homeownership rate by 3 percentage points during 1976 to 2019. Homeownership among Non-Southern married African American families fell from 62 percent to 60 percent. For 2009–2019 Southern married African American homeownership is 17 percentage points less than White families; this gap is 26 percentage points among Non-South families.

Regardless of race, region, or gender, never-married families were about 10 percentage points less likely to be homeowners in 2009–2019 than in 1976–1980. Notably, never-married Whites receive a greater return on home equity than married African Americans. Never-married Whites also have

TABLE 8.13. *Home ownership by race, marital status, and region: 1976–2019*

			South		Non-South	
	African American	White	African American	White	African American	White
Divorced, Widowed, Separated – Women						
1976–1980	0.439	0.626	0.483	0.674	0.394	0.605
1981–1990	0.454	0.629	0.504	0.676	0.395	0.607
1991–2001	0.480	0.661	0.520	0.699	0.428	0.641
2002–2008	0.536	0.703	0.578	0.741	0.482	0.683
2009–2019	0.504	0.690	0.552	0.718	0.438	0.674
Divorced, Widowed, Separated – Men						
1976–1980	0.447	0.575	0.473	0.585	0.421	0.571
1981–1990	0.453	0.581	0.485	0.606	0.419	0.568
1991–2001	0.448	0.626	0.492	0.643	0.393	0.618
2002–2008	0.501	0.677	0.549	0.701	0.445	0.664
2009–2019	0.470	0.679	0.522	0.700	0.401	0.668
Married						
1976–1980	0.646	0.807	0.671	0.813	0.616	0.804
1981–1990	0.643	0.812	0.670	0.816	0.608	0.810
1991–2001	0.671	0.841	0.703	0.845	0.626	0.839
2002–2008	0.711	0.882	0.750	0.886	0.657	0.879
2009–2019	0.660	0.864	0.703	0.867	0.597	0.862
Never-married Women						
1976–1980	0.458	0.704	0.495	0.726	0.418	0.697
1981–1990	0.412	0.653	0.474	0.674	0.343	0.645
1991–2001	0.372	0.620	0.423	0.638	0.314	0.614
2002–2008	0.399	0.644	0.440	0.650	0.352	0.641
2009–2019	0.352	0.607	0.388	0.614	0.307	0.603
Never-married Men						
1976–1980	0.523	0.722	0.578	0.726	0.466	0.720
1981–1990	0.467	0.670	0.510	0.676	0.421	0.667
1991–2001	0.438	0.636	0.485	0.645	0.383	0.633
2002–2008	0.460	0.653	0.504	0.665	0.410	0.647
2009–2019	0.410	0.619	0.451	0.637	0.361	0.610

homeownership rates that rival the homeownership rate of married African Americans.

Previously-married African American women increased their homeownership rate from 0.44 to 0.50 during 1976–2019, but the racial gap for this family type remained constant – 19 percentage points in 1976–1980 and in 2009–2019. Previously married African American men raised their

TABLE 8.14. *Mean return to home equity by race, marital status, and region: 1979–2018*

	African American	White	South African American	South White	Non-South African American	Non-South White
Divorced, Widowed, Separated – Women						
1979	$2,021	$3,220	$1,848	$3,073	$2,190	$3,285
1980–1989	$3,188	$5,239	$3,219	$4,816	$3,151	$5,442
1990–2000	$2,778	$4,386	$2,547	$3,671	$3,073	$4,752
2001–2007	$2,187	$3,274	$1,986	$2,791	$2,444	$3,531
2008–2018	$2,301	$3,418	$2,222	$3,018	$2,412	$3,650
Divorced, Widowed, Separated – Men						
1979	$2,169	$3,140	$2,182	$2,670	$2,157	$3,352
1980–1989	$3,330	$4,928	$3,313	$4,315	$3,347	$5,219
1990–2000	$2,642	$4,117	$2,535	$3,339	$2,774	$4,511
2001–2007	$2,098	$3,021	$2,032	$2,529	$2,177	$3,287
2008–2018	$2,090	$3,191	$2,071	$2,789	$2,115	$3,423
Married						
1979	$2,996	$4,277	$2,831	$3,712	$3,187	$4,542
1980–1989	$4,911	$7,061	$4,504	$6,076	$5,447	$7,552
1990–2000	$4,050	$5,795	$3,500	$4,622	$4,816	$6,408
2001–2007	$2,908	$4,202	$2,557	$3,368	$3,394	$4,652
2008–2018	$3,084	$4,375	$2,942	$3,893	$3,293	$4,645
Never-married Women						
1979	$2,152	$4,094	$2,062	$3,514	$2,242	$4,282
1980–1989	$3,114	$6,257	$3,258	$5,293	$2,954	$6,610
1990–2000	$2,087	$4,346	$1,982	$3,369	$2,208	$4,726
2001–2007	$1,489	$2,943	$1,336	$2,264	$1,661	$3,232
2008–2018	$1,486	$2,834	$1,424	$2,453	$1,563	$3,005
Never-married Men						
1979	$2,439	$4,105	$2,567	$3,468	$2,308	$4,344
1980–1989	$3,577	$6,324	$3,546	$5,234	$3,609	$6,752
1990–2000	$2,477	$4,419	$2,259	$3,420	$2,733	$4,827
2001–2007	$1,744	$2,951	$1,529	$2,269	$1,984	$3,241
2008–2018	$1,775	$2,869	$1,698	$2,544	$1,865	$3,016

homeownership rate by 2.3 percentage points, from 0.45 to 0.47 during 1976–2019, but the racial gap increased from 12 percentage points to 21 percentage points as the homeownership rate for previously married White men rose from 0.58 to 0.68.

8.4 DISCRETIONARY PROPERTY INCOME: INTEREST, RENT, DIVIDENDS, CAPITAL GAINS

The median American family does not have interest, dividends, and rental income (IDR) or capital gains income (Table 8.15). Within racial groups, men have higher mean IDR income than women, Non-South individuals and families have higher mean IDR income than Southern individuals and families and mean individual IDR income has grown since the end of the end of Jim Crow.

Non-South White family IDR income increased by 20 percent between the mid-1970s and the 2010s, while Southern White IDR income declined by 1.4 percent, from $3,506 per year to $3,458 per year. On the other hand, Non-South African American IDR income increased by 75 percent and Southern African American IDR increased by 293 percent, from $240 per year to $942 per year.

The mean value of White capital gains increased by 106 percent during 1979–2007 (Table 8.16). Non-South African American capital gains increased from $575 to $1,259 and Southern African American capital gains increased from $192 per year to $564, gains of 119 percent and 194 percent, respectively.

8.5 RACE AND PROPERTY INCOME: SOURCES OF PERSISTENT INEQUALITY

Several factors explain racial differences in property income, viz., racial differences in family savings rates, family income during the current and previous periods, inheritances and in vivo transfers, rate of return on assets, pension annuities and insurance payments, and portfolio allocation. Market discrimination is also an important determinant of racial differences in wealth. Savings from income generate wealth. Hence, discrimination in access to income will generate disparities in wealth accumulation.

8.5.1 Different Characteristics and Market Treatment

Disparity studies decompose racial differences in economic outcomes into a "characteristics" effect and a "market treatment" effect. The characteristics effect represents the fraction of the racial gap that is statistically attributable to racial differences in the average characteristics of individuals or families, for example, the average quantity and quality of education, regional location, labor market experience, and so forth. The market treatment differential represents the fraction of the racial gap that is statistically attributable to racial differences in the market rates of return to characteristics of individuals or families; for example, if an additional year of education raises White wealth by 9 percent but raises African American wealth by 6 percent, then this difference in rates of return to education contributes to the market treatment differential for wealth. In a well-specified model the market treatment differential

		Individual							
		White				African American			
		Women		Men		Women		Men	
		Non-South	South	Non-South	South	Non-South	South	Non-South	South
1964–1973	Mean	$773	$741	$1,698	$1,480	$79	$53	$230	$115
	Median	$0	$0	$0	$0	$0	$0	$0	$0
1974–1979	Mean	$1,122	$1,154	$1,929	$1,924	$175	$78	$307	$127
	Median	$0	$0	$3	$0	$0	$0	$0	$0
1980–1989	Mean	$2,472	$2,428	$2,348	$2,401	$376	$233	$459	$259
	Median	$89	$30	$86	$30	$0	$0	$0	$0
1990–2000	Mean	$2,428	$2,191	$2,626	$2,455	$616	$360	$696	$474
	Median	$69	$23	$69	$21	$0	$0	$0	$0
2001–2007	Mean	$2,135	$1,893	$2,562	$2,326	$568	$406	$730	$530
	Median	$12	$0	$13	$0	$0	$0	$0	$0
2008–2018	Mean	$1,730	$1,419	$2,397	$2,070	$451	$368	$635	$497
	Median	$1	$0	$2	$0	$0	$0	$0	$0

		Family			
		White		African American	
		Non-South	South	Non-South	South
1974–1979	Mean	$3,434	$3,506	$627	$240
	Median	$196	$69	$0	$0
1980–1989	Mean	$4,909	$4,857	$849	$517
	Median	$393	$197	$0	$0
1990–2000	Mean	$5,030	$4,607	$1,330	$892
	Median	$302	$146	$0	$0
2001–2007	Mean	$4,584	$4,088	$1,306	$946
	Median	$126	$39	$0	$0
2008–2018	Mean	$4,122	$3,458	$1,1142	$942
	Median	$41	$9	$0	$0

Source: Author's calculations, Annual Social and Economic Supple of Current Population Survey, 1965–2019. Family data start with the 1975 Survey

TABLE 8.16. *Mean and median capital gain and capital loss by race and region: 1979–2007*

	White		African American	
	Non-South	South	Non-South	South
1979	$584	$252	$575	$192
	$0	$0	$0	$0
	$0	$0	$0	$0
	$0	$0	$0	$0
1980–1989	$685	$242	$682	$200
	$0	$0	$0	$0
	$59	$35	$57	$29
	$0	$0	$0	$0
1990–2000	$1,309	$546	$1,155	$386
	$0	$0	$0	$0
	$84	$58	$78	$49
	$0	$0	$0	$0
2001–2007	$1,307	$588	$1,259	$564
	$0	$0	$0	$0
	$111	$73	$104	$62
	$0	$0	$0	$0

Sources: Author's calculations. Data are ASEC, Current Population Survey, 2000–2008. Data are $2011

represents discrimination since market rates of return to productive attributes should not vary across racial groups.[4] How much this differential contributes to discrimination depends on whether "White coefficients" are the proper weights, that is, in the absence of discrimination the African American rate of return to education would be 9 percent, or if "Black coefficients" are the proper weights, that is, in the absence of discrimination the White rate of return to education would be 6 percent.

If the market treated all persons as if they were White, estimates of the market treatment differential are 26 percent (Blau and Graham, 1990), 33 percent (Altonji, Doraszelski, and Segal, 2000), or 49 percent (Oliver and Shapiro,

[4] For Altonji, Doraszelski, and Segal (2000), the explanatory variables include region, SMSA, spouse's annual work hours, age, spouse's age, number of children in the family, whether there are children in the family, dependents outside the family, health status of individual, years of schooling, spouse's years of schooling, number of marriages, tenure of current marriage, spouse's number of marriages, number of children born or adopted, spouse's number of children. For Blau and Graham (1990), the explanatory variables are age of head of household, whether head is a female, number of children, weeks worked of wife, central city residence, residence outside of SMSA central city, region, annual income, permanent income when head is 30 years of age. Oliver and Shapiro (1995) use a similar set of explanatory variables.

1995) of the White–African American wealth gap among married couples. If the market treated all persons as if they were Black, the lowest estimates of the market treatment differential for the White–African American wealth gap are 74 percent (Blau and Graham, 1990) and 78 percent (Altonji, Doraszelski, and Segal, 2000), while the highest estimate is 94 percent (Oliver and Shapiro, 1995). By comparison, the best evidence suggests that differential market treatment accounts for 50 percent of the male wage gap.[5]

8.5.2 Savings Rates

Family saving depends on family income. Earnings (wages and salaries) are the sole source of income for most families. African Americans have greater employment insecurity than Whites, even Whites with similar household earnings. This has been a labor market datum since the end of chattel capitalism.[6] Starting at least as early as 1940, a series of professional studies report higher savings rates among African Americans after adjusting for income.[7] Racial differences in employment security and labor income are responsible for racial differences in household savings behavior. Relatively more uncertain income might cause African Americans to save a relatively higher fraction of income than otherwise identical Whites. Further, racial differences in credit utilization is another factor that has lifted the African American savings rate above the White savings rate. "In the interwar and early post–World War II years, saving rates for low-income Black families exceeded those for White families."[8] During 1918–1919, African Americans were much more likely than Whites to use installment credit rather than merchant credit. Installment credit ("lay away") is used for consumer durables and usually requires a sufficiently large down payment such that, if repossession is necessary, the company does not lose any money. Merchant credit ("charge account") is used for non-durables and does not require a down payment and there is little or nothing to repossess in cases of non-payment. Olney (1998) documents that these savings differences remained true even when one controls for region, home ownership status, and income status. Further, Olney documents that African Americans were less likely than Whites to borrow money to finance a purchase.

Gittleman and Wolff (2004) find that, after adjusting for differences in income, there are no differences in either the mean or median savings rates of

[5] Darity and Mason (1998). The market treatment portion of the female racial wage differential may be smaller.

[6] Alexis (1970).

[7] See Alexis (1962) for a discussion of the earliest studies on African American–White differences in savings rates. Utilizing the Study of Consumer Purchases 1935–1936, Mendershausen (1940) is likely the first professional study to report higher savings rates among African Americans.

[8] Olney (1998). Also, Klein and Moody (1953) report that, during 1947–1949, African Americans were substantially more likely than Whites to use installment credit than merchant credit.

White and African American households.[9] Conditional on income and other explanatory variables, median savings rates among African Americans are slightly higher because savings rates rise faster with age among African Americans than among Whites.

Non-collateralized debt includes items such as credit cards and charge cards, student loans, and medical bills. Among low income households, African Americans are less likely than White households to hold such debt. The opposite is true among high income households (Hurst, Stafford, and Luoh, 1998). Since there are disproportionately more low income African American households, the racial difference in non-collateralized debt holdings would tend to raise the African American savings rate relative to the White saving rate.

Self-employment also affects wealth accumulation and savings behavior. Bradford (2003) finds identical savings rates among African American and White entrepreneurs, although African Americans have a lower rate of entrepreneurship than Whites.[10] Both African American and White entrepreneurs have a higher savings rate than workers and both groups have greater upward mobility and less downward mobility within the wealth distribution than their respective group of workers. We note, however, that the relationship between self-employment and wealth is ambiguous (Altonji and Doraszelski, 2005).[11] Past discrimination in financial, labor, and consumer markets has a negative effect on African American self-employment and thereby reduced wealth accumulation (Oliver and Shapiro, 1995; Bates, 1997). On the other hand, greater wealth accumulation provides the savings required for successful entrepreneurship.

8.5.3 Rate of Return on Assets

Ownership of risky assets, for example, corporate stock, provides a higher rate of return than ownership of safe assets, for example, a family home. When examining families that are similar with respect to a broad set of factors, such as age of head of household, presence of children, household size, marital status, education, income, expected inheritance, net worth, employment status, self-employed, eligibility for a retirement plan, homeownership, and willingness to take risk, African Americans and Whites are equally likely to own risky assets (Gutter and Fontes, 2006).[12] Persons willing to take risks are more likely to own risky assets and this does not change with race. But among persons not willing to take risks, African Americans are more likely than Whites to own

[9] Gittleman and Wolff use PSID files for 1984, 1989, and 1994.

[10] Bradford uses the 1984, 1989, and 1994 samples of the PSID.

[11] Altonji and Doraszelski find that omitting self-employment from their wealth regressions lowers the fraction of the racial wealth differential by about 15 percentage points for married couples.

[12] Hurst, Stafford, and Luoh (1998) find that, after controlling for family income, composition, and age, African American families are less likely to hold equities.

risky assets. Among families with savings sufficient to pay their bills for at least 3 months, African Americans are much more likely than Whites to own risky assets.

For 1984–1994, there are differences in the rate of return to capital for White and African American households. African Americans had higher mean rates of wealth accumulation for 1984–1994, though the differences were not always statistically different from 0 (Gittleman and Wolff, 2004: 202). For example, for 1984–1989, the mean rates of wealth accumulation were 32.2 percent and 32 percent for African Americans and Whites, respectively. However, these rates were 36 percent and 13.8 percent, respectively, for 1989–1994, and the difference was statistically different from 0. For the entire 10 year period African American mean rate of wealth accumulation was 70.7 percent which was statistically equivalent to the White rate of 50.8 percent. African Americans had lower median rates of wealth accumulation for 1984–1994 and the differences were statistically significant. For example, for 1984–1989, the median rates of wealth accumulation were 2.6 percent and 19 percent for African Americans and Whites, respectively, and this difference was significant. However, these rates were −1.9 percent and 6.9 percent, respectively, for 1989–1994 and the difference was not statistically significant. For the entire 10 year period African American median rate of wealth accumulation was 6.1 percent, which was significantly different from the White rate of 35.4 percent.

Without adjusting for current income, the mean and median savings rates are higher among White families.[13] Combined with the outcomes on the rate of wealth accumulation, this suggests equal if not higher rates of return on wealth assets among African Americans. For both African American and White families, the median rate of return on capital is 0.00 percent for each of the two subperiods and for the entire 10-year period. For African American families the mean rates of return on capital are 17.0 percent (1984–1989), 11.5 percent (1989–1994), and 27.3 percent (1984–1994). For White families the mean rates of return on capital are 9.7 percent (1984–1989), −2.2 percent (1989–1994), and 9.8 percent (1984–1994) and the racial differences for 1989–1994 and 1984–1994 are statistically significant.

African Americans at the upper end of the wealth distribution obtained higher rates of return than their White counterpart, but there are no differences among median households. Hence, the mean rate of return is higher for African

[13] For 1984–1989, 1989–1994, and 1984–1994, mean savings rates for African Americans was 3.0 percent, 5.7 percent, and 3.9 percent, and the mean savings rates for White families were 8.2 percent, 8.2 percent, and 7.6 percent, respectively. The differences were statistically significant for 1984–1989 and 1984–1994. The median African American savings rates for these three periods were 0.3 percent, 0.7 percent, and 0.5 percent, respectively, while the savings rates for White families were 3.7 percent, 2.9 percent, and 3.6 percent, respectively. The racial differentials in the median savings rates are statistically significant for all periods.

Americans than it is for Whites because of relatively higher rates of return on the capital of the most affluent African Americans relative to their White counterparts.

8.5.4 Portfolio Allocation

Compared to Whites, African Americans have a lower rate of home ownership, lower rate of business ownership, and are less likely to own stocks. For example, during 1984, 1989, and 1994, 8.5 percent, 8.3 percent, and 14.3 percent of African American families owned stock, versus 32.3 percent, 36 percent, and 44.8 percent of White and other families (Hurst, Stafford, and Luoh , 1998). Hence, home equity is a much more important source of wealth accumulation for African Americans than Whites because Whites have a more diversified asset portfolio (Blau and Graham, 1990; Hurst, Stafford, and Luoh, 1998; Gittleman and Wolff, 2004).

During the 1990s "saving and wealth accumulation are increasingly in equity-based assets and the rise in per family wealth has been disproportionately greater than rates of active saving" (Hurst, Stafford, and Luoh , 1998). These racial differences in portfolio composition may generate differences in the rate of return to financial capital. For example, during periods of rapid growth in the stock market the White rate of return to capital may rise relative to the African rate of return because Whites are more heavily invested in stock. Similarly, during periods of dramatic downturns in the stock market the White rate of return to capital may decline relative to the African American rate of return for similar reasons. Among those owning risky assets, African Americans and Whites are equal proportions of their total financial assets (dollars) invested in risky assets (Gutter and Fontes, 2006).

8.5.5 Inheritances

Over their lifetime about 30 percent of Americans will receive an inheritance, which will account for about 40 percent of wealth at the time of their death (Wolff and Gittleman, 2014). The mean value of these transfers is $216,974.[14] Racial differences in intergenerational transfers are an important cause of the large and persistent racial difference in wealth. In particular, inheritances and in vivo transfers account for more of the racial gap than other demographic and socioeconomic indicators (Hamilton and Darity, 2010).

Income differences are the largest factor explaining differences in wealth, but 75 percent of the difference in wealth is unexplained by the statistical analysis (Blau and Graham, 1990).[15] Twelve percent of White households receive an

[14] Wolff and Gittleman report $200,000 in $2007. The number in the text is reported in $2011.

[15] Blau and Graham used the National Longitudinal Survey of Young Men and Women 1976 and 1978. Young Black families have wealth levels that are 18 percent of the wealth levels of young

inheritance, but just 1 percent of African American households receive an inheritance (Gittleman and Wolff, 2004: 215). Using the 1976 National Longitudinal Surveys of Mature Men and the 1989 Survey of Consumer Finances, Menchik and Jianakoplos (1997) estimate that financial inheritances account for 10–20 percent of the average difference in African American–White household wealth.[16]

Receiving an inheritance is positively correlated with the wealth of both African American and White entrepreneurs (Altonji and Doraszelski, 2002). Further, self-employment raises the family's savings rate. Differences in inheritances explain an important fraction of the self-employment gap between African Americans and Whites (Altonji and Doraszelski, 2002).

8.6 WEALTH CHANGES FOR MATURE PERSONS

Examining the property income of mature individuals allows us to assess the cumulative effects of persistent racial discrimination on the life-chances of African Americans. By mature, we mean persons 50 years of age and above. Mature persons have arrived at their peak earnings capacity and maximal wealth accumulation after a lifetime of social and economic decision-making and opportunities. For African Americans, these decisions and opportunities have been influenced by a greater or lesser degree of discrimination over a lifetime. Hence, for otherwise identical African Americans and Whites, differences in their earnings and income from wealth during maturity reflect the combined effects of contemporary and lifetime social and economic discrimination.

Descriptions of six overlapping synthetic cohorts of new seniors (persons 50–64 years of age) are presented in Table 8.17. Except 1965, cohorts are separated by troughs of recessions. For cohort 1, individuals are aged 50 and above in 1964, 51 and above in 1965, 52 and above in 1966, and so forth. Individuals aged 50 in 1964 reached their peak earnings while Jim Crow remained the law of the land. Notably, these seniors were born during the Nadir. Cohort 2 consists of mature adults beginning with persons age 50 and above in 1973. The youngest individuals in this second cohort were at least 40 years of age at the end of Jim Crow. This a second group of workers born during the Nadir. Hence, both de jure segregation and state-tolerated violence

White families. The primary respondent in their sample was 24–34 years of age. So, these households had relatively little time to accumulate wealth on their own. Importantly, racial differences in family structure are responsible for only 5 percent of the wealth difference in households. Their regression results control for permanent income, region, location, age, weeks work, female head, education, and number of children.

[16] Menchik and Jianakoplos use the 1976 National Longitudinal Surveys of Mature Men and the 1989 Survey of Consumer Finances. The NLS76 is representative of the US male population of 45–59 years old in 1966. The SCF89 is representative of all households in 1989.

TABLE 8.17. *Format of overlapping cohorts and their distinguishing characteristics*

Cohort	Age of youngest cohort entrants in 1964	Distinguishing characteristic	Disparity Hypothesis
Cohort 1 1964–1973	50	Nadir 1 cohort: completed all education and obtained peak earnings of adult work life prior to end of Jim Crow. Birth years: 1879–1914	Maximum (complete) disparity
Cohort 2 1974–1979	40	Nadir 2 cohort: Limited job mobility prior to or after end of Jim Crow Birth years: 1888–1923	High disparity
Cohort 3 1980–1989	34	Jim Crow cohort: completed post-school on-the-job training prior to end of Jim Crow Birth years: 1895–1930	Medial disparity
Cohort 4 1990–2000	24	Migration cohort: began adult work life after end of Jim Crow Birth years: 1905–1940	Low disparity
Cohort 5 2001–2007	14	New Negro cohort: completed secondary and post-secondary education after end of Jim Crow Birth years: 1915–1950	Minimum disparity
Cohort 6 2008–2018	6	Urban cohort: completed primary, secondary, and post-secondary education after end of Jim Crow Birth years: 1958–1913	No disparity

were White public instruments used to severely and intentionally suppress educational achievement and income opportunities of these workers prior to 1964. Also, the desire to recoup on their investments in firm-specific human capital after 1964 would lower their employment mobility.

The Jim Crow cohort (cohort 3) begins in 1980. This cohort includes young adults who were at least 34 years of age in 1964 and these workers are likely to have completed their schooling and post-school on-the-job training prior to the demise of Jim Crow. The quality and quantity of their education, on-the-job training, and labor market opportunities remained extraordinarily limited relative to Whites, but superior to African Americans of the Nadir 2 cohort. The Migration cohort (cohort 4) begins in 1990, with individuals who were no less than 24 years of age in 1964. The youngest workers in this cohort began their adult work-life at the end of Jim Crow. Hence, some of their on-the-job training was received in a desegregated environment and would likely be of a higher quality then the on-job-training provided to the youngest members of previous cohorts. The New Negro cohort (cohort 5) utilizes persons at least 50 years of age during 2000; hence, the youngest members of the cohort were 14 years old in 1964 and would have completed their secondary education, post-secondary education, and on-the-job training during the post-Jim Crow era. Finally, the Urban cohort (cohort 6) consists of persons age 50 and above in 2008. The youngest members of the cohort were born as Jim Crow was coming to an end, their education was completed after the end of Jim Crow. Collectively, the cohorts include individuals born between the Nadir (1877–1922) and early years of the post-war Civil Rights movement (1950).

For Nadir 1 cohort we merge annual data from the 1965 to 2019 surveys. For Nadir 2 cohort we merge annual data from 1974 to 2019 surveys, while we merge data for 1981 to 2019 surveys for the Jim Crow cohort, 1991 to 2019 surveys for the Migration cohort, 2001 to 2019 surveys for the New Negro cohort, and 2009 to 2019 surveys for the Urban cohort. Therefore, for each cohort (except the Urban cohort) we follow the youngest individuals from age 50 to the earliest retirement years and we also allow each cohort to fully overlap with one other cohort.

Consider the final column of Table 8.17. As we move from the Nadir 1 cohort to the Urban cohort, there are reductions in the racial gap in the quantity and quality of education, on-the-job training, and actual labor market experience and opportunities.

The declining disparity hypothesis predicts a continuous secular reduction in the African American–White racial gap in property income (and weekly wages). A strongly continuous decline implies that the racial gap in property income is consistently smaller for each new cohort. There should be no racial discrimination observed for the Urban cohort. A weakly continuous decline in racial income disparity means that the gaps may have stagnated some years, but they never increased. More than one full generation beyond the end of Jim Crow, there should be little or no racial discrimination for the Urban cohort of mature persons. An alternative hypothesis is non-continuous change in racial income disparity: there are periods when racial disparity is declining and periods when its increasing, with no predetermined secular trend.

Alternative gender and racial income ratios are presented in Tables 8.18 and 8.19. Each age-group includes five income categories: weekly wage; interest, dividends, and rent (IDR); interest, dividends, rent, capital gains, and home equity (IDRCH); interest, dividends, rent, and social security (IDRSS); and private pension income (Pension). The ratio of means is presented for age-group and each type of income. The cohorts are arranged in the columns, from the first cohort (Nadir 1) to the last cohort (Urban).

For new seniors (persons 50–54 years old), veteran seniors (persons 55–59 years old), and pre-retirees (persons 60–64 years old), there is declining weekly wage gender disparity among African Americans but not among Whites. For example, African American women veteran seniors within the Nadir 1 cohort

TABLE 8.18. *Gender income disparity among mature persons*

	African American						White					
Ages 50–54	**Nadir 1**	**Nadir 2**	**Jim Crow**	**Migration**	**New Negro**	**Urban**	**Nadir 1**	**Nadir 2**	**Jim Crow**	**Migration**	**New Negro**	**Urban**
Weekly wage	0.77	0.77	0.79	0.79	0.81	0.82	0.61	0.59	0.59	0.60	0.61	0.61
IDR	0.55	0.55	0.59	0.72	0.73	0.77	0.70	0.64	0.87	0.84	0.81	0.77
IDRCH	0.95	0.95	0.95	0.89	0.89	0.92	0.95	0.95	0.94	0.90	0.91	0.96
IDRSS	1.12	1.00	1.04	1.06	1.02	1.12	0.77	0.72	0.90	0.86	0.84	0.81
Pension	0.35	0.34	0.30	0.26	0.36	0.41	0.34	0.29	0.28	0.28	0.35	0.36
Ages 55–59	**1965**	**1974**	**1981**	**1991**	**2001**	**2009**	**1965**	**1974**	**1981**	**1991**	**2001**	**2009**
Weekly wage	0.74	0.73	0.75	0.75	0.78	0.80	0.59	0.56	0.56	0.57	0.59	0.60
IDR	0.84	0.90	0.90	0.93	0.70	0.99	0.62	0.67	0.90	0.78	0.79	0.73
IDRCH	0.95	0.93	0.94	0.86	0.82	0.95	0.95	0.92	0.89	0.82	0.90	0.95
IDRSS	0.70	0.72	0.74	0.77	0.69	0.77	0.61	0.66	0.86	0.77	0.77	0.74
Pension	0.71	0.56	0.55	0.48	0.63	0.71	0.56	0.35	0.33	0.34	0.45	0.56
Ages 60–64	**1965**	**1974**	**1981**	**1991**	**2001**	**2009**	**1965**	**1974**	**1981**	**1991**	**2001**	**2009**
Weekly wage	0.67	0.68	0.70	0.70	0.71	0.73	0.58	0.55	0.54	0.55	0.57	0.60
IDR	0.67	0.80	0.90	0.84	0.71	0.74	0.57	0.81	0.92	0.87	0.78	0.74
IDRCH	0.92	0.88	0.91	0.90	0.91	0.93	0.94	0.92	0.89	0.87	0.91	0.95
IDRSS	0.82	0.79	0.81	0.85	0.81	0.79	0.71	0.83	0.87	0.84	0.83	0.82
Pension	0.77	0.62	0.55	0.60	0.72	0.78	0.48	0.35	0.32	0.35	0.47	0.55
Ages 65–69	**1965**	**1974**	**1981**	**1991**	**2001**	**2009**	**1965**	**1974**	**1981**	**1991**	**2001**	**2009**
Weekly wage	0.72	0.72	0.73	0.80	0.88	0.85	0.57	0.53	0.52	0.52	0.54	0.56
IDR	0.68	0.71	0.70	0.63	0.65	0.69	0.62	0.80	0.86	0.74	0.69	0.69
IDRCH	0.87	0.84	0.82	0.85	0.94	0.95	0.88	0.84	0.82	0.82	0.86	0.88
IDRSS	0.75	0.75	0.77	0.79	0.81	0.83	0.68	0.76	0.77	0.74	0.74	0.76
Pension	0.53	0.47	0.49	0.57	0.65	0.65	0.39	0.32	0.30	0.35	0.43	0.49

Weekly wage	0.73	0.60	0.57	0.63	0.77	0.77	0.53	0.51	0.50	0.49	0.50	0.49
IDR	0.69	0.63	0.63	0.65	0.68	0.69	0.72	0.80	0.82	0.74	0.69	0.66
IDRCH	0.81	0.78	0.78	0.82	0.84	0.88	0.85	0.83	0.81	0.81	0.82	0.82
IDRSS	0.72	0.75	0.76	0.79	0.80	0.81	0.69	0.74	0.75	0.73	0.73	0.73
Pension	0.54	0.47	0.52	0.58	0.62	0.65	0.34	0.29	0.29	0.31	0.34	0.36
Ages 75+	**1965**	**1974**	**1981**	**1991**	**2001**	**2009**	**1965**	**1974**	**1981**	**1991**	**2001**	**2009**
Weekly wage	0.84	0.76	0.74	0.72	0.75	0.80	0.54	0.52	0.52	0.51	0.53	0.56
IDR	0.67	0.64	0.61	0.52	0.49	0.52	0.74	0.75	0.76	0.71	0.66	0.64
IDRCH	0.85	0.84	0.82	0.79	0.77	0.77	0.81	0.80	0.80	0.80	0.79	0.80
IDRSS	0.77	0.80	0.80	0.80	0.80	0.80	0.75	0.78	0.80	0.79	0.79	0.79
Pension	0.44	0.41	0.44	0.45	0.48	0.51	0.29	0.28	0.27	0.27	0.28	0.29

IDRCH does not include capital gains/losses during 2010–2019.
Source: Author's calculations. ASEC of the CPS, 1965–2019

TABLE 8.19. *Racial income disparity among mature persons*

	Women						Men					
Ages 50–54	**Nadir 1**	**Nadir 2**	**Jim Crow**	**Migration**	**New Negro**	**Urban**	**Nadir 1**	**Nadir 2**	**Jim Crow**	**Migration**	**New Negro**	**Urban**
Weekly wage	0.81	0.85	0.86	0.87	0.84	0.87	0.65	0.65	0.64	0.66	0.64	0.64
IDR	0.26	0.24	0.20	0.28	0.29	0.30	0.33	0.28	0.30	0.33	0.32	0.29
IDRCH	0.53	0.53	0.50	0.55	0.52	0.53	0.53	0.53	0.49	0.55	0.54	0.56
IDRSS	0.92	0.86	0.75	0.82	0.88	1.00	0.63	0.62	0.65	0.66	0.73	0.73
Pension	1.23	1.20	1.03	1.04	1.07	1.22	1.22	1.04	0.97	1.12	1.05	1.05
Ages 55–59	**1965**	**1974**	**1981**	**1991**	**2001**	**2009**	**1965**	**1974**	**1981**	**1991**	**2001**	**2009**
Weekly wage	0.79	0.85	0.86	0.88	0.87	0.86	0.63	0.66	0.64	0.66	0.66	0.65
IDR	0.29	0.24	0.19	0.30	0.27	0.30	0.22	0.18	0.19	0.25	0.31	0.22
IDRCH	0.54	0.50	0.49	0.55	0.51	0.54	0.54	0.49	0.47	0.52	0.56	0.54
IDRSS	0.82	0.79	0.59	0.77	0.79	0.98	0.72	0.72	0.68	0.77	0.88	0.94
Pension	1.07	1.08	1.08	1.02	1.07	1.07	0.84	0.68	0.65	0.73	0.77	0.84
Ages 60–64	**1965**	**1974**	**1981**	**1991**	**2001**	**2009**	**1965**	**1974**	**1981**	**1991**	**2001**	**2009**
Weekly wage	0.73	0.80	0.82	0.85	0.87	0.83	0.63	0.65	0.63	0.66	0.71	0.68
IDR	0.23	0.20	0.19	0.24	0.27	0.28	0.19	0.20	0.20	0.25	0.29	0.28
IDRCH	0.57	0.49	0.48	0.52	0.56	0.58	0.58	0.51	0.47	0.50	0.56	0.59
IDRSS	0.79	0.68	0.63	0.78	0.89	0.93	0.69	0.71	0.68	0.77	0.91	0.97
Pension	1.07	1.02	0.98	1.04	1.07	1.07	0.67	0.57	0.57	0.59	0.69	0.75
Ages 65–69	**1965**	**1974**	**1981**	**1991**	**2001**	**2009**	**1965**	**1974**	**1981**	**1991**	**2001**	**2009**
Weekly wage	0.75	0.81	0.90	1.02	1.06	1.00	0.59	0.60	0.64	0.66	0.65	0.65
IDR	0.16	0.15	0.19	0.25	0.25	0.24	0.14	0.17	0.23	0.30	0.27	0.24
IDRCH	0.51	0.47	0.49	0.56	0.58	0.56	0.51	0.47	0.49	0.54	0.54	0.52
IDRSS	0.70	0.65	0.67	0.75	0.80	0.83	0.64	0.65	0.68	0.70	0.74	0.76
Pension	0.86	0.84	0.95	1.04	1.04	1.00	0.63	0.58	0.59	0.64	0.69	0.76

Weekly wage	0.80	0.86	0.85	0.95	1.03	1.19	0.58	0.72	0.74	0.75	0.67	0.75
IDR	0.13	0.13	0.15	0.21	0.22	0.23	0.14	0.16	0.20	0.23	0.22	0.22
IDRCH	0.46	0.46	0.48	0.54	0.58	0.59	0.49	0.49	0.50	0.53	0.56	0.56
IDRSS	0.65	0.64	0.66	0.75	0.78	0.81	0.62	0.64	0.65	0.69	0.71	0.73
Pension	0.87	0.83	0.95	1.11	1.15	1.19	0.54	0.52	0.53	0.59	0.63	0.67
Ages 75+	**1965**	**1974**	**1981**	**1991**	**2001**	**2009**	**1965**	**1974**	**1981**	**1991**	**2001**	**2009**
Weekly wage	0.81	0.91	0.97	1.03	1.07	1.00	0.52	0.63	0.68	0.74	0.77	0.70
IDR	0.13	0.15	0.16	0.19	0.22	0.24	0.14	0.17	0.20	0.26	0.29	0.30
IDRCH	0.52	0.54	0.55	0.59	0.63	0.67	0.50	0.51	0.54	0.59	0.64	0.69
IDRSS	0.61	0.64	0.66	0.71	0.74	0.76	0.59	0.63	0.65	0.70	0.73	0.75
Pension	0.77	0.78	0.89	1.00	1.10	1.17	0.52	0.53	0.56	0.61	0.65	0.67

IDRCH does not include capital gains/losses during 2010–2019.
Source: Author's calculations. ASEC of the CPS, 1965–2019

earned 74 percent of the weekly wage earned by African American men veteran seniors within cohort 1 (see Table 8.18). This ratio increased slowly to 80 percent for the Urban cohort. The White gender ratio for veteran seniors was 59 percent of the Nadir 1 cohort and 56 percent of the Nadir 2 and Jim Crow cohorts before recovering to 60 percent for the Urban cohort.

For new retirees (persons 65–69 years old) and veteran retirees (persons 70–74 years old), there is declining weekly wage gender disparity among African Americans but not among Whites. Gender disparity among elders (persons 75+ years old) increases among African Americans, moving from 84 percent to 80 percent between the Nadir 1 and Urban cohorts, and constant among Whites, moving from 54 percent among the Nadir 1 cohort to 56 percent among the Urban cohort but falling to 51–53 percent for the middle cohorts.

Except for African American new and veteran retirees, there is no evidence of declining gender disparity across cohorts for IDRCH income. African American women new retirees earned 87 percent of African American men new retiree IDRCH income among the Nadir 1 cohort and 95 percent among the Urban cohort. The White ratio was 88 percent for the first and last cohorts but 82–86 percent for the middle cohorts.

Gender disparity in private pension income declined for African American new retirees, veteran retirees, and elders, but was stagnant or sporadically changed among Whites. For example, African American women new retirees earned $0.53 on each dollar of private pension income earned by African American men new retirees within the Nadir 1 cohort. This ratio declined to $0.47 on each dollar of male income for the Nadir 2 cohort before continuously rising to $0.65 on each dollar for the New Negro and Urban cohorts. White women new retirees earned $0.39 on each dollar of private pension income earned by White men new retirees within the Nadir 1 cohort. This ratio declined to $0.32 on each dollar of male income for the Nadir 2 cohort and $0.30 for the Jim Crow cohort, before continuously rising to $0.49 on each dollar for the Urban cohort.

There is declining racial wage disparity among elderly women of all age-groups. There is declining racial wage disparity among elderly men among pre-retirees, new retirees, veteran retirees, and elders. For example, African American women pre-retirees within the Nadir 1 cohort earned 73 percent of the weekly wage earned by White women pre-retirees within cohort 1 (see Table 8.19). This ratio increased to 87 percent for the New Negro cohort before declining to 83 percent for the Urban cohort. The male racial wage ratio for pre-retirees was 63 percent of the Nadir 1 cohort, 65 percent of the Nadir 2, and 63 percent of the Jim Crow cohort before rising to 71 percent and 68 percent for the New Negro and Urban cohorts, respectively.

For new retirees, veteran retirees, and elders, there is evidence of declining racial disparity across cohorts for IDRCH income. African American women new retirees earned 51 percent of White women new retiree IDRCH income among the Nadir 1 cohort and 56 percent, 58 percent, and 56 percent among the Migration, New Negro, and Urban cohorts, respectively. For veteran retirees, the male ratio was 49 percent for the Nadir 1 cohort and slowly increased to 56 percent for the New Negro and Urban cohorts.

Racial disparity in private pension income declined for new retirees, veteran retirees, and elders for both men and women and for pre-retiree men. For example, African American women new retirees earned $0.86 on each dollar of private pension income earned by White women new retirees within the Nadir 1 cohort. This ratio declined to $0.84 on each dollar of White female pension income for the Nadir 2 cohort before settling at parity for the Urban cohort. African American new retirees earned $0.63 on each dollar of private pension income earned by White men new retirees within the Nadir 1 cohort. This ratio declined to $0.58 on each dollar of White male income for the Nadir 2 cohort, before continuously rising to $0.76 on each dollar of White male private pension income for the Urban cohort.

8.7 SUMMARY AND DISCUSSION

This chapter shows the following. The recessions of 1974–1975, 1981–1982, and The Great Recession of December 2007–June 2009 greatly undermined wealth accumulation among African Americans. Progress in African American wealth accumulation has been concentrated in the South. Specifically, home ownership rates are higher in the South; home ownership rates declined outside the South during 1974–2018; home ownership declined within the South after the Great Recession; and The Great Recession reduced African American home ownership and net worth more than it reduced White home ownership and net worth. African American home ownership was lower during 2009–2019 than during the late 1970s.

African American homeownership, participation in pension plans, and property income are far below the levels of Whites. Estimates suggest that disadvantageous treatment of African Americans within the market, that is, discrimination, explain 26–94 percent of White–Black racial wealth disparity.

The African American savings rate is at least as high as the White savings rate for families with the same level of earnings (income). To the extent that the family's savings rate is determined by future-orientation, deferred gratification, frugality, and similar behaviors, there is no evidence to support the notion that African American families have a greater incidence of dysfunctional values than White families. The African American return on assets is at least as high as the White return on assets. African American–White differences in wealth are not strongly related to differences in rates of return on assets or a preference for investing in risky assets that provide above average rates of return. African American families are less likely to own risky assets than White families, but among those owning risky assets African Americans have a similar share of high yielding risky assets. Racial differences in inheritances and in vivo transfers explain the greatest portion of racial wealth disparity. By some measures of property income, there is moderately lower racial disparity among recent cohorts than among more distant cohorts. Progress in reducing racial disparity in property income has not been impressive.

9

Individual Wage and Employment Disparity

The two generations since the fall of Jim Crow are characterized by major social and economic changes that have differing effects on changes in family income and earnings: family size has decreased; family structure has changed, viz., more single parent families and fewer married couple families; married women are more likely to be labor market participants; the quality and quantity of education has increased for adult members of families; and the regional and urban distribution of families has changed. Importantly, also, women's labor force participation has changed dramatically since the middle 1960s (Simms and Malveaux, 1986). These social and economic changes have caused changes in the family income and earnings and, simultaneously, changes in family income and earnings have caused social and economic changes. These changes were not identical for Black and White families. Family income and earnings changes are important, but family changes may hide trends in individual income and earnings.

Racial disparity in wages and other labor market outcomes is lower among women than among men. Mostly, this is because the labor market behavior and outcomes of women changed dramatically between 1974 and 1991: greater labor force participation, higher wages, higher wages relative to men, and higher levels of paid employment (less time in unpaid work at home).

At the onset of the early 1970s African American women had higher labor force participation than White women, that is, African Americans were more likely to be working for pay or looking for paid work. Both married and young adult African American women were much more likely to be labor market participants than married and young adult White women. But, during 1974–1991 the entry of White women into the labor market far outpaced the entry of African American women into the labor market. Among Black women aged 20–24 years, 57 percent were labor force participants in 1972 and 59 percent were labor force participants in 1983 (Jones, 1985) (see Table 9.1).

TABLE 9.1. *Labor force participation of women, by race and age, 1972–1983*

Age	Black women	White women	Difference in increase
16–19	32 percent to 33 percent	48 percent to 55 percent	6 points higher among White women
20–24	57 percent to 59 percent	49 percent to 71 percent	20 points higher among White women
25–34	61 percent to 72 percent	46 percent to 79 percent	22 points higher among White women
35–44	61 percent to 73 percent	58 percent to 68 percent	−2 points higher among White women
45–54	57 percent to 62 percent	53 percent to 62 percent	4 points higher among White women
55 & above	No change	No change	Equal

Source: Jones (1985)

By comparison, labor force participation for White women of this same age and time period moved from 49 percent to 71 percent. Similarly, among women aged 25–34 years, Black labor force participation increased from 61 percent to 72 percent and White labor force participation increased from 46 percent to 79 percent. Workers in their early 20s and early 30s are relatively low wage workers; hence, with the more rapid increase in labor force participation of low wage White women (who also had less experience than African American women) the ratio of Black female wages relative to White female wages will increase – perhaps giving the false impression of a decrease in racial discrimination.

There was no change in the labor force participation of women aged 55 and above during 1972–1983. Also, Black teenagers (persons 16–19 years of age) did not have a noticeable increase in labor force participation – moving from 32 percent in 1972 to 33 percent in 1983. White teenage labor force participation moved from 48 percent to 55 percent. Mostly, teenagers work at or near the minimum wage. So, the more rapid movement of White teenagers into the labor force would have also caused the Black–White female wage ratio to increase, that is, move toward equality and give the false impression of declining discrimination during 1972–1983. Instead, this period has an equalization of wages for workers at the bottom of the economic ladder due to the relatively greater labor force participation of low wage White women. Labor force participation also increased by 11 percent for both groups of women aged 35–44, with Black women moving from 61 to 73 percent and White women moving from 58 to 68 percent. Similarly, among women of 45–54 years of age, African American labor force participation increased from 57 percent in 1972 to 62 percent in 1983, while White female labor force participation increased from 53 to 62 percent. Hence, for the highest earning age groups, women of 35–54 years of age, African American women had equal or higher labor force participation and greater labor market experience. This, too, would contribute to the false conclusion that racial inequality among women has been solved.

Post-1965, the labor market participation of Black women has been different from the labor market participation of White women because African American women were less likely to be married, but when married more likely to have husbands with earnings insufficient to support a family, and less likely to have property income. The change in the labor market supply of women became less dramatic in the late-1990s and into the 2000s. During the most recent years racial disparity among women began to mirror the patterns among men.

9.1 INDIVIDUAL RACE–GENDER WAGE AND EMPLOYMENT DISPARITY: 1964–PRESENT

Consider persons 25–64 years of age. Persons under 25 may be in the process of continuing their education; they are not fully committed to the labor market. Persons older than 64 may be in retirement or making labor market changes in anticipation of retirement and therefore are not fully committed to the labor market. The average weekly wage of African American women increased from $406 to $731 between the middle 1960s and the 2010s (see Table 9.2). For 1964–2018, mean weeks worked increased from 27 weeks to 34 weeks. The nonparticipation rate, that is, the fraction of women neither working in the market nor seeking employment, declined from 43 percent to 28 percent. The increase in labor force participation led to a large increase in the employment–population ratio and an increase in the unemployment–population ratio. The former rose from 54 percent to 66 percent, while the latter increased from 3 percent to 6 percent.

Notably, nonparticipation by African American women in the labor market declined by 6 percentage points between 1974–1979 and 1980–1989 – a positive outcome during a period mostly noted for its negative outcomes. Most of the participants moved into paid work as the employment–population ratio increased by 5 percentage points.

The Great Recession ended four decades of labor market progress for African American women. Between 2001–2007 and 2008–2018 mean weekly wages for African American women were stagnant, mildly rising from $729 to $731, and weeks worked declined from 36 to 34 weeks. Between 2002–2007 and 2009–2019 the employment–population ratio for African American women declined by 3 percentage points, from 0.69 to 0.66, as the unemployment–population ratio increased by 1 percentage point and the non-participation rate rose by 2 percentage points.

TABLE 9.2. *Individual labor market outcomes by race and gender: 1964–2018, ages 25–64*

African American Women	1964–1973	1974–1980	1981–1989	1990–2000	2001–2007	2008–2018
Weekly Wage	$406	$525	$559	$634	$729	$731
Weeks Worked Last Year	27	28	31	34	36	34
Employment–Pop. Ratio	0.54	0.56	0.61	0.67	0.69	0.66
Unemployment–Pop. Ratio	0.03	0.05	0.07	0.05	0.05	0.06
Nonparticipation Rate	0.43	0.38	0.32	0.28	0.26	0.28
African American Men						
Weekly Wage	$694	$826	$760	$814	$911	$901
Weeks Worked Last Year	42	38	36	38	37	35
Employment–Pop. Ratio	0.83	0.74	0.70	0.71	0.70	0.67
Unemployment–Pop. Ratio	0.05	0.08	0.10	0.07	0.07	0.09
Nonparticipation Rate	0.11	0.16	0.18	0.20	0.22	0.24
White Women						
Weekly Wage	$526	$558	$598	$713	$843	$875
Weeks Worked Last Year	23	26	31	36	36	36
Employment–Pop. Ratio	0.45	0.53	0.62	0.71	0.71	0.70
Unemployment–Pop. Ratio	0.02	0.03	0.03	0.03	0.02	0.03
Nonparticipation Rate	0.53	0.44	0.35	0.27	0.26	0.27
White men						
Weekly Wage	$1,095	$1,166	$1,122	$1,195	$1,378	$1,317
Weeks Worked Last Year	46	44	44	44	44	42
Employment–Pop. Ratio	0.90	0.86	0.84	0.84	0.83	0.80
Unemployment–Pop. Ratio	0.02	0.04	0.05	0.04	0.04	0.05
Nonparticipation Rate	0.06	0.09	0.10	0.11	0.13	0.15

Income figures are inflation-adjusted using the consumer price index, all urban consumers (March $2011). All families are Non-Latinx. Families include all age-groups. Employment status covers 1965–2019. Wages and weeks work refer to 1964–2018.
Source: Author's calculations. Data are March Current Population Survey, Annual Social & Economic Supplement, 1965–2019

Weekly wages of African American men rose from $694 in 1964–1973 to $826 during 1974–1979. But, 1974–1989 was an extended period of decline in the weekly wages of African American men, moving from $826 to $760. Average weeks worked dropped from 38 weeks to 36 weeks. The employment–population ratio declined from 0.74 to 0.70 and the unemployment–population ratio increased during the late 1970s and 1980s, rising from 8 percent to 10 percent. The nonparticipation rate increased from 16 percent to 18 percent.

Although the wages of African American men began a long recovery in the 1990s, all employment outcomes declined continuously between 1965–1974 and 2009–2019. Weeks worked declined by 7 weeks; the employment–population ratio dropped by 16 percentage points; and nonparticipation increased by 13 percentage points.

Gender equality among Blacks and among Whites increased between 1964–1973 and 2008–2018. During 1964–1973, African American women earned just $0.59 for every dollar earned by African American men (Table 9.3). By 2008–2018, this ratio was $0.81. During 1965–1974 African American women worked 15 weeks per year less than African American men. By 2009–2019 the gender employment gap was one week. The gender difference in the nonparticipation rate declined from 32 to 4 percentage points. The employment–population and unemployment population ratios also moved to near equality. During 1965–1974 the employment–population ratio for African American women was 29 percentage points less than the rate for African American men. For 2009–2019, the employment–population ratio for Black women rate was 1 percentage point less than the rate for Black men.

The trend toward gender equality among Whites is about one generation behind African Americans. During 2008–2018 White women earned $0.66 for every dollar earned by White men, about the same as the African American ratio during the 1970s. Similarly, the White nonparticipation gender gap declined from 45 percent to 10 percent, the same as the African American nonparticipation gender gap in the 1980s.

Men and women have had dissimilar changes in racial disparity. The African American–White weekly wage ratio was 0.77 for women and 0.63 for men during the late 1960s. By 1974–1979 these ratios were 0.94 and 0.71, respectively. Male and female racial disparity increased after the 1970s. The male wage ratio declined from 0.71 to 0.68 between 1974–1979 and 2008–2018 and the employment–population racial gap increased from 0.11 to 0.13. The female racial wage ratio decreased by 10 percentage points after the 1970s, even as White women went from being 9 percentage points less likely to be employed than African American women (1975–1980) to 4 percentage points more likely to be employed relative to African American women (2009–2019).

9.2 REGIONAL CHANGES AND RACE–GENDER DISPARITY

Regardless of race or region, gender inequality steadily declined steadily during 1964–2018 (see Tables 9.4–9.7). Gender inequality is lower among African

TABLE 9.3. *Changes in labor market inequality by race and by gender, 1965–2019*

	Gender Inequality					
African Americans	**1964–1973**	**1974–1979**	**1980–1989**	**1990–2000**	**2000–2008**	**2009–2018**
Weekly Wage	0.59	0.64	0.73	0.78	0.80	0.81
Weeks Worked Last Year	−15	−10	−6	−4	−2	−1
Employment–Pop. Ratio	−0.29	−0.18	−0.10	−0.04	−0.01	−0.01
Unemployment–Pop. Ratio	−0.01	−0.02	−0.03	−0.02	−0.01	−0.02
Nonparticipation Rate	0.32	0.22	0.14	0.07	0.04	0.04
Whites						
Weekly Wage	0.48	0.48	0.53	0.60	0.61	0.66
Weeks Worked Last Year	−23	−18	−13	−9	−8	−6
Employment–Pop. Ratio	−0.45	−0.33	−0.22	−0.14	−0.12	−0.10
Unemployment–Pop. Ratio	−0.01	−0.01	−0.02	−0.01	−0.01	−0.02
Nonparticipation Rate	0.47	0.35	0.25	0.16	0.14	0.12
Racial disparity						
Women						
Weekly Wage	0.77	0.94	0.93	0.89	0.86	0.84
Weeks Worked Last Year	5	2	0	−1	0	−2
Employment–Pop. Ratio	0.09	0.03	−0.02	−0.04	−0.02	−0.04
Unemployment–Pop. Ratio	0.02	0.03	0.04	0.03	0.03	0.03
Nonparticipation Rate	−0.11	−0.06	−0.03	0.01	0.00	0.01
Men						
Weekly Wage	0.63	0.71	0.68	0.68	0.66	0.68
Weeks Worked Last Year	−4	−6	−7	−7	−6	−7
Employment–Pop. Ratio	−0.06	−0.11	−0.14	−0.13	−0.13	−0.13
Unemployment–Pop. Ratio	0.02	0.04	0.05	0.04	0.03	0.04
Nonparticipation Rate	0.05	0.07	0.08	0.09	0.09	0.09

Income figures are inflation-adjusted using the consumer price index, all urban consumers (March $2011). All families are Non-Latinx. Families include all age-groups.

Source: Author's calculations. Data are March Current Population Survey, Annual Social & Economic Supplement, 1965–2019

TABLE 9.4. *Individual labor market outcomes by race and gender: 1964–2015, South, ages 25–64*

African American Women	1965–1973	1974–1980	1981–1990	1991–2000	2001–2008	2009–2015
Weekly Wage	$318	$445	$501	$583	$695	$716
Weeks Worked Last Year	28	29	32	35	36	34
Employment–Pop. Ratio	0.56	0.58	0.63	0.68	0.70	0.67
Unemployment–Pop. Ratio	0.03	0.05	0.07	0.05	0.05	0.06
Nonparticipation Rate	0.41	0.37	0.30	0.26	0.25	0.27
African American Men						
Weekly Wage	$557	$707	$682	$761	$869	$880
Weeks Worked Last Year	42	39	37	39	38	35
Employment–Pop. Ratio	0.84	0.77	0.73	0.74	0.72	0.67
Unemployment–Pop. Ratio	0.04	0.06	0.09	0.06	0.06	0.08
Nonparticipation Rate	0.11	0.16	0.17	0.19	0.21	0.24
White Women						
Weekly Wage	$498	$536	$585	$689	$822	$855
Weeks Worked Last Year	23	26	31	35	35	34
Employment–Pop. Ratio	0.45	0.53	0.61	0.69	0.69	0.67
Unemployment–Pop. Ratio	0.01	0.02	0.03	0.02	0.02	0.03
Nonparticipation Rate	0.53	0.45	0.36	0.29	0.29	0.30
White Men						
Weekly Wage	$996	$1,103	$1,079	$1,156	$1,337	$1,293
Weeks Worked Last Year	45	44	43	44	43	41
Employment–Pop. Ratio	0.88	0.85	0.83	0.84	0.82	0.79
Unemployment–Pop. Ratio	0.02	0.03	0.04	0.03	0.03	0.04
Nonparticipation Rate	0.08	0.10	0.11	0.12	0.14	0.16

Income figures are inflation-adjusted using the consumer price index, all urban consumers (March $2011). All families are Non-Latinx. Families include all age-groups.

Source: Author's calculations. Data are March Current Population Survey, Annual Social & Economic Supplement, 1965–2019

TABLE 9.5. *Individual labor market outcomes by race and gender: 1964–2018, Non-South, ages 25–64*

African American Women	1965–1973	1974–1980	1981–1989	1990–2000	2001–2007	2008–2018
Weekly Wage	$508	$614	$629	$700	$772	$754
Weeks Worked Last Year	26	27	30	33	35	33
Employment–Pop. Ratio	0.52	0.54	0.58	0.65	0.67	0.64
Unemployment–Pop. Ratio	0.03	0.06	0.07	0.05	0.06	0.06
Nonparticipation Rate	0.45	0.40	0.35	0.30	0.27	0.29
African American Men						
Weekly Wage	$842	$959	$855	$882	$964	$929
Weeks Worked Last Year	42	38	35	36	37	34
Employment–Pop. Ratio	0.82	0.72	0.67	0.68	0.68	0.66
Unemployment–Pop. Ratio	0.06	0.10	0.11	0.09	0.08	0.09
Nonparticipation Rate	0.11	0.17	0.20	0.22	0.23	0.25
White Women						
Weekly Wage	$538	$567	$604	$724	$854	$886
Weeks Worked Last Year	22	26	31	36	37	36
Employment–Pop. Ratio	0.45	0.53	0.63	0.71	0.72	0.71
Unemployment–Pop. Ratio	0.02	0.03	0.03	0.03	0.03	0.03
Nonparticipation Rate	0.54	0.44	0.34	0.26	0.25	0.25
White Men						
Weekly Wage	$1,131	$1,192	$1,142	$1,213	$1,399	$1,330
Weeks Worked Last Year	46	45	44	44	44	42
Employment–Pop. Ratio	0.90	0.86	0.84	0.84	0.83	0.80
Unemployment–Pop. Ratio	0.03	0.04	0.05	0.04	0.04	0.05
Nonparticipation Rate	0.06	0.09	0.10	0.11	0.12	0.14

Income figures are inflation-adjusted using the consumer price index, all urban consumers (March $2011). All families are Non-Latinx. Families include all age-groups.

Source: Author's calculations. Data are March Current Population Survey, Annual Social & Economic Supplement, 1965–2019

Gender Inequality						
African American	1965–1973	1974–1979	1980–1989	1990–2000	2001–2007	2008–2018
Weekly Wage	0.57	0.63	0.73	0.77	0.80	0.81
Weeks Worked Last Year	−14	−10	−6	−4	−1	−1
Employment–Pop. Ratio	−0.29	−0.18	−0.10	−0.05	−0.02	−0.01
Unemployment–Pop. Ratio	−0.01	−0.01	−0.02	−0.01	−0.01	−0.02
Nonparticipation Rate	0.30	0.21	0.13	0.07	0.04	0.03
White						
Weekly Wage	0.50	0.49	0.54	0.60	0.62	0.66
Weeks Worked Last Year	−22	−17	−12	−9	−8	−7
Employment–Pop. Ratio	−0.42	−0.32	−0.22	−0.15	−0.13	−0.12
Unemployment–Pop. Ratio	0.00	−0.01	−0.01	−0.01	−0.01	−0.01
Nonparticipation Rate	0.45	0.34	0.25	0.17	0.15	0.14
Racial Disparity						
Women						
Weekly Wage	0.64	0.83	0.86	0.85	0.85	0.84
Weeks Worked Last Year	6	3	1	0	2	0
Employment–Pop. Ratio	0.10	0.05	0.02	0.00	0.01	0.00
Unemployment–Pop. Ratio	0.02	0.03	0.04	0.03	0.03	0.03
Nonparticipation Rate	−0.12	−0.08	−0.06	−0.03	−0.04	−0.03
Men						
Weekly Wage	0.56	0.64	0.63	0.66	0.65	0.68
Weeks Worked Last Year	−2	−4	−6	−5	−5	−6
Employment–Pop. Ratio	−0.03	−0.08	−0.11	−0.10	−0.10	−0.12
Unemployment–Pop. Ratio	0.02	0.03	0.05	0.03	0.03	0.04
Nonparticipation Rate	0.03	0.05	0.06	0.07	0.07	0.08

Income figures are inflation-adjusted using the consumer price index, all urban consumers (March $2011). All families are Non-Latinx. Families include all age-groups.

Source: Author's calculations. Data are March Current Population Survey, Annual Social & Economic Supplement, 1965–2019

TABLE 9.7. *Changes in labor market inequality by race and by gender: Non-South, 1964–2018*

	Gender Inequality					
African American	**1964–1973**	**1974–1979**	**1980–1989**	**1990–2000**	**2001–2007**	**2008–2018**
Weekly Wage	0.60	0.64	0.74	0.79	0.80	0.81
Weeks Worked Last Year	−16	−11	−6	−3	−2	−1
Employment–Pop. Ratio	−0.30	−0.18	−0.09	−0.03	−0.01	−0.01
Unemployment–Pop. Ratio	−0.02	−0.04	−0.04	−0.03	−0.02	−0.03
Nonparticipation Rate	0.34	0.23	0.15	0.08	0.04	0.04
White						
Weekly Wage	0.48	0.48	0.53	0.60	0.61	0.67
Weeks Worked Last Year	−24	−19	−13	−8	−7	−6
Employment–Pop. Ratio	−0.46	−0.34	−0.22	−0.13	−0.11	−0.09
Unemployment–Pop. Ratio	−0.01	−0.01	−0.02	−0.02	−0.02	−0.02
Nonparticipation Rate	0.48	0.36	0.24	0.15	0.13	0.11
Racial Disparity						
Women						
Weekly Wage	0.95	1.08	1.04	0.97	0.90	0.85
Weeks Worked Last Year	3	1	−2	−3	−2	−3
Employment–Pop. Ratio	0.07	0.01	−0.05	−0.07	−0.05	−0.07
Unemployment–Pop. Ratio	0.02	0.03	0.04	0.03	0.03	0.03
Nonparticipation Rate	−0.09	−0.04	0.00	0.04	0.02	0.04
Men						
Weekly Wage	0.74	0.80	0.75	0.73	0.69	0.70
Weeks Worked Last Year	−4	−7	−8	−8	−7	−8
Employment–Pop. Ratio	−0.08	−0.15	−0.17	−0.17	−0.15	−0.15
Unemployment–Pop. Ratio	0.03	0.05	0.06	0.05	0.04	0.04
Nonparticipation Rate	0.05	0.09	0.10	0.11	0.11	0.10

Income figures are inflation-adjusted using the consumer price index, all urban consumers (March $2011). All families are Non-Latinx. Families include all age-groups.
Source: Author's calculations. Data are March Current Population Survey, Annual Social & Economic Supplement, 1965–2019

Americans. Changes in racial disparity vary by region, with the South showing the greatest progress and progress over the longest period – but, there has been long-term stagnation in the movement toward equality in both regions and for both men and women.

Outside of the South, all progress for African American men and women occurred during 1964–1979. There were extraordinary increases in inequality during 1974–2018. The weekly wage ratio for African American and White women increased from 0.95 to 1.08 during 1964–1979, but this ratio declined sizably to 0.85 by 2008–2018. There is a similar pattern for male racial wage inequality; the weekly wage ratio increased from 0.74 to 0.80 during the 1960s and 1970s. Nevertheless, the male wage ratio was 0.70 during 2008–2018.

Within the South, progress for African American men and women occurred during 1964–1979. Specifically, the male racial wage ratio rose from 0.56 to 0.64 during 1964–1979. This ratio remained more or less fixed at 0.64 during the 1990s and throughout the 2000s, before rising to 0.68 during 2008–2018. The male racial gap in the employment–population ratio steadily increased from 3 percentage points in 1965–1974 to 12 percentage points during 2009–2019. Similarly, during the post-Jim Crow era the male racial gap in weeks worked steadily increased from 2 weeks to 1.5 months. The female racial wage ratio rose from 0.64 to 0.83 during 1964–1979, but did not change very much during the 1980s, 1990s, 2000s, and 2010s. The female racial gap in the employment–population ratio steadily decreased from 10 percentage points in favor of African American women during 1965–1974 to equality during the 1980s, 1990s, 2000s, and 2010s. Similarly, during the post-Jim Crow era the female racial gap in weeks decreased from 6 weeks in favor of African Americans during 1965–1974 to equality from the 1990s forward.

9.3 EDUCATION AND LABOR MARKET CHANGES AMONG AFRICAN AMERICANS

Post-Jim Crow, wages and employment collapsed for African American men with the lowest level of education. For Black men with less than 12 years of education, weeks worked were cut in half from 41 during 1964–1973 to 20 during 2008–2018 – a loss of 4 months of employment per year (Table 9.8). The probability of being employed was more than cut in half as the employment–population ratio plunged from 81 percent to 38 percent. For 25–64 year-old African American males with less than 12 years of education, the probability of not having a job and not seeking employment, that is, the nonparticipation rate, grew steadily from 13 percent in 1965–1974 to 50 percent in 2009–2019.

Wage progress was better for African American men with the highest level of education, though there were employment problems for these men. For Black men with at least 16 years of education, that is, a bachelor's degree or higher,

TABLE 9.8. *Labor market outcomes by years of education: African American men, ages 25–64, 1965–2018*

Less than 12 years	1964–1973	1974–1979	1980–1989	1990–2000	2001–2007	2008–2018
Weekly Wage	$608	$672	$601	$579	$580	$539
Weeks Worked Last Year	41	35	30	27	25	20
Employment–Pop. Ratio	0.81	0.67	0.58	0.50	0.48	0.38
Unemployment–Pop. Ratio	0.05	0.08	0.11	0.09	0.09	0.12
Nonparticipation Rate	0.13	0.25	0.30	0.40	0.43	0.50
12 years						
Weekly Wage	$792	$872	$722	$692	$743	$713
Weeks Worked Last Year	43	41	38	38	36	32
Employment–Pop. Ratio	0.86	0.79	0.73	0.71	0.67	0.61
Unemployment–Pop. Ratio	0.04	0.09	0.11	0.09	0.08	0.10
Nonparticipation Rate	0.06	0.09	0.14	0.20	0.24	0.29
13–15 years						
Weekly Wage	$867	$935	$849	$875	$896	$838
Weeks Worked Last Year	43	41	40	42	40	37
Employment–Pop. Ratio	0.86	0.79	0.77	0.78	0.75	0.71
Unemployment–Pop. Ratio	0.04	0.08	0.08	0.06	0.06	0.08
Nonparticipation Rate	0.07	0.10	0.11	0.13	0.17	0.20
At least 16 years						
Weekly Wage	$1,069	$1,253	$1,100	$1,222	$1,388	$1,320
Weeks Worked Last Year	46	45	44	45	45	43
Employment–Pop. Ratio	0.92	0.88	0.85	0.86	0.85	0.83
Unemployment–Pop. Ratio	0.02	0.04	0.05	0.04	0.04	0.05
Nonparticipation Rate	0.05	0.06	0.08	0.08	0.10	0.11

Income figures are inflation-adjusted using the consumer price index, all urban consumers (March $2011). All families are Non-Latinx. Families include all age-groups.
Source: Author's calculations. Data are March Current Population Survey, Annual Social & Economic Supplement, 1965–2019

weeks worked declined from 46 to 45 between 1964–1974 and 1975–1980 and gradually declined to 43 during 2009–2019. Similarly, the employment–population ratio declined from 0.92 to 0.83 between 1965–1974 and 2009–2019. It is quite problematic also that the nonparticipation rate for the most educated African American males increased continuously during 1965–2019, from 5 percent to 11 percent. The late 1970s and 1980s presented challenges for college educated Black males, as their weekly wages declined from $1,253 to $1,100, weeks work fell by 1 week, the probability of employment dropped by 3 percentage points, the unemployment–population ratio increased by 1 percentage point, and nonparticipation rose by 2 percentage points.

Labor market outcomes for African American male high school graduates (men with exactly12 years of education) and men with some college (13–15 years of education) followed similar trends. Mean weekly wages for African American men with just 12 years of education rose from $792 to $872 during 1964–1979. Thereafter, the mean declined to $692 during the 1990s. There was a recovery during the 2000s, but the weekly wage in 2008–2018 was $713, less than the weekly wage of $792 in 1964–1973. For African American men with some college, mean weekly wages were $867 in the late 1960s and $838 during 2008–2018.

Nonparticipation has increased and the probability of employment has decreased consistently for male high school graduates and men with some college. Among African American male high school graduates, nonparticipation rose from 0.06 in 1965–1974 to 0.29 in 2009–2019, while nonparticipation rose from 0.07 in 1965–1974 to 0.20 in 2009–2019 for men with some college education. Similarly, the employment–population ratio has fallen from 0.86 in 1965–1974 to 0.61 in 2009–2019 for high school graduates and from 0.86 to 0.71 for men with some college education.

Trends in weekly wages and employment for African American women also varied according to years of education, but the changes were dissimilar to male labor market outcomes (Table 9.9). Women with less than 12 years of education earned $418 per week during 2008–2018, compared to $287 per week in 1964–1973. The weekly wages for women with just 12 years of education have also increased, moving from $472 (1964–1973) to $518 (2008–2018). However, the wages of high school graduates declined from $540 to $518 during 1974–2018. The weekly wages of women with some college (13–15 years of education) improved between 1964–1973 and 1974–1979, moving from $592 to $642, but then declined to $611 during 1980–1989 before closing higher, at $652, during 2008–2018. Weekly wages for women with at least 16 years of education have increased from $866 in 1964–1973 to $1,067 in 2008–2018, despite dipping from $872 in 1974–1979 to $870 in 1980–1989.

Similar to men, for 1965–2019 women with less than 12 years of education experienced a large reduction in the probability of employment (9 percentage points), a reduction in weeks worked (5 weeks), and an increase in

TABLE 9.9. *Labor market outcomes by years of education: African American women, 1965–2018, ages 25–64*

Less than 12 years	1964–1973	1974–1979	1980–1989	1990–2000	2001–2007	2008–2018
Weekly Wage	$287	$362	$364	$390	$421	$418
Weeks Worked Last Year	24	22	20	20	22	19
Employment–Population Ratio	0.47	0.43	0.40	0.40	0.42	0.36
Unemployment–Population Ratio	0.03	0.05	0.07	0.06	0.08	0.09
Nonparticipation Rate	0.50	0.52	0.53	0.54	0.50	0.56
12 years						
Weekly Wage	$472	$540	$525	$518	$559	$518
Weeks Worked Last Year	30	31	32	33	33	30
Employment–Population Ratio	0.61	0.62	0.64	0.65	0.64	0.58
Unemployment–Population Ratio	0.03	0.06	0.08	0.06	0.06	0.07
Nonparticipation Rate	0.36	0.31	0.28	0.29	0.30	0.35
13–15 years						
Weekly Wage	$592	$642	$611	$652	$698	$654
Weeks Worked Last Year	33	35	37	39	39	36
Employment–Population Ratio	0.66	0.71	0.74	0.76	0.74	0.69
Unemployment–Population Ratio	0.03	0.05	0.07	0.05	0.05	0.06
Nonparticipation Rate	0.31	0.24	0.19	0.19	0.21	0.25
At least 16 years						
Weekly Wage	$866	$872	$870	$983	$1,114	$1,067
Weeks Worked Last Year	41	42	43	43	43	41
Employment–Population Ratio	0.85	0.85	0.86	0.85	0.84	0.80
Unemployment–Population Ratio	0.01	0.03	0.03	0.03	0.03	0.04
Nonparticipation Rate	0.14	0.12	0.10	0.12	0.13	0.16

Income figures are inflation-adjusted using the consumer price index, all urban consumers (March $2011). All families are Non-Latinx. Families include all age-groups.
Source: Author's calculations. Data are March Current Population Survey, Annual Social & Economic Supplement, 1965–2019

nonparticipation (6 percentage points). However, for women with at least 12 years of education access to employment increased during 1965–2008, with the Great Recession ushering in a reversal to this progress. Prior to 2009, nonparticipation declined, while weeks worked and the employment–population ratio increased for high school graduates and women with some college education. For example, among African American women of 25–64 years of age with a high school diploma, the employment population increased from 0.61 in 1965–1974 to 0.64 in 2002–2008 – with most of the increase occurring during 1974–2000. For Black women with some college education, the probability of nonparticipation was 0.31 in 1965–1974 but 0.21 during 2002–2008, with all of the improvement occurring during 1965–1990. Among women with a college degree, access to employment was more or less stable during 1965–2008. However, for the most recent period (2009–2019) the employment–population ratio dropped 4 percentage points for women.

9.4 GENERATIONAL DIFFERENCES IN ECONOMIC WELL-BEING

Middle-aged African American males, that is, men 35–54 years of age, earned $962 per week in 2008–2018, after starting at $714 in 1964–1973 (Table 9.10). The late-1970s and 1980s were periods of decline for the mean weekly wages for middle-age African American males, as weekly wages moved from $870 (1974–1979) to $836 (1980–1989). Further, middle-age African American males have had a long-term reduction in employment. The nonparticipation rate has more than doubled from 9 percent (1965–1974) to 21 percent (2009–2019). The unemployment–population rate has increased from 4 percent to 8 percent. The employment–population ratio has declined from 86 employed men per 100 men to 71 employed men per 100 men. The average number of weeks worked has dropped by 1.5 months, declining from 43 weeks in 1965–1974 to 37 weeks in 2009–2019. The Great Recession is responsible for a 2 percentage point decline in employment for middle-aged African American males, as the employment–population ratio decreased from 0.73 (2002–2008) to 0.71 (2009–2019).

Wage and employment changes for young African American males (men 25–34 years of age) and for senior African American males (men 55–64 years of age) have followed the same pattern as middle-age African Americans. However, the negative effects have been relatively larger for young men and relatively smaller for senior men.

Middle-aged African American women have attained both greater weekly earnings and greater employment since the end of Jim Crow. They earned $785 per week in 2008–2018, rising continuously from $401 in 1964–1973. The long-term increase in weekly wages has been matched by a long-term increase in employment. The nonparticipation rate has fallen from 40 percent to 24 percent. The employment–population ratio has risen from 57 employed women per 100 women to 73 employed women per 100 women during 2001–2008,

TABLE 9.10. *Labor market outcomes by age, African American men and women, 1964–2018*

			Women			
25–34 years of age	1964–1973	1974–1979	1980–1989	1990–2000	2001–2007	2008–2019
Weekly Wage	$460	$559	$540	$555	$642	$610
Weeks Worked Last Year	26	30	31	34	37	35
Employment–Pop. Ratio	0.53	0.60	0.62	0.68	0.71	0.68
Unemployment–Pop. Ratio	0.05	0.09	0.11	0.08	0.08	0.09
Nonparticipation Rate	0.42	0.31	0.28	0.24	0.21	0.22
35–54 years of age						
Weekly Wage	$401	$528	$596	$690	$766	$785
Weeks Worked Last Year	29	29	33	36	38	36
Employment–Pop. Ratio	0.57	0.59	0.66	0.72	0.73	0.71
Unemployment–Pop. Ratio	0.03	0.04	0.06	0.05	0.05	0.06
Nonparticipation Rate	0.40	0.37	0.28	0.24	0.22	0.24
55–64 years of age						
Weekly Wage	$308	$405	$467	$595	$761	$773
Weeks Worked Last Year	24	21	22	24	28	27
Employment–Pop. Ratio	0.45	0.41	0.43	0.46	0.52	0.51
Unemployment–Pop. Ratio	0.02	0.02	0.02	0.02	0.02	0.03
Nonparticipation Rate	0.53	0.57	0.55	0.52	0.45	0.46
			Men			
25–34 years of age						
Weekly Wage	$704	$795	$682	$689	$780	$728
Weeks Worked Last Year	43	40	37	40	38	36
Employment–Pop. Ratio	0.86	0.77	0.71	0.74	0.72	0.69
Unemployment–Pop. Ratio	0.06	0.11	0.13	0.10	0.09	0.12
Nonparticipation Rate	0.06	0.09	0.12	0.14	0.17	0.18

35–54 years of age						
Weekly Wage	$714	$870	$836	$887	$952	$962
Weeks Worked Last Year	43	40	39	39	39	37
Employment–Pop. Ratio	0.86	0.78	0.76	0.73	0.73	0.71
Unemployment–Pop. Ratio	0.04	0.07	0.09	0.07	0.07	0.08
Nonparticipation Rate	0.09	0.14	0.14	0.18	0.19	0.21
55–64 years of age						
Weekly Wage	$611	$755	$730	$867	$1,039	$1,025
Weeks Worked Last Year	38	32	28	28	29	28
Employment–Pop. Ratio	0.73	0.59	0.52	0.53	0.54	0.53
Unemployment–Pop. Ratio	0.04	0.05	0.05	0.03	0.03	0.05
Nonparticipation Rate	0.24	0.36	0.43	0.44	0.43	0.42

though declining to 71 per 100 women during the most recent years. The average number of weeks worked has increased by almost two months, rising from 29 weeks in 1965–1974 to 36 weeks in 2009–2019.

Among young adult African American women (25–34 years of age), weekly wages, weeks worked, and employment increased during 1964–2018, while the nonparticipation rate dropped by 20 percentage points. The unemployment–population ratio increased to 9 percent during the 1970s and to 11 percent during the 1980s; the weekly wage declined from $559 to $540 during 1974–1989. Senior African American women (ages 55–64) experienced the most rapid wage gains, moving from $308 to $773. The unemployment–population ratio was constant at 2 percent, until after the Great Recession when it rose to 3 percent. During 1965–2019, weeks worked rose (3 weeks), the probability of employment increased (6 percentage points), and the nonparticipation rate decreased by 7 percentage points.

9.5 PERSISTENT DISCRIMINATION

There are earnings and employment differentials between men and women and between Whites and African Americans. Group differences in labor market outcomes are the result of group differences in skill as well as differences in the treatment of groups within the labor market. Group differences in skill may also occur because of differential labor market treatment, as some skill is provided through employment, promotion, and formal and informal skill transfer (on-the-job training). Also, group differences in skill may occur because of group differences in access to education and informal sources of training. Persistent discrimination means that, over a very long period of time, a worker's social identity (race, ethnicity, gender) is an important element of the decisions to hire, pay, train, promote, and lay off workers.

Persistent racial, gender, and ethnic discrimination means: (1) persons with identical ability and effort do not obtain identical skill; and (2) identically skilled persons do not receive identical labor market outcomes – all other things being equal. Racial differences in health, wealth, preschool resources, and prenatal treatment will affect skill accumulation and ability. We bypass this major issue and concentrate on racial differences in market treatment, given skill differences that may themselves be the product of current and past discrimination against a group or wealth differences between groups.

We use more than five decades of data to examine the relationship between competition and persistent racial discrimination in the labor market.[1] The

[1] The data are a sample of noninstitutionalized persons from the Current Population Survey Annual Social and Economic Supplement for 1965–2019. Years of education and probability of employment are for the survey year, while the natural logarithm of weekly wages is for the work-year, that is, the year prior to the survey. All workers are 16–64 during the work-year. Institutionalized persons are not included in the sample. The sample excludes persons who are

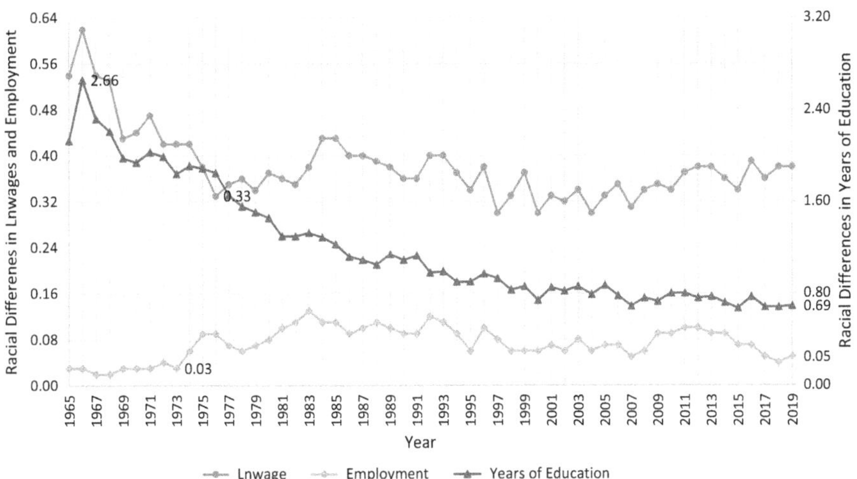

FIGURE 9.1. Racial differences in years of education, Lnwages, and employment: men, 16–64 years of age, 1965–2020

relationship between male racial differences in years of education, the natural logarithm of weekly wages, and probability of employment are presented in Figure 9.1. The same information for women is provided in Figure 9.2.

From the mid-1960s (the end of Jim Crow) through 1976, the male racial gap in the natural log of weekly wages decreased as the male racial gap in years of education decreased. For example, during 1966, White men averaged 2.66 more years of education than African American men and White men had a wage advantage of 0.62 log points (86 percent). Both groups of men had rising levels of education during the 1960s and 1970s, but the growth in years of education was faster for African American men. By 1976, White men averaged 1.85 more years of education than African American mean and White men had a wage advantage of 0.33 log points (about 39 percent). The decrease in male racial wage inequality from the middle of the 1960s to 1976 is consistent with the decreasing racial gap in skill and decreasing labor market discrimination.

This progress did not hold. From 1976 to 1985, the White male wage advantage increased from 0.33 log points to 0.43 log points, even though the White male education advantage declined from 1.85 years to 1.23 years. By

self-employed, retired, enrolled in school, did not seek paid work because of obligations to take care of their home or family, currently in the military, unable to work because of health problems, or who did not seek paid employment for other reasons. All persons are Non-Latinx African Americans and Non-Latinx Whites. The full econometric model is $Y_i = \beta_0 + \delta\text{African} + \beta_1\text{age} + \beta_2\text{age}^2 + \beta_3\text{education} + \beta_4\text{education}^2 + \beta_5\text{education*age} + \beta_6\text{married} + \beta_7\text{widowed} + \beta_8\text{divorced} + \beta_9\text{separated} + \beta_{10}\text{veteran} + \sum_{t=}^{T}\text{year}_t + u_i$, where $i = 1, 2, \ldots, n$ individuals. Separate equations are for each gender–regional group. $\hat{\delta}$ is the statistic report in Tables 9.11 and 9.12. Mostly, it is significant with $p < 0.01$.

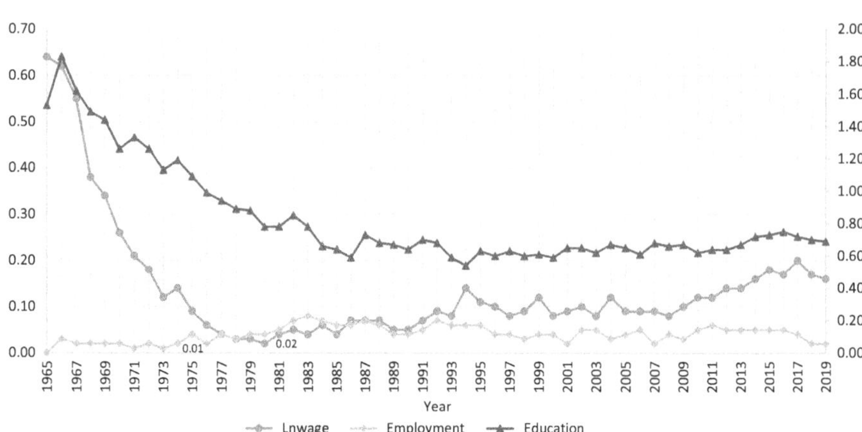

FIGURE 9.2. Racial differences in years of education, Lnwages, and employment: women, 16–64 years of age, 1965–2019

2016, the male racial wage gap was 0.39 log points (higher than the 1976 gap) and the male racial gap in years of education was 0.77 years. For the 43 years from 1976 to 2019, the White male wage advantage did not decrease (and, at times, grew substantially) while the White male education advantage continuously declined.

The White male advantage in employment is unresponsive to the decrease in the White male advantage in years of education. From the mid-1960s to 1983, the White male employment–population rate advantage grew from 3 percentage points to 13 points, though the White male advantage in years of was decreasing. By 2019, White men were 7 percentage points more likely to be employed than African American men. As the White male educational advantage was cut in half between 1965 and 2019, the White male employment advantage doubled. A 7 percentage point advantage is equivalent to a "deep recession-equivalent" racial disadvantage for African American males.

The weekly wage differential for White women declined from 0.64 log points (about 90 percent) in the mid-1960s to 0.02 log points (about 2 percent) in 1980, while White women's advantage in years of education declined from 1.53 years to 0.78 years (see Figure 9.2). The White female advantage in years of education continued to decline for the next 14 years, reaching 0.54 years in 1994. But, the wage advantage for White women grew during 1980–2019, from 0.02 log points (2.02 percent) to 0.17 log points (18.5 percent). During the 2010s, the White female advantage in years of education rose slightly from 0.54 years to 0.75 years – but this is far from sufficient to explain the very large increase in the White female weekly wage advantage.

Starting in the mid-1960s and continuing to 1980, the White female racial wage advantage declined in response to a relatively faster years of education growth among African American women, growth in the labor force participation of low wage White women, and, perhaps, lower wage discrimination against African American women. This relationship did not hold from 1980–2019; racial discrimination increased: White women's educational advantage declined as White women's wage advantage rose dramatically.

The White female advantage in employment is unresponsive to the decrease in the White female advantage in years of education. From 1965 to 1983, the White female employment–population rate advantage grew from 0 percentage points to 8 percentage points, as the racial gap in years of education was decreasing. By 2016, White women were 5 percentage points more likely to be employed than African American women. So, as the education gap was cut in half between the mid-1960s and 2016, the White female employment doubled. A 5 percentage point advantage is a "recession-equivalent" racial disadvantage for African American women. The White female employment advantage declined to 2 percentage points by 2019.

Figures 9.1 and 9.2 establish a prima facie case for persistent racial wage and employment discrimination within competitive labor markets. We use multiple regression analysis to ascertain if there is a stronger case. Racial differences in weekly wages of men and women are presented in Table 9.11 for several statistical models. Racial weekly wage differences are calculated separately for time period, region, and gender groups: Southern men, Non-Southern men, Southern women, and Non-Southern women for 1964–2018.

The unadjusted wage differential is the average racial wage difference without accounting for racial differences in skill, marital status, veteran status, or trends within each period. The Southern unadjusted male race wage differential for 2008–2018 is –0.358, that is, the average weekly wage for African American males is 0.358 log points (43 percent) less than the average weekly wage for White males. The next row presents the wage differential for workers of identical age and years of education. Regardless of race, wages are higher for persons with higher education and greater years of experience (age). For African American and White males with identical years of education and experience, the 2008–2018 Southern wage differential is –0.253 log points; Southern African American males earn 28.4 percent less than White males with equal years of education and work experience.

The third row examines the racial wage differential for men with the same years of education, age, and marital status. Marital status is also a well-known determinant of wages. For example, currently married and previously married (divorced, widowed, and separated) males earn higher wages than never-married males. In comparison to never-married men, marriage allows men to specialize in market work, while wives specialize in home work. Married males may also have a stronger commitment to work than never-married men. Finally, weekly wages may be higher for married males because they have higher levels of unmeasured skill than unmarried. By accumulating more skill than unmarried men, because they are more committed to market work, or because they have higher levels of unmeasured skill than never-married men of

TABLE 9.11. *Racial wage differentials, by gender and region, 1964–2018*

	1964–1973	1974–1979	1980–1989	1990–2000	2001–2007	2008–2018
Men, South						
Unadjusted	−0.569	−0.432	−0.402	−0.345	−0.335	−0.359
Education, Age	−0.360	−0.272	−0.291	−0.229	−0.229	−0.253
Education, Age, Marriage	−0.323	−0.229	−0.247	−0.186	−0.180	−0.202
Education, Age, Marriage, Veteran, Trend	−0.327	−0.226	−0.246	−0.192	−0.180	−0.202
Men, Non-South						
Unadjusted	−0.253	−0.197	−0.242	−0.244	−0.286	−0.349
Education, Age	−0.179	−0.155	−0.196	−0.170	−0.196	−0.238
Education, Age, Marriage	−0.161	−0.129	−0.158	−0.134	−0.146	−0.189
Education, Age, Marriage, Veteran, Trend	−0.162	−0.129	−0.158	−0.133	−0.146	−0.193
	1965–1973	**1974–1979**	**1980–1989**	**1990–1900**	**2001–2007**	**2008–2018**
Women. South						
Unadjusted	−0.540	−0.175	−0.129	−0.132	−0.079	−0.132
Education, Age	−0.376	−0.097	−0.068	−0.046	0.003	−0.037
Education, Age, Marriage	−0.377	−0.099	−0.068	−0.040	0.009	−0.025
Education, Age, Marriage, Veteran, Trend	−0.397	−0.100	−0.068	−0.046	0.008	−0.016
Women, Non-South						
Unadjusted	−0.002	0.143	0.102	0.027	−0.004	−0.110
Education, Age	0.058	0.178	0.131	0.086	0.075	0.007
Education, Age, Marriage	0.040	0.152	0.106	0.074	0.073	0.014
Education, Age, Marriage, Veteran, Trend	0.027	0.153	0.105	0.072	0.073	0.020

Source: Author's calculations, CPS ASEC 1965–2019

the same education and experience levels, married men will be more productive and obtain higher pay and have a greater likelihood of employment. Or, it may be the case that persons with higher earnings ability are more likely to marry.

White males have higher rates of marriage than African American males. Therefore, after controlling for marital status (along with education and experience), African American men earn 0.201 log points (22.3 percent) less than White males of equal education, experience, and marital status.

Finally, the fourth row of each panel controls for military service ("Veteran") and factors affecting the trend rate of growth of wages ("Trend"). Military service may have a positive effect on wages. Veterans learn leadership, teamwork, and the ability to work under extreme duress. These are productivity enhancing skills. If African Americans and Whites differ in military experience, this will alter the racial wage differential. The trend rate of growth of wages is affected by differences in economic policy, international trade, the composition of employment opportunities, changes in macroeconomic activity, and so forth. These factors may have differential racial and gender effects on workers.

For male workers with the same years of education, experience, marital status, military experience, and trend changes, during 2008–2018 Southern African American men earn 20.2 log points (22.4 percent) less than otherwise identical Southern White males. The unadjusted differential reported in row 1 is the gross wage differential, the average wage difference between African Americans and Whites. The differential reported in row 4 is the racial wage differential that remains after we have accounted for racial differences in skill – our measure of racial wage discrimination. We conclude that racial discrimination in the labor market explains (–0.202/–0.359) = 56 percent of the 2008–2018 Southern male racial weekly wage differential.[2]

For both men and women, both regions, and all time periods, accounting for differences in skill characteristics (especially education and experience) lowers the racial wage differential. Jim Crow was a Southern institution. Its destruction produced a sizable reduction in wage discrimination against African American men. Adjusting for education, experience, marital status, military experience, and the wage trend, the Southern male racial wage discrimination declined from 0.327 log points (38.7 percent) during 1964–1973 to about 0.231 log points (26 percent) during 1974–1979. For 2008–2018 Southern male weekly wage racial discrimination is only slightly lower (0.202) than where it was during the 1970s.

For Non-Southern men, the adjusted racial wage differential is 0.162 log points (17.6 percent) for the period immediately at the end of Jim Crow and 0.132 log points (14.1 percent) during the 1970s. There was an increase in

[2] Economists have far more refined estimates of racial wage discrimination, but this estimate is similar to the best studies.

discrimination against Southern and Non-Southern Black men during the 1980s, as the racial Southern wage gap rose from 0.231 log points to 0.246 log points and the Non-Southern racial wage increased from 0.132 log points to 0.158 log points. Racial discrimination against African American men fell during the 1990s, when joblessness fell to its lowest level since the years before the 1974–1975 recession. Non-Southern male weekly wage racial discrimination (0.193) is higher than any other period of 1964–2019.

The changes in the racial wage discrimination among women is dissimilar to the pattern for men, though the racial wage differential was lower. During 1964–1973, African American women had greater labor force participation than White women; hence, African American women had greater experience than White women of the same age and years of education. This would tend to lower the female racial wage differentials. During the 1970s and 1980s, White women entered the labor force at a faster rate than African American women. Indeed, the labor force participation of White women without a college degree had the most rapid growth. This, too, would tend to lower the racial wage differential.

The 2008–2018 unadjusted racial wage differential for women is –0.132 log points, that is, the average wage for African American women is 14.1 percent less than the average weekly wage for White women. Southern African American women earn about (0.037 log points) 3.77 percent less than White women of the same age and years of education. Among Southern women during 2008–2018, African American women earned 2.5 percent less than White women of equal education, age, and marital status. Finally, accounting for education, experience, marital status, military experience, and trend changes, Southern African American women earn 1.6 percent less than otherwise identical White women. For Non-Southern women, the adjusted racial wage differential is 2.7 percent in favor of African American women for the period immediately at the end of Jim Crow and 2 percent in favor of African American women during the most recent period.

Racial differentials in the probability of employment are presented in Table 9.12. Without adjusting for skill, the 2009–2019 Southern African American males are 7.1 percentage points less likely to be employed than White males. The probability of employment for African American males is 5.4 percentage points less than White males with equal years of education and work experience. Controlling for marital status, education, and age reduces the African American probability of employment differential to 4.4 percentage points. The 2009–2019 employment differential for Southern Black men is 5 percentage points less than the probability of employment for White males of the same age, years of education, marital status, veteran status, and trend; discrimination against Black males accounts for at least 70.4 percent (–0.050/–0.071) of the Southern male racial employment differential and 79.8 percent (–0.067/–0.084) of the Non-Southern male racial employment differential.

The unadjusted racial employment differential for Southern men increased from 1.7 percentage points to 6.5 percentage points between 1965–1974 and

TABLE 9.12. *Racial differential in probability of employment, by gender and region, 1965–2019*

	1965–1974	1975–1980	1981–1990	1991–2001	2002–2008	2009–209
Men, South						
Unadjusted	−0.017	−0.065	−0.077	−0.064	−0.054	−0.071
Education, Age	−0.013	−0.046	−0.063	−0.054	−0.044	−0.054
Education, Age, Marriage	−0.004	−0.035	−0.056	−0.050	−0.038	−0.044
Education, Age, Marriage, Veteran, Trend	0.003	−0.033	−0.056	−0.049	−0.037	−0.050
Men, Non-South						
Unadjusted	−0.043	−0.101	−0.116	−0.096	−0.070	−0.084
Education, Age	−0.041	−0.093	−0.105	−0.085	−0.060	−0.067
Education, Age, Marriage	−0.036	−0.086	−0.098	−0.080	−0.053	−0.058
Education, Age, Marriage, Veteran, Trend	−0.031	−0.084	−0.099	−0.083	−0.053	−0.067
Women, South						
Unadjusted	−0.037	−0.026	−0.050	−0.039	−0.026	−0.026
Education, Age	−0.007	−0.006	−0.035	−0.026	−0.016	−0.011
Education, Age, Marriage	−0.019	−0.017	−0.041	−0.028	−0.017	−0.011
Education, Age, Marriage, Veteran, Trend	−0.019	−0.017	−0.041	−0.030	−0.016	−0.011
Women, Non-South						
Unadjusted	−0.004	−0.033	−0.056	−0.047	−0.046	−0.052
Education, Age	0.009	−0.027	−0.052	−0.041	−0.038	−0.036
Education, Age, Marriage	−0.003	−0.040	−0.062	−0.045	−0.039	−0.035
Education, Age, Marriage, Veteran, Trend	−0.002	−0.040	−0.063	−0.047	−0.038	−0.039

Source: Author's calculations, CPS ASEC 1965–2019

1975–1980 and peaked at 7.7 percentage points during the 1980s. For the 1990s and early 2000s, the unadjusted racial differential fell from 6.4 to 5.4 percentage points. However, after the Great Recession, Southern African American males were 7.1 percentage points less likely to have employment than White males.

Among Southern women during 2009–2019, African American women were about 1.1 percentage points less likely to be employed than White women of equal education, experience, and marital status, military experience, and trend changes. Employment discrimination accounts for at least 42 percent of the Southern racial differential in employment. For Non-Southern women the racial wage differential is 3.9 percentage points. Employment discrimination against African American women accounts for nearly all of the Non-Southern racial differential in employment.

All other things equal, across business cycles, African American men and women are paid lower wages and have less access to employment than White men and women. Racial identification is not a skill. It does not determine productivity. There should be no wage and employment differentials based on racial identity. Yet, discrimination makes a substantial contribution to racial disparity. For example, suppose the average White male earns $33.00 per hour and because of racial discrimination the average African American male earns $22.00 per hour, where social discrimination produces differences in skill accounting for half of the racial wage differential and racial discrimination within the labor market accounts for half of the racial wage differential. Over the course of a work year of 2,080 hours, the White worker would earn $68,640 and the African American worker would earn $45,760, a difference of $22,880 per year. There are 47,000,000 African Americans, about 70 percent are between the ages of 15 and 64, 50 percent are men, and 65 percent of men are employed. Hence, there are about 10,692,500 employed African American men. In this example, social and market discrimination reduces total African American male income by $22,880 × 10,692,500 = $244,644,400,000 per year. This is an over-simplified calculation. Suppose it is wrong by 50 percent; hence, the true cost of weekly wage discrimination against Black men is $122,322,200,000. Suppose also that the cost of racial discrimination against Black women is only 40 percent of the cost of racial discrimination against Black men, that is $48.9 billion per year. Together, social and market discrimination costs African Americans $171 billion per year in weekly wages. If so, who gets this $171 billion that is produced but not received by African American men and women?

9.6 SUMMARY AND DISCUSSION

Individual wages, employment, and labor force participation vary according to gender, region, and skill-related attributes, such as years of education and years of labor market experience. The recessions of 1974–1975, 1981–1982, and

2007–2009 hampered and undermined individual labor market gains since 1964–1973.

The labor market progress of African American men and women has been concentrated in the South. 1974–1989 was a period of weekly wage decline for males, especially African Americans. For men and women, racial wage and employment inequality increased consistently during 1974–1989 and 2008–2019. For African American and White women, gender inequality declined throughout the Post-Jim Crow era. For African American and White women, weekly wages and employment increased throughout the Post-Jim Crow era. These changes hold true when we examine racial disparity for men and women of the same age group and years of education. Racial discrimination explains a large proportion the racial differences in wages and employment.

10

African American Cultural Diversity

Social Identity, Ethnicity, and Nativity

At the height of the US civil rights movement in the mid-1960s, foreign-born persons were less than 1 percent of the African American population (Kent, 2007). African Americans were Southern, English-speaking, native-born for several generations, and self-identified as Black-only. The foreign-born share of the African American population increased by a factor of 7 between 1960 and 1980, and this sub-group tripled between 1980 and 2005 (Kent, 2007: 4). Today, African Americans remain disproportionately Southern, but immigration has increased Spanish- and French-speaking ethnic groups, increased the fraction of persons self-identifying as mixed-race, and expanded the number of first and second generation Black Americans.

Some Black immigrants, for example, Creole- and French-speaking Haitian immigrants, along with Spanish-speaking Caribbean immigrants, have less desirable labor market outcomes than native-born African Americans. There are straightforward explanations for why this group of immigrants might be expected to have relatively lower wages, employment, and labor force participation: lower labor market characteristics, such as years of education; difficulties reading, writing, understanding, or speaking English; inferior information regarding labor market opportunities; an education that is inconsistent with American labor market requirements; or anti-immigrant labor market discrimination in combination with anti-Black labor market discrimination.

Other Black immigrant groups, for example, English-speaking Caribbean and African immigrants, have superior labor market outcomes and higher labor market attributes. The relative economic success of these immigrants is used by some individualists to claim racial discrimination against Black Americans is not a major economic problem. Rather, the claim is that the relative success of Caribbean-English and African immigrants indicates that interracial inequality between native-born African Americans and Whites is caused by some inferiority among native-born African Americans – not by racial discrimination within the labor market or within the skill accumulation process.

In addition to ethnic and national origin heterogeneity, African Americans also differ by self-identified social identity. Although the overwhelming majority of African Americans self-identify as Black-alone, a minority self-identifies as mixed-race. Mixed-race self-identification has been increasing at least since the mid-1990s and varies across regions and among ethnic groups. To the extent that there is an American preference for Whiteness or light skin shade, labor market outcomes will vary among African Americans according to skin shade and according to self-identification as Black-alone or self-identification as mixed-race. Further, in addition to treatment in the labor market, racial self-identification among African Americans is also related to differences in ethnicity, in particular, Latinx versus Non-Latinx, nativity, and region.

10.1 AMERICA'S AFRICAN DIASPORA LABOR FORCE: DESCRIPTIVE STATISTICS

For all Americans, about 10 percent of the 1994–2000 labor force was first or second generation immigrants. This number grew to 14–18 percent during the 2000s. The Latinx population accounted for a little over 10 percent of the US labor force during 1994–2000 and close to 14 percent during the first decade of the twenty-first century.

The African American labor force has similar trends. Black Latinx consist of native-born self-identified Black Latinx, along with self-identified Black immigrants of Mexican, Caribbean-Spanish, and South American origins. Latinx represent about 6 percent of all working-age African Americans, up from 2.5 percent during 1994–2000 (Table 10.1). During the 1990s, first and second generation immigrants were 10.3 percent of working-age African Americans. By 2009–2019, first and second generation immigrants were 17.6 percent of working-age African Americans. First generation American hemisphere immigrants grew from 6 to 8 percent of the African American labor force during 1994–2019, while second generation immigrants grew from 2 to 3 percent. First and second generation African immigrants increased from 1.07 percent and 0.16 percent to 4.79 percent and 0.74 percent, respectively, of the working-age African American population during 1994–2019. Other Immigrants are persons with unspecified national origins; this group has expanded from 2 percent of working-age African Americans to 4 percent during 1994–2019.

African American ethnic diversity varies strongly by region (Table 10.2). For 2009–2019, the working-age populations of the Northeast (41 percent first and second generation immigrant) and West (22 percent first and second generation immigrant) are the most diverse, while the Northcentral and Southern regions are the least diverse, 10.7 and 13.7 percent first and second generation immigrant, respectively. First generation Caribbean immigrants, that is,

TABLE 10.1. *Ethnicity of working-age African Americans: 1994–2019*

	1994–2000	2001–2008	2009–2019
Native-born, 3rd	0.8890	0.8450	0.7850
Native-born Latinx , 3rd	0.0081	0.0152	0.0256
Caribbean-English, 2nd	0.0087	0.0117	0.0163
Caribbean-Spanish, 2nd	0.0047	0.0047	0.0069
Haiti, 2nd	0.0027	0.0043	0.0065
Africa, 2nd	0.0016	0.0030	0.0074
Other immigrant, 2nd	0.0070	0.0089	0.0155
Canada	0.0004	0.0004	0.0005
Mexico	0.0014	0.0051	0.0081
Caribbean-English	0.0316	0.0366	0.0336
Caribbean-Spanish	0.0095	0.0109	0.0145
Haiti	0.0152	0.0169	0.0170
South America	0.0012	0.0032	0.0036
Africa	0.0107	0.0240	0.0479
Oceania	0.0000	0.0000	0.0001
Asia	0.0020	0.0038	0.0044
Europe	0.0044	0.0047	0.0019
N	58,978	117,671	169,164

Source: Author's calculations. All persons are 16–64 years of age during the work year

Caribbean-English, Caribbean-Spanish, and Haitian immigrants, have remained about 1/5 of the Northeast African American labor force during 1994–2019.

Black Latinx consists of self-identified Blacks who are also native-born Latinx, along with Mexican, Caribbean-Spanish, and South American immigrants. Black Latinx are a rising percentage of working-age African Americans in every region of the country. Within the Northeast, the representation of Black Latinx increased from 8.2 percent (1994–2000) to 10.1 percent (2001–2008) to 14.4 percent (2009–2019). The Black Latinx population has increased from 3 percent to 10 percent of the working-age African American population in the West, while rising from 1 percent to 3 percent of the Black labor force in the Midwest and South.

African and Haitian immigrants are rising portions of the Northeastern and Western and Northeastern and Southern working-age African American populations, respectively. African immigrants have increased from 2.5 percent to 8 percent in the Northeast and West, while Haitians have risen from 5 percent to 6 percent in the Northeast and have remained steady at about 2 percent of the South.

Black immigrants are moving to the South (Table 10.3). Fifty-three percent of African Americans lived in the South during the 1990s, with 21 percent, 18

TABLE 10.2. *Ethnicity of working-age African Americans, by region: 1994–2019*

1994–2000	Northeast	Northcentral	West	South
Native-born, 3rd	0.6760	0.9630	0.8850	0.9370
Native-born Latinx , 3rd	0.0282	0.0029	0.0084	0.0030
Caribbean-English, 2nd	0.0279	0.0022	0.0058	0.0049
Caribbean-Spanish, 2nd	0.0120	0.0029	0.0047	0.0030
Haiti, 2nd	0.0084	0.0006	0.0006	0.0018
Africa, 2nd	0.0022	0.0020	0.0032	0.0010
Other immigrant, 2nd	0.0111	0.0051	0.0214	0.0040
Canada	0.0007	0.0004	0.0006	0.0003
Mexico	0.0009	0.0015	0.0052	0.0010
Caribbean-English	0.1120	0.0040	0.0142	0.0166
Caribbean-Spanish	0.0364	0.0010	0.0075	0.0036
Haiti	0.0391	0.0017	0.0025	0.0136
South America	0.0041	0.0001	0.0013	0.0006
Africa	0.0209	0.0070	0.0218	0.0068
Oceania	0.0001	0.0000	0.0000	0.0000
Asia	0.0011	0.0021	0.0084	0.0013
Europe	0.0078	0.0017	0.0102	0.0033
N	12,399	10,600	4,858	31,121
2001–2008				
Native-born, 3rd	0.6000	0.9360	0.8230	0.9010
Native-born Latinx , 3rd	0.0411	0.0072	0.0252	0.0070
Caribbean-English, 2nd	0.0370	0.0029	0.0093	0.0064
Caribbean-Spanish, 2nd	0.0140	0.0019	0.0042	0.0025
Haiti, 2nd	0.0127	0.0007	0.0007	0.0032
Africa, 2nd	0.0047	0.0025	0.0047	0.0021
Other immigrant, 2nd	0.0104	0.0069	0.0261	0.0059
Canada	0.0006	0.0005	0.0010	0.0002
Mexico	0.0062	0.0035	0.0167	0.0035
Caribbean-English	0.1250	0.0049	0.0193	0.0204
Caribbean-Spanish	0.0359	0.0022	0.0113	0.0054
Haiti	0.0432	0.0022	0.0028	0.0162
South America	0.0109	0.0004	0.0032	0.0015
Africa	0.0366	0.0207	0.0344	0.0183
Oceania	0.0001	0.0000	0.0001	0.0000
Asia	0.0048	0.0033	0.0101	0.0024
Europe	0.0066	0.0027	0.0077	0.0040
N	23,105	24,431	12,713	73,469

2009–2019	Northeast	Northcentral	West	South
Native-born, 3rd	0.5340	0.8770	0.7270	0.8490
Native-born Latinx , 3rd	0.0569	0.0156	0.0532	0.0136
Caribbean-English, 2nd	0.0448	0.0052	0.0078	0.0120
Caribbean-Spanish, 2nd	0.0193	0.0007	0.0070	0.0048
Haiti, 2nd	0.0183	0.0006	0.0017	0.0054
Africa, 2nd	0.0111	0.0066	0.0112	0.0058
Other immigrant, 2nd	0.0176	0.0116	0.0537	0.0091
Canada	0.0006	0.0002	0.0012	0.0005
Mexico	0.0096	0.0058	0.0260	0.0050
Caribbean-English	0.1050	0.0062	0.0109	0.0230
Caribbean-Spanish	0.0464	0.0040	0.0087	0.0086
Haiti	0.0381	0.0015	0.0015	0.0177
South America	0.0118	0.0009	0.0015	0.0021
Africa	0.0655	0.0563	0.0724	0.0352
Oceania	0.0001	0.0001	0.0010	0.0001
Asia	0.0047	0.0057	0.0103	0.0029
Europe	0.0015	0.0011	0.0038	0.0019
N	25,936	26,455	16,999	99,774

percent, and 8 percent in the Northeast, Midwest, and West, respectively. By 2009–2019, 15 percent of working-age African Americans lived in the Northeast, 16 percent lived in the Northcentral states, 11 percent lived in the West, and 59 percent lived in the South. Non-Latinx native-born African Americans remain strongly tied to the South, with 58–60 percent of the population residing in the South during the entirety of 1994–2019. The regional distribution of native-born Latinx African Americans is becoming increasingly Southern, rising from 21 percent in 1994–2000 to 30 percent during 2009–2019, as their Northeast representation fell from 62 percent to 38 percent. The Southern distribution of South American and Caribbean-Spanish increased by 6 percent and 12 percent, respectively. A strong majority of Haitian immigrants reside in the South (58 percent) and the South is the major region of residence for African immigrants (40 percent). Caribbean-English immigrants are strongly bi-regional: Northeast (declining from 65 percent to 58 percent) and South (rising from 29 percent to 38 percent).

Except for the residual category, Other Black immigrants, Caribbean-English and African immigrants have the highest weekly wages, $867 and $807, respectively, rising from $743 to $784 during the 1990s. Non-Latinx native-born African Americans have mean wages of $728, but there has been no wage growth during 2001–2019.

TABLE 10.3 *Characteristics of alternative working-age African American ethnic groups: 1994–2019*

	Non-Latinx Native-born			Latinx Native-born			Mexico		
	1994–2000	2001–2008	2009–2019	1994–2000	2001–2008	2009–2019	1994–2000	2001–2008	2009–2019
Weekly wage	$652	$729	$728	$615	$693	$675	$454	$509	$543
Northeast	0.1460	0.1400	0.1340	0.6200	0.4960	0.3830	0.1210	0.2150	0.2110
Northcentral	0.1920	0.1930	0.1830	0.0701	0.0834	0.0881	0.1880	0.1180	0.1220
West	0.0852	0.0923	0.0938	0.0994	0.1680	0.2290	0.3100	0.3000	0.3240
South	0.5770	0.5750	0.5890	0.2100	0.2520	0.3000	0.3820	0.3660	0.3430
Metro. $\geq$ 500k	0.2580	0.2610	0.2520	0.5530	0.5190	0.4510	0.4530	0.4670	0.4070
Metro. $\leq$ 100k	0.1450	0.1470	0.1280	0.0369	0.0326	0.0395	0.0497	0.0691	0.0818
Married	0.3300	0.3220	0.2820	0.2980	0.3170	0.2360	0.3940	0.5310	0.5660
Divorced	0.1110	0.1150	0.1050	0.0642	0.0665	0.0667	0.0390	0.0454	0.0506
Widowed	0.0284	0.0260	0.0225	0.0223	0.0147	0.0088	0.0029	0.0048	0.0024
Separated	0.0607	0.0475	0.0395	0.0570	0.0532	0.0379	0.0586	0.0517	0.0430
Never married	0.4700	0.4900	0.5510	0.5580	0.5490	0.6500	0.5060	0.3680	0.3380
Education	12.3	12.6	13.0	11.7	12.2	12.7	9.1	9.4	10.2
Age	36.0	37.1	37.9	31.2	32.0	31.1	30.3	32.9	36.3
Emp/Pop	0.6240	0.6180	0.5860	0.5420	0.5830	0.5820	0.7060	0.7360	0.6930
Unem/Pop	0.0727	0.0738	0.0824	0.0767	0.0688	0.0834	0.0725	0.0515	0.0393
Health	0.1190	0.1200	0.1310	0.1010	0.0864	0.0784	0.0368	0.0195	0.0368
Veteran	0.0988	0.0838	0.0650	0.0506	0.0575	0.0382	0.0056	0.0057	0.0114
Job unionized	0.1210	0.0892	0.0055	0.0416	0.0562	0.0080	0.0517	0.0705	0.0061
Non-labor income	7.1240	7.2210	6.7190	6.8200	6.1520	4.6410	2.9330	1.6400	0.2510
Self-employed	0.0265	0.0299	0.0229	0.0172	0.0267	0.0163	0.0193	0.0366	0.0684
Male	0.4530	0.4530	0.4590	0.4570	0.4330	0.4440	0.7060	0.5920	0.5550
N (wage)	36,451	79,155	90,987	675	1,963	3,431	78	564	805
N	52,252	115,711	141,409	1,086	2,981	5,368	107	760	1,150

	South America			Caribbean-Spanish			Caribbean-English		
	1994–2000	2001–2008	2009–2019	1994–2000	2001–2008	2009–2019	1994–2000	2001–2008	2009–2019
Weekly wage	$561	$710	$652	$655	$642	$602	$743	$848	$867
Northeast	0.6140	0.6290	0.5880	0.7020	0.6000	0.5680	0.6490	0.6230	0.5570
Northcentral	0.0191	0.0240	0.0421	0.0189	0.0352	0.0465	0.0226	0.0237	0.0310
West	0.0938	0.0940	0.0408	0.0675	0.0969	0.0598	0.0383	0.0498	0.0326
South	0.2740	0.2530	0.3300	0.2120	0.2680	0.3250	0.2900	0.3030	0.3800
Metro. ≥ 500k	0.6840	0.6260	0.5780	0.7130	0.7050	0.6380	0.6000	0.6810	0.6730
Metro. ≤ 100k	0.0229	0.0184	0.0125	0.0075	0.0195	0.0239	0.0187	0.0114	0.0187
Married	0.4830	0.5390	0.5370	0.4500	0.4910	0.4160	0.4250	0.4440	0.4650
Divorced	0.0794	0.0526	0.0717	0.0986	0.1080	0.1110	0.1060	0.1070	0.1120
Widowed	0.0000	0.0170	0.0060	0.0193	0.0169	0.0186	0.0211	0.0198	0.0212
Separated	0.0423	0.0779	0.0536	0.0786	0.0622	0.0691	0.0663	0.0514	0.0553
Never married	0.3950	0.3140	0.3320	0.3530	0.3220	0.3860	0.3820	0.3770	0.3460
Education	12.1	12.5	12.6	11.1	11.4	11.7	12.5	12.8	13.4
Age	35.1	37.5	38.9	37.8	38.5	39.8	37.9	40.0	43.0
Emp/Pop	0.6710	0.7600	0.7160	0.5980	0.6450	0.6570	0.7080	0.7250	0.7130
Unem/Pop	0.0437	0.0495	0.0560	0.0730	0.0654	0.0689	0.0647	0.0518	0.0676
Health	0.0565	0.0383	0.0348	0.0906	0.0839	0.0867	0.0575	0.0555	0.0571
Veteran	0.0082	0.0123	0.0170	0.0333	0.0288	0.0231	0.0421	0.0256	0.0317
Job unionized	0.1660	0.0705	0.0027	0.0758	0.0445	0.0053	0.1080	0.0928	0.0129
Non-labor income	3.4120	3.2720	3.7670	6.8210	4.4750	2.5820	5.5660	5.1710	4.6930
Self-employed	0.0215	0.0892	0.0705	0.0239	0.0518	0.0393	0.0575	0.0506	0.0482
Male	0.4630	0.5250	0.4570	0.4510	0.4480	0.4730	0.4500	0.4380	0.4250
N (wage)	82	352	405	623	1,110	1,488	1,514	3,473	3,887
N	115	471	540	925	1,599	2,105	2,053	4,583	5,170

	Haiti			Africa		
	1994–2000	2001–2008	2009–2019	1994–2000	2001–2008	2009–2019
Weekly wage	$573	$682	$679	$784	$852	$807
Northeast	0.4720	0.4550	0.4000	0.3570	0.2850	0.2440
Northcentral	0.0195	0.0223	0.0146	0.1160	0.1560	0.1980
West	0.0141	0.0153	0.0088	0.1740	0.1380	0.1520
South	0.4950	0.5070	0.5760	0.3530	0.4220	0.4070
Metro. $\geq$ 500k	0.4190	0.5090	0.6840	0.5780	0.3940	0.3420
Metro. $\leq$ 100k	0.0050	0.0138	0.0158	0.0152	0.0275	0.0421
Married	0.4930	0.5130	0.4950	0.5100	0.5280	0.5390
Divorced	0.0797	0.0621	0.0736	0.0495	0.0729	0.0704
Widowed	0.0240	0.0168	0.0250	0.0111	0.0128	0.0186
Separated	0.0405	0.0491	0.0432	0.0481	0.0493	0.0372
Never married	0.3630	0.3590	0.3630	0.3810	0.3370	0.3350
Education	11.4	12.1	12.7	13.8	13.5	13.6
Age	37.6	39.2	40.9	34.9	36.0	38.4
Empl/Pop	0.6560	0.7250	0.6950	0.7370	0.7360	0.7010
Unem/Pop	0.0921	0.0574	0.0654	0.0466	0.0506	0.0653
Health	0.0676	0.0468	0.0582	0.0327	0.0365	0.0422
Veteran	0.0091	0.0096	0.0156	0.0041	0.0096	0.0074
Job unionized	0.1320	0.1100	0.0070	0.1900	0.0680	0.0061
Non-labor income	3.9480	4.0050	4.6070	3.3590	4.0370	3.2720
Self-employed	0.0367	0.0282	0.0264	0.0632	0.0470	0.0421
Male	0.5120	0.5000	0.4840	0.6140	0.5560	0.5210
N (wage)	670	1,599	1,721	459	2,513	6,533
N	939	2,079	2,363	622	3,327	8,814

Mean years of education for working-age Non-Latinx White Americans during 2009–2019 is 13.7. Caribbean-English immigrants, African immigrants, and Non-Latinx native-born African Americans have 13.4, 13.5, and 12.9 mean years of education, respectively.

Mexican immigrants were the least educated African Americans throughout 1994–2019, but they experienced a large gain in education, 1.1 years, as their mean education increased from 9.1 years (late 1990s) to 10.2 years (2009–2019). Haitian immigrants also attained a large increase in education, moving from high school dropouts (11.4 years) to high school graduates (12.7 years).

For most Black ethnic groups, property income is lower during the post-Great Recession years (2009–2019) than it was during the 1994–2008 era when property income was rising. For example, Non-Latinx native-born African American property income is $7,124 (1994–2000), $7,239 (2001–2008), and $6,719 (2009–2019). Caribbean-English property income declined by $873 during 1994–2019, dropping from $5,566 to $4,693. Caribbean-Spanish immigrants had the largest drop in property income, falling from $6,821 in the late 1990s to just $2,582 during the most recent period. African immigrants had a smaller decline, falling from $3,359 to $3,272. Haitian immigrants saw their non-labor income increase from $3,948 (1994–2000) to $4,005 (2001–2008) to $4,607 (2009–2019).

10.2 RACIAL IDENTITY AMONG AFRICAN AMERICANS

Enumerator established mixed-race identification was first recorded on the decennial census of 1850 with "mulatto," when enumerators were instructed to identify some Africans by this category (see Chapter 2). The 1860 census also included Black and mulatto categories. The 1870 and 1880 censuses made it clear that mulatto categorization by enumerators covered persons with one Black parent and one White parent, as well as quadroons, octoroons, and any person who had any trace of African blood; the enumerator established mulatto category was used to exclude persons from Whiteness. The 1890 census required enumerators to separately identify various Black–White mixed-race Africans: Black, mulatto, quadroon, octoroon; also, persons of Non-White–Black heritage were to be identified as Black. After the *Plessy* v. *Ferguson* case of 1896, mixed race identification was not included on the 1900 census, though both Black and mulatto were included on the 1910 and 1920 censuses. For the 1930, 1940, and 1950 censuses all persons of African descent were described as Negro and any person who appeared mixed with African ancestry was labeled Negro. For 1960–1990, census respondents selected their own race, but were limited to one category. Following the massive immigration of the 1980s and 1990s, census respondents were allowed to select multiple racial categories for the 2000, 2010, and 2020 censuses.

TABLE 10.4. *Self-identity of working-age African Americans, 2003–2019*

2003–2008	All	Northeast	Northcentral	West	South
Black-only	0.971	0.966	0.965	0.920	0.983
Black–Other	0.008	0.007	0.009	0.021	0.006
Black–White–Other	0.004	0.006	0.004	0.011	0.002
Black–White	0.017	0.022	0.022	0.049	0.009
N	93,424	15,385	16,864	9,113	52,062
2009–2019					
Black only	0.948	0.939	0.938	0.877	0.967
Black–Other	0.009	0.008	0.008	0.029	0.007
Black–White–Other	0.006	0.006	0.006	0.016	0.004
Black–White	0.036	0.047	0.048	0.073	0.023
N	169,164	25,936	26,455	16,999	99,774

The overwhelming majority of African Americans self-identify as Black-alone (Table 10.4). Three percent of African Americans self-identified as mixed-race in 2003–2008 and, for the most recent period, 5.2 percent of African Americans self-identify as mixed-race: 3.6 percent are Black–White, 0.9 percent are Black–American Indian, Black–Asian, or Black–Hawaiian (hereafter, collectively referred to as "Black–Other"), and the remainder (0.6 percent) self-identify as Black–White–American Indian, Black–White–native Alaskan, Black–White–Asian, or Black–White–native Hawaiian (hereafter, collectively referred to as "Black–White–Other").

Both Latinx and immigrant representation among African Americans increased during 1994–2019. The share of first and second generation immigrants moved from 10.29 percent to 13.98 percent to 18.94 percent, while the Black Latinx share rose from 2.49 percent to 3.91 percent to 5.87 percent (Table 10.1). The rise in immigrants and Latinx is correlated with the rise in mixed-race self-identification. For example, for 2009–2019 the Southern and Northcentral states have the fewest immigrants (13.74 percent and 10.74 percent, respectively) and the fewest Latinx (3.41 percent and 2.70 percent, respectively) and the highest percentage of African Americans who self-identify as Black-only, 97 percent and 94 percent, respectively. At 12.3 percent, the West has the largest fractions of self-identified mixed-race persons. While the fraction of Black–White and Black–White–Other persons hovers just over 5 percent in the Northcentral and Northeastern states, nearly 9 percent of the African American labor force in the West and 2.7 percent in the South are mixed-White.

Racially assimilated persons, that is, self-identified mixed-race persons, are 3 percent of working-age Non-Latinx African Americans who have resided in

TABLE 10.5. *African American racial identity, by ethnic group and generation: 2003–2019*

	Third+ Generation		Second Generation				
	Non-Latinx	Latinx	Carib-Spanish	Carib-English	Haiti	Africa	Other
Black-only	0.9710	0.8430	0.9120	0.9650	0.9870	0.9560	0.7770
Black–Other	0.0068	0.0266	0.0060	0.0065	0.0000	0.0072	0.0746
Black–White–Other	0.0033	0.0238	0.0121	0.0039	0.0000	0.0011	0.0188
Black–White	0.0182	0.1040	0.0704	0.0249	0.0125	0.0350	0.1170
N	307,540	6,890	1,989	4,335	1,515	1,801	4,302
			First Generation				
Black-only			0.9050	0.9870	0.9960	0.9930	0.8710
Black–Other			0.0068	0.0034	0.0007	0.0010	0.0200
Black–White–Other			0.0136	0.0021	0.0000	0.0001	0.0188
Black–White			0.0746	0.0078	0.0029	0.0060	0.0878
N			4,706	12,126	5,510	13,307	7,642

the United States for at least three generations, but almost 15 percent of working-age Black Latinx who have resided in the United States for at least three generations (Table 10.5). Non-Latinx African American immigrants have Black-only self-identification rates equal to or greater Non-Latinx natives: second generation immigrants, Caribbean-English 97 percent, Haiti 99 percent, and Africa 96 percent; Other immigrants, a residual group including Black immigrants from Mexico, Canada, Europe, Asia, and Oceania, has a Black-only self-identification rate of 78 percent; and 91 percent of working-age Caribbean-Spanish immigrants self-identify as Black-only. Except for Caribbean-Spanish, the Black-only self-identification rate is higher among first generation immigrants than it is among second generation immigrants, suggesting that integration into American society also encourages racial assimilation among immigrants.

In part, mixed-race self-classification is a subjective means of personal expression regarding one's ancestral heritage. It may also be the case that mixed-race self-identification is an acculturation strategy that seeks to arbitrage differences in economic inequality associated with the market and social premia obtained by White-only individuals relative to Black-only individuals. Consequently, a mixed-race self-identity strategy may not get a person into an advantaged group (e.g., White-only in the United States) but it may allow an individual to successfully distance himself from a disadvantaged group (e.g., Black-only in the United States) (Golash-Boza and Darity, 2008).

Mixed-race self-identification and Latinx ethnicity are rising and interrelated trends among African Americans. For example, 3.9 percent of African

TABLE 10.6. *Latinx ethnicity by racial group, 2003–2016*

	Percent Latinx by Racial Group				
Year	White	African American	Amer. Ind. Alas. Nat.	Asian	Hawaii Pac. Isl.
2003	0.141	0.039	0.202	0.021	0.152
2004	0.143	0.038	0.228	0.017	0.118
2005	0.147	0.036	0.239	0.013	0.110
2006	0.150	0.039	0.216	0.023	0.119
2007	0.155	0.039	0.211	0.023	0.104
2008	0.157	0.038	0.240	0.021	0.136
2009	0.160	0.039	0.241	0.026	0.110
2010	0.163	0.044	0.207	0.027	0.158
2011	0.165	0.048	0.205	0.026	0.122
2012	0.171	0.064	0.271	0.042	0.176
2013	0.174	0.068	0.269	0.033	0.185
2014	0.177	0.077	0.241	0.033	0.226
2015	0.181	0.068	0.299	0.034	0.237
2016	0.184	0.064	0.335	0.032	0.218

Source: Author's calculations, Annual Social and Economic Supplement (ASEC) of the Current Population Survey (CPS), 2003–2016

Americans were Latinx in 2003 (Table 10.6). By 2016, the Latino share of the African American population was 6.4 percent. During this same period, Latinos rose from 14 percent to 18 percent of the White population, from 20 percent to nearly 34 percent of the American Indian and Alaskan Native population, from 15 percent to about 22 percent of the Hawaiian and Pacific Islander population, and from 2.1 percent to 3.2 percent of the Asian population.

As Table 10.7 demonstrates, Latinx ethnicity has virtually no effect on self-identity as White. During 2003, 98.4 percent of Latinx Whites self-identified as White-only, and 98.7 percent of Non-Latinx Whites self-identified as White-only. There were minimal changes in these numbers by 2016. Although Latinx ethnicity is far less prevalent among African Americans than Whites, Black Latinos are far more likely than White Latinos to identify as mixed-race. Among Non-Latinx Blacks, 97.7 percent and 95.9 percent identified as Black-only in 2003 and 2016, respectively. Among Latinx Blacks, 82.7 percent and 78.3 percent identified as Black-only in 2003 and 2016, respectively. In addition, Latinx ethnicity reduces the intensity of Asian American identity, but Latinx ethnicity appears to increase single race identity among the American Indian and Alaskan Native populations as well as the Hawaiian and Pacific Islander groups.

Table 10.8 shows that Black–Other and Black–White–Other persons have higher weekly wages ($774 and $758, respectively) than Black-alone and

TABLE 10.7. *Single-race self-identification by Latinx Ethnicity, 2003–2016*

	Single race, Latinx					Single race, Non-Latinx				
			Am. Ind.		Hawaii			Am. Ind.		Hawaii
Year	White	Black	Ak. Nat.	Asian	Pac. Isl.	White	Black	Ak. Nat.	Asian	Pac. Isl.
2003	0.984	0.827	0.668	0.732	0.810	0.987	0.977	0.421	0.960	0.771
2004	0.978	0.815	0.551	0.570	0.510	0.986	0.979	0.410	0.955	0.707
2005	0.980	0.861	0.559	0.506	0.606	0.985	0.976	0.402	0.950	0.652
2006	0.979	0.843	0.500	0.574	0.649	0.985	0.975	0.413	0.949	0.657
2007	0.984	0.875	0.648	0.606	0.637	0.986	0.978	0.463	0.953	0.711
2008	0.986	0.851	0.692	0.742	0.784	0.985	0.972	0.475	0.948	0.709
2009	0.984	0.830	0.662	0.747	0.849	0.985	0.970	0.483	0.950	0.760
2010	0.983	0.821	0.582	0.808	0.863	0.985	0.971	0.508	0.947	0.716
2011	0.984	0.847	0.595	0.702	0.484	0.984	0.967	0.503	0.946	0.734
2012	0.981	0.851	0.732	0.804	0.762	0.981	0.963	0.461	0.939	0.745
2013	0.976	0.795	0.716	0.780	0.825	0.982	0.957	0.506	0.941	0.875
2014	0.974	0.811	0.604	0.580	0.836	0.982	0.957	0.538	0.941	0.847
2015	0.976	0.810	0.677	0.601	0.936	0.982	0.954	0.562	0.945	0.854
2016	0.975	0.783	0.710	0.724	0.812	0.981	0.959	0.551	0.949	0.749

Source: Author's calculations, Annual Social and Economic Supplement (ASEC) of the Current Population Survey (CPS), 2003–2016

TABLE 10.8. *Descriptive statistics of working-age African Americans by social identity*

2003–2008	Black-alone	Black–Other	Black–White–Other	Black–White
Northeast	0.181	0.158	0.278	0.227
Northcentral	0.176	0.195	0.195	0.218
West	0.092	0.244	0.284	0.272
South	0.550	0.402	0.243	0.283
Latinx	0.035	0.089	0.278	0.255
Native-born	0.891	0.924	0.862	0.867
Metropolitan area ≥ 5,000,000	0.274	0.214	0.315	0.233
Metropolitan area ≤ 100,000	0.128	0.110	0.085	0.109
Married	0.337	0.359	0.384	0.262
Divorced	0.111	0.132	0.071	0.080
Widowed	0.024	0.004	0.003	0.009
Separated	0.048	0.038	0.041	0.034
Never-married	0.479	0.467	0.501	0.615
Education	12.6	13.0	13.1	12.2
Age	37.4	37.1	33.1	29.6
Emp/Pop	0.623	0.625	0.672	0.606
Unemp/Pop	0.071	0.066	0.071	0.075
Labor Force	0.306	0.309	0.257	0.319
Health	0.112	0.149	0.090	0.060
Veteran	0.074	0.111	0.064	0.048
Job covered by union	0.067	0.079	0.037	0.068
Non-labor income	6.993	8.756	8.148	7.033
Self-employed	0.032	0.057	0.060	0.044
Male	0.457	0.481	0.469	0.473
Weekly wage	$742	$774	$758	$686
N (wage)	61,378	701	337	1,335
N	89,937	1,021	471	1,995

Descriptive statistics of working-age African Americans by racial identity

2009–2019	Black-alone	Black–Other	Black–White–Other	Black–White
Northeast	0.176	0.148	0.191	0.230
Northcentral	0.166	0.139	0.176	0.223
West	0.093	0.304	0.286	0.202
South	0.564	0.409	0.347	0.345
Latinx	0.057	0.149	0.305	0.263
Native-born	0.865	0.919	0.834	0.827
Metropolitan area ≥ 5,000,000	0.298	0.195	0.212	0.240
Metropolitan area ≤ 100,000	0.111	0.084	0.085	0.120
Married	0.312	0.304	0.300	0.255

(continued)

(*continued*)

2009–2019	Black-alone	Black–Other	Black–White–Other	Black–White
Divorced	0.102	0.101	0.120	0.065
Widowed	0.022	0.019	0.017	0.006
Separated	0.041	0.025	0.045	0.027
Never-married	0.522	0.551	0.518	0.647
Education	13.0	13.3	13.2	12.5
Age	38.2	36.2	36.1	30.1
Emp/Pop	0.601	0.611	0.630	0.611
Unemp/Pop	0.080	0.081	0.083	0.080
Labor Force	0.683	0.697	0.715	0.693
Health	0.120	0.125	0.110	0.074
Veteran	0.058	0.080	0.054	0.036
Job covered by union	0.006	0.005	0.002	0.002
Non-labor income	6.224	6.851	7.968	5.492
Self-employed	0.025	0.015	0.039	0.029
Male	0.462	0.465	0.432	0.468
Weekly wage	$736	$731	$696	$668
N (wage)	104,825	1,177	710	4,019
N	160,124	1,755	1,049	6,006

Non-labor income includes property income, insurance income, public and private transfer payments, public and private pensions.
Source: Author's calculations

Black–White persons ($742 and $686, respectively). Between 2003–2008 and 2009–2019, the employment–population ratio fell for most identity groups: Black-alone (62 percent and 58 percent, respectively), Black–Other (63 percent and 61 percent), Black–White–Other (67 percent and 63 percent), and Black–White (61 percent and 61 percent). Fifty-six percent and 41 percent of Black-alone and Black–Other African Americans, respectively, live in the South. Black–White and Black–White–Other persons are more evenly distributed throughout the country. For 2009–2019 only 5.4 percent of Black-alone persons are Latinx, but Latinx are 15 percent, 31 percent, and 26 percent of Black–Other, Black–White–Other, and Black–White persons. Eighty-seven percent of Black-alone, 92 percent of Black–Other, and 83 percent of working-age Black–White–Other African Americans and Black–White African Americans are native-born. Finally, Black–White–Other persons have the highest annual non-labor income ($7,968), while Black–White persons have the lowest annual non-labor income ($5,492) and Black–Other and Black-only persons have $6,851 and $6,224, respectively.

10.3 INEQUALITY AND AFRICAN AMERICAN IMMIGRANTS

10.3.1 Wage Disparities, Immigrant Men

Wage and employment differentials for alternative groups of African American men and women are reported in Table 10.9. The comparative group is native-born Non-Latinx White men and women. The table includes wage and employment differentials for Non-Latinx and Latinx African Americans of third and higher generation, first and second generation Black immigrants from various countries, Black immigrant citizenship status, and period and age of arrival in the United States. The differentials reported in the table are for men and women with the statistically same years of education, age, marital status, national region of residence, size of city residence, health status, military veteran status, non-labor income, children under 18 years of age, period of employment, and state of employment.[1]

African American males earn lower wages than White males. For example, Latinx and Non-Latinx African American males who have been in the United States for at least three generations earn 0.156 log points (14.4 percent) and 0.211 log points (19 percent) less, respectively, than otherwise identical native-born Non-Latinx White males. Second generation Black male immigrants have earnings penalties similar to those of third and higher generations. For example, second generation Caribbean-Spanish immigrant males have an earning penalty of 0.142 log points (13.2 percent), while second generation African immigrants have an earnings penalty of 0.176 log points (16.1 percent).

Assimilation should improve the labor market outcomes of immigrants. First generation Black immigrants are less assimilated into the American political economy than their children, that is, second generation immigrants. Also, the labor market outcomes of first generation immigrants are affected by their age and period of arrival in the United States. Immigrants who arrived as children are more assimilated than immigrants who arrived as adults. Immigrants who arrived during the 1990s may have different labor market outcomes than those who arrived in the United States during the late 1970s and 1980s; cohorts differ in the factors pushing them to emigrate from their country of origin, the factors

[1] For robustness checks, we tried several other specifications: (1) omit state fixed effects; (2) omit state fixed effects and identify first and second generation African immigrants by their country of origin and whether African immigrants are from English-speaking, French-speaking, or Other-language countries; (3) omit state fixed effects and split education into amount of education received in the United States and amount of education received in the country of origin; (4) include state fixed effects, language of country of origin of African immigrants, and United States versus foreign education; and (5) all of the changes in (4) plus state*trend interaction terms. The probability of employment results reported in the table are for a linear probability model. We also estimated a logit model. There are no substantive changes in the results for these alternative specifications.

TABLE 10.9. *Racial disparity in natural logarithm of weekly wages and probability of employment (selected coefficients)*

	Weekly Wages		Employment	
	Men	Women	Men	Women
Non-Latinx, generation 3+	−0.211***	−0.0186***	−0.0915***	−0.0242***
	[0.0030]	[0.0028]	[0.0014]	[0.0014]
Hispanic, generation 3+	−0.156***	0.0313*	−0.0976***	−0.0537***
	[0.0197]	[0.0165]	[0.0094]	[0.0082]
Caribbean-English, 2nd generation	−0.146***	0.0141	−0.115***	−0.072***
	[0.0237]	[0.0221]	[0.0108]	[0.0106]
Caribbean-Spanish, 2nd generation	−0.142***	0.0463	−0.103***	−0.0783***
	[0.0358]	[0.0330]	[0.0159]	[0.0150]
Haiti, 2nd generation	−0.12**	−0.0436	−0.145***	−0.0997***
	[0.0491]	[0.0490]	[0.0198]	[0.0196]
African, 2nd generation	−0.176***	−0.0638	−0.115***	−0.0406**
	[0.0409]	[0.0398]	[0.0175]	[0.0179]
Other Immigrant, 2nd generation	−0.159***	−0.022	−0.0604***	−0.0138
	[0.0237]	[0.0236]	[0.0112]	[0.0107]
Immigrant Citizen	−0.159	0.0366***	0.0274***	0.0703***
	[0.0237]	[0.0138]	[0.0070]	[0.0073]
Caribbean-English, 1st generation	0.0355	0.0545**	−0.079***	−0.0277***
	[0.0141]	[0.0213]	[0.0104]	[0.0103]
Caribbean-Spanish, 1st generation	−0.145	−0.091***	−0.0275**	−0.0688***
	[0.0204]	[0.0258]	[0.0127]	[0.0128]
Haiti, 1st generation	−0.24	−0.0411*	−0.0756***	−0.0114
	[0.0257]	[0.0250]	[0.0123]	[0.0127]
Africa	−0.315	−0.0023	−0.0748***	−0.0476***
	[0.0248]	[0.0244]	[0.0108]	[0.0118]
Other Immigrant, 1st generation	−0.279	−0.0272	−0.0272**	−0.0556***
	[0.0223]	[0.0243]	[0.0111]	[0.0120]
Arrived Pre-1965	−0.242	0.0162	−0.017	0.245***
	[0.0228]	[0.0763]	[0.0279]	[0.0308]
Arrived 1966–1973	−0.159	−0.0208	−0.0285	0.267***

Arrived 1974–1979	−0.182	−0.0262	−0.023	0.266***
	[0.0596]	[0.0757]	[0.0279]	[0.0306]
Arrived 1980–1989	−0.157	−0.0369	−0.0208	0.257***
	[0.0601]	[0.0739]	[0.0267]	[0.0294]
Arrived 1990–2000	−0.186	−0.0796	−0.0328	0.196***
	[0.0582]	[0.0736]	[0.0263]	[0.0292]
Arrived 2001–2007	−0.166	−0.115	−0.0354	0.157***
	[0.0577]	[0.0759]	[0.0275]	[0.0304]
Arrived 2008–2018	−0.157	−0.197**	−0.102***	0.0964***
	[0.0689]	[0.0819]	[0.0318]	[0.0342]
Arrived 2019	−0.0691	0.0461	−0.0568**	0.207***
	[0.0622]	[0.0762]	[0.0286]	[0.0313]
Arrived as Child (≤ 12)	0.106***	0.058**	−0.0404***	−0.0622***
	[0.0270]	[0.0257]	[0.0125]	[0.0129]
Arrived as Young Teen (13–17)	0.136***	0.0714**	−0.0115	−0.0278**
	[0.0281]	[0.0278]	[0.0136]	[0.0139]
Arrived as Emerging Adult (18–25)	0.0176	0.0411*	−0.00225	−0.0135
	[0.0249]	[0.0235]	[0.0118]	[0.0125]
Arrived as Young Adult (26–34)	−0.113***	−0.0751***	−0.00915	−0.00286
	[0.0255]	[0.0241]	[0.0120]	[0.0129]
Arrived as Advanced Adult (35–44)	−0.173***	−0.0653**	0.00512	0.0346**
	[0.0299]	[0.0289]	[0.0141]	[0.0151]
Arrived as Middle-Aged Adult (45– 54)	−0.221***	−0.0264	−0.00356	0.0831***
	[0.0400]	[0.0414]	[0.0207]	[0.0207]
Arrived as Senior Citizen (55–64)	−0.116	−0.293***	−0.0755	0.0359
	[0.1061]	[0.1022]	[0.0513]	[0.0385]
R^2	0.4603	0.3372	0.3245	0.2149
N	670,946	678,650	816,683	925,799

The dependent variables are the natural log of weekly wages and a binary variable where employment = 1 if a person is working and 0 if the person is not working. The explanatory variables are African American ethnicity, age of arrival, citizenship status, education, age, marital status, region, size of city, health status, military veteran status, children under 18 years of age, non-labor income, period and state fixed effects. Native-born Non-Latinx Whites are the comparative group. Robust standard errors are reported in brackets. $^{*}p < 0.10$; $^{**}p < 0.05$; $^{***}p < 0.01$.

Source: Author's calculations. Annual Social and Economic Supplement of the CPS, 1994–2019

pulling them to immigrate to the United States, and the conditions of the labor market when they arrived in the United States.

Ignoring age of arrival and cohort effects, first generation African immigrants have a wage penalty of 0.279 log points (24.3 percent), which is greater than the 16.1 percent penalty of second generation African immigrants. First and second generation Haitian immigrants have wage penalties of 0.315 log points (27 percent) and 0.12 log points (11.3 percent), respectively, while the penalties for first and second generation Caribbean-Spanish immigrants is 0.24 log points (21.3 percent) and 13.2 percent, respectively. Caribbean-English immigrants exhibit a dissimilar pattern: first generation immigrants have a penalty of 0.145 log points (13.5 percent) and second generation immigrants has a penalty of 0.146 log points (13.5 percent).

Immigrants arriving as emerging adults (18–25 years of age) have about 15 years less time in the United States than immigrants arriving as children (less than or equal to 12 years of age). The wage penalties experienced by first generation Black male immigrants decline with length of time in the United States, though they are not eliminated (as one would expect in a labor market with no racial discrimination) and tend to become very similar to the wage penalties of third generation Non-Latinx African Americans (as one would expect in a labor market with substantial racial discrimination). Caribbean-English and African men who arrived in the United States as emerging adults during 1990–2000 earn 29.3 and 42.7 percent less, respectively, than native-born Non-Latinx White males.[2] Caribbean-English male immigrants who arrived in the United States as children during 1990–2000 have a wage penalty of 20.5 percent, the same penalty as African men of the same cohort and age of arrival. Caribbean-Spanish and Other immigrant men of the 1990s cohort who arrived in the United States as children have a 30 percent wage penalty, while Haitian men have a wage penalty of 37.5 percent. Immigrant men from those groups have penalties of 39 percent (Caribbean-Spanish), 46 percent (Other), and 46 percent (Haitian).

Citizenship raises the earnings of Black male immigrants by 3.6 percent.

10.3.2 Wage Disparities, Immigrant Women

Non-Latinx African American women who have been in the United States for at least three generations earn 0.0186 log points (1.8 percent) less than otherwise identical native-born Non-Latinx White women. Latinx African American women who have been in the United States for at least three generations earn 0.0313 log points (3.2 percent) more than native-born Non-Latinx White

[2] This effect is the sum of the log points for the first generation effect (–0.145) + the cohort effect (–0.166) + the age of arrival effect (0.0176). The sum of the log points is converted into percentages.

women. Second generation Black women immigrants have weekly wages that are statistically identical to White women.

Caribbean-English women who arrived in the United States as children and emerging adults during 1990–2000 earn 3.3 percent and 1.6 percent more, respectively, than native-born Non-Latinx White women. Caribbean-Spanish women immigrants arriving in the United States as children and those arriving in the United States as emerging adults during 1990–2000 have wage penalties of 11.3 and 13 percent, respectively. Haitian immigrant women arriving in the United States during 1990–2000 have wage penalties of 6.3 percent and 8 percent when they arrive as children and emerging adults. African women immigrants arriving in the United States during 1990–2000 have wage penalties of 2.4 percent and 4.1 percent as childhood and young adult arrivals.

Citizenship raises the earnings of Black women immigrants by 3.6 percent.

10.3.3 Employment Disparities, Immigrant Men

Employment differentials for alternative groups of African American men and women are reported in columns 3 and 4 of Table 10.9, where each column is analogous to the wage differentials of columns 1 and 2. Non-Latinx and Latinx African American males who have been in the United States for at least three generations are about 9.5 percentage points less likely to be employed than otherwise identical native-born Non-Latinx White males. Second generation Black male immigrants have employment differentials similar to those of third and higher generations. For example, second generation Caribbean-Spanish immigrant males have 10.3 percentage points lower employment, while second generation African and Caribbean-English immigrants have 11.5 percentage points lower employment. Second generation Haitian male immigrants have a 14.5 percentage points lower probability of employment than otherwise identical native-born Non-Latinx White males. Second generation Other immigrant men have the lowest employment differential, 6 percentage points less than native-born Non-Latinx White males.

Caribbean-English, Haitian, and African men immigrants arriving in the US at 18–25 years old in 1990–2000 have 11 percentage points lower probability of employment, while those arriving as children have 15 percentage point disadvantage relative to native-born Non-Latinx White men. Caribbean-Spanish and Other immigrant men who arrived in the United States as emerging adults and children during 1990–2000 have 6 and 10 percentage point points lower employment, respectively, than native-born Non-Latinx White males. Other immigrant men who arrived in the United States as emerging adults and children during 1990–2000 have 12 and 6 percentage points lower probability of employment than native-born Non-Latinx White men.

Citizenship raises the probability of employment by Black immigrant men by 2.7 percentage points.

10.3.4 Employment Disparities, Immigrant Women

Non-Latinx and Latinx African American women who have been in the United States for at least three generations are 2.2 and 5.4 percentage points less likely to be employed, respectively, than otherwise identical native-born Non-Latinx White women. Second generation Black immigrant women have employment differentials similar to those of third and higher generations. For example, second generation Caribbean-English and Caribbean-Spanish immigrant women have 7.2 and 7.8 percentage points lower employment, while second generation African immigrant women have 4.1 percentage points lower employment. Second generation Haitian immigrant women have 10 percentage points lower probability of employment than otherwise identical native-born Non-Latinx White women. Second generation Other immigrant women have the smallest employment disadvantage, 1.4 percentage points.

Black immigrant women arriving with the 1990s cohort have a greater probability of employment than native-born Non-Latinx White women. First generation Caribbean-English immigrant women arriving as children and emerging adults have 10.6 and 15.5 percentage points higher employment rates, while Haitian immigrant women have 12 and 17 percentage point higher employment than native-born Non-Latinx White women. The employment rates for first generation Caribbean-Spanish are 6.5 percentage points (arrived as children) and 11.4 percentage points higher (arrived as emerging adults) native-born Non-Latinx White women. First generation employment rates for Other and African immigrant women are 8 percent (child arrivals) and 13 percent (emerging adult arrivals) higher than the comparative group of White women.

Citizenship raises the probability of employment by Black women immigrants by 7 percentage points.

10.4 INEQUALITY AND INTENSITY OF AFRICAN AMERICAN IDENTITY

Racial wage differentials for alternative groups of African American men and women are presented in Table 10.10. The differentials are for men and women who self-identify as Black-only, Black–Other, Black–White–Other, and Black–White, where the comparative group is native-born Non-Latinx White men and women. The "All" specification includes all immigrant and native-born African Americans, while the "Immigrant" specification includes first generation Black immigrants. The "Caribbean-Spanish and Other-immigrant" includes first and second generation Black immigrants from those two groups. The "Latinx and Other" specification includes first, second, and third generation or higher Latinx, as well as first and second generation Other immigrants.

Regardless of which sample of African American men are compared to native-born Non-Latinx White males, the results provide evidence of an

TABLE 10.10. *Racial disparity in natural logarithm of weekly wages by intensity of racial self-identity (selected coefficients)*

	Men			
	All	Immigrants	Caribbean-Spanish and Other	Latinx and Other
Black-only	−0.210***	−0.233***	−0.201***	−0.181***
	[0.0029]	[0.0197]	[0.0169]	[0.0135]
Black–Other	−0.228***	−0.378***	−0.213**	−0.198***
	[0.0317]	[0.1137]	[0.0921]	[0.0759]
Black–White–Other	−0.254***	−0.240***	−0.238***	−0.241***
	[0.0477]	[0.0713]	[0.0700]	[0.0648]
Black–White	−0.139***	−0.176***	−0.160***	−0.152***
	[0.0196]	[0.0493]	[0.0423]	[0.0356]
R^2	0.4602	0.4665	0.4688	0.4687
N	670,946	598,411	591,835	593,167
		Women		
Black-only	−0.0174***	−0.00921	−0.0178	0.0071
	[0.0027]	[0.0218]	[0.0176]	[0.0130]
Black–Other	−0.0381	−0.0625	0.0746	0.0891
	[0.0282]	[0.1513]	[0.0749]	[0.0610]
Black–White–Other	−0.0316	−0.275**	−0.190*	−0.187***
	[0.0374]	[0.1168]	[0.1059]	[0.0719]
Black–White	0.00672	−0.0233	−0.0121	−0.0223
	[0.0189]	[0.0472]	[0.0418]	[0.0349]
R^2	0.3372	0.3397	0.3407	0.3406
N	678,650	583,436	576,796	578,614

All persons are 16–64 years of age. These are ordinary least squares regression, where the dependent variables are the natural log of weekly wages. The explanatory variables are African American social identity, age of arrival, citizenship status, educational status (11 years or less, 13–15 years, 16 years, 17 years or more), age, age 2, age 3, marital status, region, size of city, health status, military veteran status, children under 18 years of age, non-labor income, period fixed effects, and state fixed effects. Native-born Non-Latinx Whites are the comparative group. Robust standard errors are reported in brackets. $^{*}p < 0.10$; $^{**}p < 0.05$; $^{***}p < 0.01$.
Source: Author's calculations. Annual Social and Economic Supplement of the Current Population Survey, 2003–2019

identity gradient: self-identified Black–White African American men have the smallest wage penalties; Black–Other men have larger wage penalties than Black-only African American men and Black–White–Other men have larger wage penalties than Black–White men. Black-only men have wage penalties ranging from 0.181 log points (17 percent) for Latinx and Other African American men to 0.233 log points (21 percent) for African American immigrants. Black–White men have wage penalties ranging from 0.139 log points (13 percent) for all African American men to 0.176 log points (16 percent) for African American immigrants. Self-identified Black–White–Other men usually have the largest wage penalties: 22.4 percent (All), 21.2 percent (Caribbean-Spanish and Other), and 21.4 percent (Latinx and Other).

Except for Black–White–Other women, there is a small penalty or no wage penalty for African American women relative to native-born Non-Latinx White women. Black-only women have wage penalties ranging from no significant effect to 1.7 percent (All). Black–White–Other women have wage penalties of 21 percent (Immigrants, Caribbean-Spanish and Other and Latinx and Other) and 22 percent (All).

Self-identified Black-only African American men have the worst employment outcomes relative to native-born Non-Latinx White males; the employment penalties are 9.4 percentage points (All), 7.5 percentage points (Immigrants), 7 percentage points (Caribbean-Spanish and Others), and 8.5 percentage points (Latinx and Others) (Table 10.11). Black–White men have more favorable employment outcomes, with a penalty of 3 percentage points (All) and advantage of 6.4 percentage points (Immigrants). Black–Other and Black–White–Other men have wage penalties of 6.3 percentage points and 3.8 percentage points, respectively, when all men are considered, while Black–Other men have an employment advantage of 7.1 percentage points when immigrants are compared to native-born Non-Latinx White men.

Black–Other women have a wage penalty of 3.2 percentage points (All), but no penalty when the analysis compares Latinx and Other African American women to White women. The Black–Other employment penalties are 18 percentage points (Immigrants) and 8 percentage points (Caribbean-Spanish and Other). Self-identified Black-only women have employment penalties of 3–5 percent relative to native-born Non-Latinx White women. Black–White women have employment penalties of 3.2 percent (All), 3.5 percent (Latinx and Other), and 6.4 percent (Immigrants), but have no penalty for Caribbean-Spanish and Other women. Black–White–Other women have 4.2 percentage points (All) and 7.3 percentage points (Latinx and Other) lower employment than native-born Non-Latinx White women.

10.5 SUMMARY AND DISCUSSION

African Americans are an ethnically diverse population: 20 percent of working age persons are first or second generation immigrants. About 6 percent are Latinx. More than 2 percent are Haitian. Caribbean-English and African immigrants are 5 and 5.5 percent of the Black population. Five percent of African Americans self-identify as mixed race.

TABLE 10.11. *Racial disparity in probability of employment, Black identity groups*

	All	Immigrants	Caribbean-Spanish and Other	Latinx and Other
Men				
Black-only	−0.0936***	−0.0749***	−0.0692***	−0.0845***
	[0.0014]	[0.0096]	[0.0080]	[0.0065]
Black–Other	−0.0634***	0.071*	−0.0181	−0.0183
	[0.0136]	[0.0385]	[0.0309]	[0.0284]
Black–White–Other	−0.0382*	−0.0458	−0.0195	−0.0414
	[0.0218]	[0.0554]	[0.0442]	[0.0382]
Black–White	−0.0302***	0.0637***	0.0125	−0.0173
	[0.0090]	[0.0233]	[0.0197]	[0.0163]
R^2	0.3245	0.3086	0.3102	0.3105
N	816,683	710,292	702,499	704,513
Women				
Black-only	−0.0261***	−0.0453***	−0.0426***	−0.0489***
	[0.0013]	[0.0103]	[0.0080]	[0.0061]
Black–Other	−0.0317**	−0.178***	−0.0811**	−0.0437
	[0.0133]	[0.0558]	[0.0368]	[0.0317]
Black–White–Other	−0.0421**	−0.0841	−0.0621	−0.0732*
	[0.0200]	[0.0632]	[0.0483]	[0.0376]
Black–White	−0.0322***	−0.0642**	−0.0251	−0.0349**
	[0.0086]	[0.0267]	[0.0208]	[0.0167]
R^2	0.2148	0.1989	0.1993	0.1998
N	925,799	785,073	775,997	778,931

All persons are 16–64 years of age. This is a linear probability model where dependent variable is a binary variable where employment = 1 if a person is working and 0 if the person is not working. The explanatory variables are African American social identity, age of arrival, citizenship status, educational status (11 years or less, 13–15 years, 16 years, 17 years or more), age, age 2, age 3, marital status, region, size of city, health status, military veteran status, children under 18 years of age, non-labor income, period fixed effects, and state fixed effects. Native-born Non-Latinx Whites are the comparative group. Robust standard errors are reported in brackets. *$p < 0.10$; **$p < 0.05$; ***$p < 0.01$.

Source: Author's calculations. Annual Social and Economic Supplement of the Current Population Survey, 2003–2019

The Northeast is the most diverse region, where 40 percent of the African American working age population consists of first or second generation immigrants: 14.5 percent are Latinx; 6 percent are Haitian. Caribbean-English and African immigrants are 15 and 8.0 percent of the Black population, respectively. Six percent of Northeastern African Americans self-identify as mixed race.

The West is the second most diverse region, where Africans are 8 percent of the Black population and Latinx are 10 percent of the African American population. Thirteen percent of Western African Americans self-identify as mixed race.

Caribbean-English and Africans are the most affluent African American ethnic groups, with average weekly wages of $867 and $807, respectively, and 13.4 and 3.6 average years of education. Caribbean-English and Africans are the most affluent African American ethnic groups, with average weekly wages of $867 and $807, respectively, and 13.4 and 3.6 average years of education. Black–Other and Black–White–Other are the most affluent social identity groups, with average weekly wages of $774 and $758, respectively, and 13.0 and 3.1 average years of education. Four percent of Non-Latinx African Americans are mixed race, but 22 percent of Latinx African Americans are mixed race.

Despite the great ethnic, nativity, and identity group diversity among African Americans, African American men and women have similar wage and employment outcomes. Native-born Non-Latinx African American men have a 20 percent weekly age penalty and 9 percentage point employment penalty relative to native-born Non-Latinx White men; other groups of Black men have similar outcomes. Non-Latinx African American women have a 2 percent weekly age penalty and 2 percentage point employment penalty relative to native-born Non-Latinx White women; other groups of Black women have similar outcomes.

PART IV

STRUCTURAL RACISM, 1965–PRESENT

11

Structural Racism and Persistent Disparity

The 1964 Civil Rights Act made it illegal to discriminate in hiring, firing, compensation, or the terms, conditions, and privileges of employment because of an individual's race, color, religion, sex, or national origin. Enforcement of the Act reduced discrimination in labor market activities, especially in the South and especially during the first decade after passage of the act (1964–1973). However, at least one-half of today's Black–White inequality in compensation and employment cannot be explained by racial differences in observable labor market attributes, such as education, age, region of residence, marital status, etc. (see Chapters 9 and 10). An important question is whether these large residuals in racial wage and employment disparity can be explained by difficult to observe differences in attributes or whether they are caused by racial discrimination within labor market processes. Further, racial differences in observed skills may be caused by racial differences in wealth, as well as racially differential treatment in schools and other organizations which produce skill.

Racial discrimination in the labor market exists when there is differential treatment of workers because of non-essential racial differences in characteristics, that is, equally skilled persons are treated differently within the market because of their "race." Racial discrimination may affect all elements of the labor market process: establishment of employment pools and hiring practices and requirements, wages and salaries, training and promotion opportunities, employment segregation within and between firms, evaluations, layoffs, working conditions and benefits, hours of work, and work schedule.

Racial inequality in labor market outcomes refers to racial differences in compensation, hours, and working conditions. There is debate among economists regarding how much of this inequality is due to racial discrimination *within the labor market*. Consider the fact that African American men earn about $0.66 for every dollar obtained by White men. The issue is how much of this inequality in pay is caused by the racial differences in skill (and therefore productivity) versus racially differential treatment in the labor market for equally skilled persons.

It is fruitful to note the distinction between racial discrimination in the labor market versus non-labor market discrimination that contributes to racial inequality in labor market outcomes. No discrimination within the labor market means that individuals are employed, promoted, and paid in strict accordance with their level of skill and performance. However, non-labor market discrimination may produce racial differences in skill. For example, there are a variety of activities that may affect skill development prior to entering the labor market. These activities include racially differential access to high quality schools, access to information and capital via interpersonal relationships such as marriage, membership in private clubs, religious affiliation, and differential parental resources (time, money, and education) because of past market discrimination against African American parents.

Accordingly, racial inequality in labor market outcomes may occur for five reasons:

1. racial discrimination within the labor market;
2. racial discrimination in non-labor market activities that affect skill development and access to information and capital;
3. differences in the behaviors and values of individuals and families that affect skill accumulation;
4. differences in the innate abilities of individuals; and
5. racial differences in wealth.

Explanations of racial inequality and racial discrimination are developed from theories of the distribution of income. In the United States, the dominant economic narrative and its derivative policies regarding racial inequality largely ignore structural racism, offering instead an individualist perspective on economic inequality. This reasoning is committed to the notion that racially-based inequalities in economic well-being are primarily the outcome of individual decisions by workers regarding the acquisition of skills, labor force participation, employment, hours, occupational selection, and risk-taking. Therefore, racial differences in employment and economic status are explained as the result of differences in the individual's marketable skills, behaviors, and culture.

Economists who take this individualist position discount racial discrimination as a substantive force in the labor market (Heckman, 1998, 2011). Within this framework, "race" is confined to non-market activities and often race is not distinguished from values, behaviors, or culture. When it comes to persistent racial inequality, the individualist framework is supported by a largely Libertarian argument: competition will ensure that persons with identical skills and market-functional values and behaviors will receive identical treatment in the market. By extension, this view holds that individuals or racial groups who achieve superior economic well-being are endowed with advanced market-functional values, behaviors, and culture. Groups that have lower levels of economic well-being have inferior market-functional attributes. Despite the popularity of the individualist framework, the empirical evidence has not provided strong support for this perspective.

Although the innate abilities of individuals may differ quite markedly, the distributions of innate ability are the same for large aggregations of individuals such as racial groups. There is also strong evidence that Black–White income inequality cannot be explained by Black–White differences in family values and behaviors (Mason, 2004). The empirical evidence also shows that there are long periods where racial earnings inequality is stagnant or increasing, while racial difference in skill is decreasing, for example, 1880–1910 and 1974–present. Thus, it is possible that nearly all of the Black–White racial inequality in earnings can be attributed to discrimination, either within the labor market or in non-labor market activities that affect skill accumulation and other vital aspects of income attainment, and racial differences in wealth.

Stratification economics emphasizes an important alternative to individualist economics and provides important insights into the nature of structural racism. Stratification economics takes seriously the idea that people with identical skills and market-functional behaviors will *not* necessarily receive identical treatment in the labor market. Stratification economics emphasizes the rivalrous nature of the competitive process: firms strategically compete with other firms within the same industry (by lowering the unit cost of production), firms strategically interact with other firms in different industries (by entering and exiting industries in response to profitability), managers compete with workers over control of the labor process and distribution of the fruits of production (by struggling over the wage rate, working conditions, task assignment, and the effort level of workers), and individual and social groups of workers compete with other individual and social groups of workers. Market power does not necessarily imply the absence of competition but may be a necessary requirement to successfully compete.

Diversity and heterogeneity are inherent elements of the competitive process. Hence, persons of identical skill may not receive identical treatment in the market; regardless of race, otherwise identical workers may receive differential wages, access to employment, promotion, and training, and working conditions. Competition reproduces persistent market inequality. But competitively reproduced labor market inequality in combination with racial identity actions creates persistent racial discrimination in the labor market.

Within the stratification framework, race is an economic strategy for determining access to resources and opportunities. Chattel and servitude capitalisms produced and bequeathed to racialized managerial capitalism a resilient legacy of racialized competition within the labor market. At the center of this racialized competition are racial norms governing manager–worker interactions; these norms tend to exclude African Americans from the highest paying jobs.

11.1 SOURCES OF PERSISTENT INEQUALITY AND RACIAL DISCRIMINATION

11.1.1 Involuntary Joblessness

Chronic joblessness is endemic to capitalist economies; it is not an aberrant outcome that occurs because wages and prices are inflexible, public assistance is too high, or there is some other impediment to competition (Keynes, 1936; Kalecki, 1954; Shaikh, 2016). The economy may not produce sufficient employment opportunities because of insufficient investment spending in response to fundamental uncertainty regarding future economic activity, declining profitability, or other features of the competitive process. Consequently, some people will be underemployed or unemployed regardless of their education, family background, intelligence, attitude toward hard work, or other individual characteristics.

Persistent involuntary joblessness in a competitive capitalist economy creates the possibility that individual productive capacity is not the only factor determining who works and who does not work – jobs may be allocated according to factors other than the productivity related characteristics of workers. Structural racism is intimately connected to involuntary joblessness; within limits, hiring managers may disproportionately exclude Black applicants and production managers may disproportionately layoff Black employees without worry of being penalized by the market.

Racialized employment and layoff decisions create racial differences in the probability of employment. Differences in observable characteristics explain 20–30 percent and 25–58 percent of the men's and women's racial employment gap, respectively. The "unadjusted" racial differential is the raw difference in employment rates (see Table 11.1, a modification of Table 9.12). For example, during 2009–2019, the Southern African American male employment rate was 7.1 percentage points lower than the Southern White male employment rate. The "adjusted" differential is the racial difference in employment rates for persons of the same observable characteristics, viz., years of education, age, marital status, military service status, region, gender, and annual economic trend. During 2009–2019 the employment rate of Southern African American men was 5 percentage points lower than the employment rate of Southern White men with the same observable characteristics. "Percent explained" is the percentage of the unadjusted racial differential that is explained by racial differences in the observed characteristics of workers. For example, racial differences in observed characteristics explain 29.6 percent of the 2009–2019 Southern male unadjusted racial employment gap $= \left(1 - \frac{0.050}{0.071}\right) * 100$. For Southern men, the racial employment gap was 1.7 percentage points in 1965–1974 and observed characteristics explained all of the racial gap. During the late 1970s, the Southern male employment gap increased and

TABLE 11.1. *Racial differential in probability of employment, percent explained, 1965–2019*

	1965–1974	1975–1980	1981–1990	1991–2001	2002–2008	2009–2019
Men, South						
Unadjusted	−0.017	−0.065	−0.077	−0.064	−0.054	−0.071
Adjusted	0.003	−0.033	−0.056	−0.049	−0.037	−0.050
Percent explained	117.6	49.2	27.3	23.4	31.5	29.6
Men, Non-South						
Unadjusted	−0.043	−0.101	−0.116	−0.096	−0.070	−0.084
Adjusted	−0.031	−0.084	−0.099	−0.083	−0.053	−0.067
Percent explained	27.9	16.8	14.7	13.5	24.3	20.2
Women, South						
Unadjusted	−0.037	−0.026	−0.050	−0.039	−0.026	−0.026
Adjusted	−0.019	−0.017	−0.041	−0.030	−0.016	−0.011
Percent explained	48.6	34.6	18.0	23.1	38.5	57.7
Women, Non-South						
Unadjusted	−0.004	−0.033	−0.056	−0.047	−0.046	−0.052
Adjusted	−0.002	−0.040	−0.063	−0.047	−0.038	−0.039
Percent explained	50.0	−21.2	−12.5	0.0	17.4	25.0

"Unadjusted" is raw differential in probability of employment. "Adjusted" is racial differential of employment for persons of the same education, age, marital status, veteran status, and annual trend. Modification of Table 9.12.
Source: Author's calculations, CPS ASEC 1965–2019

observed characteristics explain less than half of the gap. During 1981–2019, observable characteristics explained 23–32 percent of the employment gap.

For each period, the Non-Southern male racial employment gap is larger than the African American–White Southern employment gap and the percent explained is lower. For most periods, observed characteristics explain 20 percent or less of the Non-Southern male racial employment gap. There are similar patterns among women.

11.1.2 The Wage–Productivity Ratio and Bargaining Power

Competition creates a tendency toward an equal rate of profit among regulating firms between industries and an equal selling price among firms within an industry. Firms may use different vintages of and different types of capital equipment, have differences in labor–management relations, have differences in sources of capital and raw materials, have differential working conditions, and have different marketing goals. Workers with identical characteristics may have differences in pay because of differences in the wage–productivity strategy of their firms of employment.

Competition does not ensure that workers will automatically share in productivity gains; the hourly wage–hourly productivity ratio $\left(\beta = \frac{\textit{hourly wage}}{\textit{hourly productivity}}\right)$ is variable across firms, industries, and time. For example, some firms may focus on a high productivity approach via a high wage–high labor effort strategy while others focus on a low cost approach using a low wage–low effort strategy. Among other factors, this ratio is proportional to the relative strength of workers' bargaining power, the competitive structure of firms, and managerial strategy. From 1980 to 2014, productivity grew by about 80 percent while real wages and earnings either did not keep pace or declined (see Figure 3.1). Real average wages did not keep pace with productivity growth and real median weekly earnings of full-time workers declined for most of the period. Companies had the ability to pay higher wages between 1974 and 2014, but workers lost the ability to make them pay, especially workers below the highest wage levels.

The 1974–1975 and 1981–1982 recessions were turning points in the struggle against racial discrimination within the labor market. At the end of servitude capitalism (1966), White male workers aged 16–64 had an advantage of 2.57 years of education (see Figure 3.2). This advantage shrunk to 1.95 years in 1975, to 1.29 years in 1982, to 0.95 years in 1992, to 0.68 years in 2007, and grew to 0.76 years in 2016. Hence, the racial difference in years of education declined between the mid-1960s and the mid-1970s and continued to decline between the mid-1970s until the present. Also, the racial gap in the quality of education declined during 1970–1900 (see Chapter 4).

The decline in the racial gap in the quantity and quality of education was reflected in the decline in the racial wage differential between 1960 and 1980;

thereafter, the skills gap continued to decline while the racial wage gap showed no discernable trend. From 1980 to 2015, there was virtually no progress toward closing the racial wage gap despite continued progress in closing the gaps in the quantity and quality of education: African American men earned 29 percent less than White men in 1974–1979 and 32 percent less than White men in 2009–2018 (see Chapter 9). Similarly, during 1880–1910, the racial gap in skills decreased while racial discrimination in the labor market increased (see Table 4.4).

Together, these trends are consistent with the stratification perspective that bargaining power and racial identity are important factors for determining the distribution of income in competitive markets. All workers lost bargaining power relative to management between 1980 and 2016, and Black workers lost bargaining power relative to White workers. Median wages stagnated while productivity was increasing, and racial wage inequality was constant or increasing during a period when racial skill inequality was declining.

11.1.3 Persistent Inequality

The average wage rate for each job is determined by the ability of firms to pay (productivity) and the ability of workers to make firms pay (bargaining power).[1] Firms within the same industry may have different competitive characteristics and they may face workers with different degrees of bargaining power. The competitive characteristics of firms set limits on wages. Suppose, for example, we have a group of identical workers: they have equal years of education and training, cognitive ability, years of experience, communication skills, motivation to work, etc. These identical workers may receive different pay for doing the same work because they are employed at firms that are differentiated by the ability to pay and by the ability of workers to make firms pay. In this case, identical workers who perform the same job at the same firm will receive similar pay. However, identical workers who perform the same job at firms with less competitive characteristics or who are part of workforces with lower bargaining power will receive lower pay. Different pay for equal skill is the competitive norm as each firm utilizes the technology and managerial strategy that yields the strongest competitive advantage.

Average wage for job ← ability to pay, ability to make pay

[1] Botwinick (1993) is the seminal reference for wage inequality. Shaikh (2016) provides the details for the discussion of competition. Mason (1995, 1999) are the references for competition, wage inequality, and racial discrimination in the labor market.

The competitive characteristics of a firm include many factors: the size and quality of its workforce, the level of its fixed capital investment, its capital-to-labor ratio, strategic advantages in obtaining physical inputs, strategic advantages in selling its goods and services, and quality of its workforce. Workers employed at larger, more capital-intensive firms, and with greater amounts of fixed capital investment will receive above average pay. Increases (decreases) in the quality of labor used to produce the output of firms will raise (lower) the wage rate. Similarly, strong product demand pressures will tend to raise (lower) the wage rate at firms growing above (below) their planned rate of growth.

It is also the case that workers who are members of a workforce with above average bargaining power will receive above average pay. The bargaining power of workers is strongly related to what fraction of the workforce is organized, the quality of worker organization, and the form, scope, ideology, and structure of worker organization.[2] In addition, the legal process that covers the treatment of workers, minimum wage payments, and the institutional framework for bargaining determines bargaining power. Unorganized workers who do not share salary information will have the lowest average wage rate and (perhaps) the greatest level of wage inequality.

ability to make pay ← relative power of labor v. capital
← bargaining power of workers
← quantitative extent of organization, quality of organization, form of worker organization, scope of organization, ideology of organization, and structure of organization

11.1.3.1 Conflict Effect

Worker inequality lowers bargaining power, which in turn reduces the firm's average wage rate. Movements away from egalitarian wages, hours, working conditions, on-the-job training, hiring, lay off, and promotion opportunities disrupt class cohesion among workers. Racial conflict outside of the workplace also limits coalition building within the workplace; hence, a socially homogeneous workforce may be more cohesive than a socially heterogeneous workforce. Also, the racial composition of the workforce is an important economic variable if the match in social identity between journeymen and incoming

[2] Variations in form refer to union versus employee associations, while variations in scope refer to industrial versus trade union. Further, ideological differences might include business unionism versus social unionism. Finally, organizational structure refers to whether the workers' organization is democratically or autocratically organized. Google "Coalition of Immokalee Workers" for information on innovative worker–community organization that has dramatically increased the bargaining power for workers with limited education and skill.

workers is an important factor in the relative efficiency of on-the-job training (Thurow, 1975; Pedulla and Pager, 2019). These considerations suggest that neither managers nor workers are indifferent to the identity composition of the workforce and the nature and extent of identity inequalities among workers. To lower bargaining power, managers will seek a diverse workforce with wide inequalities in remuneration and employment opportunities. However, too much social heterogeneity and inequality may lower productivity. To raise bargaining power, workers will seek egalitarian remuneration and employment opportunities. Managers may favor a homogeneous workforce as a strategy to increase worker effort. But too much social homogeneity lowers community support for workers (when the firm's operating community is heterogeneous) and may reduce product demand (and thereby lower wages). The actual social composition of the labor force, that is, its racial–ethnic, gender, or other diversity, depends on the contending interests between and among workers and managers; the substantive point is that both managers and workers have strong economic interests in the identity composition of the workforce.

11.1.3.2 Racial Exclusion Effect

Both workers and managers enter the US labor market with socially constructed and historically persistent racial identities. The intra- and interindustry allocation of workers is mediated by the racialized practices of managers and workers, especially in high wage jobs (Williams 1987, 1991; Darity, 1989). The utilization of ascriptive characteristics, such as race and gender, as labor allocation mechanisms provides the operative framework for formalizing racial domination (Mason, 1995). Hiring other-group workers into a labor force alters the average wage, the average rate of effort extraction, and the employment stability of dominant group workers.

Differences in pay for otherwise identical workers will encourage intense competition among workers for the highest paying jobs. Workers will participate in strategic identity coalitions that seek to limit competition from other social groups. Race and gender are two of the more salient ascriptive characteristics for establishing coalitions. Racial identity matters because it is a cultural coalescing force used by workers to improve their relative positions in the labor queue (Darity, 1989). If so, we might expect that White (male) employment density has a positive correlation with the wage differential when race is a sorting mechanism in a labor surplus economy with a hierarchical job structure (Mason, 1995, 1999).

11.1.4 Identity and Exclusion

Managers are not identity-free professionals, focused solely on how to use their discretion to craft decisions that most efficiently combine identity-free workers, capital, and material to produce marketable outputs. Managers are racialized economic agents; the application of managerial discretion and resources is connected to the manager–worker racial identity match. Racial identity affects managerial discretion in hiring and evaluation of applicants. Additionally, racial identity affects managerial decisions related to the labor process: remuneration, promotion, and allocation of workers to alternative tasks, on-the-job training opportunities, information, and managerial resources that affect the productivity of the enterprise.

Production managers observe attributes of workers that are unobserved by hiring managers and executives. Production managers have information on their own abilities and knowledge of workers that is unobserved by hiring managers and executives. Production managers possess information on situational logistics and the effectiveness of rules that is unobserved by hiring managers and executives. Because production managers possess unobserved information, productive efficiency requires managerial discretion in the allocation of information, financial resources, and decision-making authority.

Worker productivity may be changed by managerial policy. For example, employers may pay workers an efficiency wage, that is, a wage that exceeds the best available wage in alternative employment opportunities, as inducement for workers to increase their work effort (Weiss, 2016). Employers may also raise productivity by hiring high quality managers (Shaw, 2019). Workers employed at firms with better supervisors or efficiency wages will have higher productivity and compensation than workers with identical individual characteristics employed at firms with lower quality supervisors or who do not have an efficiency wage policy. To the extent that workers of different racial and ethnic groups have differential access to higher paying firms, the average level of compensation will vary across these groups

Workers, too, are racialized agents. Workers value the racial identity match with managers (Cook and Heyes, 2021). For example, White applicants are 11 percent more likely to accept a job offered by a White manager than an otherwise identical job offered by a Black manager. Black applicants are 17 percent less likely to accept a job offered by a White manager than the same job offered by a Black manager. If White workers are the majority of applicants, then identity preferences shaping their racial supply will create a competitive advantage for the employment of White managers.

The manager–worker racial identity match has an impact on critical decisions within the labor process (Giuliano, Levine, and Leonard, 2011). For example, an African American worker matched with an African American manager lowers the worker's probability of dismissal by 19 percent, and there is a similar effect for Latinx manager–worker and Asian manager–worker identity matches. Matching an African American worker with an African American manager increases the probability of promotion by 79 percent. A White worker matched with White manager reduces the probability of quitting by 4 percent, with a similar effect for African American manager–worker, Latinx manager–worker, and Asian manager–worker identity matches.

Hiring decisions are influenced by the manager–applicant racial identity match and the racial context of the hiring decision (Daskalova, 2018). When deciding alone, hiring managers discriminate based on negative assessment of an applicant belonging to a different racial group. When hiring as part of a group, discrimination is driven by own-group favoritism. In particular, group hiring decisions with a racially homogeneous decision group is associated with favoritism toward own-group candidates. An expectation of own-group favoritism by other members of a homogenous hiring group can lead a manager to engage in positive discrimination in favor of an applicant in joint decisions even if the individual manager does not positively discriminate in favor of the own-group in individual decisions; discrimination in joint decisions may occur if a manager expects that other own-group colleagues are racially biased. However, group hiring decisions with a racially diverse group of decision-makers is associated with no difference in treatment of own- and other-group candidates.

Worker productivity may be changed by managerial actions. Managerial favoritism for own-group workers has an impact on hiring, wages, and productivity (Dickinson, Masclet, and Peterle, 2018). Potential workers are evaluated during the hiring process, where both ability and identity are important in managerial evaluation of applicants. Holding identity constant, lower productivity workers are ranked lower than high productivity workers. Decision-makers rank own-group applicants higher than other-group applicants. The subjective rankings gap between own- and other-group applicants is greater when the applicants are homogenous than when they are heterogenous (in terms of productive ability). Favoritism continues to exist when workers differ in productivities, but favoritism is lower in the presence of heterogeneous productivities.

The racial identity match also affects wage offers. Own-group workers are more likely to be offered a high wage than other-group workers. Evidence from the Dickinson, Masclet, and Peterle economic experiment indicates that the wage differential is higher when there is less opportunity for employment discrimination, that is, there is greater wage discrimination when worker ability is randomly assigned by a computer than when workers are ranked by decision-makers: wage discrimination increases when decision-makers lack the opportunity to discriminate in evaluating workers. Wage favoritism is lower in heterogeneous treatment (workers have differing abilities) than homogeneous treatment (workers have identical ability). There is a tradeoff between employment and wage discrimination, given the absence of information on productivity.

Productivity is not a fixed attribute based solely on a worker's productive characteristics; there is also an endogenous component to productivity. Dickinson, Masclet, and Peterle confirmed the efficiency wage insight: regardless of the worker–manager identity match, workers offered higher wages reciprocate with greater work effort. Additionally, the manager–worker identity match affects productivity: own-group workers provide higher effort than other-group workers. The worker–worker identity match matters:

workers provide higher effort when paired with other members of their own-group. Workers selected via ranking treatment provide greater effort than those selected via random treatment: workers provide greater production effort when they are aware that hiring managers ranked them above other workers. Finally, racially biased managers may create racial differences in worker productivity by providing more information and managerial resources to own-group workers relative to other-group workers (Glover, Pallais, and Pariente, 2017).

By raising the productivity of the enterprise, discrimination can be profit-increasing for the firm. Du Bois (1935) noted that the White racial contract combined racial discrimination in public goods provision with racial discrimination in wages and employment. Nevertheless, discrimination by for-profit competitive firms may generate spillover costs for society (Dickinson, Masclet, and Peterle, 2018). There are social costs associated with market discrimination. The social cost of discrimination by firms increases when unemployed workers perceive that the hiring process is racially biased; employers are more likely than workers to be targets of protest actions. The social costs of discrimination are higher in heterogeneous worker treatments (differences in workers' wage–effort relationship) than homogeneous worker treatments.

11.1.5 Instrumental Racial Discrimination: Competition and Persistent Racial Discrimination

Racial discrimination can be profit-increasing. Firm managers are in a continuous competitive rivalry with their workforce. Competitive survival and profit-increasing behavior establishes constant pressure for managers to increase work effort, to reduce the wage-to-productivity ratio, to trade lower firm wages for the promise of a higher social wage, and to increase managerial discretion regarding labor allocation. Within an industry, the competition between workers and managers is most intense at high-cost firms. Across industries, the competition between workers and managers is most intense in those companies with the least resistance to entry by potential rivals. Each firm selects a managerial strategy consistent with its competitive rivalry with other firms and its internal competition with workers. The average wage rate paid by firms to equally skilled workers will differ because firms have differing competitive structures and differing managerial strategies, both within and between industries.

Persistent discrimination is linked to job competition (Darity and Williams, 1985; Darity, 1989; Mason, 1995, 1999). Racial identity is a coalescing force among workers and between workers and managers. Racial groups have unequal access to those who control resources and to those embedded into positions of power and authority (Williams, 1987, 1991). African American workers have less power among workers and less power in social interactions with managers and, therefore, have a more difficult time than Whites in gaining access to the most desirable jobs.

Notably, there is nothing within the stratification perspective that automatically links decreases in the racial skills gap to decreases in the racial wage and employment gaps. Measured over time or across regions, the racial skills gap may decline even as the racial wage and employment gaps increase. Hence, the stratification perspective is consistent with the stagnation of racial disparity among males over the period from 1974 to the present, while, during the same period, there was considerable improvement in the relative educational attainment of Blacks. Similarly, during the nadir of Jim Crow, roughly the years 1877–1914, the racial skills gap decreased while the racial gap in occupational status increased (Darity, Guilkey, and Winfrey, 1996; Darity, Dietrich, and Guilkey, 2001).

11.1.6 Automatic Associations, Instrumental Discrimination, and Managerial Resources

Instrumental discrimination means that social group discrimination, viz., racial discrimination in hiring, employment, pay, promotion, skill acquisition, and layoffs, is a profit-increasing labor market strategy that is consistent with vigorous competition (Reich, 1981; Williams, 1987; Mason, 1995, 1995; Darity, Mason, and Stewart, 2006; Darity, Hamilton, and Stewart, 2015; Githinji, 2015). Managers may make race-conscious decisions but explicit bigotry is not necessary for instrumental discriminations. All that is necessary is for managers to have racially influenced automatic associations, which is often called implicit racial bias.

Implicit discrimination is "*unintentional* and outside of the discriminator's awareness" (Bertrand, Chugh, and Mullainathan, 2005; Papillon, 2014). Chattel capitalism and servitude capitalism created ubiquitous, deeply rooted, and often unexamined racial associations (Green, 1998; Bobo, 2011; Equal Justice Initiative, 2018; Payne, Vuletich, and Brown-Iannuzzi, 2019). Both the massive racial inequality in wealth, income, and power, along with the binary associations between "Black" and negative attributes, on the one hand, and "White" and positive attributes, on the other hand, were created and continuously reproduced during 1619–1965 and transmitted to racialized managerial capitalism. With automatic associations: (1) economic agents have "unconscious mental association between members of a social group and a given (usually negative) attribute" (Gallo, Grund, and Reade, 2013: 136; and (2) agents unconsciously act on this information during the process of making economic decisions. Further, this social psychology approach argues that discrimination will occur even when there is an absence of explicitly bigotry. The decision-making context may activate psychological associations between race and other socioeconomic attributes; and implicit racial associations are pliable. Automatic associations, that is, implicit bias, are embedded in the instrumental racialism associated with the formation of racial identity norms.

Automatic associations are binary racial correlations that are strongly embedded within an individual's cognitive processes. For example, "Black" and "bad," "immigrant" and "poor English," or "White" and "smart" are subjective race–attribute correlations. Implicit bias (also called "automatic associations" or "unconscious bias") may have a substantively large and persistent impact on racial differences in labor market outcomes, such as employment, compensation, promotion, working conditions, and layoffs. Chattel and servitude capitalisms provide historical roots for automatic associations. In particular, for counties and states more dependent on slavery in 1860, contemporary White citizens have higher pro-White implicit bias Geographic differences and contemporary Black citizens have lower pro-White implicit bias (Payne, Vuletich, and Brown-Iannuzzi, 2019). Persistent inequality transmits these racial associations from the past into the present.

Persons may not be conscious of their implicit biases; hence, when explicitly asked they may even deny the objective reality of these subjective correlations. These biases enter into the decision-making process when decisions are made under time pressure or other cognitive load stresses, when there is inattentiveness to task, and when there is ambiguity in the decision-making environment (Bertrand, Chugh, and Mullainathan, 2005; Papillon, 2014).

Suppose job interviewers are all White and a significant fraction of them associate "Black" with "lower than average preparation." The employers receive a large number of resumes (say, 400) for an open position and these resumes must be evaluated in a very short period of time (say, 30 days). In addition to evaluating resumes, job interviewers must carry out all of their other employment activities, which may also have pressing deadlines. As a first cut, resumes are shorted into a "yes" pile and a "no" file. In this environment, resumes with African American identifiers are more likely to enter the "no" file because interviewers have insufficient time to carefully read each resume; hence, the stress of a pressing deadline encourages shortcuts in decision-making, viz., sub-consciously acting on the subjective belief that African Americans have lower preparation than Whites.

An alternative scenario is that there is sufficient time but there are distractions from the task of selecting the best candidates to interview. Instead, they are social cues that distract from the candidate selection process. For example, evaluation of the resumes contains social cues that racially identify the candidate without providing additional information on the candidate's qualifications. For example, Black applicants may have obtained training at an academic institution that is a weak identity match for White reviewers, for example, a Historically Black College or University such as Florida A&M University, rather than a predominately White institution such as Michigan State University. Or African American applicants may have majored in an academic discipline that is a dissonant identity match for White evaluators, such as African American Studies, rather than a discipline that is a stronger identity match for White evaluators, such as Classical Studies. The social cues on the resumes introduce ambiguity into the decision-making process, that is, it is possible to disproportionately reject Black applicants for reasons other than race per se, though the resumes contained the social cues that trigger implicit bias in decision-making.

11.1.7 Racial Discrimination in the Labor Market

Workers do not enter into employment with a fixed level of productivity, rather they may have a fixed set of productivity-linked attributes, for example, the quality and quantity of formal education, general and specific experience prior to hiring, etc. A given set of worker characteristics may yield differing productivity according to variation in the effort extraction process: variations in manager policy and behavior may produce variations in worker productivity. Racially biased managers will reduce the quality of manager–worker interactions and thereby reduce the productivity of individuals affiliated with subaltern groups.

Glover, Pallais, and Pariente (2017) consider new cashiers employed by a single employer (French grocery store chain) with multiple sites of employment (stores). The store has a large number of racial minority workers of North African and Sub-Saharan origin (28 percent), who are identified by their names. Individual cashiers are hired by the chain's central office and individual store's chief cashier. Store managers have no role in the hiring cashiers. New cashiers have six-month contracts and their work schedules are determined by a computer program, "which assigns shifts to meet predicted demand, taking into account the preferences of more senior workers" (p. 1221). Both racial majority and racial minority workers work with different managers on different days, labor under similar conditions, and are similarly skilled. However, the schedules of new cashiers are posted several weeks in advance; hence, both new cashiers and managers know in advance the worker–manager matches for future dates of employment at a particular store. Data on new cashier absences, time worked, scanning speed, and time taken between customers are collected on a daily bias. These data, along with managerial observations on workers' performance and customer relations, determine whether a new cashier will be offered a longer contract at the expiration of their initial six-month contract. About 30–40 percent of new cashiers are offered a longer contract.

Manager bias is assessed by an implicit association test (IAT), a social psychology test of automatic associations that has become the primary metric of unconscious bias used in empirical studies (Greenwald and Krieger, 2006). In this case, the test assesses implicit association between traditionally French- or North African-sounding names and words indicating worker competence or incompetence. The bias score increases with the intensity of managerial association of North African names with words indicating poor work performance. On average, managers took the IAT 17 months after the study's data were collected.

For a one standard deviation increase in managerial bias, as measured by the IAT, Glover, Pallais, and Pariente (2017) find the following results:

1. the minority absence rates increase by 1 percentage point, an effect that is 70% of the mean absence rate;
2. minority cashiers are less willing to work after their scheduled time, in particular, minority work time is reduced by 3.3 minutes, which is 1/12 of a standard deviation;
3. minority workers scan 0.28 fewer items per minute, about 10 percent of the standard deviation of 2.9 articles per minute; and
4. the customer line moves slower for minority workers, as North African-named cashiers spend about 1.2 more seconds (one tenth of a standard deviation or 4% longer) between customers.

The impact of managerial bias is greatest during the latter portion of the contract and its effects are concentrated in less diverse stores. Surprisingly, there is no statistically significant relationship between managerial bias and the average performance of all workers; "biased managers (insignificantly) improve majority worker performance."

Cleaning is the least pleasant duty of cashier workers. Perhaps, contrary to expectations, North African named cashiers are less likely to be assigned to cleaning when working with a biased manager. Assignment to cleaning requires a manager to ask a cashier to close down a register and switch to cleaning, that is, extra-contact between workers and managers. If biased managers seek to avoid contact with minority workers, then minority workers will be less likely to be assigned to cleaning and less likely to work after hours when asked by mangers. Managers are likely to have contact with racial minority members in stores where they are a large share of the workforce; hence, the negative effects of managerial bias are concentrated in stores with a below average percentage of minority workers.

The quality of manager–worker interactions has a significant effect on worker productivity. Workers who remembered the names of a manager scanned 1.5 more articles per minute than when working with a manager whose name they were not able to recall.[3] For a one standard deviation in managerial bias, North African named worker were about 1.5 percentage points less likely to remember the manager. The impact of managerial bias

[3] This positive memory effect is independent of cofounding factors. "Workers did not perform better when working with managers they had been scheduled to work with more often …, nor does the effect of remembering the manager on worker performance decrease when we control for the amount of time spent working together … or manager fixed effects …" Mas and Moretti (2009) similarly find that cashiers exert more effort when their performance is being noticed by coworkers they value. In particular, Mas and Moretti find that, among workers in a large supermarket chain, worker effort responds positively to peers who see them but not to peers who do not see them. Worker effort also has a greater response to peers with whom they frequently interact.

declines by 25 percent if the sample is limited to the days a minority worker remembers the manager. Importantly, “minorities do not report that biased managers disliked them or assigned them to unpleasant tasks” (p. 1223).

For a given set of worker characteristics, manager–worker interactions make racial minority workers less productive. Racial discrimination during the labor process may provide an explanation for discrimination during the hiring process. The central office is responsible for hiring workers and providing longer contracts after the end of the initial six months contracts of new cashiers. Managers initiate employee discrimination, that is, lower productivity by North African named workers because of reduced contact with managers. Executives do not observe the quantity or quality of time managers allocate to workers. Executives only observe the realized productivity of workers and the characteristics. Hence, if firms use racial affiliation during the hiring process to infer potential productivity during the laboring process, racial minority workers will need superior characteristics to be equally likely to be hired as a majority worker with lower characteristics and, when paired with unbiased managers, minority workers will need higher realized productivity than majority workers.

Glover, Pallais, and Pariente (2017) find that, on days when matched with an unbiased manager, minority workers have fewer absences, more articles scanned per minute, less inter-customer time, and served more customers. On days when matched with a biased manager, there are no productivity effects associated with minority workers. “[W]hen they work with unbiased managers, minorities serve 9% more customers than majorities. While the average minority is at the 53rd percentile of average worker performance, on days with unbiased managers she is at the 79th percentile” (p. 1224).

11.1.8 Wage Differentials and Structure

Persistent racial discrimination in the labor market occurs because of racial differences in access to the highest paying jobs. Labor compensation depends on the characteristics of workers (education, experience, etc.) and the characteristics of firms (firm size, capital intensity, economic sector, extent of unionization, etc.). Both the characteristics of workers and the characteristics of firms influence the productivity of labor – the ability to the pay. In particular, larger firms and firms operating in the private sector pay higher wages. In the competition for jobs, African Americans tend to be excluded from positions with higher pay.

Southern African American women are less likely to be employed in the private sector than Southern White women, 77.5 percent and 80 percent, respectively (Table 11.2). This is also true for men: 83.5 percent and 85.4 percent of Southern African American and White men, respectively, are employed in the private sector. Outside of the South, African American men are less likely to work in the private sector than White men, 84.1 percent and

TABLE 11.2. *Sector of employment and composition of employment*

	Women			
	Non-South		South	
	African American	White	African American	White
Private Sector	0.814	0.816	0.775	0.800
Government	0.186	0.184	0.225	0.200
	Men			
	Non-South		South	
Private Sector	0.841	0.869	0.835	0.854
Government	0.159	0.131	0.165	0.146

All workers are 16–64 years of age, paid private and public sector employees, not self-employed, and Non-Latinx.
Source: Author's calculations, Annual Social and Economic Supplement of Current Population Survey, 2011–2018

86.9 percent, respectively. Non-Southern African American and White women are about equally likely to work in the private sector, 81.4 percent and 81.6 percent, respectively.

There are race–gender differences in the distribution of workers according to the size of the firm in the private sector (Table 11.3). For all workers and for both regions of the country, the major employers are firms that employ 1,000 or more workers. For example, 47–48 percent of African American women and 39–40 percent of White women work at the largest firms, while 45 percent and 38 percent of African American and White men are employed by firms with 1,000 or more employees. The median White worker labors at a firm with 100–499 employees, while the median African American worker provides labor services to firms with 500–999 employees.

The public sector provides more advantageous employment for women. For both African American and White women, public sector wages are 12–13 percent greater than private sector wages for women with the same observable characteristics. Male wages in the public sector are lower than male wages for the private sector, especially for White men. African American men in the Non-Southern and Southern public sectors earn 4.3 and 1.8 percent less, respectively, than Black men in the private sector. The differentials for White men are 9.3 percent (Non-South) and 6.4 percent (South).

African American workers encounter less inequality in the public sector than in the private sector (Table 11.4). For men of the same age, years of education, year of employment, and region, African Americans employed in the private sector earn 26 percent (Non-South) to 28 percent (South) less than their White competitors; African American men employed in the public sector earn 11–13 percent less than their White competitors. Among women of the same age,

TABLE 11.3. *Size of firm and composition of employment: private sector*

	Women			
	Non-South		South	
	Black	White	Black	White
Less than 10 employees	0.098	0.154	0.099	0.173
10–49 employees	0.132	0.177	0.142	0.184
50–99 employees	0.079	0.076	0.081	0.074
100–499 employees	0.155	0.139	0.134	0.128
500–999 employees	0.064	0.057	0.065	0.054
1,000 or more employees	0.471	0.397	0.478	0.386
	Men			
	Non-South		South	
Less than 10 employees	0.124	0.162	0.120	0.171
10–49 employees	0.152	0.178	0.146	0.174
50–99 employees	0.082	0.087	0.081	0.081
100–499 employees	0.136	0.144	0.141	0.137
500–999 employees	0.056	0.053	0.060	0.053
1,000 or more employees	0.451	0.376	0.453	0.384

All workers are 16–64 years of age, paid private sector employees, not self-employed, and Non-Latinx.
Source: Author's calculations, ASEC of Current Population Survey, 2011–2018

years of education, year of employment, and region, Non-Southern and Southern African American women employed in the private sector earn 1.8 percent and 7.3 percent less, respectively, than their White competitors; Non-Southern and Southern African American women employed in the public sector earn 11.2 percent and 4.4 percent more, respectively, than their White competitors.

Large private sector firms and public organizations provide higher pay than smaller firms (Tables 11.5 and 11.6). The size of firm premium presented in each row is relative to a worker of the same region, age, race, gender, years of education, year of employment, and sector, employed in a firm with less than 10 employees ("mom-and-pop shop"). For example, Non-Southern and Southern African American women working at private sector firms with 10–49 employees earn 13.9 percent and 11.8 percent more than identical African American women working at mom-and-pop shops.

For all race–gender groups and for both sectors of employment, the wage premium tends to increase with the number of employees. For instance, Non-Southern African American men working at public sector organizations with 10–49 employees earn 24.2 percent more than Black men working for mom-

TABLE 11.4. *Public sector and racial wage differentials*

	Public sector							
	African American women				White women			
	Non-South		South		Non-South		South	
Public Sector	0.119	***	0.130	***	0.129	***	0.132	***
	[0.0157]		[0.0110]		[0.0182]		[0.0139]	
N	15,518		25,192		13,213		19,627	
R^2	0.277		0.274		0.282		0.273	
	African American men				White men			
Public sector	−0.0428	***	−0.0187	*	−0.0923	***	−0.0636	***
	[0.0055]		[0.0080]		[0.0056]		[0.0081]	
N	138,279		59,094		144,954		62,971	
R^2	0.287		0.277		0.358		0.336	
	Race							
	Women							
	Private				Public			
African American	−0.018	*	−0.073	***	0.112	***	0.044	***
	[0.0074]		[0.0066]		[0.0143]		[0.0108]	
N	123,872		66,021		29,925		18,265	
R^2	0.2873		0.2733		0.2366		0.2256	
	Men							
African American	−0.263	***	−0.276	***	−0.109	***	−0.132	***
	[0.0075]		[0.0067]		[0.0146]		[0.0124]	
N	135,388		69,343		22,779		13,255	
R^2	0.3673		0.3464		0.2888		0.2721	

All workers are 16–64 years of age, paid private and public sector employees, not self-employed, and Non-Latinx. Ordinary least squares regression where dependent variable is the natural logarithm of weekly wages and explanatory variable are race, region, age, age^2, years of education, and year of employment fixed effects. Separate equations are estimated for men and women. Standard errors in parentheses. * $p < 0.05$, ** $p < 0.01$, *** $p < 0.001$.
Source: Author's calculations, ASEC of CPS, 2011–2018

and-pop organizations. This size differential increases to 42.3 percent of Non-Southern African American men employed at public sector organizations with at least 1,000 employees. This pattern does not hold in the same way for Southern Black men working in the public sector; there is a 17.2 percent differential for organizations with at least 1,000 employees but no differential for smaller organizations.

TABLE 11.5. *Firm size differentials by race–gender and region: men*

	Black							
	Non-South				South			
Employees	Private		Public		Private		Public	
10–49	0.164	***	0.242	***	0.145	***	−0.084	
	[0.0080]		[0.0407]		[0.0119]		[0.0637]	
50–99	0.268	***	0.253	***	0.259	***	0.026	
	[0.0102]		[0.0401]		[0.0153]		[0.0642]	
100–499	0.354	***	0.293	***	0.326	***	−0.039	
	[0.0085]		[0.0370]		[0.0131]		[0.0559]	
500–999	0.398	***	0.320	***	0.390	***	0.0002	
	[0.0113]		[0.0387]		[0.0173]		[0.0580]	
1,000+	0.407	***	0.423	***	0.353	***	0.172	**
	[0.0069]		[0.0357]		[0.0103]		[0.0525]	
N	111,299		26,980		46,817		12,277	
R^2	0.314		0.247		0.295		0.243	
	White							
	Non-South				South			
	Private		Public		Private		Public	
10–49	0.092	***	0.168	***	0.100	***	0.226	***
	[0.0071]		[0.0355]		[0.0109]		[0.0579]	
50–99	0.154	***	0.236	***	0.174	***	0.294	***
	[0.0088]		[0.0362]		[0.0136]		[0.0596]	
100–499	0.202	***	0.265	***	0.209	***	0.256	***
	[0.0076]		[0.0328]		[0.0115]		[0.0540]	
500–999	0.218	***	0.268	***	0.264	***	0.292	***
	[0.0104]		[0.0354]		[0.0157]		[0.0580]	
1,000+	0.229	***	0.315	***	0.221	***	0.376	***
	[0.0062]		[0.0308]		[0.0093]		[0.0503]	
N	124,355		20,599		53,182		9,789	
R^2	0.375		0.296		0.351		0.281	

All workers are 16–64 years of age, paid private and public sector employees, not self-employed, and Non-Latinx. Ordinary least squares regression where dependent variable is the natural logarithm of weekly wages and explanatory variable are race, region, age, age², years of education, and year of employment fixed effects. Separate equations are estimated for men and women. Standard errors in parentheses. * $p < 0.05$, ** $p < 0.01$, *** $p < 0.001$.
Source: Author's calculations, ASEC of CPS, 2011–2018

More often than not, the employee size premium is larger for African American workers than it is for White workers, though Southern African American men working in the public sector are a clear exception. Consider private firms and public organizations with 100–499 employees. Non-Southern

TABLE 11.6. *Firm size differentials by race–gender and region: women*

	Black			
	Non-South		South	
Employees	Private	Public	Private	Public
10–49	0.139 ***	0.175	0.118 ***	0.198 *
	[0.0278]	[0.161]	[0.0212]	[0.0993]
50–99	0.179 ***	0.342 *	0.199 ***	0.184
	[0.0313]	[0.167]	[0.0243]	[0.102]
100–499	0.258 ***	0.310 *	0.258 ***	0.251 **
	[0.0270]	[0.145]	[0.0212]	[0.0910]
500–999	0.300 ***	0.369 *	0.332 ***	0.329 ***
	[0.0335]	[0.148]	[0.0257]	[0.0945]
1,000+	0.279 ***	0.467 ***	0.284 ***	0.493 ***
	[0.0232]	[0.136]	[0.0180]	[0.0842]
N	12,573	2,945	19,204	5,988
R^2	0.274	0.244	0.268	0.23
	White			
	Non-South		South	
	Private	Public	Private	Public
10–49	0.043	0.236	0.104 ***	0.139
	[0.0283]	[0.179]	[0.0224]	[0.115]
50–99	0.128 ***	0.264	0.231 ***	0.191
	[0.0332]	[0.181]	[0.0260]	[0.118]
100–499	0.170 ***	0.332 *	0.207 ***	0.112
	[0.0288]	[0.165]	[0.0222]	[0.105]
500–999	0.184 ***	0.263	0.233 ***	0.187
	[0.0367]	[0.170]	[0.0283]	[0.110]
1,000+	0.191 ***	0.425 **	0.235 ***	0.294 **
	[0.0238]	[0.155]	[0.0187]	[0.0966]
N	11,033	2,180	16,161	3,466
R^2	0.275	0.269	0.27	0.239

All workers are 16–64 years of age, paid private and public sector employees, not self-employed, and Non-Latinx. Ordinary least squares regression where dependent variable is the natural logarithm of weekly wages and explanatory variable are size of firm, race, region, age, age^2, years of education, year of employment, sector, and region. Standard errors in parentheses. * $p < 0.05$, ** $p < 0.01$, *** $p < 0.001$.

Source: Author's calculations, Annual Social and Economic Supplement of Current Population Survey, 2011–2018

African American men employed in the private and public sectors earn 35.4 percent and 29.3 percent more, respectively, than African Americans employed at mom-and-pop firms and organizations. Non-Southern White men employed in the private and public sectors earn 20.2 percent and 26.5 percent more, respectively, than Whites employed at mom-and-pop firms and organizations. Southern African American women employed in the private and public sectors earn 25.8 percent and 25.1 percent more, respectively, than African Americans employed at mom-and-pop firms and organizations. Southern White women employed in the private and public sectors earn 20.7 percent and 11.2 percent more, respectively, than Whites employed at mom-and-pop firms and organizations.

For both regions of the country, African American men have larger private sector employment size wage premiums than African American women, though the opposite is true for the public sector. There is a similar pattern for Non-Southern White men and women, but not for Southern White men and women. Consider firms and organizations with 500–999 employees. Relative to the same race–gender group employed in mom-and-pop shops, Non-Southern African American men have private and public sector premiums of 39.8 percent and 32 percent, while the Southern premiums are 39 percent and 0 percent, respectively. By comparison, Non-Southern African American women have private and public sector premiums of 30.0 percent and 36.9 percent, while the Southern premium is 33 percent for both sectors. Non-Southern White men have private and public sector premiums of 21.8 percent and 26.8 percent, while the Southern premiums are 26.6 percent and 29.2 percent, respectively. Non-Southern White women have private and public sector premiums of 17.0 percent and 33.2 percent, while the Southern premiums are 20.7 percent and an imprecisely measured 11.2 percent, respectively.

There is less racial inequality among public sector organizations than private sector firms (Tables 11.7 and 11.8). The Black racial wage differential presented in each row is relative to a White worker of the same region, age, gender, years of education, year of employment, and sector. Consider private sector firms and public organizations with at least 1,000 employees. Southern African American women earn 10.7 percent less and 3.88 percent more, respectively, than identical White women working at employers of the same size. Similarly, Non-Southern African American women working at private sector firms and public organizations earn 7.45 percent less and 8.03 percent, respectively, more than White women. Southern African American men earn 26.8 percent and 13.4 percent less, respectively, than White men. Non-Southern African American men working at private sector firms and public organizations earn 26.4 percent and 11.2 percent less, respectively, than identical White men working with employers with at least 1,000 employees.

Within the private sector, there is greater inequality in the South. Consider firms with 100–499 employees. Non-Southern and Southern African American men earn 29.4 and 31.9 percent less, respectively, than White men. Non-Southern and Southern African American women earn 7.1 and 13.1 percent less, respectively, than White women. Within the public sector, there is greater inequality among Non-Southern men than in the South. For example, among organizations with 100–499 employees, African American men earn

TABLE 11.7. *Race differentials by firm size, gender, region, and sector: women*

	<10	10–49	50–99	100–499	500–999	1,000+
Non-South, Private Sector						
Black	0.018	0.006	−0.062 *	−0.071 ***	−0.065 *	−0.075 ***
	[0.0264]	[0.0200]	[0.0244]	[0.0172]	[0.0257]	[0.0105]
N	19,191	21,893	9,657	17,549	7,162	48,420
R^2	0.189	0.264	0.27	0.267	0.315	0.357
Non-South, Public Sector						
Black	0.003	−0.054	0.143	0.085	0.124 *	0.080 ***
	[0.186]	[0.0933]	[0.100]	[0.0522]	[0.0609]	[0.0158]
N	458	1,333	1,487	4,427	2,254	19,966
R^2	0.085	0.231	0.25	0.262	0.276	0.236
South, Private Sector						
Black	−0.065 **	−0.089 ***	−0.126 ***	−0.131 ***	−0.119 ***	−0.107 ***
	[0.0221]	[0.0169]	[0.0225]	[0.0161]	[0.0242]	[0.00943]
N	9,898	11,347	5,227	8,857	3,888	26,804
R^2	0.171	0.238	0.246	0.26	0.279	0.353
South, Public Sector						
Black	−0.239 *	0.0008	−0.119	0.014	0.061	0.039 ***
	[0.119]	[0.0688]	[0.0690]	[0.0449]	[0.0493]	[0.0118]
N	234	486	452	1,392	911	14,790
R^2	0.08	0.214	0.237	0.196	0.239	0.225

TABLE 11.8. *Race differentials by firm size, gender, region, and sector: men*

	<10	10–49	50–99	100–499	500–999	1,000+
Non-South, Private Sector						
Black	−0.258 ***	−0.296 ***	−0.277 ***	−0.294 ***	−0.288 ***	−0.264 ***
	[0.0238]	[0.0191]	[0.0257]	[0.0187]	[0.0293]	[0.0107]
N	22,277	24,176	11,626	19,527	7,351	50,431
R^2	0.268	0.363	0.336	0.333	0.346	0.435
Non-South, Public Sector						
Black	−0.236	−0.192 *	−0.198 *	−0.151 **	−0.207 **	−0.112 ***
	[0.187]	[0.0885]	[0.0940]	[0.0514]	[0.0643]	[0.0161]
N	467	1,198	1,072	2,641	1,306	16,095
R^2	0.207	0.37	0.25	0.347	0.376	0.27
South, Private Sector						
Black	−0.309 ***	−0.299 ***	−0.247 ***	−0.319 ***	−0.340 ***	−0.268 ***
	[0.0207]	[0.0174]	[0.0227]	[0.0169]	[0.0258]	[0.0098]
N	10,952	11,489	5,616	9,853	3,921	27,512
R^2	0.261	0.338	0.307	0.301	0.339	0.418
South, Public Sector						
Black	−0.069	−0.123	−0.169 *	−0.181 ***	−0.174 **	−0.134 ***
	[0.123]	[0.0632]	[0.0755]	[0.0443]	[0.0613]	[0.0138]
N	196	520	428	1,047	558	10,506
R^2	0.076	0.182	0.18	0.256	0.256	0.284

15.1 percent and 18.1 percent less, respectively, than White men. Except for mom-and-pop operations, African American women employed in the public sector obtain equal or higher wages than White women, though the African American advantage is greater outside of the South. For example, among organizations with 100–499 employees, there is no statistically significant difference in the wages of African American and White women in either region. But, among public sector organizations with 500–999 employees, Non-Southern African American women earn 12.4 percent more than White women and there is no racial difference in the South.

11.2 SUMMARY AND DISCUSSION

This chapter had made three inter-related points: (1) increases in productivity do not guarantee increases in wages, especially for those in the middle and bottom half of the wage distribution; (2) closing the racial skills gap is not sufficient to close the wage and employment gaps experienced by African Americans; and (3) usually, the economy cannot provide a job to every person willing and able to work. Structural racism has its roots in involuntary unemployment and competitive differentiation, leading to the current state of affairs in which equally skilled but racially distinct workers have unequal access to employment.

Stratification economics takes seriously the notion that persons of identical skill and market-functional behaviors will not necessarily receive identical treatment within the labor market. Persistent racial discrimination is consistent with vigorous labor market competition. As specified by the racial stratification framework, racial identity is a form of strategic behavior that determines access to resources and opportunities. Understanding race as a competitive economic strategy allows us to examine the link between job competition and racial discrimination in the labor market.

Stratification economists link persistent discrimination to job competition (Darity and Williams, 1985; Darity, 1989; Mason, 1995, 1999). Racial identity is a coalescing force among workers and between workers and managers. Racial groups have unequal access to those who control resources and to those embedded into positions of power and authority (Williams, 1987, 1991). African American workers have less power among workers and less power in social interactions with managers and, therefore, have a more difficult time than Whites in gaining access to the most desirable jobs.

Equally skilled workers may receive different pay for doing the same work because they are employed at firms that are differentiated by the capacity to pay and by the capacity of workers to make firms pay. Workers who perform the same jobs at some firms may receive differences in pay because of differential access to managerial resources. Additionally, equally skilled workers who perform the same job at firms with less competitive characteristics, or who are part of a workforce with lower bargaining power, will receive lower pay.

Competing racial identities and different pay for equal work is the competitive norm as each firm utilizes the technology, managerial strategy, and marketing strategy that provides the strongest competitive advantage.

Differences in pay for equally skilled workers will encourage intense competition among workers for the highest paying jobs and will spur greater labor effort among those workers who are able to obtain these types of jobs. Workers will participate in strategic identity coalitions that seek to limit competition from other social groups. Race and gender are two of the more salient ascriptive characteristics for establishing coalitions. Racial identity matters because it is a culturally coalescing force used by workers to improve their relative positions in the labor queue (Darity, 1989). For example, White male employment density is correlated positively with the wage differential. Regardless of race, individual remuneration increases with the density of White male employment for a job (Mason, 1995, 1999).

12

The Criminal Legal System and Hate Crimes

African Americans and Latinx are 14.5 percent and 18 percent, respectively, of the US population. However, African Americans make up 40.1 percent of persons arrested for violent crimes, such as murder and non-negligent manslaughter, rape, robbery, and aggravated assault, and 30.8 percent of persons arrested for property crimes, such as burglary, larceny-theft, motor vehicle theft, and arson. Latinx are 26.5 of persons arrested for violent crimes and 17.4 percent of persons arrested for property crimes.

Empirical research frequently focuses on the relationship between arrests and race, since many criminal offenses are unreported. For otherwise identical persons, for example, persons of the same age, education, region, and marital status, this research tends to find that African Americans are more likely to be arrested than Whites (Myers, 1980; Gyimah-Brempong, 1986; Myers and Sabol, 1987; Cornwell and Trumbull, 1994; Cox, 2010). Just as African Americans are disproportionately arrested and jailed, they have lower wages and employment than White Americans. Individualistic explanations of both disparities in arrests and labor market outcomes often suggest that the measured racial inequalities are not caused by differential racial treatment in the criminal legal system and the labor market, respectively. Rather, from this perspective, African Americans are more likely to be arrested (and jailed) because they have more criminogenic factors (bad families, bad neighborhoods, bad peers, bad schools, bad culture) and African Americans have lower wages and access to employment because they have inferior skills or behavior.

Stratification economics offers an alternative perspective: racial disparities in criminal legal system outcomes are causally related to racial differences in treatment by police, prosecutors, courts, probation officers, and parole officers.

Parts of this chapter were originally published as Mason, Myers, and Simms (2022).

Just as racial discrimination within the labor market contributes to the profitability of firms within competitive markets, racial discrimination in the criminal legal system (a public monopoly with no competitors) contributes to the racialized goals of the agents and agencies operating within that system.

12.1 CRIMINAL LEGAL SYSTEM: RACIALIZED AGENTS AND AGENCIES

The individualist analysis of crime assumes that criminal legal system agents (police, prosecutors, judges, parole and probation officers, prison officials) are identity-free public servants, focused solely on efficiently providing public safety. Simultaneously, it is often implicitly assumed that African Americans citizens have a higher cultural propensity for crime than White citizens.[1] Both assumptions are false: criminal legal system agents have racial identities and these identities affect the productivity of social interactions; African American identity is not defined by a high propensity for crime; and officer-citizen identity matches are strategic interactions that influence policing and other criminal legal system outcomes. Incorporating the economics of identity into the analysis of race and crime yields insights that improve our understanding of persistent racial bias in criminal legal system outcomes.

12.1.1 Policing and Racial Threat

Sociological and criminological research indicates that police are concerned with efficient social control and have racial threat goals in addition to their concern for the efficient provision of public safety. The racial threat perspective examines the empirical consequences for criminal legal system and policing policies when competing racial groups have unequal political economic power. This approach assumes that the racial group with greater political economic power uses that power to exercise social control over subordinate racial groups. Hence, racial discrimination within the racial threat perspective has an instrumental objective – social control – and, thereby, is not necessarily the result of incorrect or insufficient information (prejudice, statistical discrimination) or irrational negative feelings (bigotry, "tastes" for discrimination). Within the racial threat perspective, the criminal legal system operates to protect the power and privilege of a political economic elite relative to subordinate groups and a dominant racial elite (Whites) relative to subaltern groups,

[1] Research on racial profiling by police is of interest because African Americans are oversampled in police stops (relative to their share of the population). Differences in the probability of stops by race are efficient if, all other things equal, there are racial differences in the probability of guilt. See, for example, the statistical discrimination argument of Knowles, Persico, and Todd (2001) and similar research. Equilibrium with statistical discrimination implies an equal probability of guilt, that is, an equal "hit rate," for African Americans and Whites, though a higher search rate for African Americans who are observationally the same as White drivers.

in particular, African American and other Non-White racial and ethnic minorities.

The empirical content of the racial threat perspective is summarized by three interrelated empirical observations.

i. *Percent Minority Effect*. An economic or racial elite's average assessment of racial threat increases with the fraction of Non-White racial and ethnic minorities within the relevant geographical area but decreases with the extent of segregation of Non-White racial and ethnic minorities. The positive Percent Minority effect occurs because, (a) the dominant group is threatened by greater political or economic competition, (b) an enhanced expectation of violence is attributed to the stigmatized group, and (c) there are other negative stereotypical assessments (Stults and Baumer, 2007). The negative racial segregation effect embodies the notion that greater interracial contact within an area increases racial animosity, when greater contact is associated with greater political and economic competition (Blumer, 1958).
ii. The *Demand for Crime Control* increases with the assessment of a racial threat by the economic or racial elite.
iii. The intensity of the *Law Enforcement Response* by the criminal legal system increases with the strength of the Demand for Crime Control by the economic or racial elite. This response may consist of changes in one or multiple enforcement activities, for example, increasing the size of the police force, greater public expenditures on policing activities, or greater arrest and imprisonment of members of the subaltern group.

Bringing these three observations together, there is an increase in the size of the police force, greater expenditures on policing activities, and greater arrest and imprisonment of racial and ethnic minorities as the percent minority increases within a particular location. For the most part, the empirical literature tends to affirm these hypotheses (Stults and Baumer, 2007; Dollar, 2014). In particular, Feigenberg and Miller (2021) establish that, within the county of a given state, there is a relationship between the severity of punishment and the density of African Americans in the county's population. The severity of punishment peaks when the African American population reaches 30–37 percent, at which point punishment is 15–27 percent more severe than in an all-White jurisdiction. Thereafter, the severity of punishment declines.

Ethnic and racial minorities will have a strategic response to White identity actions (Darity, Mason, and Stewart, 2006). Since racial and ethnic minorities are aware that the dominant group views the members of subaltern groups as a racial threat, Non-White persons strategically respond by attempting to limit the actions of the dominant group. Empirical studies of racial threat suggest a positive correlation between the racial density of the police and the racial density of the population: political representation within the local government increases with Percent Minority population and this change in political representation produces change in the demographic composition of the police force. For example, the election of an African American mayor leads to an increase in Percent Minority police (Hopkins and McCabe, 2012). Subaltern groups do not have to have a political majority to influence criminal legal system policy. When the Percent Minority population reaches 25–30 percent, Non-White racial and ethnic minorities are able to exercise substantive influence on political decisions regarding the exercise of social control (Stults and Baumer, 2007).

Policing differs by the racial and ethnic identity of officers, especially by the officer–citizen identity match (Eitle, Stolzenberg, and D'Alessio, 2005; Close and Mason, 2006, 2007; Feigenberg and Miller, 2020). Racially discriminatory behavior during officer–citizen interactions is less surprising when one considers that there is some degree of racial discrimination by White officers against Black colleagues (Rim, Ba, and Rivera, 2020). When a police–suspect interaction occurs, White officers are more likely than Black officers to make an arrest; both Black and White officers are more likely to arrest Black citizens than White citizens; and Black officers are more likely to arrest a Black citizen than a White officer (Brown and Frank, 2006). These outcomes are similar to Close and Mason (2007), who also find that both Black and White officers search Black drivers too often – though the excess searches are higher among White officers. Black officers are less likely than White officers to make unnecessary traffic stops and, thus, more likely than White officers to write traffic citations or equipment violations rather than taking no action against a stopped driver or charging stopped drivers with a crime (Close and Mason, 2006).

12.1.2 Organizational Identity

Racially biased policing is a practice embedded in the police organizational context. Because each troop has a set of command and troop rules/norms, the use of police discretion varies across troops (or precincts for municipal police). As the demographic composition of a police troop changes, the organization's social context changes in important ways that shape the policing process, for example, by creating an organizational identity that provides more disproportionately favorable or unfavorable outcomes for some citizen groups (Watkins-Hayes, 2011).

Racial identity is a produced good (Stewart, 1995). Law enforcement officers can be guided to substitute professional identities over pre-existing racial identities (Stewart, 2009; Oberfield, 2012). An organizational identity is imposed on agents through rules, procedures, institutional oversight, and cultural norms. Watkins-Hayes (2009) suggests that there is a process of "racialized professionalism" among street-level bureaucrats, in particular, law enforcement officers, such that police seek to integrate their racial identity into "their understanding and operationalization of their work and their goals for what it should accomplish" (Watkins-Hayes, 2011: 237).

Darity, Mason, and Stewart (2006) show that agents construct racialized social identity norms through repeated social interactions governed by a process of own-group altruism and other-group antagonism. Whether or not an agent becomes an "individualist," that is, one who attempts to engage in social interactions without conforming to a racial identity and without being seen by others as a member of the same or a different racial group, is shaped by the fraction of other agents who are either "individualists" or persons with a racialized identity. In a society governed by strong and persistent racial identity norms, police are more likely to be "racialized" police than "individualist" police. So, although professional (police department) and organizational (precinct) identities limit variation in policing outcomes that are associated with differences in the racial and ethnic identity of officers and matches between police and citizens, law enforcement officers still have sufficient discretion to engage in racialized decision-making. For example, police searches of drivers and, hence, the efficient provision of public safety, are governed by an individual law enforcement officer's use of bureaucratic discretion in combination with the possibly contending norms of racial identity, professional identity, and organizational identity.

Stimulating a person's social identity has an effect on the actions taken by that person, specifically, moving the person toward actions that are consistent with the norms for their identity-group (Benjamin, Choi, and Strickland, 2010). If African American and Latinx officers are particularly responsive to accusations that police are unjust in their interactions with African American and Latinx citizens, then raising the fraction of African American and Latinx officers within the troop increases the probability that every officer within the troop will have professional interactions with other officers who stress the importance of racially unbiased policing. Stimulating the professional identity of the troop will make all the troop's officers less likely to engage in biased policing; continuous contact by White officers with individual minority officers can change the behavior (if not the attitudes and preferences) of White officers (Sklansky, 2006).

12.1.3 Officer Identity

Individual police officers have both a law enforcement (or "blue") identity and a racial identity. Hence, the racial composition of police departments may yield startling responses to public policy changes and to activist demands by racial and ethnic minorities to change departmental culture and racial composition. Racial identity reactions to changes in the intensity of other-race identity strategies are counter-intuitive. For example, a national increase in anti-Islamic hate crimes raises the cost of being Muslim; yet, when faced with this rising cost, Arab Americans opted to move away from a White racial identity and to increase self-identification as Black or other (Mason and Matella, 2014). In the same way, an increase in White antagonism against African Americans raises the cost of being Black; yet, when faced with this rising cost, African Americans chose to increase the intensity of Black racial identity by increasing the probability of a Black-alone racial identity relative to self-identifying as mixed-race (Mason, 2017).

African American civilian protests against police abuse of authority raise the cost of unprofessional law enforcement behavior. Thus, we should expect a reduction in police abuse of authority and unnecessary use of force. African American civilian protests may raise the cost of unprofessional police behavior by increasing political oversight and regulation of police, inspiring greater media attention to police–citizen interactions and encouraging greater civic involvement by citizens concerned with police efficiency and racial justice. But African American protests against police abuse of authority is also a racial identity action; hence, we would expect an identity reaction from White police – an increase in actions associated with an increase in the intensity of White racial identity. It seems perverse to observe increases in an action when costs are rising, unless one considers that social identity norms may be used to allocate access to resources and authority. African American civilian protests against police abuse of authority are demands for greater access to police power and resources. Such demands may be seen as a racial threat to White police power and, thereby, greater social control by White police over protesting populations, regardless of their reasonableness or ability to increase justice.

Cunningham and Gillezeau (2019) provide an event study of the effect of African American social protests from 1964 to 1971 on police killings in the following years. There were more than 700 uprisings during this period. The timing of the first uprising in a county is the treatment variable. This study finds that, in the short run (1–4 years after an uprising), there are an extra 0.6–1.2 lethal interventions per year by police against Non-White citizens in counties that experienced an uprising. In the long run (5–9 years after treatment) there are an extra 1–1.7 Non-White deaths per year. Also, in the short-run, there are an extra 0.7–0.8 White deaths per year. There are no significant long run effects for White civilians. The cumulative effects over nine years after a riot is that police kill an additional 3.8–6.6 White citizens and 9–15.1 Non-White citizens. More granular analysis reveals that the statistically significant results are driven by rioting in Midwestern and Western states.

Cunningham and Gillezeau find no change in a county's trend of criminal activity after a riot: uprisings did not cause an increase in a county's violent or non-violent criminal activity. The trend in the number of police employed per 1,000 residents was unaffected by the timing of a county's first racial uprising. However, the number of police killed per year does increase after an uprising. On average, an additional 0.582 officers are killed in event year 2. This number continues to increase in the short run and is statistically significant in event year 5. The authors offered no guidance on the causes of the increase in police line of duty deaths; for example, whether the riot increased community hostility toward police; whether there was an increase in risky behavior among police

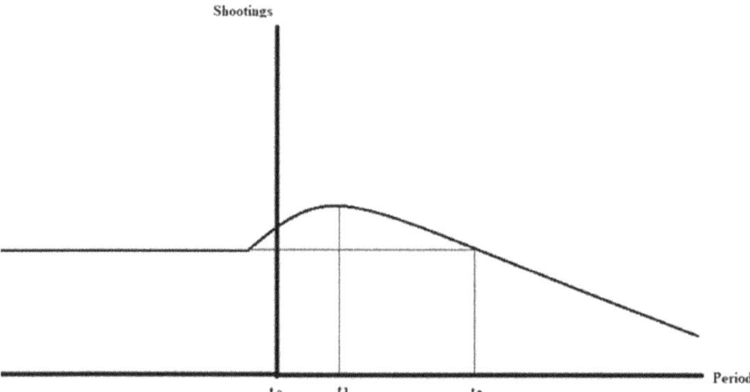

t_0 = threat of affirmative action, t_1 = start of dominance of diversity effect, t_2 = start of net positive benefit period

FIGURE 12.1. Trend of police shootings after threat to after racial composition of force

during the post-uprising period; or whether the post-uprising increase in police killing of civilians pushed citizens to respond to police hostility. The latter scenario is consistent with an identity response (protection against police) as a reaction to the police's identity response (more civilian killings in response to the racial threat of an uprising against police).

Cox, Cunningham, and Ortega (2020) add insight on police identity reactions to perceived racial threats to White control over the racial composition of the police force. Specifically, they find that the threat of an affirmative action lawsuit to hire more Non-White police has contradictory effects on police shootings of African American citizens. There is a short run backlash effect, police react to the racial threat of an affirmative action lawsuit with more aggressive policing of African American citizens, resulting in an increase in the number of Black shootings. Also, there is a long run diversity effect; as the department becomes more diverse, there will be a decrease in the number of Black shootings.

Per Figure 12.1, backlash may begin shortly before t_o and it dominates the diversity affect up to t_1. At t_1, backlash effect = diversity effect. After t_1, diversity effect dominates backlash effect. $Shooting_j \leq Shootings_o$ for all $t \geq t_2$. Event history analysis shows that shootings begin rising one year before threat and peak year of threat and that shootings decline to their pre-threat level about two years after the affirmative action lawsuit. The negative effects for shootings of Non-White civilians are statistically significant for years 6 through 11 after the affirmative action lawsuit.

The police backlash reaction to racial uprisings and to affirmative action lawsuits indicates that racial discrimination in law enforcement is due to instrumental discrimination. Further, the results also indicate that full policy impacts take time. The short run impact may be misleading. Policies seeking to change social norms should account for an identity backlash from agents benefitting from the currently existing norms.

12.2 HATE CRIMES: ECONOMIC CAUSES AND IMPACT ON RACIAL IDENTITY

A hate crime occurs when there is a "criminal offense against a person or property motivated in whole or in part by an offender's bias against a race, religion, disability, sexual orientation, ethnicity, gender, or gender identity."[2] Hate crimes are outcomes of citizen–citizen interactions; hence, police murder, beatings, and other abuses of force are not included in the count of hate crimes. Hate crime victimization varies by race and ethnicity. There are 5.93 hate crimes per 100,000 Non-Latinx African Americans, 0.53 hate crimes per 100,000 Non-Latinx Whites, and 0.34 hate crimes per 100,000 Latinx.[3] Hate crimes have a terrorizing effect, as the "victims include not only the crime's immediate target but also others like them. Hate crimes affect families, communities, and at times, the entire nation."[4] Examining hate crimes helps us understand the relationship between racial identity and violence within the population that supplies the police, judges, prosecutors, and other agents of the criminal legal system.

Federal hate crimes legislation was passed in 1968 and the Federal Bureau of Investigation has collected data since 1996. Historically, hate crimes have been the result of instrumental racism, rather than mere prejudice or bigotry. For example, the intimidation and murder associated with anti-Black lynchings of the mid-nineteenth to mid-twentieth centuries were intended to suppress the vote of African Americans (Wells, 1909). False criminal accusations, typically the lynched Black male was alleged to have raped a White women, provided "an excuse to get rid of Negroes who were acquiring wealth and property and thus keep the race terrorized" (Wells, 1970: 56).[5] Myers and Radhakrishna (2018: 2) warn that, "Public policies designed to improve the social and economic well-being of marginalized groups may have the unintended consequence of provoking animosities among non-protected group members."

The perpetrator of a hate crime is motivated by a desire to make the victim worse off and is willing to spend resources and incur costs to commit the crime

[2] See U.S. Department of Justice, www.justice.gov/hatecrimes/learn-about-hate-crimes. Last accessed December 15, 2022.

[3] These rates are calculated from the 2018 Population Estimates, US Census Bureau (www.census.gov/newsroom/press-releases/2019/estimates-characteristics.html) and the 2018 Hate Crime Statistics, Federal Bureau of Investigation (https://ucr.fbi.gov/hate-crime/2018/topic-pages/tables/table-1.xls). Both last accessed December 15, 2022.

[4] United States Department of Justice, "Learn about hate crimes," available at: www.justice.gov/hatecrimes/learn-about-hate-crimes. Last accessed December 15, 2022.

[5] Hate crimes are correlated with the number of firms owned by African-Americans, Asians, Indian, and Latinx (Geisler, Enomoto, and Djaba, 2019). This is consistent with instrumental racism. Using county data for the state of Kentucky, the authors find that the number of Black-owned firms, Hispanic-owned firms, Asian-owned firms, and Asian Indian-owned firms decrease in response to the number of hate crimes. But, the number of White-owned firms is unresponsive to the number of hate crimes in the county.

(Gale, Heath, and Ressler, 2002). Self-identified White persons are more likely to be the perpetrator when a hate crime has occurred.[6] The mean income of the Non-Latinx White majority is higher than the mean income of most racial and ethnic minorities. If a racial or ethnic minority group succeeds in raising its income relative to the White majority, this might excite racial envy among the White majority, motivating some Whites to commit money, time, and other resources to supply hate crimes against the minority group.[7] Gale, Heath, and Ressler find that hate crimes are highly responsive to changes in a state's Black–White household income ratio: a 1 percent increase in the racial index of household income will increase hate crimes by 4.4 percent (nation), 5.7 percent (South), and 3.17 percent (Non-South).[8] Except for hate crimes, a 1 percent increase in the Black–White household income ratio will decrease the supply of crime by 1.11 percent (nation), 0.71 percent (South), and 1.09 percent (Non-South).

The supply of hate crimes within a state increase with: a decrease in the market wage rate; an increase in the unemployment rate (reduction in the opportunity cost of time); and an increase in the percentage of the state's population that is 15–19 years of age (Medoff, 1999).[9] Education (the fraction of the state's population age 25 and above with at least a high school diploma) has an ambiguous effect: it raises the wage rate and thus reduces the incentives to engage in hate-crimes, but lowers the time and goods cost of producing hate (education increases efficiency of producing hate) and thus increases the incentives to engage in hate-crimes. An increase of $1 in a state's full-time hourly wage rate lowers hate-crimes by 31.4 crimes per 100,000 persons. Hate-crimes have diminishing returns to increases in a state's unemployment rate.

Both hate crimes and anti-Black racial slurs increased during the Great Recession (Anderson, Crost, and Rees, 2020). Racist internet searches increased by 5.5 percent and 6.1 percent for a one standard deviation increase in pre-manufacturing and real estate share of employment, respectively. Hate crimes against African Americans increased by 55 percent and 51 percent for a one standard deviation increase in the pre-manufacturing and real estate shares of employment, respectively.

[6] For their examination of crimes reported to the Los Angeles Police Department during 2000–2007, DeAngelo, Gittings, and Pena (2018) report that "Whites are more likely to assault and use weapons against Blacks and Hispanics than Blacks and Hispanics are to assault or use weapons against Whites. On the other hand, Blacks and Hispanics are typically more likely to commit robbery (crimes which we characterize as being often related to economic motives) against Whites than the reverse."

[7] Gale et al. modify Becker's model of the family, where another family member's utility is included in the utility function. When the family head is altruistic (envious) there is positive (negative) marginal utility associated with another family member's utility.

[8] The t-statistics from the random effects specification are 3.43 (national), 1.62 (South), and 2.78 (Non-South) for n = 148, 52, and 96, respectively.

[9] Law enforcement activity has a positive but insignificant effect.

There are also group identity effects for hate crimes. Having a White supremacist group within a county increases hate crimes perpetrated by Whites against Non-Whites by 22–25 percent (Mulholland, 2013). Importantly, Mulholland finds that White supremacist groups appear to operate as social movements, rather than as gangs, or criminal institutions enforcing contracts and resolving disputes, or as organized crime enterprises. White supremacists "organize to stop the perceived degradation of western culture" (Mulholland, 2013: 110).

Hate crimes are identity actions. Including envy (Gale, Heath, or Ressler) or hate (Medoff) into economic analyses of these crimes is justified by the history of slavery and Jim Crow in shaping White attitudes toward Black life (Wells, 1909). There is a continuing impact of slavery on the racial attitudes of White Americans today, more than a century and a half after the US Civil War. For example, Gunadi (2019) finds that a 1 percentage point increase in the fraction of enslaved persons within a county's 1860 population "is associated with 0.018 more hate crime incidents per 100,000 population directed at" African Americans (Gunadi, 2019: 1). This a 5.8 percent increase in anti-Black hate crimes.[10]

Racialization of a social group increases as more intense social stigma is directed toward the group. Variation in hate crimes targeted at a group is one metric of variation in social stigma. In this way, hate crimes contribute to racialization (Mason and Matella, 2014). Public and private reaction to the Al Qaeda attacks of September 11, 2001 provided an increase in the intensity of US stigmatization of persons with Islamic religious affiliation and Arab ethnicity. Mason and Matella use the fraction of all hate crimes directed at Muslims as a measure of stigmatization after 9/11. Comparing 2002–2012 to 1996–2001, they find that "a one percentage point increase in anti-Muslim hate crimes is associated with a 9% increase in the odds an Arab or Islamic American will self-identify as Non-White, that is, either Black or Other-race. The point estimates for native-born persons and immigrants are 28% and 7%, respectively."

12.3 POLICE ABUSE OF FORCE

Excessive police use of force has been an endemic and enduring issue of concern among African American citizens for decades. For example, as servitude capitalism was coming to an end the Black Panther Party for Self-Defense's Ten-Point Program of 1966 emphasized eliminating excessive and deadly use of force by law enforcement officers. Also, police abuse of force was examined by non-economists in the Kerner Commission report of 1967 (Gooden and Myers,

[10] Gunadi also finds that the 1860 intensity of slavery also contributes to contemporary hate crimes against Jews and members of the LGBT community.

2004). Nevertheless, until recently, economists have had to say little on this issue.

The first published study in an economics journal on the police use of force examined citizens' allegations of excessive force by the Chicago police department from 2011 to 2015 (Ajilore and Shirey, 2017). Citizens' complaints ranged from objections to police placing hands on citizens to various categories of excessive force, where excessive force complaints include instances with and without the use of a firearm and with and without injury.[11] Ajilore and Shirey estimated two probabilities: the probability that a complaint against the police is an excessive force complaint; and the probability that a police complaint is sustained.

African American men are 12.3 percent more likely than White men to file excessive force complaints (relative to all other complaints) and African American male officers are 2.2 percent less likely than White male officers to be the subject of excessive force complaints. African American male citizens are 19.5 percent less likely than White men and women to have their excessive force complaints sustained. The south side of Chicago is 93 percent African American and covers 50 percent of the city's land area. African American men who reside on the south side are 22.7 percent less likely than White men and women to have their excessive force complaints sustained.

Another early and influential economics study separates use of force into nonlethal uses of force and officer-involved shootings (Fryer, 2019). Nonlethal uses of force include seven items: put hands on a civilian, force to a wall, handcuff, draw a weapon, push to the ground, point a weapon, and pepper spray or strike with a baton. Using the New York City Stop, Question, and Frisk Program dataset for 2003–2013 and taking into account civilian demographics, encounter characteristics, and civilian behavior, along with fixed characteristics of precincts and years of observation, and comparing racial and ethnic minorities to White civilians, the odds ratio for being subjected to nonlethal force increases by 17.8 percent (African American) and 12.2 percent (Latinx).[12] Importantly, Fryer reports that there are differences in nonlethal uses of force according to the officer–citizen racial identity match, though he does not explain this finding.

[11] The data are the Chicago extract of the Citizens Police Data Project (2016), a national dataset of police interactions with the public.

[12] The odds ratio is the probability force is used on a stopped citizen divided by the probability that force is not used on a stopped citizen. The odds ratio increased by 5.1 percent (Asian) and 37.2 percent (Other race), though the increase for Asians was not statistically significant. Using the Police–Public Contact Survey dataset for 1996 to 2011 and controlling for civilian demographics, encounter characteristics, civilian behavior, and year of interaction and comparing racial and ethnic minorities to White civilians, the odds ratio for being subjected to nonlethal force increases by 177 percent (African American), 182 percent (Latinx), and –24.2 percent (insignificant, Other race).

Fryer's analysis of officer-involved shootings (OIS) uses data from the Houston police force for 2000–2015. First, Fryer selects all observations where there is an officer-involved shooting. Second, with the help of the Houston police department, Fryer constructs a control group, a matched benchmark sample where there is not an officer-involved shooting for a set of police–citizen interactions "in which lethal force is more likely to be justified: attempted murder of a public safety officer, aggravated assault on a public safety officer, resisting arrest, evading arrest, and interfering in an arrest" (p. 1213). Fryer finds that African Americans and Latinx are 27.4 percent less likely and 21.1 percent more likely, respectively, to be shot by police than Non-Latinx, Non-Black persons, though these results are not statistically significant, that is, the estimated results are not measured sufficiently precisely to be distinguished from 0.

Consequently, the conclusions from Fryer's study are there is a positive correlation between non-lethal use of force and status as a Non-White citizen; there is no correlation between lethal use of force (officer-involved shootings) and status as a Non-White citizen.[13]

There are multiple reasons for Fryer's counterintuitive results on the lethal use of force. First, as Ajilore and Shirey (2017) explain, some shootings occur with lower uses of force and others do not. The former might capture interactions where there was an escalation of force while the latter does not. Failure to incorporate this information omits important information related to officer-involved shootings and this error may be correlated with the officer's race, the citizen's race, or the officer–citizen racial identity match. Second, there are officer-involved deaths of civilians that do not involve the use of a firearm; these deaths are not included in Fryer's analysis. Third, drawing and pointing a gun at a citizen without firing is not a shooting, but both are exceptional acts of force. It would be helpful to explicitly account for use of a firearm, even if no shooting occurs, since both drawing and pointing a gun at a citizen indicates that an officer is prepared to use deadly force. Fourth, police undercount the number of officer-involved deaths (Swaine and McCarthy, 2016; Lee et al., 2017).

Public policymakers are concerned about allegations of racially discriminatory behavior in *officer-involved deaths and severe beatings* of civilians, which exceed the number of officer-involved shootings. There are incremental steps from no force to lethal force (Headley and Wright, 2019): police–citizen interactions where there are no arrests and no force; no arrests and force; arrest but no force; and both arrests and force (Headley and Wright, 2020). Empirical examination of officer-involved deaths and other extreme uses of force should be undertaken within the context of both incremental steps in the use of force

13 See Knox, Lowe, and Mummolo (2020) for an exploration of the assumptions that must be made for a causal study of racially biased policing when using administrative data on police–citizen interactions.

TABLE 12.1. *Police involved deaths, US: 2015 and 2016*

	2015		2016	
	Total	Percent	Total	Percent
Gunshot	1,017	0.887	1,011	0.925
Taser	50	0.044	22	0.020
Struck by vehicle	31	0.027	21	0.019
Death in custody	47	0.041	37	0.034
Other	1	0.001	2	0.002
Unknown	0	0.000	0	0.000
Total	1,146	1.000	1,093	1.000

Source: *The Guardian*. "The Counted: People Killed by the Police in the US." Available at: www.theguardian.com/us-news/ng-interactive/2015/jun/01/the-counted-police-killings-us-database. Last accessed November 20, 2020

and bivariate outcomes of arrests and use of force. Otherwise, one may not have an appropriate benchmark for measuring the impact of the racial identity of civilians (and other variables of interest) on the probability an officer uses lethal force.[14]

The Guardian newspaper found twice as many national police-involved-deaths as the Federal Bureau of Investigation (FBI) (Swaine and McCarthy, 2016). The FBI (using reports from local authorities) counted 442 deaths for 2015. *The Guardian* counted 1,146. About 89 percent of 2015 deaths and 93 percent of 2016 deaths were caused by gunshots (Table 12.1).

Based on *The Guardian*'s report, New York City carried out a detailed examination of police-involved deaths. Mary T. Bassett, Ph.D., identified 105 law enforcement related deaths in New York City from 2010 to 2015, versus just 46 deaths publicly reported for the same period.[15] There were 61 legal interventions, that is, law enforcement delivered the deadly force; 31 arrest-related deaths (deaths which occurred during the process of pursuit, apprehension, or in custody); and 13 community/bystander deaths (deaths to persons who were not intended suspects, for example, persons hit by police

[14] Further, there are two kinds of officer-involved deaths: (1) an officer kills a suspect after lesser uses of force do not subdue the suspect or after the interaction gets out of control; and (2) an officer kills a suspect after arriving on scene and making a split-second decision. A single equation binary dependent variable analysis may be appropriate for the second case. But an ordered logit, multivariate logit, or similar regression is appropriate for the first case. If there was an arrest along with use of force, a simultaneous equation model is necessary.

[15] Mary T. Bassett, Ph.D., Commissioner, New York City Department of Health and Mental Hygiene, January 2014 to August 2018, analyzed law enforcement deaths for 2010 to 2015. The draft was completed in 2017. She concludes that the city undercounts deaths involving police.

bullets, pedestrians killed from vehicle accidents during police activity, etc.) (Lee et al., 2017).

One-third of legal intervention deaths were not assigned legal intervention ICD-10 codes, often because law enforcement involvement was not indicated on the death certification.[16] The incidence of legal intervention death was significantly higher among Non-Latinx Blacks than Non-Latinx Whites. There were no Non-Latinx White deaths categorized as legal intervention where the decedent was unarmed; whereas six (18 percent) Non-Latinx Black decedents and five (38.5 percent) Latinx decedents were unarmed.

Both criminology and economic research indicate that the ecology of police–citizen interaction is an important variable for explaining outcomes of these interactions. The racial composition of the area of interaction is one measure of the ecology of stop. If police engage in "enforcement redlining," that is, providing a lower quality of law enforcement in African American or Latinx areas than White areas, then studies that omit the ecology of police–citizen interactions may obscure important race effects on the probability of use of force.

There is an increase in police use-of-force when an officer's peer has been injured on the job (Holz, Rivera, and Ba, 2019). Injuries to peers on the job increase the use of force by 7 percent and increase the probability an officer will injure a suspect by 10 percent in the week following the injury. For this study, the officer's peer group consisted of officers admitted into the police academy during the same month and year.[17] Notably, the increases in use of force and injuries to citizens are larger when the injured peer is of the same race. The increases in use-of-force are driven by increases in the lower level of force, but the 7 percent estimate may be a lower bound estimate since the intensity of connections formed during the academy may decrease with time and injuries to co-workers yield a greater response than injuries to peers in other districts.[18] Use-of-force incidents against African American civilians increase the week after an African American citizen is responsible for injuring an officer's police academy peer. There are no increases in use of force against Latinx citizens after a Latinx civilian injures an officer's peer or White citizens after a White civilian injures an officer's peer.[19]

[16] ICD-10-CM codes, external causes of morbidity, legal intervention includes, "Any injury sustained as a result of an encounter with any law enforcement official, serving in any capacity at the time of the encounter, whether on-duty or off-duty. Includes: injury to law enforcement official, suspect and bystander." See www.icd10data.com/ICD10CM/Codes/V00-Y99/Y35-Y38. Last accessed December 15, 2022.

[17] Academy peers currently working in the same police district are excluded, in order to prevent contamination from correlated shocks to civilian noncompliance.

[18] Additional findings show that peer injury causes a 15 percent increase in citizen complaints against officers for failure to provide service.

[19] Holz, Rivera, and Ba (2019) note that African Americans are 81 percent of Chicago's use-of-force victims and 80 percent of persons who injure an officer.

Hoekstra and Sloan (2022) confirm the importance of racial identity for policing and the officer–citizen identity match, factors that have been strongly emphasized by African American economists. They find that, "[T]he type of white person attracted to the police force is systematically different from the typical Black person when it comes to the likelihood of using force" (p. 4). Hoekstra and Sloan examined millions of 911 calls for two separate cities, one predominately White and African American and the other predominately White and Latinx. In both cases, officers do not select the calls to which they will respond; instead; officers are assigned to calls by the dispatcher and must respond unless they are presently engaged in another activity. Race is assessed from the address from which the call originated, based on the geocode in a Census Block Group. Other studies have found that there is an increase in the probability of the use of force when officers know the race of the civilian prior to interaction (Wexler, 2020).

For all uses of force, Hoekstra and Sloan found that White officers are 0.0429 percentage points more likely to use force than African American officers, an increase of 40 percent relative to the mean use of force for all officers and an increase of more than 55 percent relative to the mean use of force for African American officers. For gun use of force, they find that White officers are 0.004,63 percentage points more likely to use force than African American officers, an increase of 61 percent relative to the mean gun use of force by all officers and an increase of more than 136 percent relative to the mean gun use of force by African Americans officers.

For all uses of force and for opposite race police–citizen interactions, the analysis indicates that White officers are 0.0618 percentage points more likely to use force than African American officers during an interaction with an African American citizen, an increase of 60 percent relative to the mean use of force for all officers. The increase in use of force when for White officer–Black citizen interaction are concentrated in police beats with high rates of use of force: the odds for these interactions increase by 82 percent in beats with high rates.

For gun use of force, White officers are 0.0369 percentage points more likely than African American officers to use force on African American citizens, an increase of 520 percent relative to the mean gun use of force for all officers. Again, opposite race effects for gun use of force are concentrated in police beats with high rates of use of force. Hoekstra and Sloan (2022, p. 26) conclude that the opposite-race effect for gun use of force "seems largely driven by much higher rates of gun force used by White officers in mostly-Black neighborhoods, compared to Black officers."

Although there are no racial differences between White and African American officers in gun force used in White neighborhoods, White officers use gun force five times as often in neighborhoods that are at least 80 percent African American. The probability of all uses of force is causally related to the officer–citizen racial identity match: an opposite race identity match increases the use of force by 30–60 percent. This is driven by the behavior of White officers in African American neighborhoods, as African American officers use modest force in both White and African American neighborhoods but White officers substantially increase their use of force when they are dispatched to calls in Black neighborhoods.

Similarly, the Latinx and White officer–citizen identity match also influences an officer's use of force. Overall, White and Latinx officers use force at the same rate. Officers dispatched to calls of a different ethnic group are more than two times as likely to increase the use of force; White officers dispatched to Latinx neighborhoods increase their use of force more than Latinx officers dispatched to Latinx neighborhoods. For all uses of force and for opposite ethnicity police–citizen interactions, findings indicate that White officers are 0.0649 percentage points more likely than Latinx citizens to use force against Latinx citizens, an increase of 75 percent relative to the mean use of force for all officers. Hoekstra and Sloan (2022, p. 29) conclude, "the rate at which white officers use force increases by more as those officers are dispatched to more Hispanic neighborhoods, compared to Hispanic officers."

There are collateral effects to police use of force. Ang (2020: 1) "finds that exposure to police violence leads to persistent decreases in GPA, increased incidence of emotional disturbance and lower rates of high school completion and college enrollment. These effects are driven entirely by Black and Hispanic students in response to police killings of other minorities and are largest for incidents involving unarmed individuals." Legewie and Fagan (2019: 1) "find that exposure to police surges significantly reduced test scores for African American boys, consistent with their greater exposure to policing. The size of the effect increases with age, but there is no discernible effect for African American girls and Hispanic students."

Finding and maintaining policies that successfully reduce officer-involved deaths (especially deaths of racial and ethnic minority citizens) has been the subject of four major national commissions: 1931 Wickersham Commission, 1968 Kerner Commission Report, 2015 President's Task Force on Twenty-First Century Policing, and the 2018 Commission on Civil Rights' Report on Police Use of Force (Headley and Wright, 2019). Nevertheless, there is no national standard for collecting and comparing the use of force data across police departments. Using the Fatal Encounters dataset, which has tried to catalog every police-involved gun death since 2000, Jennings and Rubado (2017) found that 6 percent of police agencies require filing a report when a gun is drawn but not fired. This reporting requirement lowers civilian gun deaths without increasing the gun deaths of police officers. Departments with a firearm display report requirement had 0.322 fewer deaths per 100,000 residents in comparison to departments without the policy, a reduction of 18.4 percent from the mean of 1.75 deaths per 100,000 residents. The paperwork requirement for police threatening a civilian with a drawn gun lowers gun deaths because: (1) it is a deterrent to unnecessary use of force because of additional demands on an officer's time; (2) it implies police leaders are committed to avoiding gun draws; and (3) it is part of a commitment to best practices among agencies that have this requirement.

12.4 MASS INCARCERATION

During the ascendant period of mass incarceration (1980–2008), increases in crime were responsible for about 20 percent of the increase in incarceration (Raphael and Stoll, 2013). Other factors explain most of the increase in incarceration: an increase in the average length of sentence given that a criminal violation has occurred accounts for one third of incarceration growth and the probability of imprisonment given that a criminal was convicted tripled.

An incarceration regime is a government's set of criminal charging, sentencing, probation, incarceration, and parole policies. With a rehabilitative incarceration regime, a large increase in crime is associated with a small increase in incarceration: there is a high rate of probation and parole, alternative sentences to incarceration, a low rate of conviction, and short sentences for mild offenses, for example, smoking weed is de-criminalized. With a punitive incarceration regime, a small increase in crime causes a large increase in incarceration: there is a low release rate (low probability of probation and parole), high probability of incarceration if convicted – especially for nonviolent offenses, limited alternatives to incarceration, and a conviction rate that exceeds the rate of persons released from person. With a low release rate and high conviction rate, the incarceration rate will grow.

Mass incarceration arises and persists as an outcome of a vicious cycle: too many persons are incarcerated within a punitive incarceration regime; there is a policy-induced rise in crime among excessively punished social groups; and more persons are incarcerated by an excessively punitive system (Temin, 2018). As the criminal legal system becomes more punitive, admissions rise above releases. The rising crime leads to greater incarceration and, thereby, more induced crime. The system comes to rest in a high crime rate, high incarceration rate equilibrium. This high crime rate, high incarceration rate equilibrium means the criminal legal system is a major stratifying institution in American society (Phelps and Pager, 2016). The incarceration rate grows as convictions exceed releases and incarceration may rise even if criminal activity is not increasing.

Induced crime is additional crime caused by the collateral damage of incarceration – economic exclusion of returning citizens from attractive income and wealth opportunities and social exclusion from beneficial networks, creates conditions that make crime relatively more attractive. Mass incarceration reduces marriage, disrupts families and social networks, reduces parental involvement with children, has a negative effect on employment and pay, hurts skill accumulation among children of incarcerated persons, and reduces voting and other civic participation, while increasing criminal knowledge (Phelps and

TABLE 12.2. *Federal mass incarceration policies*

Year	Policy
1971	Nixon War of Drugs
1984	Sentencing Reform Act (War on Drugs, Tough on Crime, Fight "Crack Epidemic")
1986	Anti-Drug Abuse Act
1988	Life sentence without parole for defendants with two or more felony drug convictions
1994	Clinton crime bill – massive increase in police and tougher sentences
1990s	More minimal sentence laws, more "3 strikes" laws, greater prosecutorial power (rather than judges and courtrooms)

Pager, 2016). The collateral damage of mass incarceration is concentrated in families with low wealth and income and in neighborhoods with high percentages of racial and ethnic minorities.

Hence, a correlation between race and crime, for example, a positive correlation between African American status and the probability of incarceration, does not necessarily imply that relatively greater single parent families or greater family dysfunctional behavior causes relatively greater incarceration; rather, the direction of causation might be that relatively greater incarceration causes racial differences in family structure and functioning.

The era of mass incarceration was initiated in 1971 with the Nixon administration's "war on drugs." Thereafter, a series of increasingly punitive federal and state laws were passed (Table 12.2). Because of these laws, mandatory imprisonment increased, sentence length increased, and probation and parole became less frequent. America's population of incarcerated persons grew continuously before peaking in 2008. America's incarceration rate is still the highest in the world, 810 prison or jail inmates for every 100,000 residents aged 18 and older (Gramlich, 2021).

Data may not accurately reflect the strength of relationship between mass incarceration and drug laws. Federal prisoners (about 10% of those imprisoned) are predominately convicted of drug convictions. But, for states,

> the importance of public prosecutors and plea bargains contaminates this inference because the listed crimes in state prisons were produced in plea bargains. Since drug laws are so severe, plea bargains were driven toward lesser charges that did not fall under the drug laws. The results of the plea bargains do not indicate why prisoners were originally arrested, and most prisoners who would be freed in a policy shift are not violent people. (Temin, 2018: 324)

Imprisonment protects society from harmful persons; it is also a process for warehousing economically marginal persons, especially men. Utilizing census data for 1850–1980, Myers and Sabol show that "black imprisonment (and

Northern imprisonment in general) [is inversely linked to] manufacturing output and [directly linked to] black unemployment" (Myers and Sabol, 1987, 189). Further, the influx of Southern African Americans into Northern cities during the peak years of the Great Migration (1940–1970) increased the African American population percentage within commuting zones. These racial composition changes induced changes in the childhood environment of commuting zones (Derenoncourt, 2022). Among other changes, the overall change in childhood environment included increased spending on police, higher incarceration rates, and more crime. These threat effect responses to higher percentages of African Americans within commuting zones "explains 43% of the upward mobility gap between Black and White men in the region today."

An increasingly punitive incarceration regime was the federal, state, and local governmental response to the African American social protests of the 1960s and 1970s. From 1971 to 1994, governmental concern for greater racial control (instrumental discrimination explicitly expressed via the so-called War on Drugs) encouraged more severe sentences for a given crime rate. Legal scholar Michelle Alexander (2010) provides an intersectional refinement of this argument: mass incarceration is an attack against African American males designed to win votes of poor and working-class Whites. Alexander argues that the criminal legal system has labeled racial and ethnic minority males "criminals" and then used that categorization as a rationale for "discrimination, exclusion, and social contempt" (p. 2). It is perfectly legal to discriminate against returning citizens (convicted felons) in an extensive range of social and economic activities: labor and housing markets, voting and political participation, access to educational assistance and institutions, access to public assistance, denial of jury service, etc. Petach and Pena (2020) provide empirical support for the "Alexander hypothesis"; localities "with higher levels of inequality experienced larger increases in the overall incarceration rate" and the increase in the White/Non-White poverty ratio is associated with an expansion in Non-White incarceration rates but no change in White incarceration rates.

Some institutions and practices create incentives that work against reform of the criminal legal system. For example, mass incarceration increases the profits of private prisons, creating a strong incentive for the prison oligopolies to lobby against criminal legal system reform.[20] Just 8 percent of federal and state prisoners are housed in private prisons, but that number has been increasing during the last two decades. Also, prosecutors are paid by counties, while prisons are financed by the state; hence, prosecutors have no incentive to

[20] The companies are CoreCivic (formerly, Corrections Corporation of America or CCA), the GEO group (formerly, Wackenhut Securities), Management and Training Corporation (MTC), and Community Education Centers (CEC). The Obama administration made a decision to cease using private prisons, but the Trump administration reversed that decision. For private imprisonment enrollment numbers, see Muhitch and Ghandnoosh (2021).

consider the relative costs of imprisonment and non-imprisonment when requesting jail time for convicted persons.

Individual social and economic factors that contribute to incarceration, such as educational and labor market opportunities, are well studied and continue to be a focus of contemporary research. For example, Booker T. Washington (President, Tuskegee University) and Julius Rosenwald (philanthropist) built 5,357 schools, shops, and teacher homes across the rural South between 1912 and 1932. Statistical analysis shows "that full exposure to one of the new primary schools built as part of the Rosenwald program reduces the probability of incarceration by 1.9 percentage points" (Eriksson, 2020: 1). Also, raising a state's minimum wage rate by $1 per hour leads to approximately 12–25 fewer incarcerations per 100,000 state residents (Ghosh, Hoover, and Liu, 2020). Increasingly, scholars are also interested in the impact of racial differences in wealth on racial differences in incarceration. Zaw, Hamilton, and Darity (2016) show that family wealth and the probability of individual incarceration are inversely related. Even so, for a given level of wealth, African Americans are more likely to experience incarceration than Whites and Latinx. They also show that there is a racial wealth gap among persons who will be incarcerated in the future as well as among those previously incarcerated.

Incarcerated persons pay two prices for their conviction: time costs and financial sanctions associated with being convicted for a criminal activity; and collateral consequences (invisible punishments) for formerly incarcerated citizens returning to society (Chiteji, 2017). The invisible punishment imposed on returning citizens includes lower labor market earnings and substantial criminal legal system debt beyond the financial sanctions associated with a criminal conviction. States and localities impose numerous fines, fees, and surcharges on individuals as their case makes its way through the justice system, including charging the individual for the time spent in jail. Incarceration reduces wealth accumulation; thereby, extending punishment from youth to old age (Chiteji, 2014).

Mass incarceration imposes costs on law abiding citizens: (1) it makes law abiding citizens less safe because it locks up too many nonviolent criminals, who then become potentially violent because of their exposure to violence in prison; (2) it is costly to taxpayers, reallocating tax revenue from schools, health care, and public amenities; (3) it reduces the economic resources available to families through the costs of incarceration and the reduced employment prospects for individuals when released from prison; and (4) it gives prosecutors increasing amounts of power to fight crime, which endangers all of our civil liberties (Forman, 2010).

Mass incarceration affects family structure and family function (Myers, 2000). More than half of all prisoners have children under the age of 18 and nearly two thirds of incarcerated women have children and lived with their children prior to being jailed (Cox, 2012; Sykes and Pettit, 2014). Forty-five percent of prisoners were living with their children prior to imprisonment (Sykes and Pettit, 2014: 128). Women with longer sentences may face termination of parental rights and have their children placed in foster care. Persons convicted of some felonies (such as drug violations) may be ineligible for a variety of public assistance programs, such as Temporary Assistance to Needy Families, public housing, and public sector employment. The "ban the box" movement seeks to remove the check box that asks if job applicants have a criminal record, since divulging this information will lower the probability a returning citizen will be hired. Ban-the-Box policies could raise the probability of public employment for those with a previous conviction by 30 percent, which would have a disproportionately positive impact on African Americans given racial disparities in convictions (Craigie, 2021).

Most incarcerated persons are male and most of them were fathers prior to incarceration. In support of the Darity–Myers discussion of African American male marginalization, Liu (2018) finds that a one percentage point increase in the incarceration rate of Black males: (1) reduces the probability of marriage for young African American women by 2–3 percentage points; (2) increases the probability a Black child is born to an unmarried mother and lives in a mother-only family by 4.5 and 3.5 percentage points, respectively; and (3) reduces the probability that young African American men and women will attain at least one year of college by 4.4 and 3.2 percentage points, respectively (Table 12.3).[21] Finally, Liu finds that one standard deviation in the punitiveness of sentencing policies in areas where a person lived during childhood increases racial disparity in the racial income gap by 0.7 percent, holding parental income constant.[22]

Incarceration of men increases the childcare costs, care work, social stigma, and mental health costs of their wives and partners, resulting in lower wages, hours, and employment for the women directly affected by male incarceration (Craigie, 2021). Mueller-Smith (2015) also finds that incarceration reduces earnings, employment, and marriage among formerly incarcerated persons and incarceration increases the probability of divorce. When felons are readmitted to society, criminal activity increases by 4–7 percentage points per quarter for each additional year spent incarcerated. Incapacitation reduces both

[21] See also Foster and Hagan (2009) for empirical results which support and complement Liu's analysis of the intergenerational effects of parental incarceration.

[22] Chetty et al. (2020) do not reference the Darity–Myers discussion of Black male marginalization, though they find evidence consistent with Black male marginalization. Specifically, conditioning on parental income African American young adults have marriage rates that are 30 percentage points lower than White young adults. This intergenerational marriage gap is correlated with gender-specific gaps in intergenerational mobility. Conditioning on parental income; Black males have wages that are 7 percentiles lower than White males, are much less likely to be employed, work 9 hours per week less than White males, have a substantial higher probability of incarceration than White males, and the college attendance rate is 7 percentage points lower. The intergenerational racial gaps among women are smaller or nonexistent.

TABLE 12.3. *Incarceration effects on socioeconomic outcomes*

Group	Percentage point change	
Impact of 1 percentage point increase in African American male incarceration rate		
African American women, 18–34 years of age		
Probability of marriage, some college	−3.1	
Probability of marriage, no college	−2.6	
Probability of marriage, man with ≥ years of education, some college	−1.9	
Probability of marriage, man with ≥ years of education, no college	−2.9	
Probability Black child is born out of wedlock	4.5	
Probability Black child lives in mother-only family	3.5	
At least 1 year of college, black males, 22–24 years old	−4.4	
At least 1 year of college, black females, 22–24 years old	−3.2	
Impact of a one standard deviation increase in punitiveness of sentencing policies in areas where individuals lived during childhood		
Change in racial gap in income ranks for Black and White	Percentile change	
men (conditional on parental income)	0.7	
Percentage point change at margin of incarceration		
	Extensive	Intensive
Probability of marriage, black women w/college > 0	−4.1	
Probability of marriage, black women w/college = 0		−4.1
Probability Black child is born out of wedlock	4.5	7.3
Probability Black child lives in mother-only family by age 15	3.5	6.9

Source: Liu (2018)

felonies and misdemeanors. However, felonies increase among readmitted persons who were formerly incarcerated for felonies and for misdemeanors. Among the new types of crimes committed by readmitted felons, property crimes, drug possession, and drug manufacturing and distribution increase by 1.5, 1.3, and 0.45 percentage points, respectively, per quarter for each additional year spent incarcerated (Mueller-Smith, 2015: 46).

12.5 SUMMARY AND DISCUSSION

Economic analysis of racial identity as a social norm must be a pillar of economic analysis of criminal legal system agents, policies, and practices. Racial differences in treatment by police, prosecutors, courts, probation officers, and parole officers are a source of racial disparities in criminal legal system outcomes. This is instrumental discrimination caused (at least in part) by racial threats associated with increasing racial competition for resources as the percent minority increases within a jurisdiction. Racial threat effects will cause an increase in the size of the police force, greater expenditures on policing activities, and greater arrest and imprisonment of racial and ethnic minorities as the percent minority increases within a city. In response, as the percentages of racial and ethnic minorities within a jurisdiction increase, they use the political process to increase own-group representation and better treatment among police.

There is evidence that, as African American civilian activists protest against police abuse of authority, police agencies respond with more aggressive policing; there is an increase in lethal interventions by police against African Americans for up to 9 years after first local uprising against the police. Further, there is both a backlash effect and a diversity effect by police agencies in response to affirmative action lawsuits forcing the agency to hire more ethnic and racial minority police. The backlash effect is an increase in the number of shootings of Black citizens. The diversity effect is a decrease in the number of shooting of Black citizens as more Black officers are hired. Initially, the backlash effect dominates the diversity effect, but over time the diversity effect dominates the backlash effect.

Hate crimes are the result of instrumental discrimination; in particular, public policies that raise the relative economic well-being of marginalized may inspire envy or hate among some members of the dominant group. Hate crimes increase with racial economic competition: a decrease in racial inequality, a decrease in the market wage rate, an increase in the unemployment rate, and presence of a White supremacist group in the county. In turn, the increase in hate crimes creates an incentive for more intensive racialization among the targeted social group.

Officer-involved deaths and severe beatings of civilians increase when an officer's peer has been injured on the job, especially in the week after an African American civilian has injured a White officer. Use of force also increases when officers know the race of a civilian prior to interaction following an emergency call, when White officers interact with African American citizens, when White officers are dispatched to an African American neighborhood.

It is important to note that police abuse of force has a negative academic and behavioral influence on African American and Latinx youth, especially Black boys. In the same way, mass incarceration has had deleterious effects on African American families: reducing the probabilities of marriage and attending college and increasing racial inequality and increasing the probability a child is born to an unmarried mother.

PART V

RESTATEMENT AND DISCUSSION

13

Restatement and Discussion

This manuscript includes a historically complex economic analysis of structural racism and its transformations across alternative periods of US political economic development. Exclusion is a central quality of Black life in the US political economy. During the era of chattel capitalism, Africans were commodities, wholly excluded from ownership of their own life, time, and activities, standing before the law, representation in the political system, or ownership of productive assets. Under chattel capitalism, Africans were not citizens, workers, consumers, or even people; they were commodities, that is, fixed capital inputs into the production process whose utilization and mobility were wholly determined by capitalist agricultural producers. From 1619 to 1865, the wealth produced by African commodities was appropriated by Whites.

Chattel capitalism was ended by a war – the ultimate government policy, not by competitive market forces undermining the structural racism. The slave trade and chattel enslavement were based on instrumental discrimination: differential treatment, viz., commodification of Africans, because it was profitable, not because capitalist farmers had an inexplicable "taste for discrimination (bigotry)" or statistical discrimination (prejudice).

Capitalist agricultural production with enslaved Africans required the formation of racial identity norms. Racial identity norms were constructed to provide differential access to assets: Blacks were persons who could be and were enslaved and without wealth accumulation, without citizenship, and without personhood; Whites were persons ineligible for enslavement, disenfranchisement, or removal of personhood. Enslaver-initiated violence against Africans (hate crimes) enforced racial identity norms. Police tracked and sought to return Africans seeking to escape enslavement.

Finally, until The Great Migration and Urbanization of the 1910s, 90 percent of Blacks lived in the South – marking that region as the site of the most intense racism.

During the transition from chattel capitalism to servitude capitalism, Blacks were transformed from Africans to African Americans. They were no longer eligible for chattel enslavement; nevertheless, for 100 years (1865–1965) African Americans were excluded from effective citizenship. White appropriation and monopolization of Black citizenship was the core element of structural racism. Servitude capitalism was based on instrumental discrimination: convict leasing, debt peonage, sharecropping, and the chain gang were policies that held down Black wages and wealth accumulation, reduced public expenditure on services to the African American community, and provided for public infrastructure under conditions akin to enslavement. The racial identity norms of servitude capitalism restricted Black access to courts, restricted Black bargaining power in employment, and hampered wealth accumulation. Lynching – the ultimate hate crime - was used to enforce racial identity norms, with about one African American lynched per week during servitude capitalism. Police were participants in hate crimes and the major policies of servitude capitalism.

For a brief period (1868–1873), the federal policies of Reconstruction made a substantial contribution to African American progress. But the Long Recession of 1873–1896 and the rise and consolidation of Jim Crow (1877–1896) created the Nadir – the lowest point of the African American struggle to abolish structural racism. During the Nadir (1877–1917) the federal government retreated from commitments to protect African American civil rights, while state governments became increasingly hostile. Further, regardless of race, both state and local governments were pro-capital and hostile to workers.

Self-help is a major element of African American culture; during servitude capitalism, this cultural tradition was the foundation of African American economic progress, educational progress, and building group institutions (religious progress) (see Table 4.3). Labor market discrimination increased during 1880–1910; yet, African Americans closed the skills gap with Whites (see Table 4.4). The job competition perspective suggests that labor market discrimination increased because Blacks were becoming more competitive.

African American self-help was also expressed in The Great Migration and Urbanization (1914–1965). In particular, African Americans moved out of low wage areas with limited opportunities (rural South) to higher wage areas with more opportunities (urban South and urban Non-South). Blacks begin to move to urban areas decades before they began to move out of the South. Urban residents were 13–14 percent of the total African American population during 1870–1880, increasing to more than 27 percent by 1910 and rising to 73 percent by 1960 (Price, 1970). The fraction of African Americans living in the South declined from 90 percent in 1910 to 54 percent in 1965.

Despite massive self-help among African Americans, the competitive forces of the market did not bring an end to Jim Crow. Rather, in combination with African Americans self-help, President Roosevelt's New Deal programs (1933–1939), changes in federal hiring and the military's utilization of Black troops (1939–1945), and President Johnson's Great Society programs (1964–1968) brought about the demise of servitude capitalism and the rise of racialized managerial capitalism.

The rise of racialized managerial capitalism has not ended the political economic exclusion of African Americans. The enduring legacies of Black exclusion during chattel and servitude capitalisms are now embedded in racialized managerial capitalism, where exclusion takes the form of differential socioeconomic opportunities due to massive racial wealth disparity, formation of racial identity norms governing access to public and private resources, racial differences in access to managerial power and resources, and racial disparity in access to employment and high wage jobs. Relatively greater exclusion from justice in the criminal legal system is manifested in greater likelihood of exposure to abuse of police authority, officer-involved dates, mass incarceration, and hate crimes.

Similar to changes that occurred during the Nadir, for the decades since the 1973–1975 recession, African American–White wage and family income inequality has remained stagnant, despite unambiguous progress in the average quantity and quality of African American education relative to White Americans (see Chapter 5). This progress was due do African American self-help, school desegregation, and increases in the years of free education. Yet, the Black–White college degree gap has increased since the demise of Jim Crow; this increase is explained by racial wealth differences.

An important change occurred in African American family structure during the era of racialized managerial capitalism: a major increase in the fraction of men and women in their 20s and 30s who have never-married (see Chapter 6). A fall in marriage-eligible men is a major factor responsible for this change. Per the Darity-Myers index of African American male marginalization, we can increase the rate of marriage-eligible men (and, therefore, increase marriage) by increasing their earnings and employment, reducing premature deaths and disability, increasing college enrollment, reducing contact with the criminal legal system and reducing incentives for criminal behavior, and reducing premarital births and dissolution of unions when children are present. This perspective suggests that it is changes in economic well-being that causes changes in family structure, not the reverse. Further, family functioning is different from family structure. The empirical data suggests that, on average, African American families have strong family functioning.

The recessions of 1974–1975, 1981–1882, and 2007–2009 were impediments to African American relative and absolute progress since the end of servitude capitalism. For the Non-South, median African American family income stagnated and declined during 1967–2018 and the poverty rate increased during 1967–2018, especially during 1967–1989. Within the South, median African American family income rose during 1967–2018, though median income stagnated during 1974–2000, and the poverty rate declined from 36 percent to 21 percent during 1967–2018, even as there was stagnation during 1974–1989.

African American mean family wealth is 6–8 percent of White mean family wealth. About one of every three African American families has zero or negative net worth. Both numbers were more or less unchanged during 1984–2017. The African American savings rate is at least as high as the White savings rate for families with the same level of earnings (income). Racial differences in inheritances and in vivo transfers explain the greatest portion of racial wealth disparity.

The labor market progress of African American men and women has been concentrated in the South: 1974–1989 was a period of weekly wage decline for males, especially African Americans. For men and women, racial wage and employment inequality increased consistently during 1974–1989 and 2008–2019. Racial discrimination explains a large proportion of the racial differences in wages and employment. Native-born Non-Latinx African American men have a 20 percent weekly wage penalty and 9 percentage point employment penalty relative to native-born Non-Latinx White men; other groups of Black men have similar outcomes. Non-Latinx African American women have a 2 percent weekly wage penalty and 2 percentage point employment penalty relative to native-born Non-Latinx White women; other groups of Black women have similar outcomes.

Experimental and observational data, as well as analyses using automatic associations data show that the manager–worker racial identity match influences hiring, pay, and access to managerial resources. Explanations of racial inequality in labor market outcomes depend on the wage–productivity relationship. The manager–worker racial identity match may affect productivity and wages in two ways: managers may use higher pay and better promotion opportunities to raise the productivity and wages of own-group workers; and managers provide time, assistance, or other resources to own-group workers and thereby increase their productivity, employment stability, and opportunities for promotion.

Also, stratification economists link persistent discrimination to job competition. Equally skilled workers may receive different pay for doing the same work because they are employed at firms that are differentiated by the capacity to pay and by the capacity of workers to make firms pay. Equally skilled workers who perform the same job at firms with less competitive characteristics, or who are part of a workforce with lower bargaining power, will receive lower pay.

Racial differences in treatment by police are a source of racial disparities in criminal legal system outcomes. Racial threat effects are associated with an increase in the size of the police force, greater expenditures on policing activities, and greater arrest and imprisonment of African Americans and Latinx as the percent minority increases within a jurisdiction. In response, racial and ethnic minorities use the political process to increase own-group representation and better treatment among police.

As African American civilian activists protest against police abuse of authority, police agencies respond with more aggressive policing; there is an increase in lethal interventions by police against African Americans for up to nine years after first local uprising against police. Further, there is both a backlash effect (more police shootings) and a diversity effect (fewer police shootings) by police agencies in response to affirmative action lawsuits forcing the agency to hire more ethnic and racial minority police. Initially, the backlash effect dominates the diversity effect but over time the diversity effect dominates the backlash effect.

Hate crimes, too, are the result of instrumental discrimination, increasing with racial economic competition: a decrease in racial inequality, a decrease in the market wage rate, an increase in the unemployment rate, and presence of a White supremacist group in the county. Increases in hate crimes create an incentive for more intensive racialization among the targeted social group.

Officer abuse of force increases when an officer's peer has been injured on the job, especially in the week after an African American civilian has injured a White officer. Use of force also increases when officers know the race of a civilian prior to interaction following an emergency call, when White officers interact with African American citizens, and when White officers are dispatched to an African American neighborhood.

Finally, police abuse of force has negative academic and behavioral effects on African American and Latinx youth, especially Black boys. Also, mass incarceration has had deleterious effects on African American families: reducing the probabilities of marriage and attending college and increasing racial inequality and the probability a child is born to an unmarried mother.

Eliminating structural racism requires a transformative political agenda that will: (1) persistently maintain the economy at full employment or provide income to households with persons unable to work; (2) aggressively attack labor market discrimination against racial minorities; (3) massively redistribute wealth and income from the most affluent to middle income and poor Americans, with relatively greater benefit for racial and ethnic minorities; (4) eliminate institutional policies and organizational practices that stigmatize racial, ethnic, and religious groups; and (5) expand the scope and scale of collective African American self-help. Achieving these changes is a daunting but not impossible task. For decades, an army of scholars and activists has put forward specific ideas and broad agendas seeking to eradicate structural racism.[1] We can turn society and the future of work toward greater social inclusivity and a more equitable distribution of material prosperity by carefully applying these ideas and incorporating them into political action and local, state, and national policy.

[1] See for example Section 4.4.3, as well as Du Bois (1940), Hamilton and Darity (2010), Darity and Hamilton (2012), Aja et al. (2013), Nembhard (2014), Movement for Black Lives (2016), Albisa et al. (2020), and Darity and Mullen (2020).

References

Aja, Alan with Daniel Bustillo, William Darity Jr., and Darrick Hamilton. (2013). "Jobs instead of austerity: A bold policy proposal for economic justice." *Social Research: An International Quarterly*, 80(3):781–794.

Ajilore, Olugbenga and Shane Shirey. (2017). "Do #all lives matter? An evaluation of race and excessive use of force by police." *Atlantic Economic Journal*, 45 (2):201–212.

Akerlof, George A. (2002). "Behavioral macroeconomics and macroeconomic behavior." *American Economic Review*, 92(3):411–433.

Akerlof, George A. and Rachel E. Kranton. (2000). "Economics and identity." *The Quarterly Journal of Economics*, 115(3):715–753.

Albisa, Cathy and Ben Palmquist with Brittany Scott, Sean Sellers, and Marigo Farr. (2020). *A New Social Contract: Collective Solutions Built by and for Communities*. New York: Partners for Dignity and Rights. Available at: https://dignityandrights.org/initiative/new-social-contract. Last accessed December 15, 2022.

Alexander, Michelle. (2010). *The New Jim Crow: Mass Incarceration in the Age of Colorblindness*. New York: The New Press.

Alexis, Marcus. (1962). "Some Negro–White differences in consumption." *The American Journal of Economics and Sociology*, 21(1):11–28.

(1970). "Patterns of black consumption 1935–1960." *Journal of Black Studies*, 1 (1):55–74.

Altonji, Joseph and Ulrich Doraszelski. (2005). "The role of permanent income and demographics in Black/White differences in wealth." *Journal of Human Resources*, XL(1):1–30.

Altonji, Joseph, Ulrich Doraszelski, and Lewis M. Segal. (2000). "Black/white differences in wealth." *Economic Perspectives*, 24(1):38–50.

Anderson, Bernard. (1996). "The ebb and flow of enforcing executive order 11246." *The American Economic Review*, 86(2):298–301.

Anderson, D. Mark, Benjamin Crost, and Daniel I. Rees. (2020). "Do economic downturns fuel racial animus?" *Journal of Economic Behavior and Organization*, 175:9–18.

Andrews, Evan. (2019). "8 Things You May Not Know about the Battle of the Bulge," History. A&E Television Networks, LLC. December 6, 2019. Available at: www.history.com/news/8-things-you-may-not-know-about-the-battle-of-the-bulge. Last accessed December 15, 2022.

Ang, Desmond. (2020). "The Effects of Police Violence on Inner-City Students," Kennedy School of Government. Harvard. Working paper. June 7, 2020.

Antman, Francisca and Brian Duncan. (2015). "Incentives to identify: Racial identity in the age of affirmative action." *The Review of Economics and Statistics*, 97(3):710–713.

The Aspen Institute. (2004). "Structural Racism and Community Building." Available at: www.racialequitytools.org/resourcefiles/aspeninst3.pdf. Last accessed March 25, 2022.

Austen-Smith, David and Roland G. Fryer, Jr. (2005). "An economic analysis of 'acting white'." *The Quarterly Journal of Economics*, 120(2):551–583.

Bates, Timothy M. (1997). *Race, Self-employment, and Upward Mobility: An Ilusive American Dream*. Washington, DC: Woodrow Wilson Center Press.

Baum, Dan. (2016). "How to win the war on drugs." *Harper's Magazine*, April 2016. Available at: https://harpers.org/archive/2016/04/legalize-it-all/Bonczar. Last accessed February 4, 2022.

Becker, Gary S. (1957). *The Economics of Discrimination*. Chicago: University of Chicago Press.

Bell, Derrick. (1992). *Faces at the Bottom of the Well: The Permanence of Racism*. New York: Basic Books.

Benjamin, Daniel J., James J. Choi, and A. Joshua Strickland. (2010). "Social identity and preferences." *American Economic Review*, 100(4):1913–1928.

Bernstein, Jared. (1995). *Where's the Payoff? The Gap between Black Academic Progress and Economic Gains*. Washington, DC: Economic Policy Institute.

Bertrand, Marianne, Dolly Chugh, and Sendhil Mullainathan. (2005). "Implicit discrimination." *American Economic Review*, 95(2):94–98.

Bertrand, Marianne and Sendhil Mullainathan. (2004). "Are Emily and Greg more employable than Lakisha and Jamal? A field experiment on labor market discrimination." *American Economic Review*, 94(4):991–1013.

Bianchi, Suzanne M. and Daphne Spain. (1986). *American Women in Transition*. New York: Russell Sage Foundation.

Billingsley, Andrew. (1992). *Climbing Jacob's Ladder: The Enduring Legacies of the African American Family*. New York: Simon and Shuster.

Blackmon, Douglass. (2012). "Slavery by Another Name." *PBS*. March 8, 2022.

Blair, Irene V., Charles M. Judd, and Kristine M. Chapleau. (2004). "The influence of Afrocentric facial features in criminal sentencing." *Psychological Science*, 15(10):674–679.

Blair, Irene V., Charles M. Judd, Melody S. Sadler, and Christopher Jenkins. (2002). "The role of Afrocentric features in person perception: Judging by features and categories." *Journal of Personality and Social Psychology*, 83(1):5–25.

Blau, Francine and John W. Graham. (1990). "Black–white differences in wealth and asset composition." *The Quarterly Journal of Economics*, 105(2):321–339.

Blumer, Herbert. (1958). "Race prejudice as a sense of group position." *The Pacific Sociological Review*, 1(1):3–7.

Bobo, Lawrence D. (2011). "Somewhere between Jim Crow & post-racialism." *Daedalus*, 140(2):11–36.

Bodenhorn, Howard N. (2002). "The Mulatto advantage: The biological consequences of complexion in rural antebellum Virginia." *The Journal of Interdisciplinary History*, 33(1):21–46.

(2003). "The complexion gap: The economic consequences of color among free African-Americans in the rural antebellum south." *Advances in Agricultural Economic History*, 2:41–73.

Bodenhorn, Howard N. and Christopher S. Ruebeck. (2003). "The Economics of Identity and the Endogeneity of Race." Cambridge, MA: National Bureau of Economic Research Working Paper 9962.

(2007). "Colourism and African-American wealth: Evidence from the nineteenth-century South." *Journal of Population Economics*, 20(3):599–620.

Bonczar, Thomas P. (2003). "Prevalence of Imprisonment in the US Population, 1974–2001." *Bureau of Justice Statistics*. NCJ 197976. August.

Bound, John and Richard Freeman. (1992). "What went wrong? The erosion of relative earnings and employment among young black men in the 1980s." *The Quarterly Journal of Economics*, 107(1):201–232.

Boushey, Heather. (2002). "The Effects of the Personal Responsibility and Work Opportunity Reconciliation Act on Working Families." Economic Policy Institute. March 2, 2002. Available at: www.epi.org/publication/webfeatures_viewpoints_tanf_testimony/. Last accessed December 15, 2022.

Bowen, William G. and Derek Bok. (1998). *The Shape of the River: Long Term Consequences of Considering Race in College and University Admissions*. Princeton, NJ: Princeton University Press.

Bowman, P. J. (1989). "Research perspectives on Black men: Role strain and adaptation across the adult life cycle." In Reginald Lanier Jones (ed.), *Black Adult Development and Aging*. Oakland, CA: Cobb & Henry Publishers, pp. 117–150.

(1988). "Postindustrial displacement and family role strains: Challenges to the black family." In Patricia Voydanoff and Linda C. Majka (eds.), *Families and Economic Distress: Coping Strategies and Social Policy*. New York: Sage Publications, Inc., pp. 75–96.

Bowman, Phillip J. and Reliford Sanders. (1998). "Unmarried African American fathers: A comparative life span analysis." *Journal of Comparative Family Studies*, 29 (1):39–56.

Bradford, William D. (2003). "The wealth dynamics of entrepreneurship for black and white families in the US." *Review of Income and Wealth*, 49(1):89–116.

Breitman, George (ed.). (1965). *Malcolm X Speaks: Selected Speaks and Statements*. New York: Grove Press.

Brodkin, Karen. (1998). *How Jews Became White Folks & What that Says about Race in America*. New Brunswick, NJ: Rutgers University Press.

Brown, Robert A. and James Frank. (2006). "Race and officer decision making: Examining differences in arrest outcomes between Black and White officers." *Justice Quarterly*, 23(1):96–12.

Burgin, Audrieanna T. (2021). "Parental wealth on educational attainment." Essays on educational attainment and labor outcomes. Doctoral dissertation, Florida State University.

Burma, John H. (1946). "The measurement of Negro 'passing'." *American Journal of Sociology*, 52(1):18–22.

Cammett, Ann. (2014). "Deadbeat dads & welfare queens: How metaphor shapes poverty law." *Boston College Journal of Law & Social Justice*, 34:233.

Carpenter, Seth B. and William M. Rodgers III. (2004). "The disparate labor market impacts of monetary policy." *Journal of Policy Analysis and Management*, 23 (4):813–830.

(2005). "The disparate labor market impacts of monetary policy." *Labor History*, 46 (1):57–77.

Carper, N. Gordon. (1976). "Slavery revisited: Peonage in the South." *Phylon*, 37(1):85–99.

Cherry, Robert. (1976). "Racial thought and the early economics profession." *Review of Social Economy*, 34(2):147–162.

Chetty, Raj, Nathaniel Hendren, Maggie R. Jones, and Sonya R. Porter. (2020). "Race and economic opportunity in the United States: An intergenerational perspective." *The Quarterly Journal of Economics*, 135(2):711–783.

Chiteji, Ngina. (2007). "To have and to hold: An analysis of young adult debt." In Sheldon Danziger and Cecilia Elena Rouse (eds.), *The Price of Independence: The Economics of Early Adulthood*. New York: Russell Sage Foundation, pp. 231–258.

(2010). "Wealth in the extended family: An American dilemma." *Du Bois Review*, 7 (2):357–379.

(2014). "Does incarceration affect inequality during old age?" Institute for Research on Poverty, University of Wisconsin, Spring/Summer.

(2017). "Prodigal sons: Incarceration, punishment, and morality." *Faith & Economics*, 70(Fall):3–49.

Chiteji, Ngina S. and Darrick Hamilton. (2002). "Family connections and the black–white wealth gap among middle-class families." *The Review of Black Political Economy*, 30(1):9–28.

(2005). "Family matters: Kin networks and asset accumulation." In Michael Sherraden (ed.), *Inclusion in the American Dream: Assets, Poverty, and Public Policy*. New York: Oxford University Press, pp. 87–111.

Churchill, Ward and Jim Vander Wall. (1990). *The COINTELPRO Papers: Documents from the FBI's Secret Wars Against Domestic Dissent*. Boston: South End Press.

Citizens Police Data Project. (2016). Available at: https://cpdb.co/data/AB9XY8/citizens-police-data-project. Last accessed April 27, 2016.

Close, Billy R. and Patrick L. Mason. (2006). "After the traffic stops: Officer characteristics and enforcement actions." *The BE Journal of Economic Analysis & Policy*, 6 (1):1–43.

(2007). "Searching for efficient enforcement: Officer characteristics and racially biased policing." *Review of Law & Economics*, 3(2):263–321.

Coleman, Major G. (2003). "Job skill and black male wage discrimination." *Social Science Quarterly*, 84(4):892–906.

College Entrance Examination Board. (2016). "College Bound Seniors Report: Total Group Profile [National] Report," 1996 to 2004, 1996–97 through 2006–07, and 1986-87 through 2015–2016.

Collins, William J. and Robert A. Margo. (2003). "Historical Perspectives on Racial Differences in Schooling in the United States." National Bureau of Economic Research, Working paper 9770.

Cook, Nicolai and Anthony Heyes. (2021). "A boss like me." Social Science Research Network. Available at: https://ssrn.com/abstract=3958790. Last accessed December 15, 2022.

Cornwell, Christopher and William N. Trumbull. (1994). "Estimating the economic model of crime with panel data." *The Review of Economics and Statistics*, 76 (2):360–366.

Cox, Oliver C. (1940). "Sex ratio and marital status among Negroes." *American Sociological Review*, 5(6):937–947.

Cox, Robynn J. A. (2010). "Crime, incarceration, and employment in light of the great recession." *The Review of Black Political Economy*, 37(3–4):283–294.

(2012). "The impact of mass incarceration on the lives of African American women." *Review of Black Political Economy*, 39(2):203–212.

Cox, Robynn J. A., Jamein P. Cunningham, and Alberto Ortega. (2020). "Impact of affirmative action legislation on police killings of civilians." University of Memphis. Working paper presented at the Association for Public Policy and Management Conference, November 2020.

Craigie, Terry-Ann. (2021). "Men's incarceration and women's labor market outcomes." *Feminist Economics*, 27(4):1–28.

Craigie, Terry-Ann, Samuel L. Myers, Jr. and William A. Darity, Jr. (2018). "Racial differences in the effect of marriageable males on female family headship." *Journal of Demographic Economics*, 84(3):231–256.

Crenshaw, Kimberle Williams. (1988). "Race, reform, and retrenchment: Transformation and legitimation in antidiscrimination law." *Harvard Law Review*, 101(7):1331–1387.

Cullen, James. (2018). "The History of Mass Incarceration." Brennan Center for Justice, July 20, 2018. Available at: www.brennancenter.org/our-work/analysis-opinion/history-mass-incarceration. Last accessed December 15, 2022.

Cunningham, Jamein P. and Rob Gillezeau. (2019). "Don't shoot! The impact of historical African American protests on police killing of civilians." *Journal of Quantitative Criminology*, 37(1):1–34.

Darity, William A. (1987). "Abram Harris: An odyssey from Howard to Chicago." *The Review of Black Political Economy*, 15(3):4–40.

Darity, Jr., William. (1989). "What's left of the economic theory of discrimination?" In Steve Shulman and William Darity, Jr. (eds). *The Question of Discrimination: Racial Inequality in the U.S. Labor Market*. Middletown, CT: Wesleyan University Press, pp. 335–374.

(1994). "Many roads to extinction: Early AEA economists and the Black disappearance hypothesis." *History of Economics Review*, 21(1):47–64.

Darity, Jr., William, Jason Dietrich, and David K. Guilkey. (1997). "Racial and ethnic inequality in the United States: A secular perspective." *American Economic Review: Papers and Proceedings*, 87(2):301–305.

(2001). "Persistent advantage or disadvantage?: Evidence in support of the intergenerational drag hypothesis." *The American Journal of Economics and Sociology*, 60(2):435–470.

Darity, Jr., William, David K. Guilkey, and William Winfrey. (1996). "Explaining differences in economic performance among racial and ethnic groups in the USA: The data examined." *American Journal of Economics and Sociology*, 55 (4):411–425.

Darity, Jr., William and Darrick Hamilton. (2012). "Bold policies for economic justice." *The Review of Black Political Economy*, 39(1):79–85.

Darity, Jr., William, Darrick Hamilton, and James B. Stewart. (2015). "A Tour de Force in understanding intergroup inequality: An introduction to stratification economics." *Review of Black Political Economy*, 42(1–2):1–6.

Darity, Jr., William and Patrick L. Mason. (1998). "Evidence on discrimination in employment: Codes of color, codes of gender." *The Journal of Economic Perspectives*, 12(2):63–90.

Darity, Jr., William, Patrick L. Mason, and James B. Stewart. (2006). "The economics of identity: The origin and persistence of racial norms." *Journal of Economic Behavior and Organizations*, 60(3):283–305.

Darity, Jr., William and Kirsten Mullen. (2020). *From Here to Equality*. Chapel Hill, NC: University of North Carolina Press.

Darity, Jr., William and Rhonda M. Williams. (1985). "Peddlers forever?: Culture, competition, and discrimination." *The American Economic Review Papers and Proceedings*, 75(2):256–261.

Daskalova, Vessela. (2018). "Discrimination, social identity, and coordination: An experiment." *Games and Economic Behavior*, 107:238–252.

Dawson, Michael C. (2001). *Black Visions: The Roots of Contemporary African-American Political Ideologies*. Chicago: University of Chicago Press.

DeAngelo, Gregory, Kaj R. Gittings, and Anita Alves Pena. (2018). "Interracial face-to-face crimes and the socioeconomics of neighborhoods: Evidence from policing records." *International Review of Law and Economics*, 56:1–13.

Derenoncourt, Ellora. (2022). "Can you move to opportunity? Evidence from the Great Migration." *American Economic Review*, 112(2):369–408.

Derenoncourt, Ellora, Chi Hyun Kim, Moritz Kuhn, and Moritz Schularick. (2021). "The racial wealth gap: 1860–1920." Princeton University: Working paper, August 29, 2021.

Diamond, John B. and James P. Huguley. (2014). "Testing the oppositional culture explanation in desegregated schools: The impact of racial differences in academic orientations on school performance." *Social Forces*, 93(2):747–777.

Dickinson, David L., David Masclet, and Emmanuel Peterle. (2018). "Discrimination as favoritism: The private benefits and social costs of in-group favoritism in an experimental labor market." *European Economic Review*, 104:220–236.

Diffey, Louisa and Sarah Steffes. (2017). "Age Requirements for Free and Compulsory Education. 50-State Review." Denver, Colorado: Education Commission of the States. Available at: https://files.eric.ed.gov/fulltext/ED577460.pdf. Last accessed December 15, 2022.

Dimarche, Ketsia Stephanie. (2020). "Parental wealth, personality traits, immigrant status and education attainment." Essays on the economic outcomes of children of immigrants. Doctoral dissertation, Florida State University.

Dollar, Cindy Brooks. (2014). "Racial threat theory: Assessing the evidence, requesting redesign." *Journal of Criminology*, 983026(4).

Donohue III, John J. and James Heckman. (1991). "Continuous versus episodic change: the impact of civil rights policy on the economic status of blacks." *Journal of Economic Literature*, 32(4):1603–1643.

Du Bois, William E. B. (1899). *The Philadelphia Negro: A Social Study*. Philadelphia: University of Pennsylvania Press.

(1903). "Of the dawn of freedom." In *The Souls of Black Folk*, Chicago: A. C. McClurg & Co.

(1908). *The Negro American Family*. The Atlanta University Publications, 13. Atlanta, GA: Atlanta University Press.

(1935). *Black Reconstruction in America: An Essay toward a History of the Part Which Black Folk Played in the Attempt to Reconstruct Democracy in America, 1860–1880*. New York: The Free Press.

(1940). *Dusk of Dawn: An Essay toward an Autobiography of a Race Concept*. New York: Harcourt, Brace & Co.

Economic Policy Institute, State of Working America Data Library, "Union Coverage" (2021).

Eitle, David, Lisa Stolzenberg, and Stewart J. D'Alessio. (2005). "Police organizational factors, the racial composition of the police, and the probability of arrest." *Justice Quarterly*, 22(1):30–57.

Elliott, Diana B., Kristy Krivickas, Matthew W. Brault, and Rose M. Kreider. (2012). "Historical Marriage Trends from 1890–2010: A Focus on Race Differences." Social, economics, and housing Statistics Division, United States Census Bureau, Working Paper Number 2012-12.

Equal Justice Initiative. (2017). "Lynching in America: Confronting the legacy of racial terror, third edition." Montgomery, AL. Available at: https://eji.org/reports/lynching-in-america/. Last accessed December 15, 2022.

(2018). "Slavery in America: The Montgomery Slave Trade." Available at: https://eji.org/reports/slavery-in-america/. Last accessed December 15, 2022.

Eriksson, Katherine. (2020). "Education and incarceration in the Jim Crow South: Evidence from Rosenwald schools." *Journal of Human Resources*, 55(1):43–75.

Executive Order 8802. (1941). Available at: www.blackpast.org/african-american-history/executive-order-8802-1941-2/. Last accessed December 15, 2022.

Fairclough, Adam. (1983). "Was Martin Luther King a Marxist?" *History Workshop*, 15:117–125.

Farley, Reynolds. (2004). "Racial integration in the public schools, 1967 to 1972: Assessing the effect of governmental policies." *Sociological Focus*, 8(1):3–26.

Federal Bureau of Investigation (FBI). (2020). "What we investigate: Civil rights, hate crimes." Available at: www.fbi.gov/investigate/civil-rights/hate-crimes. Last accessed December 15, 2022.

Feigenberg, Benjamin and Conrad Miller. (2020). "Racial disparities in motor vehicle searches cannot be justified by efficiency." National Bureau of Economic Research, working paper 27761. August.

(2021). "Racial divisions and criminal justice: Evidence from Southern State Courts." *American Economic Journal: Economic Policy*, 13(2):207–240.

Ferguson, Ronald. (2008). *Toward Excellence with Equity: An Emerging Vision for Closing the Achievement Gap*. Cambridge, MA: Harvard Education Press.

Figlio, David N. (2005). "Names, expectations and the black-white test score gap." NBER Working Paper No. 11195.

Fletcher, Michael A. (2012). "Black jobless rate is twice that of whites." *Washington Post*, December 14.

Fogel, Robert William. (1989). *Without Consent or Contract: The Rise and Fall of American Slavery*. New York: W. W. Norton.

Fordham, Signithia and John U. Ogbu. (1986). "Black students' school success: Coping with the burden of 'acting white'." *The Urban Review*, 18(3):176–206.

Forman, Jr., James. (2010). "Why care about mass incarceration?" *Georgetown Law Faculty Publications and Other Works*. 370. Available at: https://scholarship.law.georgetown.edu/facpub/370. Last accessed December 15, 2022.

Foster, Holly and John Hagan. (2009). "The mass incarceration of parents in America: Issues of race/ethnicity, collateral damage to children, and prisoner reentry." *The Annuals of the American Academy of Political and Social Science*, 623:179–194.

Franklin, Benjamin. (1751). "Observations concerning the increase of mankind." Founders Online, National Archives, available at: https://founders.archives.gov/documents/Franklin/01-04-02-0080. [Original source: *The Papers of Benjamin Franklin*, vol. 4, July 1, 1750, through June 30, 1753, ed. Leonard W. Labaree. New Haven: Yale University Press, 1961, pp. 225–234.] Last accessed December 15, 2022.

Frazier, E. Franklin. (1939). *The Negro Family in the United States*. Chicago: University of Chicago Press.

Freeman, Richard B. (1973). "Decline of labor market discrimination and economic analysis." *The American Economic Review*, 63(2):280–286.

Fryer, Jr., Roland G. (2019). "An empirical analysis of police differences in police use of force." *Journal of Political Economy*, 127(3):1210–1261.

Galbraith, James K. and William A. Darity, Jr. (1994). *Macroeconomics*. Boston: Houghton Mifflin Company.

Gale, Lewis R., Will Carrington Heath, and Rand W. Ressler. (2002). "An economic analysis of hate crimes." *Eastern Economic Journal*, 28(2):203–216.

Gallo, Edoardo, Thomas Grund, and J. James Reade. (2013). "Punishing the foreigner: Implicit discrimination in the Premier League based on oppositional identity." *Oxford Bulletin of Economics and Statistics*, 75(1): 136–156.

Geisler, Karl R., Carl E. Enomoto, and Theophilus Djaba. (2019). "Hate crimes and minority-owned businesses." *Review of Black Political Economy*, 46(1):3–21.

Gershenson, Seth, Cassandra M. D. Hart, Joshua Hyman, Constance Lindsay, and Nicholas W. Papageorge. (2021). "The long-run impacts of same-race teachers." National Bureau of Economic Research, Working Paper 25254.

Gershenson, Seth, Stephen B. Holt, and Nicholas W. Papageorge. (2016). "Who believes in me? The effect of student–teacher demographic match on teacher expectations." *Economics of Education Review*, 52:209–224.

Ghosh, Pallab K., Gary A. Hoover, and Zexuan Liu. (2020). "Do state minimum wages affect the incarceration rate?" *Southern Economic Journal*, 86(3):845–872.

Gibson, Campbell and Kay Jung. (2002). "Historical Census Statistics on Population Totals by Race, 1790 to 1990, and By Latinx Origin, 1970 to 1990, for the United States, Regions, Divisions, and States." Population Division, U.S. Census Bureau. Working Paper Series No. 56, September 2002. Available at: https://web.archive.org/web/20080725044857/www.census.gov/population/www/documentation/twps0056/twps0056.html. Last accessed December 15, 2022.

Giddings, Paula J. (1984). *When and Where I Enter: The Impact of Black Women on Race and Sex in America*. New York: HarperCollins Publishers.

Gĩthĩnji, Mwangi. (2015). "Erasing class/(re)creating ethnicity: Jobs, politics, accumulation and identity in Kenya." *The Review of Black Political Economy*, 42 (1–2):87–110.

Gittleman, Maury and Edward N. Wolff. (2004). "Racial differences in patterns of wealth accumulation." *The Journal of Human Resources*, XXXIX (1):193–227.

Giuliano, Laura, David I. Levine, and Jonathan Leonard. (2011). "Racial bias in the manager–employee relationship: An analysis of quits, dismissals, and promotions at a large retail firm." *Journal of Human Resources*, 46(1):26–52.

Glover, Dylan, Amanda Pallais, and William Pariente. (2017). "Discrimination as a self-fulfilling prophecy: Evidence from French grocery stores." *Quarterly Journal of Economics*, 132(3):1219–1260.

Golash-Boza, Tanya and William Darity, Jr. (2008). "Latino racial choices: The effects of skin colour and discrimination on Latinos' and Latinas' racial self-identifications." *Ethnic and Racial Studies*, 31(5):899–934.

Goldsmith, Arthur, William A. Darity, Jr., and Darrick Hamilton. (2007). "From dark to light: Skin color and wages among African-Americans." *Journal of Human Resources*, XLII(4):701–738.

Gooden, Susan and Samuel L. Myers Jr. (2004). "Social equity in public affairs education." *Journal of Public Affairs Education*, 10(2):91–97.

Goodman, Joshua. (2014). "Flaking Out: Student Absences and Snow Days as Disruptions of Instructional Time." National Bureau of Economic Research, Working paper 20221.

Gordon, David, Richard Edwards, and Michael Reich. (1982). *Segment Work, Divided Workers: The Historical Transformation of Labor in the United States*. Cambridge: Cambridge University Press.

Gould, Eric D. and Esteban F. Klor. (2016). "The long-run effect of 9/11: Terrorism, backlash, and the assimilation of Muslim immigrants in the West." *The Economic Journal*, 126(597):2064–2114.

Graham, Lawrence O. (1999). *Our Kind of People: Inside America's Black Upper Class*. New York: HarperCollins Publishers Inc.

Gramlich, John. (2021). "America's incarceration rate falls to lowest level since 1995." Pew Research Center. August 16, 2021. Available at: https://pewrsr.ch/2rfSmVL. Last accessed December 15, 2022.

Graves, Jr., Joseph L. (2004). *The Race Myth: Why We Pretend Race Exists in America*. New York: Dutton.

Green, Laura. (1998). "Stereotypes: Negative racial stereotypes and their effect on attitudes toward African-Americans." *Perspectives on Multiculturalism and Cultural Identity*, XI(1).

Greenfeld, Lawrence A. (1989). "Prisoners in 1988." Bureau of Justice Statistics Bulletin, Bureau of Justice Statistics, Office of Justice Programs, U.S. Department of Justice. April 1989. Available at: https://bjs.ojp.gov/content/pub/pdf/p88.pdf. Last accessed December 16, 2022.

Greenwald, Anthony G. and Linda Hamilton Krieger. (2006). "Implicit bias: Scientific foundations." *California Law Review*, 94(4):945–967.

Gunadi, Christian. (2019). "The legacy of slavery on hate crimes in the United States." *Research in Economics*, 73(4):339–344.

Gutter, Michael S. and Angela Fontes. (2006). "Racial differences in risky asset ownership: A two-stage model of the investment decision-making process." *Journal of Financial Counseling and Planning*, 17(2):64–78.

Gyimah-Brempong, Kwabena. (1986). "Empirical models of criminal behavior: How significant a factor is race?" *Review of Black Political Economy*, 15(1):27–43.

Halloran, Clare, Rebecca Jack, James C. Okun, and Emily Oster. (2021). "Pandemic Schooling Mode and Student Test Scores: Evidence from US States." National Bureau of Economic Research, Working paper 29497.

Hamilton, Darrick and William A. Darity, Jr. (2010). "Can 'baby bonds' eliminate the racial wealth gap in putative post-racial America?" *Review of Black Political Economy*, 37(3–4):207–216.

Harris, Donald. (1972). "The black ghetto as colony: A theoretical critique and alternative formulation." *The Review of Black Political Economy*, 2(4):3–33.

Headley, Andrea M. and James E. Wright, II. (2019). "National police reform commissions: Evidence-based practices or unfulfilled promises?" *Review of Black Political Economy*, 46(4):277–305.

(2020). "Is representation enough: Racial disparities in levels of force and arrests by police." Florida State University. Working Paper presented at the Association for Public Policy and Management Conference, November 2020.

Heckman, James. (1998). "Detecting discrimination." *Journal of Economic Perspectives*, 12(2):101–116.

(2011). "The American family in black & white: A post-racial strategy for improving skills to promote equality." *Daedalus*, 140(2):70–89.

Heflin, Colleen M. and Ngina Chiteji. (2014). "My brother's keeper? The association between having siblings in poor health and wealth accumulation." *Journal of Family Issues*, 35(3):358–383.

Herring, Cedric, Verna M. Keith, and Hayward Derrick Horton. (2004). *Skin Deep: How Race and Complexion Matter in the Color-Blind Era*. Chicago, IL: University of Illinois Press.

Herrnstein, Richard J. and Charles Murray. (1994). *The Bell Curve: Intelligence and Class Structure in American Life*. New York: Simon and Shuster.

Hersch, Joni. (2006). "Skin-tone effects among African Americans: Perceptions and reality." *The American Economic Review*, 96(2):251–255.

(2008). "Profiling the new immigrant worker: The effects of skin color and height." *Journal of Labor Economics*, 26(2):345–386.

Herskovitz, Melvin J. (1942). *The Myth of The Negro Past*. Boston, MA: Beacon Press.

Higginbotham, Jr., A. Leon. (1978). *In the Matter of Color: Race and the American Legal Process: The Colonial Period*. Oxford: Oxford University Press.

Hill, Robert B. (1972). *The strengths of Black families*. New York: Emerson Hall Publishers.

(1993). *Research on the African-American Family : A Holistic Perspective*. Westport, CT: Greenwood Publishing Group.

Hobbs, Allyson. (2014). *A Chosen Exile: A History of Racial Passing in American Life*. Cambridge, MA: Harvard University Press.

Hochschild, Jennifer L. and Brenna Powell. (2008). "Racial reorganization and the United States census 1850–1930: Mulattoes, half-breeds, mixed parentage, Hindoos, and the Mexican race." *Studies in American Political Development*, 22 (1):59–96.

Hoekstra, Mark and Carly Will Sloan. (2022). "Does race matter for police use of force? evidence from 911 calls." National Bureau of Economic Research, Inc, NBER Working Papers: 26774. February 2020.

Hoffman, Saul D. and Greg J. Duncan. (1995). "The effect of incomes, wages, and AFDC benefits on marital disruption." *The Journal of Human Resources*, 30 (1):19–41.

Holz, Justin E., Roman G. Rivera, and Bocar A. Ba. (2019). "Spillover effects in police use of force." Faculty Scholarship at Penn Law. 2133. Available at: https://scholarship.law.upenn.edu/faculty_scholarship/2133. Last accessed December 16, 2022.

Hopkins, Daniel J. and Katherine T. McCabe. (2012). "After it's too late: Estimating the policy impacts of Black mayoralties in U.S. cities." *American Politics Research*, 40 (4):665–700.

Houlihan, Glenn. (2021). "The Legacy of the Crushed 1981 PATCO Strike." *Jacobin*. November 5, 2021. Available at: www.jacobinmag.com/2021/08/reagan-patco-1981-strike-legacy-air-traffic-controllers-union-public-sector-strikebreaking. Last accessed December 16, 2022.

Hurst, Erik, Frank P. Stafford, and Ming Ching Luoh. (1998). "The wealth dynamics of American families, 1984–94." *Brookings Papers on Economic Activity*, 29 (1):267–338.

Ignatiev, Noel. (1995). *How the Irish became White*. New York: Routledge.

Infoplease. (2012). "Integration: 1954 to 1963." *The Columbia Electronic Encyclopedia*, 6th ed. New York: Columbia University Press. Available at: www.infoplease.com/encyclopedia/history/north-america/us/integration/1954-to-1963. Last accessed December 16, 2022.

Jennings, Jay T. and Meghan E. Rubado. (2017). "Preventing the use of deadly force: The relationship between police agency policies and rates of officer-involved gun deaths." *Public Administration Review*, 77(2):217–226.

Johnson, Rucker. (2015). "Long-run impacts of school desegregation and school quality on adult attainment." National Bureau of Economic Research Working Paper 16664.

Jones, Barbara A. P. (1985). "Black women and labor force participation: An analysis of sluggish growth rates." *Review of Black Political Economy*, 14(2–3):11–31.

Jones, Jacqueline. (1998). *American Work: Four Centuries of Black and White Labor*. New York: W. W. Norton.

Jordan, Winthrop D. (1968). *White over Black American attitudes toward the Negro, 1550–1812*, 2nd edn. Chapel Hill, NC: The University of North Carolina Press.

Kalecki, Michael. (1954). *Theory of Economic Dynamics: An Essay on Cyclical and Long-Run Changes in Capitalist Economy*. London: George Allen and Unwin.

(2009). *Theory of Economic Dynamics: An Essay on Cyclical and Long-Run Changes in Capitalist Economies*. New York: Monthly Review Press.

Katznelson, Ira. (2005). *When Affirmative Action was White: An Untold History of Racial Inequality in Twentieth-Century America*. New York: W. W. Norton.

Keith, Verna M. and Cedric Herring. (1991). "Skin tone and stratification in the black community." *American Journal of Sociology*, 97(3):760–778.

Kennedy, Randall. (2001). "Passing." *Ohio State Law Journal*, 62(3):1145–1194.

Kent, Mary Mederios. (2007). "Immigration and America's Black population." *Population Bulletin*, 62(4):3–16.

Keynes, John M. (1936). *The General Theory of Employment, Interest, and Money*. New York: Harcourt, Brace & World.

Kindig, Jessie. (2007). "March on Washington Movement (1941–1947)." December 6, 2007. Available at: www.blackpast.org/african-american-history/march-washington-movement-1941-1947/. Last accessed December 16, 2022.

King, Mary C. (2005). "Keeping people in their place: The economics of racial violence." In Cecilia Conrad, John Whitehead, Patrick Mason, and James Stewart (eds), *African Americans in the US Economy*. Lanhan, MD: Rowan & Littlefield, pp. 110–117.

King, Martin L. (1968). *Where Do We Go from Here: Chaos or Community?* Boston, MA: Beacon Press.

Klein, Lawrence R. and H. W. Mooney. (1953). "Negro–White savings differentials and the consumption function problem." *Econometrica*, 21:425–446.

Knowles, John, Nicola Persico, and Petra Todd. (2001). "Racial bias in motor vehicle searches: Theory and evidence." *Journal of Political Economy*, 109(1):203–229.

Knox, Dean, Will Lowe, and Jonathan Mummolo. (2020). "The bias is built in: How administrative records mask racially biased policing." *American Political Science Review*, 114(3):619–637.

Kochbar, Rakesh, Richard Fry, and Paul Taylor. (2011). *Wealth Gaps Rise to Record Highs between Whites, Blacks and Hispanics*. Washington, DC: Pew Research Center.

Kotlowski, Dean. (1998). "Black power–Nixon style: The Nixon administration and minority business enterprise." *The Business History Review*, 72(3):409–445.

Lee, Christopher T., Mary Huynh, Paulina Zheng, Alejandro Castro III, Francia Noel, Darlene Kelley, Jennifer Norton, Catherine Stayton, and Gretchen Van Wye. (2017). Enumeration and classification of law enforcement-related deaths – New York City, 2010–2015. Technical report, New York City Department of Health Maryland. Available at: www1.nyc.gov/assets/doh/downloads/pdf/about/law-enforcement-deaths.pdf. Last accessed December 16, 2022.

Legewie, Joscha and Jeffrey Fagan. (2019). "Aggressive policing and the educational performance of minority youth." *American Sociological Review*, 84(2):220–247.

Leonard, Jonathan. (1991). "The federal anti-bias effort." In Emily P. Hoffman (ed.), *Essays on the Economics of Discrimination*. Kalamazoo, MI: W. E. Upjohn Institute for Employment Research, pp. 85–113.

(1996). "Wage disparities and affirmative action in the 1980's." *The American Economic Review*, 86(2):285–328.

Levy, David M. (2001) "How the dismal science got its name: Debating racial quackery." *Journal of the History of Economic Thought*, 23(1):5–35.

Levy, David M. and Sandra J. Peart. (2000). "Modeling non-abstract economic man: Victorian anthropology, Punch & Piltdown." Presented at the *University of Toronto History of Economics Workshop*.

(2003). "Denying human heterogeneity: Eugenics & the birth of neoclassical economics." *Journal of the History of Economic Thought*, 25(3):261–288.

Lichter, Daniel T., Diane K. McLaughlin, George Kephart, and David J. Landry. (1992). "Race and the retreat from marriage: A shortage of marriageable men?" *American Sociological Review*, 57(6):781–799.

Lincoln, C. Eric and Lawrence H. Mamiya. (1990). *The Black Church in the African American Experience*. Durham, NC: Duke University Press.

Lindsay, Constance A. and Cassandra M. D. Hart. (2017). "Exposure to same-race teachers and student disciplinary outcomes for black students in North Carolina." *Educational Evaluation and Policy Analysis*, 39(3):485–510.

Liu, Sitian. (2018). "Incarceration of African American Men and the Impacts on Women and Children." Stanford University Working Paper.

Loury, Glenn C. (1984). "Internally directed action for black community development: The next frontier for 'the movement'." *Review of Black Political Economy*, 13 (1–2):31–46.

(1989). "Why should we care about group inequality?" In William A. Darity, Jr., and Steve Shulman (eds.). *On the Question of Discrimination*. Middletown, CT: Wesleyan University Press, ch. 9, pp. 268–290.

Loury, Linda Datcher. (2009). "Am I still too Black for you?: Schooling and secular change in skin tone effects." *Economics of Education Review*, 28(4):428–433.

Maddox, Keith B. (2004). "Perspectives on racial phenotypicality bias." *Personality and Social Psychology Review*, 8(4):383–401.

Malthus, Thomas R. (1820). *Principles of Political Economy*. London: William Pickering.

Mancini, Matthew J. (1978). "Race, economics, and the abandonment of convict leasing." *The Journal of Negro History*, 63(4):339–352.

Mandle, Jay R. (1983). "Sharecropping and the plantation economy in the United States South." *The Journal of Peasant Studies*, 10(2–3):120–129.

Mangino, William. (2010). "Race to college: The 'reverse gap'." *Race and Social Problems*, 2:164–178.

(2012). "Why do whites and the rich have less need for education?" *American Journal of Economics and Sociology*, 71(3):562–602.

(2013). "A critical look at oppositional culture and the race gap in education." *International Scholarly Research Notices*, vol. 2013, Article ID 363847, 5 pages.

(2014). "The negative effects of privilege on educational attainment: Gender, race, class, and the bachelor's degree." *Social Science Quarterly*, 95(3):760–784.

(2019). "Income returns in early career: Why whites have less need for education." *Race and Social Problems*, 11:45–59.

Marcotte, Dave E. (2007). Schooling and test scores: A mother-natural experiment. *Economics of Education Review*, 26:629–640.

Mas, Alexandre and Enrico Moretti. (2009). "Peers at work." *American Economic Review*, 99(1):112–145.

Mason, Patrick L. (1995). "Race, competition and differential wages." *Cambridge Journal of Economics*, 19(4):545–568.

(1997). "Race, culture, and skill: Interracial wage differences among African Americans, Latinos, and whites." *The Review of Black Political Economy*, 25 (3):5–39.

(1999). "Male interracial wage differentials: competing explanations." *Cambridge Journal of Economics*, 23(3):1–39.

(2004). "NEA presidential address: Identity, markets, and persistent racial inequality." *Review of Black Political Economy*, 32(1):13–36.

(2007). "Intergenerational mobility and interracial inequality: The return to family values." *Industrial Relations*, 46(1):51–80.

(ed.). (2013). *Encyclopedia of Race and Racism*, 2nd ed. New York: Macmillan Reference USA.

(2017). "Not black-alone: The 2008 presidential election and racial self-identification among African Americans." *Review of Black Political Economy*, 44 (1–2):55–76.

Mason, Patrick L. and Andrew Matella. (2014). "Stigmatization and racial selection after September 11, 2001: Self-identity among Arab and Islamic Americans." *IZA Journal of Migration*, 3:20.

Mason, Patrick L., Samuel L. Myers, Jr., and Margaret Simms. (2022). "Racial isolation and marginalization of economic research on race and crime." *Journal of Economic Literature*, 60(2):494–526.

Maxwell, Nan L. (1994). "The effect on black–white wage differences of differences in the quantity and quality of education." *Industrial and Labor Relation Review*, 47 (2):249–264.

McArthur, Colin and Sarah Edelman. (2017). *The 2008 Housing Crisis: Don't Blame Federal Housing Programs for Wall Street's Recklessness*. Washington, DC: Center for American Progress, April 13, 2017.

McDaniel, Antonio. (1990). "The power of culture: A review of the idea of Africa's influence on family structure in antebellum America." *Journal of Family History*, 15 (1):225–238.

(1994). "Historical racial differences in living arrangements of children." *Journal of Family History*, 19(1):55–77.

McNamee, Catherine B. and R. Kelley Raley. (2011). "A note on race, ethnicity and nativity differentials in remarriage in the United States." *Demographic Research*, 24 (13):293–312.

Mead, Lawrence. (1992). *The New Politics of Poverty: The Nonworking Poor in America*. New York: Basic Books.

Medoff, Marshall H. (1999). "Allocation of time and hateful behavior: A theoretical and positive analysis of hate and hate crimes." *American Journal of Economics and Sociology*, 58(4):959–973.

Menchik, Paul and Nancy Jianakoplos. (1997). "Black–White wealth inequality: Is inheritance the reason?" *Economic Inquiry*, 35(2):428–442.

Mendershausen, Hortst. (1940). "Differences in family savings between cities of different size and location, whites and negroes." *The Review of Economics and Statistics*, 22(3):122–137.

Mills, Charles W. (2015). "Bestial inferiority: Locating simianization within racism." In Wulf D. Hund, Charles W. Mills, and Silvia Sebastiani (eds). *Simianization: Apes, Gender, Class, and Race*. Munster: LIT Verlag, pp. 19–41.

Minsky, Hyman. (1992). "The capitalist development of the economy and the structure of financial institutions." The Jerome Levy Economics Institute, Working Paper No. 72.

Movement for Black Lives. (2016). "A vision for Black lives policy demands for Black power, freedom & Justice." Available at: https://policy.m4bl.org/platform. Last accessed December 16, 2022.

Moynihan, Daniel P. (1965). *The Negro Family: The Case for National Action*. Office of Planning and Research, US Department of Labor, Washington, DC: US Government Printing Office.

Mueller-Smith, Michael. (2015). "Criminal and labor market impacts of incarceration." Working Paper. Ann Arbor, MI: University of Michigan. June 8, 2015.

Muhitch, Kevin and Nazgol Ghandnoosh. (2021). "Private prisons in the United States." The Sentencing Project. Washington, DC. March 2021. Available at: sentencingproject.org. Last accessed December 16, 2022.

Mulholland, Sean E. (2013). "White supremacist groups and hate crimes." *Public Choice*, 157(1/2):91–113.

Murray, Charles. (1984). *Losing Ground: American Social Policy, 1950–1980*. New York: Basic Books.

Murray, Charles A. and Richard Herrnstein. (1994). *The Bell Curve: Intelligence and Class Structure in American Life*. New York: Free Press.

Myers, Jr., Samuel L. (1980). "Black–white differentials in crime rates." *The Review of Black Political Economy*, 10(2):133–152.

(2000). "The unintended impacts of sentencing guidelines on family structure." Revised Technical Report, Grant no: USDJ/96-CE-VX-0015. United States Department of Justice, National Institute of Justice, Washington, DC.

Myers, Jr., Samuel L. and Vanishree Radhakrishna. (2018). "Hate crimes, crimes of atrocity, and affirmative action in India and the US." A paper prepared for the Government of Karnataka International Conference: Reclaiming Social Justice, Revisiting Ambedkar, pp. 2–47.

Myers, Jr., Samuel L. and William J. Sabol (1987). "Business cycles and racial disparities in punishment." *Contemporary Economic Policy*, 5(4):46–58.

Myrdal, Gunnar. (1944). *An American Dilemma: The Negro Problem and Modern Democracy*. New York: Harper and Row Publishers.

Nakosteen, Robert and Michael Zimmer. (2019). "Latent earnings capacity and the race marriage gap." *Cogent Economics and Finance*, 7(1):1609155.

Neal, Derek A. and William R. Johnson. (1996). "The role of pre-market factors in black–white wage differences." *Journal of Political Economy*, 104(5):869–895.

Nembhard, Jessica Gordon. (2014). *Collective Courage: A History of African American Cooperative Economic Thought and Practice*. University Park, PA: The Pennsylvania State University Press.

The Neshoba Democrat. (2021). "Ronald Reagan's 1980 Neshoba County Fair speech." Philadelphia, Mississippi. Available at: https://neshobademocrat.com/stories/ronald-reagans-1980-neshoba-county-fair-speech,49123. Last accessed December 16, 2022.

Neumark, David. (2012). "Detecting Discrimination in Audit and Correspondence Studies." *Journal of Human Resources*, 47(4):1128–1157.

New York Times. (1903). "Peon holders pardon; President Roosevelt Exercises His Power in Behalf of Two Imprisoned Alabamans." September 17, 1903. Available at: www.nytimes.com/1903/09/17/archives/peon-holders-pardoned-president-roosevelt-exercises-his-power-in.html. Last accessed December 16, 2022.

(2004). "Barack Obama's Remarks to the Democratic National Convention." July 27, 2004. www.nytimes.com/2004/07/27/politics/campaign/barack-obamas-remarks-to-the-democratic-national.html. Last accessed December 16, 2022.

Nott, Josiah C. and George R. Gliddon. (1854). *Types of Mankind: or, Ethnological Researches, based upon the Ancient Monuments, Paintings, Sculptures, and Crania of Races, and upon Their Natural, Geographical, Philological and Biblical History*. Philadelphia, PA: Lippincott, Grambo & co.

Oberfield, Zachery W. (2012). "Socialization and self-selection: How police officers develop their views about using force." *Administration & Society*, 46 (4):702–730.

Oliver, Melvin and Thomas M. Shapiro. (1995). *Black Wealth/White Wealth: A New Perspective on Racial Inequality*. New York: Routledge.

Olney, Martha L. (1998). "When your word is not enough: Race, collateral, and household credit." *The Journal of Economic History*, 58(2):408–431.

Olzak, Susan. (1990). "The political context of competition: Lynching and urban racial violence, 1882–1914." *Social Forces*, 69(2):395–421.

Pager, Devah. (2003). "The mark of a criminal record." *American Journal of Sociology*, 108(5):937–975.

Papillon, Kimberly. (2014). *Brief Paper on Implicit Bias and Intent in Bureaucracies*. Reno, NV: National Judicial College.

Payne, B. Keith, Heidi A. Vuletich, and Jazmin L. Brown-Iannuzzi. (2019). "Historical roots of implicit bias in slavery." *PNAS*, 116(24):11693–11698.

Peart, Sandra J. and David M. Levy. (2001). "'Not an average human being': Racial attacks on abstract economic man in Victorian prose and images." Working paper. Berea, OH: Baldwin-Wallace College.

Pedulla, David S. and Devah Pager. (2019). "Race and networks in the job search process." *American Sociological Review*, 84(6):983–1012.

Petach, Luke and Anita Alves Pena. (2020). "Local labor market inequality in the age of mass incarceration." *Review of Black Political Economy*, 48(1):7–41.

Phelps, Michelle S. and Devah Pager. (2016). "Inequality and punishment: A turning point for mass incarceration?" *The Annuals of the American Academy of Political and Social Science*, 663(1):185–203.

Pien, Diane. (2010, February 11). *Black Panther Party's Free Breakfast Program (1969–1980)*. BlackPast.org. Available at: www.blackpast.org/african-american-history/black-panther-partys-free-breakfast-program-1969-1980/. Last accessed December 13, 2022.

Price, Daniel O. (1970). "Urbanization of the blacks." *The Milbank Memorial Fund Quarterly*, 48(2):47–67.

Rangel, Marcos A. (2015). "Is parental love colorblind? Human capital accumulation within mixed families." *The Review of Black Political Economy*, 42(1–2):57–86.

Raphael, Steven and Michael A. Stoll. (2013). *Why Are So Many Americans in Prison?* New York: Russell Sage Foundation.

Reich, Michael. (1981). *Racial Inequality: A Political Economic Analysis*. Princeton, NJ: Princeton University Press.

Rim, Nayoung, Bocar Ba, and Roman Rivera. (2020). "Disparities in police award nominations: Evidence from Chicago." *AEA Papers and Proceedings*, 110:447–451.

Rodgers III, William M. and William E. Spriggs. (1996). "What does the AFQT really measure: Race, wages, schooling and the AFQT score." *The Review of Black Political Economy*, 24(4):13–46.

Roediger, David R. (1991). *The Wages of Whiteness: Race and the Making of the American Working Class*. New York: Verso.

(2005). *Working toward Whiteness: How America's Immigrants became White, the Strange Journal from Ellis Island to the Suburbs*. New York: Basic Books.

Roosevelt, Theodore. (1910). "The New Nationalism." A Speech Delivered at the Dedication of the John Brown Memorial Park in Osawatomie, Kansas, August 31, 1910. Available at: https://nationalsecurity.gmu.edu/wp-content/uploads/2019/03/New-Nationalism-Speech-Theodore-Roosevelt.pdf. Last accessed December 16, 2022.

The Royal Society. (2022). "'Types of Mankind': Science and Race in the 18th and 19th Centuries." Available at: https://web.archive.org/web/20150402222040/https:/royalsociety.org/exhibitions/2012/black-history-month/types-of-mankind/. Last accessed December 14, 2022.

Ruebeck, Christopher S., Susan L. Averett, and Howard N. Bodenhorn. (2009). "Acting white and acting black: Mixed-race adolescents' identity and behavior." *The B.E. Journal of Economic Analysis & Policy*, 9(1):1–42.

Ruggles, Steven. (2021). "Components of race differences in men's first marriage rates in the United States, 1960–2019." University of Minnesota Working Paper.

Rustin, Bayard. (1966). *A "Freedom Budget" for All Americans: Budgeting Our Resources, 1966-1975, to Achieve "Freedom From Want"*. New York: A. Philip Randolph Institute. October 1966. Available at: https://archive.org/details/freedomBudgetForAllAmericansBudgetingOurResources1966–1975To/page/n1/mode/2up. Last accessed December 16, 2022.

Shaikh, Anwar. (2016). *Capitalism: Competition, Conflict, Crises*. New York: Oxford University Press.

Shaw, Kathryn L. (2019). "Bosses matter: The effects of managers on workers' performance." *IZA World of Labor*. DOI:10.15185/izawol.456.

Simms, Margaret C. and Julianne C. Malveaux (1986). *Slipping through the Cracks: Status of Black Women*. New York: Routledge.

Sklansky, David Alan. (2006). "Not your father's police department: Making sense of the new demographics of law enforcement." *Journal of Criminal Law and Criminology*, 96(3):1209–1244.

Smith, James P. and Finis R. Welch. (1989). "Black economic progress after Myrdal." *Journal of Economic Literature*, 27(2):519–564.

Sowell, Thomas. (1975). *Race and Economics*. New York: David McKay Company.

Stampp, Kenneth M. (1965). *The Causes of Civil War*. Hoboken, NJ: Prentice-Hall.

Stanford School of Medicine. (2021). "Health History: Health and longevity since the mid-19th century." *Ethnogeriatrics*. Available at: https://geriatrics.stanford.edu/ethnomed/african_american/fund/health_history/longevity.html. Last accessed December 16, 2022.

Stewart, James B. (1994). "NEA Presidential Address, 1994: Toward broader involvement of black economists in discussions of race and public policy: A plea for a reconceptualization of race and power in economic theory." *The Review of Black Political Economy*, 23(3):13–36.

(1995). "NEA Presidential Address, 1994: Toward broader involvement of black economists in discussions of race and public policy: A plea for a reconceptualization of race and power in economic theory." *The Review of Black Political Economy*, 23(3):13–36.

(2009). "Be All That You Can Be?: Racial Identity Production in the U.S. Military." *The Review of Black Political Economy*, 36(1):51–78.

Stiglitz, Joseph and Linda Bilmes. (2008). *The Three Trillion Dollar War: The True Cost of the Iraq Conflict*. New York: W. W. Norton.

Stults, Brian J. and Eric P. Baumer. (2007). "Racial context and police force size: Evaluating the empirical validity of the minority threat perspective." *American Journal of Sociology*, 113(2):507–546.

Swaine, Jon and Ciara McCarthy. (2016). "Killings by US police logged at twice the previous rate under new federal program." *The Guardian*, December 15, 2016. Available at: www.theguardian.com/us-news/2016/dec/15/us-police-killings-department-of-justice-program, last accessed November 20, 2020.

Sykes, Bryan L. and Becky Pettit. (2014). "Mass incarceration, family complexity, and the reproduction of childhood disadvantage." *The Annuals of the American Academy of Political and Social Science*, 654(1):127–149.

Takaki, Ronald. (1990). *Iron Cages: Race and Culture in 19th Century America*. Oxford: Oxford University Press.

Temin, Peter. (2018). "The political economy of mass incarceration and crime: An analytic model." *International Journal of Political Economy*, 47(3–4):317–329.

Thurow, Lester. (1975). *Generating Inequality: Mechanisms of Distribution in the U.S. Economy*. New York: Basic Books, Inc.

Tolnay, Stewart E. and Elwood M. Beck. (1992). *A Festival of Violence: An Analysis of Southern Lynching, 1882–1930*. Champaign, IL: University of Illinois Press.

Tyson, Karolyn, William A. Darity, Jr., and Domini R. Castellino. (2005). "It's not 'a Black thing': Understanding the burden of acting White and other dilemmas of high achievement." *American Sociological Review*, 70(4):582–605.

U. S. Bureau of the Census. (2021). "Table 2. Persons 25 years old and over, by years of school completed, for the United States by divisions and States: 1940." *Educational Attainment of the Population 25 Years Old and Over in the United States: 1940 – Detailed Tables*. Available at: www.census.gov/data/tables/1940/demo/educational-attainment/p10-8.html. Last accessed December 14, 2022.

U.S. Department of Health and Human Services. (1993). *National Center for Health Statistics, Vital Statistics of the United States, Volume I, Natality*. Available at: www.cdc.gov/nchs/births.htm. Last accessed December 16, 2022.

Unicon Research Corporation. (2007). *The CPS Utilities User's Manual*. Santa Monica, CA.

United States Bureau of Labor Statistics. (2021). "Union members summary." *Economic News Release*. January 22, 2021.

United States Senate. (1976). *Supplementary detailed staff reports on intelligence activities and the rights of Americans, Book III, Final report of the select committee to study government operations with respect to intelligence activities*. Available at: https://vault.fbi.gov/cointel-pro. Last accessed December 16, 2022.

Urquhart, Brian. (1988). *Ralph Bunche: An American Odyssey*. New York: W. W. Norton.

Washington, James M. (ed.). (1986). *A Testament of Hope: The Essential Writings and Speeches*. New York: Harper Collins Publishers.

Watkins-Hayes, Celeste. (2009). "Race-ing the bootstrap climb: Black and Latino bureaucrats in post-reform welfare offices." *Social Problems*, 56(2):285–310.

(2011). "Race, respect, and red tape: Inside the black box of racially representative bureaucracies." *Journal of Public Administration Research and Theory*, 21(Suppl 2):i233–i251.

Weems, Jr., Robert E. and Lewis A. Randolph (2001). The national response to Richard M. Nixon's black capitalism initiative: The success of domestic detente. *Journal of Black Studies*, 32(1):66–83.

Weiss, Andrew. (2016). *Efficiency Wages: Models of Unemployment, Layoffs, and Wage Dispersion*. Princeton, NJ: Princeton University Press.

Wells, Ida B. (1909). "Lynching, our national crime." National Negro Conference, New York City, May 31–June 1, 1909. Available at: www.blackpast.org/african-american-history/1909-ida-b-wells-awful-slaughter/. Last accessed December 16, 2022.

(1970). *Crusade for Justice: the autobiography of Ida B. Wells*. Chicago: The University of Chicago Press.

Wexler, Noah. (2020). "Testing for police racial profiling using data on pre-stop race visibility: evidence from Minneapolis." University of Minnesota Working Paper, presented at Association for Public Policy and Management Conference, November 2020.

Williams, Eric. (1994). *Capitalism and Slavery*, 3rd ed. Chapel Hill, NC: University of North Carolina Press.

Williams, Jhacova A., Trevon D. Logan, and Bradley L. Hardy. (2021). "The persistence of historical racial violence and political suppression: Implications for contemporary regional inequality." *The Annals of the American Academy of Political and Social Science*, 694:92–107.

Williams, Rhonda M. (1987). "Capital, competition, and discrimination: A reconsideration of racial earnings inequality." *Review of Radical Political Economics*, 19(2):1–15.

(1991). "Competition, discrimination and differential wage rates: On the continued relevance of Marxian theory to the analysis of earnings and employment." In Richard R. Cornwall and Phanindra V. Wunnava (eds). *New Approaches to Economic and Social Analyses of Discrimination*. New York: Praeger, pp. 65–92.

Williams, Walter E. (1982). *The State against Blacks*. New York: McGraw-Hill.

Williamson, Samuel H. and Louis P. Cain. (2021). "Measuring Slavery in 2020 Dollars." MeasuringWorth.com. Available at: https://measuringworth.com/slavery.php#footstar. Last accessed December 23, 2022.

Wilson, William J. (1978). *The Declining Significance of Race: Blacks and Changing American Institutions*. Chicago: University of Chicago Press.

Wilson, William J. and Kathryn M. Neckerman. (1986). "Poverty and family structure: The widening gap between evidence and public policy issues." In Sheldon H. Danzinger and D. H. Weinberg (eds). *Fighting Poverty: What Works and What Doesn't*. Cambridge, MA: Harvard University Press, pp. 232–259.

Winship, Christopher and Robert D. Mare. (1991). "Economic and educational change and the decline in Black marriages." In Christopher Jencks and Paul E. Peterson (eds.), *The Urban Underclass*. Washington, DC: Brookings Institution Press.

Wolff, Edward N. and Maury Gittleman. (2014). "Inheritances and the distribution of wealth or whatever happened to the great inheritance boom?" *Journal of Economic Inequality*, 12(4):439–468.

Womack, Gabrielle C. (2017). "From 'Mulatto' to 'Negro': How Fears of 'Passing' Changed the 1930 Census." Master of Arts thesis. Boston, Massachusetts: Simmons College.

Woodward, C. Vann. (1951). *Origins of the New South: 1877–1913*. Baton Rouge, LA: Louisiana State University Press.

(1973). *The Strange Career of Jim Crow*. Oxford: Oxford University Press.

Work, Monroe N. (1922). *Negro Yearbook: An Encyclopedia of the Negro, 1921–1922*. Tuskegee, AL: The Negro Yearbook Publishing Company.

Zaw, Khaing, Darrick Hamilton, and William Darity. (2016). "Race, wealth and incarceration: Results from the national longitudinal survey of youth." *Race and Social Problems*, 8(1):103–115.

Index

Ingram Content Group UK Ltd.
Milton Keynes UK
UKHW040133050423
419672UK00002B/6